THE MAN OVERBOARD

Ask me about my journey.

www.themanoverboard.com

How a Merchant Marine Officer Survived the
Raging Storm of Alcoholism and Drug Addiction

DARRYL HAGAR

ISBN: 1-4392-2269-X
ISBN-13: 9781439222690
Library of Congress Control Number: 2009900016

Book cover design, Copyright 2009, George Foster.
Contact george@fostercovers.com for more information.
Visit www.booksurge.com to order additional copies.

'For

Two people who deeply affected my life.

Dad, you left too soon, and we miss you.

I had so much to show you yet.

I always forgave you.

Son, you saved my life.

I couldn't stop the madness.

I couldn't save myself from myself.

And then you came along, Darryl II, like an angel.

You are a true godsend.

I'll always love you both.

—Darryl Edward Hagar

CONTENTS

PREFACE

The Man Overboard is the memoir of a Merchant Marine officer who struggled with the chaos of alcoholism and drug abuse, first while attending a state maritime academy and later navigating dozens of supertankers around the world. The stories are documented by police and medical reports and by the testimonies of friends and neighbors, sheriff's deputies and police officers, doctors and lawyers, people in the shipping industry, psychotherapists, surgeons, and even members of the U.S. Coast Guard.

What follows is a description of the life of Darryl Hagar, a "drunken sailor" who survived twenty-five years in a conservative and highly regulated industry that was heavily scrutinized in the aftermath of the massive oil spill from the Exxon Valdez in 1989, caused by a captain's drinking.

Hagar served as ship's officer/ship's navigator from 1985 to 2005 on oil tankers between 500 and 900 feet long. Hagar refueled the U.S. Navy in the Persian Gulf during the Iran/Iraq tanker war in 1987–88 when Ronald Reagan was President and again in 1990–91 when President George H.W. Bush took the country to war against Iraq in Desert Storm.

"I started my career attending Maine Maritime Academy in 1981. I began sailing when guys still drank openly. After the Exxon Valdez, the real drinkers had to go underground. But alcoholism and ships go together like salt and pepper. People started hiding the booze and drinking only when off duty. I stopped drinking on board, but the moment my feet went down the gangway anything could—and did—happen," says Hagar.

The Man Overboard does not blame the oil industry, the shipping companies, the Coast Guard, or Maine Maritime Academy. Hagar does not fault his family. But neither is the book sugarcoated to protect any of the above. **The Man Overboard** depicts the wild, addicted life of a

Merchant Marine officer. There are stories of visiting prostitutes around the world, his father's suicide, multiple arrests for drunk driving, car wrecks, and medical procedures to repair the aftereffects of a drunken life.

In 1999 Hagar's son was born. For the first five years he parented as an alcoholic father. During that time Hagar continued to live in chaos and despair, until he was finally able to see the future in a different light. In 2005, after flying across country in a drunken stupor to attend a company conference, Hagar finally surrendered. He was alone, emotionally spent, spiritually bankrupt, physically exhausted, and mentally broken. He begged God to either save his life or end it.

The recovery process began, and Hagar started a new voyage that began with detox and rehab and led to full-fledged sobriety, a twelve-step program, and many moments spent on his knees. Hagar prayed to the Man Upstairs, asking for guidance and the ability to help others overcome alcoholism and all the horrific things that come with what is an unforgiving and relentless disease.

ACKNOWLEDGEMENTS

I want to express my appreciation for those who helped me not only with this book but in my life and in my recovery. First and foremost I'd like to give Bill W. and Dr. Bob credit for saving my life. Without them I'd be dead.

I'm so very grateful to my family and their spouses and children for sticking by me. Mom, Mark, Randy, Chris, and Karen Ann, I love you all very much. Jen, thank you for giving me the most precious thing in my life, my son Darryl II, who finally gave me a strong enough reason to get sober. Jen, you've been with me throughout my crazy drinking and drugging and in my recovery, and you've been a constant friend.

Thanks to all my aunts and uncles and their children. Thanks to all my friends; you helped me make it. I hope those still in the grip of alcohol and drugs will read my story and see that there's a better way to live.

I want to thank all the captains I worked under and the people who worked with me. It wasn't easy, but we hauled a lot of oil safely. To the men who worked under me, only a sailor understands a sailor; I'm sorry if I hurt any of you. I also want to thank Maine Maritime Academy, the most prestigious maritime academy in the world. I did my best and I'm proud of this fine institution. Although I struggled with substance abuse, you helped to mold the man I am today.

Thank you Nancy Adair from Mercy Hospital Recovery Center, Phil del Vecchio from The Way Home, and my two sponsors, all of whom showed me how to live life one day at a time. I hold all four of you close to my heart.

I'd like to express my gratitude to Debbie Jackson, accentonwords.net, the best editor in the world. I highly recommend her work. I want to thank

Professor Ted Sottery, Elizabeth, Suzanne, and Heidi, who proofread tirelessly. Thank you to Ben Clarke, who helped me immensely with websites and ideas, and his wife Nikki for being great friends. Thanks to Sonya Messer and Mark Girr for advice and direction, Jack Barnard and Susan Levin for their expertise, and RTIR and Steve Harrison for their terrific ideas and guidance. I'd like to thank Glen Chadbourne, cemetarydance. com, my artist and buddy, George Foster for his help in creating a really cool cover, and Jayme Proctor, my extremely talented graphic designer.

Blessings to Pastor Joel Osteen from Lakewood church in Houston. He inspired me to reach out to God, to sow seeds, and to help others in need. He helped my faith return and was an important part of my recovery. I'd like to thank all my former pastors, Don Harrington and others, and Pastor Rick Newall for baptizing me in the Sheepscot River.

Most of all I'd like to thank my heavenly Father and his son Jesus Christ, who came back to earth to take away our sins. I strayed from you for years, my Lord, but I have returned. I will do my best to help others struggling with alcoholism and addiction, so help me God.

These mariners were comprised of "hordes of rough and hardy men; rude, uneducated, brave, suffering terrific hardships with sailor-like stoicism; heavy drinkers, coarse frolickers in moral sties like the Natchez-under-the-hill of that day, heavy fighters, reckless fellows, every one, elephantinely jolly, foul-witted, profane; prodigal of their money, bankrupt at the end of the trip, fond of barbaric finery, prodigious braggarts; yet, in the main, honest, trustworthy, faithful to promises and duty, and often picturesquely magnanimous."

—Mark Twain, *Life on the Mississippi*

POSITIVELY NEGATIVE

I DRANK FOR JOY AND BECAME MISERABLE
I DRANK FOR SOCIABILITY AND BECAME ARGUMENTATIVE
I DRANK FOR SOPHISTICATION AND BECAME OBNOXIOUS
I DRANK FOR FRIENDSHIP AND BECAME ENEMIES
I DRANK TO HELP ME SLEEP AND AWAKENED EXHAUSTED
I DRANK TO GAIN STRENGTH AND IT MADE ME WEAKER
I DRANK FOR "MEDICAL REASONS" AND ACQUIRED HEALTH PROBLEMS
I DRANK TO HELP ME CALM DOWN AND ENDED UP WITH THE SHAKES
I DRANK TO GET MORE CONFIDENCE AND BECAME MORE AFRAID
I DRANK TO MAKE CONVERSATION FLOW MORE EASILY AND THE WORDS CAME OUT SLURRED AND INCOHERENT
I DRANK TO DIMINISH MY PROBLEMS AND SAW THEM MULTIPLY
I DRANK TO FEEL HEAVENLY AND ENDED UP FEELING LIKE HELL

—ANONYMOUS

AUTHOR'S NOTE

In this written account of my life I have included documentation of many of the events. Some incidents are backed up by eyewitness accounts. Yet because of extensive drug and alcohol use on my part and because not all records are readily available from the shipping companies, there may be a chance that some of the dates or the chronology of events are not exact. Additionally, pseudonyms are sometimes used in order to protect the innocent.

This memoir, however, is truthful. It is a faithful representation of the major events of my life.

—Darryl Hagar

INTRODUCTION
FROM A THERAPEUTIC PERSPECTIVE

When I first met Darryl on June 6, 2005, I was struck by the duality of his rough exterior and voice (similar to my own in its coarseness) and his sincere desire to arrest his haunting illnesses of alcohol/drug abuse and depression. He was the epitome of what a quarter century on the oceans of the world can do to a man. He was a brash, salty "Ahab" ready to take on anyone at any cost and risk.

As his potential counselor, Darryl put me through a litmus test for quality and reliability. His style was full hog on, in your face, and yet sensitive to the smallest nuance of contradiction. Though I respected the process, it was no easy task. He was searching for someone in whom he could put his trust and to whom he could reveal the inner workings of his life; he was not going to take a chance with just anyone.

At first I took his testing as a challenge to my integrity and competency as a therapist. This "testing" continues today and is, I believe, a testament to his serious desire to find a male he can connect with who will not abandon or hurt him. His assessment and reassessment is a constant for which I am grateful.

As our relationship and trust grew, ever so slowly Darryl described bits and pieces of his very hard yet very exciting life. As a child he suffered excruciating and debilitating migraines treated as best medicine could back then, with lackluster results. Darryl suffered for a long time. And twenty-plus years of hardcore alcohol abuse and poly drug abuse had taken its toll. He had a litany of physical aliments that may be related to the years of abuse his body has gone through with his active addictions. As an adult, his physical being had taken a beating, and he was hurting as a result. It showed.

Psychologically, another story emerged. Before me sat a young man with scars from twenty years of sailing the world's oceans as an active addict/alcoholic in addition to the unsettling experiences of his youth, including his father's suicide. Darryl walked this planet hard—and sometimes ran it hard—with that pain and heartache held deep within. Too preoccupied with feeding his addictions and numbing himself, he had never dealt with those events.

When he wasn't entertaining his addictive side, his personality emerged as either the consummate professional, perfectionist "worka-holic" or the shadow of a "monster" that could rip you in half with his tongue. He found himself swinging from one extreme to the other, but grew most familiar with the anger and rage within. This duality took Darryl to extremes in risky behavior and a devil-may-care, cava-lier persona. His moods varied from a virtual wild man living at a fre-netic pace to a depressed miserable fuck who shot toxic darts at anyone near.

Imagine the pain and distance that grew in his heart and spirit. He became wrenched from "God" and couldn't understand why certain things were happening to him, if indeed God did exist. His relationships became tangled and highly dysfunctional and distant. He became a man hurtling through life without any real plan or direction. What would become of him?

In our first meetings, I somehow successfully got through his rigor-ous and respectful testing. We then set on a path I hoped would give Darryl a long road of successful recovery from the active demons of his addictive ways and from emotional torture. Slowly, his teetering emo-tional state and his life in general began to take on balance. Early re-covery and sobriety, while prickly and sensitive, was at the same time eye-opening and soothing. Though he was still smarting from the rigors of the past twenty-seven years, he was also keenly aware of his most pressing needs. With a vengeance, he sought sobriety at whatever cost.

He engaged in self help (a twelve-step program) and began the pro-cess of working the steps. He also knew he needed more than just a few meetings with an individual therapist. If he was truly going to conquer his multiple addictions, he required intensive outpatient treatment. With an attitude still sharp and raw that sometimes looked for any apparent excuse to rip out at someone in anger, he lobbied hard for treatment, believing his insurance company should support his need for more intensive services. He won that battle and went on a two-and-a-half-week journey through the Mercy Hospital Recovery Center intensive outpatient program.

He came out of this experience with a stronger resolve to quiet his stabbing dependencies. While he remained sober from alcohol and illicit drugs, his behavior and attitudes ran amok. He was the proverbial "dry drunk" with a razor's edge, often leaving behind a bloody mess for himself and those he hurt. Try as he might to temper his impulsive anger, it gushed forth with reckless abandon.

Darryl then entered mid-stage recovery and began to identify some of his shortcomings and negative character traits. Simultaneously, he grew closer to his son. The boy's calm demeanor, energy, and unconditional love soothed Darryl's rage and hurt.

He began to feel feelings that had become detached from his soul. Memories and pain that had been buried and numbed poured forth as an endless litany of events and traumas. The dam had sprung a leak and was beginning to flood. The dualities were phenomenal. The stories swung from calm and soft to utter chaos and huge risk. Beautiful places and people—to the ugliness of sin and despair. Calm oceans—to vicious frozen storms at sea. These stories from his life mirrored themselves in Darryl's very skin and soul.

He grew to despise his job and felt the urgent need to detach from that lifestyle. Darryl attempted to return to work, but that experience only served to validate what he already knew. He was done. He jumped ship and fully engaged in his life and recovery. While he was studious and made a concerted effort to work hard at sobriety, old scars haunted him: his father's brutal suicide, his chaotic and wild life, his confounding loneliness.

He searched for someone or something to fill the void, but nothing worked. Darryl continued to take his anti-depressant medication and decided to join a Wellness group. His efforts, coupled with his ongoing awakening, ignited in him the idea to write his story. His book was born.

Though he was initially hesitant and nervous, we worked through that and started the journey of telling his story. He entered another stage of recovery. The process fueled a passion to work his program even more vigorously. He became willing to risk public venues beyond the self-help groups and began to speak at colleges, jails, and hospitals.

While initially he bristled at the idea, he soon warmed up to the process and became adept at telling his story. This gave Darryl a positive therapeutic energy, which he drank in with a huge thirst.

Today, Darryl moves forward independently and assuredly. He stays in touch with an authentic blend of his caring, soft self and the abrupt, hard-hitting sailor. That is Darryl. His dreams are all his now, and they are tangible and in plain sight. His feelings are intense and alive. His soul is filling with spirituality, as he defines it, and it is a great comfort to him.

Some of the emptiness and void may always be there, but Darryl has found creative methods to cope. His feelings are no longer foreign and frightening. Like a sailor lost at sea, he now sees a beacon of some distant lighthouse—pointing the way home.

Coming out of the sanctity of our therapeutic relationship of the past three years, Darryl asked for my input. I was humbled by such a request. It is with the highest levels of dignity, respect, and confidence that I write, though I don't believe words can ever portray accurately what happens between two humans on an intimate therapeutic journey together.

There are many nuances of Darryl's life and recovery that I have not covered here. I apologize both to Darryl and to the reader for those shortcomings. I defer the reader to Darryl's compelling stories.

Darryl will always occupy a place close to my heart. I fully support Darryl's pursuit of his dreams and meaningful connections in life. Live life with the full expression of all of your emotions, Darryl!

—Felix ("Phil") A. del Vecchio, LCSW, LADC, CCS
(Just a man in Maine fortunate to meet many fascinating humans.)

Phil del Vecchio is a private practice clinical social worker and psychotherapist working with young people, adults, couples, and families in Portland, Maine. He is currently an adjunct professor at a community college in South Portland. He also conducts training and is a consultant throughout greater New England. He has worked in the field of substance-abuse treatment and mental health for twenty-five years, including extensive work with dual diagnoses and Gestalt therapy. For two years he was the clinical program manager at Mercy Hospital Recovery Center (in and outpatient). He has held many other clinical management positions in the mental health and substance abuse treatment field. Before coming to Maine, he spent some time working in New Jersey. He attended Temple University in Philadelphia and Fordham University in New York City, where he obtained an MSW. The most important element in his life is his family: his wife, Joni, a clinical social worker and artist; his eleven-year-old son, Felix; and their standard poodle, Luna.

GLENN CHADBOURNE

CHAPTER ONE
THE MAN OVERBOARD

o·ver·board: —*adverb* 1. over the side of a ship, especially into the water: *to fall overboard.*
—*idiom* 2. **go overboard**, to go to extremes.

Merchant mariners all over the world know exactly what to do if a man goes overboard. The men on board sound the alarm, the ship is brought about, and—if all goes well—the man overboard is rescued.

For many years when I was serving on ships in the Merchant Marine, I was The Man Overboard, adrift in a maelstrom of alcohol and drug addiction without anyone recognizing fully that I was in imminent danger of being lost forever. For a long time, there was no ship turning around for me, no one jumping into the water to save me, no hands reaching down to pull me back aboard, no one throwing me a life ring—even when indications were that I was in the deepest kind of trouble.

I was overboard in every sense of the meaning of that word. I lived an overboard life of extremes: overboard partying, overboard womanizing, overboard irresponsibility in my personal life. My work life was just as extreme: extreme honesty, extreme dedication, and extreme perseverance and hard work. There was no in-between place in the world I had built for myself. Like many alcoholics, I'm an all-or-nothing kind of guy.

Eventually an alarm *was* sounded in my life, and the ship did turn around and come back for me, and I was rescued with the help of a twelve-step program and a Power greater than myself. But it took many years to get to that place, and my overboard life of extremes went on for a very long time. Ostensibly, that life of extremes, of The Man Overboard, started even before I was born . . .

My grandfather, Paul Jacobs, knew the life of the Merchant Marine. He was a lobsterman in his early years and then later learned how to cook when he and his father owned a restaurant. After years in business, he became a ship's cook. The men who already knew how to cook when they joined were always the favorites. Those men had been good enough to cook ashore, and all their secret recipes and dishes were vastly enjoyed by the sailors. One time there was a shoreside gourmet cook on board one of my ships, and the crew loved it each time he came back to work. My uncle Dick told me that Grampa Jacobs was a good cook, and the men loved that he had such enthusiasm for doing a good job.

Unfortunately, I never got to meet my grandfather. He died mysteriously in Boston Harbor while serving as chief cook on an oil tanker. He disappeared one night, and nobody knew exactly what happened to him. His sons pressed the Massachusetts State Police to conduct an investigation, since initially no body was found. He was finally found nine weeks later about a mile from the dock where his tanker was berthed, his body badly decomposed, the flesh completely devoured. According to the authorities, there was no foul play, but I never found final police reports regarding his death. I have newspaper articles about the investigation, but no solid evidence explaining how he died.

My mother's sister, Polly, told me what she knew about their father's death: My grandmother, Gertrude, received a phone call that Paul was missing from his ship. She was told that one end of the "plank" used to come aboard was found in the water and that Paul's flashlight was found lying on shore. They believed he "accidentally fell overboard." The Coast Guard found his body when it washed ashore at Charleston Beach. Police determined that he fell overboard, his clothes got caught on a pier, and when the cloth rotted, his body floated to the surface.

But Paul had called his wife at 1:00 a.m. from a convenience store to tell her he had cashed his paycheck, had purchased what he needed for the next cruise, and was sending the rest of his money home to her. During that conversation, he also mentioned that he hated it when the ship docked during the night, because he had to go through a dark alley to get to the little store, where the owner lived upstairs. He said, "People up here will bump you off for a five-dollar bill."

When Paul's body was found, he still had the paychecks belonging to the men under his supervision in the galley, but no cash. His watch had stopped at 1:20 a.m.

Bob Strong, an undertaker in Damariscotta, Maine, went to Boston to retrieve his body. My grandfather was buried in Sheepscot Cemetery, where his father and mother are buried. The case was closed, but with several opinions about what really happened.

My grandmother talked to me about her husband's death when I first became interested in attending Maine Maritime Academy. The night he went missing he called home to say hello as he always did. A short time later he called again, which she said was unusual. Then he called a third time. She said, "Paul, what's going on? You never call more than once!"

He disappeared the very same night. Because the gangway was upset, I assume he fell over the side and drowned. Whether or not alcohol was involved was never determined, but common sense dictates it was probably part of the story. He had been known to tip a few—some say a lot; others say not in excess.

I know when I caught a buzz while serving on a ship and got lonely and homesick, it wasn't unusual to call my sweetie three times in the same night. That's called looking for love and support, and we all know we do things differently under the influence. My grandfather could have had more than his usual couple of beers, called my grandmother, went back to the ship, and then fell drunkenly off the gangway.

It would have been ironic if fate had led me to a similar early death. I went out and got drunk many times to the point where I was practically crawling up the gangway late at night, then sleeping it off until the men came around to wake me for my turn at watch. The only difference is that during my time we had modern gangways and equipment. My grandfather's tanker had been tied to another vessel, causing an unsafe environment.

All my foolish drunken behavior had to come from somewhere. I often kid around that it was because I was born about 2:00 a.m. on April 2, 1963. Because I was nearly born on April Fools' Day, my mother always teased me that she crossed her legs so I wouldn't be born until after midnight. My father often ribbed me that he knew I would grow up to be foolish. Though we always joked about it, I somehow always felt he really meant it.

I grew up in a normal middle-class family with five children and two parents who worked hard. My father was a printer, and my mother worked as dairy manager in a local supermarket. We lived in mid-coast Maine and struggled economically like many other American families in the sixties and seventies. I can still remember my dad telling one of my brothers one night not to drink the orange juice in the refrigerator; it was very expensive and only for breakfast. Both my mother and father earned modest salaries, each a couple of hundred dollars a week. We had what we needed, but not much extra.

My siblings and I attended Sunday school at the Baptist church every week. Mom was in the choir and was also a Sunday school teacher. As a young adult, I was involved in the Baptist Youth Fellowship. Thank God my mom had the moral integrity to make us go to church every week. I later drew on that moral foundation as I fought my battles with addiction.

As a young boy I once stole a candy bar from Clarke's Spa, a local ice cream shop. It bothered me immensely for a week, so without telling anyone I went into the shop and told the owner, Bill, I'd stolen candy and wanted to pay for it. Bill said, "That'll be a quarter," and laughed. That laugh had as much impact on my life as going in and paying for stolen candy without being told. Even at that young age, I understood that Bill's laugh meant acceptance and understanding—in a small-town, Mayberry USA way.

Later, I could be called a lot of things, but I always tried my best to be honest, and I certainly could never be called a thief. All the damage I did later was primarily to myself, although everyone knows that with addiction, everyone near the addict gets hit with the overspray.

Although no one factor has been defined by science as the cause of addictive behavior, there is strong evidence that a tendency toward drug and alcohol addiction has hereditary and physiological components. And I knew early on that I was different.

In 1969, at the age of six, I started having severe migraine headaches to the point of crying, screaming, and holding my hands over my face to keep the light out. My father had experienced similar migraines as a boy, and his father had suffered the same malady. The blood vessels in the brain are thought to expand and contract abnormally in people suffering from migraines; these abnormally severe headaches are believed to be a genetic medical disorder of the brain. It seems I had been dealt the same genetic cards as my father and grandfather.

My dad decided my migraines were more severe than his had been and demanded that doctors run tests. As a young boy, I was taken to a futuristic-looking hospital room and hooked up to what I remember as suction cups and wires. They turned on a machine and recorded my brainwaves. The brain scan showed some irregular brainwave patterns.

At the age of six, I remember thinking, *Why is this happening just to me? My brothers don't have to do these weird tests. What's wrong with me?*

The migraines were debilitating. If I took my prescribed medicine plus aspirin at onset, sometimes the migraine would abate. At other times it would keep building. If I lay down quickly and there was no light or no noise around me, and if I was lucky enough to fall asleep, the medication would quiet my brain. I would then awaken feeling much better but with effects like a hangover, a dull throbbing head and upset stomach, with no vomiting.

The worst scenario occurred if I started to get a monster migraine somewhere where I wasn't able to treat it in the first twenty minutes.

Within an hour I was crying, screaming, vomiting violently, and lying down wherever I was, clutching my head and face.

One time when I was still in grammar school, I began to get a migraine at a basketball game. I went out to the school bus and lay in one of the seats waiting for the game to end. We were at another school, and they weren't going to drive me home until the game was over. Sometimes during sporting events I would go to the locker room and lie down on the floor or a bench. There were many such incidents through the years.

Thirteen years old (at left), playing hoops, 1976.

No wonder I felt different. While my team was playing basketball, I was throwing up, crying, and writhing in pain, trying to understand why I was the only boy in my school, my family, my church, who had these terrible headaches. *Why me? What did I do wrong to deserve it all?*

The headaches happened two or three times a week. At home, I went into my bedroom, which I kept in complete darkness, assumed the fetal position, cried, vomited, sobbed, and tried to sleep. I often heard my parents tell my three brothers to turn the TV down and keep as quiet as possible: "Your brother is having a hard time."

On January 28, 1970, I was sent to Maine Medical Center in Portland for tests. Three doctors and our family physician ran monopolar and bipolar tests on my brain in the electrodiagnostic laboratory. The results were inconclusive.

Not long afterward doctors decided I should take daily medications, including 15 mg of the barbiturate Phenobarbital. I took it in the morning, at bedtime, and whenever I had a migraine. Phenobarbital is used in children to prevent seizure activity, but usually only for a short time. I took it from 1971 to 1977.

Today doctors hesitate to prescribe Phenobarbital, because of its reputation for side effects in children affecting behavior and learning. I didn't have negative side effects, and the medication did help me with anxiety. I was high strung and frequently got cold sores on my lips. Stress exacerbates both cold sores and migraines.

Studies also indicate that Phenobarbital is addictive and shouldn't be prescribed to alcoholics or drug addicts. I wonder if it was the right choice for a boy who later would struggle mightily with drugs and alcohol. Naturally, doctors can't detect alcoholism in children before it occurs, but what effect does the drug have on potential alcoholics and addicts? Could it act as a trigger?

I wonder if and how the migraines, the medication, and my addictions tie in together. It's known that barbiturates can cause depression. I took strong doses of a barbiturate for six years at a young age. I was a high-strung, overachieving kid all the way through high school. Today, I suffer from depression and take a high dose antidepressant, prescribed to calm my aching heart and soul. Could Phenobarbital have played a role?

Otherwise, my childhood was a good one full of happy memories. I grew up in a normal household full of kids and pets and two parents who loved all five of their children. I have two older brothers, a younger brother, and a sister. Karen Ann was the diamond in my father's eyes; nine years after having four boys and all the rough and tumble that comes with them, my parents were delighted to have a baby girl.

My family (from left): Randy, me, Chris, Mark, Mom, Dad, and Karen Ann (in front), late 1970s.

We did many things together as a family. We rented a campsite on Damariscotta Lake every year. My father took us fishing from the time we were small up through our teen years and beyond. My dad invariably found a school of yellow or white perch, and we caught one right after the other. Those were joyous times.

My father was a terrific outdoorsman who also taught us how to hunt. He often took his four boys and put us on paths where deer were likely to cross. He taught us which way to watch according to wind direction then left us to stir the deer up and "push" them toward us.

Once, when I was sixteen, he left me on an old sawdust pile and showed me where a deer might cross. I sat there for an hour and thought, *What would you do if a deer walked out over there, right now? I'd slowly take off my gloves, slowly raise the shotgun, take the safety off, take a deep breath, aim, and pull the trigger.* Just as I was thinking this, a deer walked out in the exact spot I had imagined. I went through the routine automatically, and five seconds later I had killed the first (and only) deer of my life.

Being young and reckless, I fired shots in the air. After a short time my dad showed up, and I ran up to him, eager and elated: "I shot my first deer!"

We took the deer to a tagging station at the local convenience store. I thought I was the great white hunter, having slain his animal, and was quite proud of myself. The 20-gauge shotgun I used that day was a nice gun for a young guy learning to hunt. It was low caliber and therefore didn't kick much. I used that gun for target practice, cleaned it, and took care of it. But later, my father would take my favorite gun and use it to end his own life.

As I was growing up, my father and I shared a love for baseball. In 1975, Dad and I watched the World Series together. The Red Sox were playing the Cincinnati Reds, "the Big Red Machine." Halfway through the series, the Red Sox were down three games to two and had to win. Bernie Carbo hit a home run to bring the Red Sox back into the game, and Carlton Fisk hit his famous game-winning home run, waving it fair to tie the series three games apiece at Fenway Park.

My dad—a huge Sox fan—and I were euphoric that night, a memory that will stay with me for the rest of my life. The Red Sox, who hadn't won a World Series since 1918, went on to lose game seven to the Big Red Machine. We would have to wait some more. But my dad never saw the Red Sox in the World Series again. He died in 1983.

The Red Sox were important to more than just two people in the Hagar clan. Three years after my dad died, my grandfather and I watched the Red Sox vs. the New York Mets in the 1986 World Series. It would be most truthful to say that I *tried* to watch with my grandfather. Some nights I was in better shape than others. My cocaine addiction was so strong at that time that I was either out snorting or recuperating from being up too many nights in a row.

Grampa lived for the Red Sox. I wish I'd been further along in life so I could have really enjoyed being with him. The night before game six, I went out snorting cocaine, drinking beer, and chasing women. I got in late and slept in so I could watch the game later. The Red Sox were up three games to two and had a chance to win their first World Series in sixty-eight years. I'm sure my grandfather felt this might be his last chance to see them win the series in his lifetime. I got my mind clear for the game and sat down to watch with him, but fought falling asleep the whole time. Toward the end of the game, I passed out.

I was awakened by a yell: "Goddamn it!" The ball went down the first base line right between Bill Buckner's legs, and the winning runs were scored. I looked at my grandfather, dazed and confused, trying to figure out what had just happened. I'm sure he wasn't impressed that I couldn't stay awake to watch the Red Sox in the World Series. But my body was crashing, and I went back to sleep. My bad memories of the game have nothing to do with the Red Sox losing on an easy ground ball error, but because I couldn't straighten out long enough to enjoy my grandfather's last years.

New Englanders were known to be sarcastic about how the Red Sox had let us down year after year because they hadn't won a World Series since 1918 and because our hated rivals, the New York Yankees, had won several times. But people outside New England don't understand the love we have for the Boston Red Sox, who are adored here as much as the Maine lobster. I have a Red Sox flag mounted on the front of my house that flies in rain, sleet, and snow, day and night, spring, summer, fall, and winter.

In 2004, the Red Sox were again in the World Series, and I was home from sea, watching and drinking my way through every game. I'm sure just about all of New England, including my mom (their number two fan behind me), would like to thank John Henry and the new ownership for finally breaking the curse and bringing home the trophy where it belongs. We finally got some quality, relentless ownership that in the end brought us the glory we sought. John Henry and his partners made all of New England proud.

I later said that the Red Sox got my grandfather—who passed away in 1990 while I was at sea in the Gulf of Mexico—and they got my father, but they didn't get me. All we wanted during our lifetimes was to see the Red Sox finally win a World Series.

In addition to being a Sox fan, my father was a proud man with a high school education. When I was young, he was paid about $200 a week for printing the county newspaper. I remember the distinctive smell of ink and watching as he set up type on the printing machines, as he measured to ensure the print would fit evenly on each page, and as he printed out paper after paper.

My father was a hardworking man who loved his family. He liked to work on our cars and around the house; every year he cut wood for our fireplace, planted a vegetable garden, and landscaped our yard. At night he liked to relax and watch the news and other TV shows of the time. He was a good man, well liked around our community. But looking back, I now understand that he had some deep, dark mental health issues. It didn't help that he was stressed by raising five kids on a salary fit for a young, inexperienced printer rather than the highly skilled expert he was.

Dad was a loner and didn't like public events. He attended our soccer games because he was comfortable outdoors. He also played baseball at night with my brothers and me to help us practice for our Little League games, but as a boy I didn't understand why he wouldn't go to my basketball games in the gym.

Every night my mom made a nice sit-down supper, and we ate to-gether. I'll also never forget all seven of us watching *The Waltons*. It was like watching our own family, and it made us feel close. Sometimes I watch that show today, and it brings back fond memories—but it also brings sadness. As a young man I didn't know that one of my parents was struggling so badly he would eventually take his own life.

I have mainly good memories of my high school years. At that time I was a good athlete and a tremendous long-distance runner. I lettered in soccer, basketball, and golf in ten out of twelve seasons, and I lettered in track my final year of high school, losing only one race that season.

Conference Track Champion, two-mile event, 1981.

I twice bested the kid who placed second in the state two-mile race in 1981.

That year I qualified to run at regionals, but I de-cided to go on my senior class trip instead. Coach was understandably disap-pointed; not running in the regionals disqualified me to participate in the state championships. I was at an elite level athletically and could have gone further in my track career. But partying on the passenger ship Caribe from Portland to Halifax with my class-mates took precedence over becoming a state champion and the chance to become a world-class runner. I probably had the potential. But my decision-making was already beginning to be ruled by alcohol.

The first time I ever got drunk was in 1977 at a party organized by seniors on the soccer team. We were at an ocean-side cottage owned by someone's parents, who were unaware a kegger was going down on their property. Everybody who was anybody at Lincoln Academy High School was there, including all the pretty high school girls and my older brothers. People were running around in togas having a good time. It was then that I drank the first alcohol of my life, a bottle of Boone's Farm wine. My buddy and I swigged it down, and I was suddenly all warm inside, a little dizzy, and started acting silly. It felt good, so we drank beer too. I was fifteen.

I hadn't eaten anything for awhile. Someone had set the keg up with a big plastic bowl under the tap to catch the spill. The last thing I remember before passing out was picking up the plastic bowl and gulping down the contents. I looked to the side as I was drinking, and a couple of seniors pointed at me and laughed as I poured beer down my throat and the front of my shirt. The next thing I remember was waking up in a dark room on the floor, vomiting. I had blacked out the very first time I got drunk.

But I learned no lessons from my first alcoholic episode.

STATE OF MAINE

GLENN CHADBOURNE

CHAPTER TWO
DRIFTING INTO DARKNESS

The Hardy Boys, Nancy Drew, The Chronicles of Narnia, the books of J.R.R. Tolkien—and as I got older, the works of Stephen King and Tom Clancy—fueled my imagination growing up. As a kid I was always reading, which spurred me on to take my education further.

My parents supported my dream and pushed me toward attending Maine Maritime Academy. There are similar state academies in California, Massachusetts, New York, and Texas and a national academy in Kings Point, New York, that have trained thousands of young people to serve as ship's officers in the nation's Merchant Marine fleet.

Most people don't realize the importance of the U.S. Merchant Marine, especially its service during wartime and in helping the economy run smoothly during peacetime. Every day, the Merchant Marine transports passengers and cargo in and out of U.S. waters on a fleet of ships run by both private interests and the U.S. government. About 95 percent of all U.S. imports and exports come into and leave our great country on civilian-manned merchant ships. The men who operate the ships are known as "merchant mariners."

The Merchant Marine is not part of the U.S. military, although in time of war it acts as an auxiliary to the Navy. The U.S. Merchant Marine provides transportation of up to 90 percent of all war materials during wartime. Most tanks, jeeps, ammunition, troops, and fuel go over to war zones on civilian merchant ships.

I always thought—and still do—that Maine Maritime Academy is superior to the other maritime academies. And I want to be completely clear that the stories that follow, especially those involving the use of alcohol and drugs and other irresponsible behavior, are the exception and not the rule at MMA. The academy should not be viewed negatively because of my addictions.

In 1980 I was enticed by my parents and a family friend, an MMA grad and the chief engineer of a supertanker, to take a tour of the academy. The chief engineer seemed like a great guy and said he wanted only the best for me, so I agreed to go. He was a hard-working man who had grown up in an affluent family. When his dad passed away, he received a large inheritance; he had also worked for Gulf Oil, which paid extremely well. He told me he had so much money he didn't know what to do with it all. I was seventeen and impressionable. My mind was racing: *Wow!*

The chief engineer was a bit of a renegade. He picked me up in his souped-up gold Pontiac Trans Am, evoking images from *Smokey and the Bandit*. He brought his nephew, who was interested in the marine engineering program. We drank a few beers on the way to Castine. At one point we pulled over, and the chief engineer asked, "Do you want to do a line of cocaine?"

I was bowled over. I thought, *If you're doing some, I'm right behind you.* The three of us did a few lines. All the while I imagined the life I'd lead: the money, cool sports cars, big house, and scantily clad women at big parties.

That day a switch went off inside my brain that allowed cocaine to make decisions in my life for twenty-seven years. The kid who paid for the only thing he had ever stolen, a 25¢ candy bar, went from experimenting with cocaine to partying with it once a month to selling and using weekly to smoking crack several times a week with prostitutes and junkies around the globe. I got away from the church and moved to the dark side. I remained there until 2005, when I thought about ending my life to put myself out of my misery.

But at seventeen, I continued to study hard. More than once, my Latin teacher said in front of the class, "Darryl isn't the smartest guy in the world, but he'll do well in life, because he's a hard worker." She was right. With all my hard work, good grades, and several letters of recommendation from prominent people in the community, I was accepted into Maine Maritime Academy. I was still running fifty miles a week, was stick thin, and was physically ready for the intense two-week boot camp.

My parents took me to Castine, three hours northeast of Portland along the Maine coast. I hadn't even started shaving seriously, so I was more than apprehensive; I was shaking in my boots. I moved forward on automatic pilot with this crazy idea of being an officer and a seaman.

We arrived at the thirty-five-acre campus overlooking Castine Harbor. There were many large brick buildings, athletic fields, and a huge gymnasium. The waterfront complex had more buildings, a sprawling boatyard, and docks. When we approached the waterfront, we couldn't miss the crown jewel of the academy: the T/V State of Maine. The 500-foot training vessel, previously called the USNS Upshur, had been used for troop transport to Korea and Vietnam.

Maine Maritime Academy is a world-class institution with world-class instructors and equipment. The instruction is hands on. But first I'd have to get through boot camp. My parents and I went to the gymnasium to sign in, and I said my goodbyes. Mom and Dad smiled proudly and assured me I'd be okay.

I was whisked away, fitted for Navy-style dungarees and combat boots, and told to stand in line to get my head shaved. I was then told to leave my gear in the gym and to head to the football field, where we'd meet our drill instructor and his midshipmen assistants. The regiment was organized in a "wedge" comprised of nine senior class cadets headed by a regimental commander. The wedge helped run the school, making sure the midshipmen attended morning colors, were correctly dressed, and that strict regimental behavior was observed.

The academy ran on a demerit system. If a midshipman exceeded a hundred demerits in a year, he was expelled. The wedge handed out demerits and indoctrinated incoming freshmen, officially known as "mugs." The unofficial term was "maggots," and it was widely used. Hazing was prevalent and wasn't considered cruel or offensive. We were training to see if we had the mettle to serve aboard vessels around the world; hazing quickly exposed the weak.

We were put in formation and divided into Alpha, Bravo, Charlie, and Delta companies, which we belonged to for four years. I was placed in Bravo Company with forty guys and a few girls. There were about six females in my class who were put through the same rigorous training as the males.

After 160 freshmen stood at attention in columns and rows, our sixty-year-old ex-Marine drill sergeant walked onto the field. I felt like I was in a Hollywood movie. He was chewing on an unlit cigar, sported a crew cut, and wore a Marine sergeant's drill cap. He started yelling about how it was his responsibility to separate the men from the boys, the weak from the strong, and in two weeks, if we were back there standing at attention, we might have a future as officers in the U.S. Merchant Marine.

After the sergeant's talk, the regimental commander, a senior midshipman, told us what he expected of us. Rise every day at 0430 hours for a four-mile run. Shower, eat, and spend the rest of the day drilling. March, run, and exercise all day long. Eat by "squaring" our meals, which meant holding a fork full of food out, then up, then into the mouth. No talking at meals and no socializing at bedtime.

We marched down to the 500-foot training ship and one by one went onto our new home. It was old and odd-smelling. We were assigned bunks and roommates, four men to a room, with the females in their own section. We were allowed to unpack and get organized and then walked around the ship to learn about the firefighting stations, emergency gear lockers, and how to quickly exit the ship in an emergency. We spent the rest of the day training and drilling and were told to "sleep fast" at 2130 (9:30 p.m.), because we'd have a "very long day tomorrow."

Training Vessel State of Maine, returning home.

I slept soundly that night, exhausted by the stress of new people, new experiences, and a new regimental lifestyle. We had people telling us when we could eat, when we could sleep, even when we could use the head. I didn't know what to expect next, but figured at least we'd be rested for the new day.

I awoke at 0427 to the sounds of pipes hitting the metal bulkheads and loud whistles blowing over the intercom. Seniors ran through the passageways screaming, "Get out of bed! Get out of bed! You have three minutes to be dressed in shorts, sneakers, and T-shirts and be at the bottom of the gangway. Let's go! Let's go!"

I jumped out of my rack, bumping into my scurrying bunkmates, and dressed quickly. Someone had darkened the rooms and corridors to see how we'd react getting off the ship without lights. Guys were banging into each other and putting hands and arms out so they wouldn't run into something face first. The seniors hid in empty rooms, yelling at us and blowing whistles as we passed. The drill was designed to see if we could hold our composure. Some of us did better than others, and by the end of the day I knew our numbers would dwindle. By the end of two weeks we'd have significantly fewer freshmen.

On the dock the sergeant screamed at us to get into ranks. I fell in up front directly behind the sergeant, and we started our four-mile run. My heart was pounding and adrenaline rushed through my veins. I was in optimum shape and pulled up even with the sergeant. He looked over and said," Fall back behind me, now!"

I was surprised, thinking he'd like my enthusiasm and my excellent athletic condition. But the sergeant wasn't impressed. As I edged up closer again, he yelled, "Mister, I'm not gonna tell you again! Fall back!" I realized he was dead serious and kept a safe arm's length behind him.

Near the end of boot camp, the sergeant told the seniors to assemble those who had made it through; he had something important to tell us. All the "mugs" sat in the football bleachers expecting him to yell at us and tell us we needed to do better. Instead, he told us we were turning into men and women that our country, our parents, and our local communities could be proud of, that we were going to be the best Merchant Marine officers on the planet. I could tell by his voice he was pleased with our progress.

He ended his talk with something I'll remember the rest of my life: "This morning in the Mediterranean Sea, two Libyan MiG fighter jets challenged two U.S Navy F-14 Tomcat fighter jets. The F-14 Tomcats were ordered to take them out, and they quickly evaded the Russian-made MiGs, circled behind them, and blew them both out of the sky."

The sergeant pumped his fist in the air as he spoke, and the whole class went nuts. In the midst of that uproar, I had never been more proud to be an American. The sergeant couldn't have scripted a better moment for a worn out, beat up bunch of freshmen. His comments reinvigorated us, and at that moment we jelled as one. The U.S military had taught the Libyan dictator, Colonel Gadhafi, a lesson, and the sergeant had effectively used that example to boost our morale in the final days of boot camp. It suddenly all seemed worthwhile.

But there was still one last requirement to pass boot camp: jump off the training vessel into the cold waters of Castine Harbor, fully dressed, sneakers on. And that upper deck was a scary twenty-five feet above the water. The instructors lined us up and explained that if we ever needed to abandon ship in an emergency with no time to get in the life rafts, we'd have to make a similar jump.

I waited in line while one by one my classmates made the plunge, feeling as if I was about to walk the plank to my final demise. Some guys needed more encouragement than others, and a few refused completely. They were told, "No jump, no training cruise," thus no MMA and no Coast Guard license. Every one of us sucked it up and leaped.

To make matters worse, there was a large crowd on the beach. Apparently watching a bunch of apprehensive young men and women jump their way to becoming midshipmen at MMA was cheap entertainment for the town of Castine.

I was anxious and rushed the jump. I clutched my life preserver with crossed arms, but I uncrossed my legs, and my body rotated forward. My face and body slapped the water full force. I went under and realized immediately that my groin had taken the worst of the impact. As I surfaced clutching myself, the people watching laughed hysterically. I gasped for air as I swam weakly to shore and pulled myself onto the beach, my face and groin crying out in pain. A couple of seniors helped me out of the water and onto my feet, assuring me that it was over and that I'd be all right. I had completed the two-week hell period and was now officially a middie—a Maine Maritime midshipman. We were ready to start classes.

MMA was intense and challenging. Freshman year was a lot like that of any other college, except that we took seventeen to twenty-one credit hours each semester and took specialized classes, such as Nautical Science and Marine Engineering.

I continued my running career and won many races, besting older, more experienced athletes. Our team often went out for ten-mile runs, which I could complete in about sixty-five minutes. At that point in my life, I was an exceptional athlete and an overachieving student.

CHAPTER THREE
SALTWATER IN MY VEINS

During the first semester at Maine Maritime Academy, I lived isolated from campus on the training ship—away from the partying. In the beginning, life at MMA was all about studying and getting used to quasi-military life, which meant always being in uniform, marching to and from classes, and getting up early for morning colors.

Each morning, the wedge stood in a line up front, and all six hundred midshipmen lined up in formation at attention, saluting while the national anthem was played. Once attendance was taken and announcements completed, we were dismissed to class.

I had a full course load all four years at the academy. My first semester included typical though strenuous academics, plus the marine/military courses of Engineering Fundamentals, Deck Indoctrination, and Rifle Shooting.

Still in top physical condition, I also competed on the cross country team, running fifty miles a week. I won several college races that year and placed second at the Northeast College Conference on Parents Day.

On a Friday afternoon in November I went home, already having learned "college-level" drinking from some upperclassmen. The academy barber agreed to give my buddy and me a ride home if we drove. He'd been known to tip a few, and, of course, we were drinking.

About an hour into the trip, I asked the barber if he minded if I smoked. He was a great guy and said, "Hell no, Hagar, here's a lighter." My buddy and I had already planned the scenario. I lit up a joint, took a toke, and handed it to my buddy. The barber got nervous.

He said, "You know, Doc says you shouldn't be smoking that stuff and driving."

We laughed and finished the joint.

A short time later, the barber said, "Why don't we pull it over and take a leak? Doc says don't drive with a full bladder. If you ever got in a car accident, and your nuts got hit, they'd explode."

We laughed. By that time we were stoned and drunk and said, "Good idea."

We pulled over and jumped out. The barber quickly locked the driver's side door and slid into the driver's seat. Even though he was old and frail, he insisted on driving the rest of the way. We laughed and told him that was pretty smart thinking.

At home, I went out partying. I had already made plans to go deer hunting with my dad early Saturday. You'd think I'd stay in and take it easy, but I didn't get home until after 1:30.

When my dad woke me at 4:30, I wanted to tell him I didn't feel well. But I didn't want to disappoint him, so I dragged myself out of bed. It's cold in the woods in November, so I put on my long johns, wool socks, and hunting gear. As we drank coffee, Dad asked if I still wanted to go. I didn't want him to think I was turning into a drunk, so I said, "Hell, yeah!"

We loaded our shotguns with double aught buckshot and slugs. I had the 20-gauge bolt action; he had a 12-gauge pump. I followed my father single file into the woods. It was still dark, and the leaves were frozen, but there was no snow on the ground. He always put his boys in a good location and then left for hours at a time. Since it was just us this time, he picked a deer crossing on an old tote road and pointed, saying he would walk around and try to push a deer my way. He was an awesome hunter and fisherman. I knew if I paid attention, I might see a deer.

He left, and I stood there with no tree to lean against, fighting sleepiness and a hangover. I did okay for half an hour, then I literally fell asleep on my feet. The first time I woke up, the loaded shotgun was lying at my feet. *Oh, God—I dropped my gun!* I quickly bent over and picked it up.

I kept fighting sleep, but I soon woke up with my gun on the ground again. *My God, you're an idiot, Darryl!* I thought about how disappointed my father would be if he walked up and found me dozing with my gun on the ground, but he never did. I never shared the story with my family. I was embarrassed—and afraid they'd put pressure on me to stop drinking.

At the time, I thought stories like that were funny, and I used to brag to my drinking buddies about the crazy things I did.

After each long week of regimental life, I went home and uncoiled like a spring. I studied hard all week at the academy and partied hard on the weekends. There was no drug testing at MMA then. As long as your police record was clean, no problem. Unfortunately, I wasn't scared of anything back then, which made me too brazen for my own good.

The first encounter I had with the law that could have seriously jeopardized my standing at the academy, and thereby my future career as a Merchant Marine officer, happened that same November. I was home, had scored an ounce of marijuana, had gotten some beer, and my buddy and I went out partying. I borrowed my father's Ford pickup, and we pulled to the end of a quiet neighborhood. It seemed like a good place to smoke a joint and drink a beer.

But one of the residents figured that a vehicle sitting on his turn-around meant we must be up to no good. As I was rolling joints, two police cruisers stormed down on us with blue lights flashing. One blocked the front of the truck, the other blocked the rear.

"Oh, fuck—cops! Hide the weed, man! Don't worry about the beer!" I said, stuffing a case full of pot under the truck seat.

"What are you two guys up to? Get your hands up!" one of the officers said.

"We're not doing anything, Officer," I said. "We're home from Maine Maritime for the weekend, just drinking a couple of beers."

"Get out of the truck."

We got out, and the officers searched the vehicle.

"What's this? A joint on the seat? What else do we have in here?" The officer reached under the seat and pulled out the ounce of pot.

Then I noticed that the other cop was the chief of police in Damariscotta, an old family friend. He looked at me and knew I was scared. I had grown up next to him, which was my saving grace that day.

"Follow us down to the police station, Darryl," the chief said.

At the station, they sat us down, and the chief said, "You guys know you're in a lot of trouble, don't you?"

"Yes, sir, I realize we made a big mistake."

"You're not even old enough to drink. What were you thinking? Having that much marijuana is a big problem."

"I know, Chief. I'm worried that if the academy sees that on our records, we'll both be thrown out of school."

He sat there thinking. "I tell you what. I'll throw out the marijuana conviction, if you two plead guilty to underage drinking."

"Thank you, Chief. You're really helping us out of a jam. I appreciate it."

We were both convicted of underage drinking, and that was the last I heard about it. I knew we had dodged a bullet, and I intended not to repeat that mistake.

Second semester meant a move from quarters on ship up to the dormitory, a huge four-story brick building with a central courtyard. The freshmen occupied one corner, the sophomores another, the juniors a third, and those in charge, the seniors, a fourth. In the heart of the dormitory there was a common area we called "the quarterdeck" where the commander had an office and a midshipman always stood watch.

As I headed to the dorms, I crossed my fingers, hopeful I'd get buddies as bunkmates. On the quarterdeck, a group of mugs crowded around the roommate list. Had there been some kind of mistake? I couldn't even pronounce the names next to mine. There were two Malaysian students in our class; apparently they were my new roommates.

I was angry as I headed to my room. When I opened the door, sure enough, there were Ahmed and Mohammed. But as we talked my anger dissipated, and we quickly became friends.

These two young foreigners explained that they were very religious. Would I be offended if they said their Islamic prayers at various times during the day? I told them, "Absolutely not." But I soon learned that "various times" meant chanting on their knees five times a day. What would other people think? Would anybody else understand their beliefs?

That question was answered quickly. Our room was frequently raided and trashed, and pranks were played repeatedly. Someone sneaked into the room, tipped over the bunk beds, threw our clothes out the window, and dropped shaving cream bombs all over. When we were in the room, someone threw in a wad of lit firecrackers and ran. The smell lingered for hours. It was a good lesson about how pathetic and demeaning discrimination is.

Mohammed and Ahmed always apologized to me, knowing that ours was the only room being bombarded. I felt sorry for both of them—and angry. I complained to the higher-ups, and eventually the harassment stopped.

Both guys were smart and helped me with homework. When I worried about failing physics, they said, "Shoot for the sky; hit the fence. Shoot for the fence; hit the ground." I understood and squeaked by in physics with my only D of the semester.

As the year wore on, I started experimenting more with drugs and alcohol. I was like tightly wound spring, and marijuana slowed me down. I was still the same high-strung individual I'd been as a kid on Phenobarbital, and I periodically still had migraines.

My roommates knew I acted differently when I was high and asked me why. I explained that smoking and drinking alleviated stress and helped to channel my emotions. They didn't understand, because their religion prohibited alcohol. Yet they treated me the same, and we never had any problems. They knew I was involved with a big circle of influential friends, and they reaped the benefits; nobody harassed or belittled them anymore.

Every day at MMA we completed regimental duties, including cleaning the seniors' bathrooms, sweeping the dorms, and taking out trash. In the spring and summer we donned khaki Navy uniforms. In the fall and winter, black Navy uniforms. Uniforms were required 7:00 a.m. to 5:00 p.m. Casual uniforms, such as khakis and an MMA golf shirt, could be worn after hours. Our uniforms included our last name in white lettering on a blue tag, collar pins, shined shoes, a shiny brass belt buckle, and a piss-cutter hat. We also had Navy dress blue uniforms or Navy dress white uniforms for official occasions and admiral inspections.

Anybody out of uniform got ten demerits, usually handed out by the wedge, regimental commander (RC), or regimental executive officer (XO). If a midshipman missed one morning of formation, he received ten demerits. If he got caught with alcohol, fifty demerits. But if he got caught with drugs, it was an automatic expulsion with a good chance he could not reapply to MMA.

The academy was strict, but we were still an unruly, rebellious group of young men, mostly Maine boys just out of high school. Even then, I didn't have any serious disciplinary issues or problems with demerits until my junior year.

One weekend, I planned to hang out at Moosehead

In my dress blue uniform.

Lake with my buddy Moil. We left Castine on Friday and first headed south to Portland to pick up a used car he wanted to buy. We hitched a ride with another midshipman, partaking in a few joints and beers during the three-hour drive. We had a buzz going by the time we got to Portland, but thought we were still okay to drive. Moil decided to buy the car, so we got in and headed north.

We drove for an hour. Because we were partying and not really paying attention, we somehow got off the road we should have been on. When we finally noticed we were heading the wrong way, we decided to just keep heading north and "cross over" when we got to a major town. But as we continued to get stoned and drunk, common sense flew right out the window.

We'd been driving for hours, and neither one of us had a clue where we were. Moil's eyes were red and barely open, which happened whenever he got stoned. As I watched him drive, his head started nodding.

"Pull over, Moil. You're gonna kill us both! You're tired, man. Sleep, and I'll drive."

"Okay, Darryl. I *am* tired. Where the hell are we?"

"I don't know, man, it's starting to look like ski country. Sugarloaf Mountain should be to our west, unless we're that far off course. You sleep, and I'll just keep heading north."

I was buzzed and tired, but we didn't have any other option so I just drove. I was on autopilot and wasn't thinking about paying attention to the road signs; I was just watching the road. After awhile I shook my head. I couldn't believe what I had just seen. I decided not to wake up Moil until I could confirm my worst nightmare. I drove on, and sure enough, it was true.

"*Moil!* Wake up! You're not gonna believe it!"

"What? What is it?"

"The street signs just turned French!"

"What?! Did you go through the border?"

"Not that I remember, man. I've been watching the road."

"Holy fuck! We've got to turn around and talk to Border Control before they call out the troops on us! Throw out anything we have, pot pipes, beer bottles, weed, anything."

I stopped and we went through the car and chucked everything illegal. When we finished, Moil took the wheel and turned around. After a few miles, sure enough, there was the U.S./Canada border with its flashing red lights. We went to the American side first and explained that we were lost.

"Holy cow," said the American border patrol officer. "The Canadians were just getting ready to mobilize and chase you guys down. You drove right through the border without slowing down. We figured you were running drugs."

"No, sir. We go to Maine Maritime Academy."

"You better get over there and tell your story to the Canadians. They're pretty upset."

We hustled over to the Canadian side, but they weren't as forgiving. They only half believed our story and searched the vehicle up and down, underneath, in the engine, and in the trunk. When they came up empty handed, they told us to go inside.

"Officer, I was falling asleep. I swear to God I didn't know I drove through the border. I'm the world's worst driver, but my buddy drove for five or six hours and was nodding off, so I took over. Honest."

"Empty your pockets here on the table," said a Canadian border guard.

I complied. There was my driver's license, some crumpled up pieces of paper with numbers and names on them, my hunting license. Nothing illegal.

"Do you have a wallet?"

I took out my wallet, knowing I had nothing to hide. I had dabbled with cocaine, but if there was any to be snorted I would have already done it to stay awake. In those days, I used my wallet to keep business cards, numbers, paperwork, etc. It was full of stuff. The guard kept pulling things out and suddenly stopped.

In his hand was a single-edged razor blade. He smirked, looked at me, and said, "What's this?"

"That's a razor blade, Officer," I answered.

"Yeah, it's a razor blade, but what's it for?"

"It's for cutting purposes," I said

He laughed sarcastically. "Yeah, but to cut what?"

"Officer, a razor blade is a sharp object. You can cut many things with it."

He continued to look through my wallet, but finding nothing finally let us go. It's possible they believed we were telling the truth, but they probably suspected we weren't angels.

A guard asked where we were headed.

"Moosehead Lake."

"Why don't you cross back into Canada and take Route 161 up to Armstrong and then Route 173 back down to the USA to Jackman and then head east to Moosehead Lake?"

"Thanks so much, Officer. We really appreciate it."

Moil and I drove off. It wasn't long before Moil noticed we were low on gas. I hadn't noticed, which shows how out of it we were. We drove as far as we could go before running out of gas somewhere in Quebec. It was freezing, late, and after the nerve-wracking border incident, it was hard to believe we were in trouble again.

"Now what, Moil?"

"Get out and walk for help. We got no choice."

We walked several miles before coming upon a rural house in the country. We knocked on the door. An old woman and her husband peered out at us.

"We're sorry to wake you, but we got lost. The Canadian border sent us this way, and now we've run out of gas."

They said something in French and motioned us inside. They couldn't speak a word of English. We couldn't speak French. They led Moil to a spare bedroom and made up a couch for me. I couldn't believe it. Here we were, two lost American boys, half frozen, probably still smelling of beer, and they provided a place to sleep for the night. God was looking out for us.

In the morning, the old man took us to a gas station. We said our goodbyes with handshakes and hugs, and left laughing about what had been a bizarre sequence of events. We had gotten drunk, gotten stoned, bought a car, got totally lost, passed through an international border without knowing it, run out of gas, been put up for the night by two elderly Canadians who couldn't understand a word we said, and we were on our merry way to Moosehead Lake as if nothing had happened. Oh, my God: We were a pair of midshipmen in action!

Despite incidents like these, I survived freshman year academically, regimentally, physically, mentally, and emotionally. But before our sophomore year we still had to decide whether we wanted to major in marine engineering or nautical science. This decision would dictate what direction our careers would take.

Marine engineering classes focused on learning to work in the engine room, working with boilers, turbines, condensers, pumps and motors. Nautical science focused on learning how to be a deck officer and included courses on celestial, terrestrial, and electronic navigation.

Additionally, we'd take seamanship classes to learn how to tie knots and to safely work on ships, meteorology to understand weather and how to avoid big storms, including hurricanes in the Western Hemisphere and typhoons in the Eastern Hemisphere, and navigational "rules of the road" to teach us how to safely pass other ships. We would learn rules to follow in different situations, such as what signals the ship was required to sound if a ship longer than two hundred meters was underway in fog.

My father and I talked about which way I should go. I favored nautical science so I could see where the ship was going. I dreamed of being a captain on a 900-foot supertanker, navigating around the world, stopping at far-flung ports full of beautiful, exotic women, living the life of a world traveler, and making lots of money.

My father had other ideas. He suggested that I go into marine engineering; that way I would learn mechanical skills that could be used to work in power plants or paper mills. He stressed that if I grew tired of working on a ship, I could come ashore with skills that would translate to a high-paying shore job.

I understood where he was coming from, but my first love was the open sea. Growing up on the coast of Maine, the wind and saltwater were already in my veins.

CHAPTER FOUR
A SEA DOG AND HIS SINSEMILLA

The year was 1982, seven years before the Exxon Valdez supertanker accident occurred in March of 1989. In that accident, eleven million gallons of unrefined crude oil spilled out into Prince William Sound in Alaska, causing untold environmental damage. The official investigation concluded that alcohol consumption on the part of the ship's master (captain) contributed to the ship running aground. That accident brought drug and alcohol testing to the Merchant Marine, but in my freshman year at Maine Maritime Academy that was still "down the channel."

That year when I packed for my first two-month-long journey, ready and willing to be a sea dog, I decided to roll up an ounce of super strong Maine sinsemilla Afghani marijuana and put fifty joints inside two empty packs of playing cards, which I placed inside my sea bag. Nobody suspected anything, and off to sea I went.

Who knows what other drugs were on that training cruise? There was plenty of marijuana, and allegedly some freshman had a stash of LSD. Although I had experimented with LSD before, lucky for me I was never offered any on the training cruise. A couple of my classmates who used it saw stars on nights when it was completely overcast. I know at least one of them is serving as captain on a 1000-foot military pre-position ship.

Yet at the time I justified my drug use; the only time I ever smoked any grass was at the end of a long day and only if I wasn't going on duty for eight hours. Besides, I was young and foolish, and I assumed someday I'd "outgrow" my childish, crazy behavior.

The next morning we cast off the mooring lines—which were as big around as my arms—and the T/V State of Maine set sail for Virginia, with my mom, dad, and siblings waving goodbye from the dock. My first voyage was underway. Our itinerary after Norfolk was to head across the Pond with stops in Lisbon, Barcelona, and Tenerife in the Straits of Gibraltar.

We were quickly given our assignments, which were broken up into four segments: standing watch, maintenance, training, and regimental duties. We stood one segment for a week and then rotated. Standing watch involved two four-hour stints separated by eight hours.

For maintenance, we mustered with the boatswain at 0800 for eight hours of chipping and painting, greasing valves, or working on equipment. Training included classes in navigation, seamanship, rules of the road, and engineering in one of the holds set up with desks, benches, and chalkboards. We also received hands-on training in the engine room, on deck, and on the bridge. Regimental duties involved keeping the ship clean, serving meals, cleaning the galley, changing linens, and making beds.

We quickly took to the routine, but at the end of the day it was party time. Because the State of Maine was an old troop transport ship, some of the holds were set up with row upon row of bunk beds held together with chains, and some had carried ammunition in wartime. That meant there were a thousand nooks and crannies where I could smoke a joint and drink whiskey with my buddies.

The training cruise was for juniors and freshmen. Approximately 150 juniors ran the show, while the freshmen were there to learn and observe. The MMA instructors were former captains and chief engineers or former ship's officers there to train and assist.

The ship was run like any other, with a captain, chief mate, second mate, and third mate on the bridge. The second mate and third mate each took four-hour watches, with the captain on call. The captain was on the bridge at specific times: when arriving or departing port, in heavy traffic, in fog, or any other time deemed necessary. The chief mate ran ship's maintenance and anything outside on deck: dropping the anchor, telling the boatswain what to chip and paint, telling the midshipmen what needed to be done, and loading stores.

The juniors stood watch according to the field they had chosen. Deck juniors did the navigation, piloting, celestial fixes with a sextant, and plotting positions with radar. The freshmen stood watch under their supervision and were assigned helmsman and lookout duties. The captain and mates assisted and made sure all navigation and traffic situations were handled correctly and safely.

It worked the same way in the engine room. Junior midshipmen ran the watches as freshmen did the dirty work. The watch engineer made sure things ran safely and correctly. The seven-story engine room was full of motors, pumps, boilers, turbines, pipelines, superheated steam, and valves. A million things could go wrong; we had to be on our toes.

Plus, we were all taught how to tie knots, how to forecast the weather, how to conduct fire and abandon-ship drills, and other emergency procedures.

Because I was a freshman, I had to stand watches in both the engine room and on the bridge. After the cruise we'd make our decision: engineering officer or deck officer. By that time I already knew I wanted to be a deck officer, but rules were rules. I did my duty in the engine room when told, and because of that I later appreciated my counterparts in the engine room, who were always sweaty, stinky, and dirty. We called them "the black gang" or "snipes." They called us "deckie fags."

Later when I was second mate, I told the second engineer that someday when I was captain and he was chief engineer, I'd have him up to my stateroom for a few drinks and then tell him to go fix my toilet. To this day, engineers still get pissed off at that joke, but they also know who runs the ships. A lot of rhetoric between deck and engine is teasing, but some of it's real. It seems to me that it's the engineers who still hold onto the old ideas of which department is better—which means I don't have any problem defending the deck officers.

At the Norfolk Naval Station all of the midshipmen participated in fire training, involving both classroom education and simulated ship's fires. The instructors started different kinds of fires in different buildings set up like ships; the fires often involved petroleum, pipelines, and valves.

One of the fire instructors said over and over in his distinctive Southern drawl, "Gentlemen, fire can kill you!" He made this point so well that I never forgot it. Later, I was involved in several fire situations, though none ever got out of hand. The seed that man planted served me well throughout my career.

Participating in firefighting training.

After leaving Norfolk, we headed across the Atlantic for foreign shores. While we were underway, I was in the Six Hold one night getting ready for watch. I was standing in front of a row of lockers where the middies stowed their gear. It was dark and nobody was around. One of the upperclassmen ran up to me. Looking over his shoulder, he handed me a brown paper bag.

"Hey, man, hide this for me!"

"What is it?" I asked.

"Don't worry about it; I'll take care of you later."

Back then, the guy was what I thought of as "cool." I knew he was from Down East Maine; he had grown up on the coast just like I had. I quickly decided to help him.

"Okay. I'll stash it somewhere," I assured him. "When are you gonna come get it?"

"As soon as it's okay. I'll be in touch."

"Okay, man. It'll be safe. Don't worry."

"Thanks. I gotta get out of here," he said, running away.

I held onto the bag for several days, knowing there was some kind of drugs inside. I was curious. *It's too big to be a bunch of cocaine. It's probably a big stash of marijuana, but it doesn't smell up my locker. Maybe I should look and sample.*

But I was living by some warped code of honor, and I never looked in the bag. I had this weird feeling that if I didn't mess with his stuff, I would be "made," like I was in the Mafia earning my stripes.

The upperclassman came back a few days later and met me in the Six Hold.

'Hey, do you have that bag I gave you?"

"Right here." I walked over to my locker and dug it out. "I didn't even look inside, man."

He smiled. "I believe you. I'll take care of you—big time."

I knew I had just been made. This guy was one of the big guys at MMA, and I felt good that I had helped him. My sick, twisted mind enjoyed being involved in the underworld. I suspected this guy would tell other upperclassmen what I'd done, meaning I'd be able to do whatever I wanted at the academy until his class graduated. That ended up being true, and I ended up being on the inside of something I didn't need to be in on.

The same guy partied with me many times after that. One time I invited him up to my room. I locked the door, put on Eric Clapton's *Crossroads* album, and played the live version of "Cocaine." I then cut out some big fat lines, and we snorted them. If he didn't think I was the cat's meow before, he certainly did after that. The sick part was that I thought I was the coolest guy around. In reality, I was beginning a life of alcoholism and drug addiction.

That first Atlantic crossing was new and exciting. Never before had I left the sight of land on an oceangoing ship. I loved it. I loved the sea—its smell, the waves, and the big storms that tossed the training ship around like a toy boat. That's when I got hooked on that crazy, lonely life. Alcoholics are drawn to ships like preachers are drawn to churches. We're drawn to a seagoing career with its promise of wealth, women, and wine. Later, I cursed like a crusty old pirate, chased women in every port, swigged from many different bottles, and swore I had saltwater in my veins. I'd found what I was looking for, never mind that the lifestyle turned out to be dangerous for me.

I also experienced foreign countries for the first time in my life, and I found them exhilarating. When we went ashore in Lisbon and Barcelona, we were required to wear dress whites to show respect for the countries we were visiting. Yet before each night was over, our uniforms were covered with beer and lipstick, our high pressure hats were lost in some bar, and we were sneaking back to the training ship more than a little tipsy. We went up the gangway trying our best not to cause any commotion, slipped into our racks to rest, and did it all over again the next day. I loved this new life; it was what I wanted to do for the rest of my life.

In Lisbon, many of my classmates discovered prostitution. Thankfully, I was a late bloomer in that respect, and I didn't participate. But I heard plenty of stories about middies getting gassed up and visiting red light districts. There were stories of "window shopping" for women; prostitutes of different ethnic backgrounds sat in storefront windows, and a sailor could choose whomever he desired.

When we docked in Barcelona, there were tens of thousands of people partying in a street festival. There, I smoked hash and drank beer with 17 percent alcohol. If that was what Europe was all about, I wanted to see more.

Surprisingly, nothing tragic happened to anyone on board during that cruise. We had a little bit of education about prostitution, alcohol and drug abuse, how to manage a Merchant Marine officer's income. It wasn't nearly enough education on how to recognize when we were getting caught up in irresponsible, unsafe behavior. At the time it was just the way we did things, and my class and those before us eventually paid the price. Today, the Coast Guard requires drug and alcohol testing, there are "personal responsibility" classes at the maritime academies, and midshipmen are better prepared to face the challenges of going to sea.

But in those days, the ships were like the Wild Wild West. There was plenty of liquor, women, and outrageous behavior. It was exactly what I thought it would be, and I loved it. As we sailed back to the United States, I felt like I was not only becoming a man, I was on my way to becoming a captain. Yet I would never make it to the top. My drinking was like a ship dragging anchor; it slowed me down and often prevented me from moving forward.

During that first voyage, The Man Overboard had been awakened. The world should have been warned: *Hide your whiskey, hide your wives, hide your daughters, turn out the lights, and lock the doors.* A modern-day American pirate had been born.

GLENN CHADBOURNE

CHAPTER FIVE
AVOIDING A DIFFICULT QUESTION

I went back up to the academy, no longer a mug. As a sophomore I still wasn't very high up the food chain, but at least I no longer had to clean the seniors' bathrooms.

My schedule again included strenuous academics and maritime classes: Meteorology, Seamanship, Piloting/Nautical Astronomy, and Oceanography. No matter how difficult I knew it would be, I looked forward to continuing. Eventually I'd graduate, go to sea, and make that big money.

I was again training with the cross country team. Running kept me focused, and the exercise was good for my brain as well as my body. I was still high strung, and the running somehow replaced the need for marijuana. Though I sometimes still craved the high, while I was running I stayed away from it. Yet there was the occasional exception to that rule. Despite running more than fifty miles a week, I still dabbled in drugs and alcohol, especially when I got a weekend off from the cross country meets.

Back home, as winter approached, my family faced some major issues. My dad had back surgery at Togus, a Veterans Administration facility near Augusta, Maine; he'd been fighting the pain for some time and decided enough was enough.

I still went home on the weekends, but got caught up in the partying scene. I was just old enough not to have much time for my parents unless I needed something. But Dad was a good man and probably thought I was acting like a normal young man. He was proud of me and understood me wanting to go out and drink and chase women. What he didn't understand was the reason I smoked marijuana.

One Friday afternoon, I came home stoned. My eyes were bloodshot, and I'm sure I reeked of marijuana. After I said hello to my parents and siblings, we sat down for supper. Our family dinner went downhill rather quickly; my father singled me out before the first piece of bread was broken.

"I can't understand why a young guy with enough smarts to go to Maine Maritime Academy would be dumb enough to smoke pot. You'd think a person would realize that it's an illegal drug and hampers one's ability to concentrate and learn."

I was shocked. I hadn't expected a grilling. I'd been a little worried about giving myself away when I walked in the house, but after saying hello I didn't think they realized I was high. I didn't say anything back to my father. I ate my dinner and went out drinking afterward, oblivious to what I was doing to myself and to my family. His remarks did not change my behavior.

I still don't completely understand my fascination with doing illegal things, the underage drinking and taking drugs, although I didn't do anything else immoral. I had a fascination, even an obsession, with getting and staying high.

In my dress white uniform, hung over.

When a young person thinks it's cool to get screwed up all the time, like I did, it could be an indication there's potential for addiction. But at that point I didn't realize I had the addiction gene. I just saw myself as a rebel with a cause: to prove that I could get through prestigious Maine Maritime Academy—and life itself—as a renegade. My class was full of other such subversives, in part because we'd been groomed that way by upperclassmen with the same attitude.

An example of that mutinous undercurrent occurred when we were freshmen. The graduating senior class completely trashed the academy, throwing ripped up text books, chairs, and clothes into their section of the dorms. There was trash a foot deep in the hallways, toilet paper in all the trees on campus, and everywhere drunken midshipmen out of control. This was all done the night before they were to graduate with parents and officials in attendance.

One time I got stoned just before dinner. At MMA there was one mess hall and an officer was always on duty at mealtime, so we had to be in uniform and look presentable. That day I got high with my roommate and wasn't sure I should eat in the mess hall. I looked in the mirror at my extremely bloodshot eyes. *Man, I'm baked.*

But we were fearless back then, so my roommate and I walked down to the mess hall and went through the serving line. I was a little paranoid and looked around to make sure I wasn't being watched. I looked for an out-of-the-way seat where I could be incognito. Before I could sit down, I ran into my friend Grady James, a junior. He took one look at me and laughed.

"What's so funny?" I asked.

"Your eyes are so red I can tell you're stoned out of your mind."

His hysterical laughter made me even more paranoid. I said, "Fuck off!" and sat down. Nobody else said a word to me, but at that moment I decided getting stoned before dinner would not be happening on a regular basis.

There it was again—that fascination for taking drugs and blatantly walking around campus in uniform as if everything were perfectly normal.

Of course, uniforms certainly were part of everyday, normal life at MMA. In fact, not only were all the midshipmen required to wear naval style uniforms during the day, the professors were also required to wear them. All of the professors complied, except two.

The first, considered one of the country's leading experts on ships, sea captains, and the history of men at sea, taught American Oceanic History. Quite the character, he was known as "Bucko." In the old days of wooden ships, a "Bucko Mate" was the enforcer, the man who got sailors to work harder by hitting them with a wooden club. This Bucko wore the prescribed uniform, but tilted his high-pressure hat to the side, tucked one pant leg inside his boot, and left one out. He made believe he didn't know the difference, but he was a brilliant man; I think he knew exactly what he was doing. He was, in his own subtle way, being a non-conformist.

I'm not sure if the name Bucko was self-appointed or if the middies made it up, since midshipmen have been known to show ingenuity with nicknames. We called the Nuclear Engineering teacher "Wing Nut" for his big ears and the Economics teacher "The Sandman," for being so boring we constantly fell asleep in class. The Tanker Operations professor was dubbed "Crash" after he drunkenly drove down a walkway, stairs and all. I witnessed the entire event. After he came to a stop at the mess hall, he got out, put on his high-pressure cap, went inside, and ate a meal as if nothing unusual had happened.

Then there was the academy barber—my uncle, my mother's brother-in-law—known as "Shaky Dick." Like me, he liked to tip the bottle, and his hands shook so badly in the mornings we worried he'd take off a piece of someone's ear. Shaky Dick met the demise of his academy career one afternoon when the admiral unexpectedly sat down in his barber's chair. Shaky Dick had one too many noontime cocktails, and there went a legend. He was fired the same day, with no second chances.

We labeled the physics teacher "Speedo" for writing formulas at a rate of about three feet per second that stretched across the entire chalkboard and then expecting his students to soak it all in. There was also the less inventive "Wimpy" and "Stinky," and we called our 500-foot training ship the "State of Pain" instead of the "State of Maine." We were unabashedly cruel at times, but the rebellious attitudes stemmed from a bunch of teens and twenty-somethings responding to a regimental lifestyle.

While Bucko only wore the uniform incorrectly, our Psychology professor refused to wear one at all. He was a New Yorker with an overgrown Freudian beard and liberal teachings for the time. A deep thinker, he discussed everything openly. He was also a recovering drug addict and alcoholic. We were at the age of experimentation, and we bugged him to tell us about his drug-using days. He liked to talk to us about the dangers of substance abuse. One day he told us he'd only used heroin once, because he loved the high so much he knew if he used it again he'd become addicted.

I asked him, "Have you ever tried cocaine?"

"Yes, I've tried it many times. It's bad news."

"If it's bad news, why would you try it 'many' times?" I questioned. "Have you ever stayed up all night doing cocaine?"

He then said, "Darryl, I want to talk to you outside of the classroom, please."

"Um, okay." I was floored. Everyone in the classroom watched us walk into the hallway.

The professor shut the door. He asked calmly, "Darryl, do you have a cocaine problem?"

I was surprised. "No, I don't. Why would you ask me that?"

My mind was whirling. I did have the makings of a cocaine problem, but nobody had ever had the gall to ask me about it. Plus, he had asked me to step outside in front of twenty-five of my peers. What were they thinking, and what would they say to the other midshipmen outside of class? What the professor had done was unprecedented; to my knowledge, no one else had ever been put on the spot like that. He'd seen right through the questions I had asked.

"I'm just making sure you're okay. Are you sure you don't have a cocaine problem? I'd be happy to talk to you confidentially and help you through it if you do."

Not surprisingly, I lied. "No, I can assure you, I don't have a cocaine problem. I appreciate your concern, though."

Twenty-five pairs of eyes watched me walk back into a classroom where someone seemingly had pushed the mute button. I didn't say a word to anyone. When asked about it later, I told my classmates not to worry about it.

I've often wondered if I'd admitted my substance abuse that day how my life might have been different. Would I have avoided all the demons that chased me for another twenty-two years? Yet I can live with the idea that I'll never know the answer to that question. Instead, I hope to redeem the cockeyed path I took by exposing my life as a cautionary tale.

CHAPTER SIX
SCHOOL OF HARD KNOCKS

When second semester began, nothing changed; I self-medicated with marijuana again. It didn't help that we had a more challenging, heavier class load. This time, we were taking only military and maritime classes: Maritime Shipping Economics, Deck Drawing (ship design/drafting), Seamanship, Rules of the Road, Marlinspike (knots and rigging), Celestial Navigation, Tanker Operations, and a class called "Merchant Marine Officer."

So, with a defiant attitude, I continued to dabble in marijuana. Occasionally I'd score some cocaine, and a bunch of us would stay at MMA over the weekend to party. Drug use was strictly forbidden, so we stayed quietly behind locked doors. We also smoked a lot of "good Maine green bud" grown by people I knew along the coast. I'd buy seven or eight grams of what we called "high test smoke," and get the boys together to get high on study breaks. It wasn't the most efficient way to study, but I didn't care.

If caught, we knew we'd be thrown out of the academy and the Coast Guard would be notified. But we were hip to all the tricks. We smoked a one-hit pipe and to minimize the smell, we blew smoke into rolled-up towels, leaving a brown impression, our own "THC lipstick mark." We also stuffed a towel into the space at the bottom of the door so that any smoke that escaped the blow rag stayed in the room. We sometimes got stoned three or four times in a single day.

Even now, I can't say why I thought it was okay to go through life like that. I wasn't in the least ashamed of my behavior. In part I was doing what I needed to survive MMA's challenging work load, but I'm amazed I was able to get through all the dope smoking and studying at the same time.

One day Joe Bowen, one of the smartest, coolest guys I knew, asked me about it. "How are you passing all your classes and smoking this much weed? I can't believe you can do it."

I told him pot quieted my mind. I'd smoke, relax, have fun with the guys, and then hit the books. I had an uncanny ability to focus when I needed to, and even then I had an unbelievable work ethic. I still do. It's something my parents instilled in all their children, and that work ethic continues to serve me well. No matter what was going on in my life, my mission was to study, graduate from MMA, go to sea, and be successful. Whatever needed to be done, I would do it. It didn't matter if I hadn't slept or eaten; I'd hit the coffee pot running and study all night long.

I'd get high and then study. I'm sure it took me two hours to get what most people learned in one. My mind often wandered, and I had to constantly refocus. But without making excuses for my behavior or condoning substance abuse, I must acknowledge that I was doing what I needed to survive. Some people self-medicate because there really is a condition that needs medicating, such as my depression. The ideal would be to get the right kind of help, but people who need help often don't know they need it.

One day, my buddies and I found something on the training ship that led to even more frequent use of marijuana. Behind the lockers in Six Hold we found a dark blue plastic bong just shy of a yard tall, obviously a leftover from a previous cruise. Two of us got a duffel bag and transported it to the dorms. We used that bong the rest of the year.

The dorm bathrooms were "gang heads" outside our rooms with multiple showers, sinks, and toilets. One of the gang heads also had lockers, and that's where we kept the bong. When we wanted to use it, we put a towel over it and walked through the hallway to someone's dorm room. It was a short distance, but I always wondered what we'd do if one of the lieutenants making a security round ran into one of us carrying meter-long drug paraphernalia.

One afternoon I had an accident while I was smoking out of that bong. My roommate at the time, Itchy, and I filled it with water, packed it full of sinsemilla, and were getting high behind locked doors.

"Hey man, I heard about this new thing called an elevator. Have you ever heard of it?" I asked.

"No, what's that all about?"

"You get a head rush off smoking weed by hyperventilating. It's kind of like when you were a kid and you took a deep breath and held it while you brother squeezed you from behind. You would kind of pass out and then come to. Didn't you ever try that as a kid?"

"Yeah, I remember doing that," he said. "What's an elevator, though?"

"You stoop down close to the ground and light the bong. As you're taking the hit, you stand up slowly, and you'll get a head rush. I've never done it, but I've been told it's pretty wild."

"Okay. You first." Itchy smiled.

I tilted the bong, knelt down as close as I could to the floor, and lit it. I smiled and stood up slowly. The next thing I remembered was hearing a crash. I didn't know what it was.

"You're okay, man." Itchy was shaking me by the shoulders, and somehow I was on my knees coming out of a blackout.

"What happened, man? All I remember is standing up, and then I heard a loud bang."

Itchy was smiling. "You see the steel radiator over there?" He laughed.

"What about it?" I asked, surprised.

"That loud bang was your face hitting it. You passed out cold and went face first right into that thing!" He laughed again. "Your face is a mess."

I got off my knees and looked in the mirror. *Oh, hell!* My face was cut and bruised. I pleaded with Itchy to get some ice. "The officers are gonna ask me what happened to my face. Hurry up, man, so I can at least keep the swelling down!"

He was still laughing as he left. As I iced my face that afternoon, I got up every fifteen minutes to look in the mirror. I thought, *Oh God, I've done it this time!* That was the first and last time I did an elevator.

To make matters worse, Itchy decided I was the latest science exhibit; he gathered some guys for a big laugh fest, until I finally kicked them out. I sat in my room sulking and icing my face. It hadn't turned black and blue yet, so I figured maybe I could cover it up a little. My parents I could handle by staying at MMA on weekends until my face returned to normal. But I needed a good story for the academy and my professors. While I was thinking one up, I cleaned up and put on my after-hours uniform.

Itchy was still laughing at me on our way to dinner; I angrily told him to shut up. As we went through the serving line, I got quite a few looks and a few comments, but no problems. After filling up my tray, I went out into the mess hall and ran straight into Lt. Deratt.

The lieutenant asked, "What happened, Mr. Hagar? Did you get in a fight or something?"

There was a little snow and ice on the ground left over from the long Maine winter, so I said, "Oh, no, sir. I was running down the hill from the library in my uniform and dress shoes and hit an ice patch. I fell flat on my face. I was a little shaken up, but I'm better now." Lying through my teeth was becoming far too easy.

"If you get headaches or if it gets worse, I want you to get up in the night and call the doctor. You should go see him tomorrow, regardless."

I promised to see the doctor if it got any worse. Then I sat at one of the long tables as Itchy and others laughed and pointed. I avoided eye contact with all of them. I figured the situation was still manageable, but I didn't want to be seen laughing and risk having our room investigated. We still had a bong in the bathroom as tall as a two-year-old child. We didn't need any extra attention.

I continued to study, and I continued to get stoned, but I did slow down the marijuana use. Having a beat up face was humiliating, and it made me think about being more careful. But that was just one of many times I ended up beating up my own body under the influence of alcohol and drugs.

Despite my many harebrained high jinks in my first two years at the academy, my mother and father were still proud of me. After all, I was working my way through one of the world's most prestigious maritime academies.

Of course, they knew only a little about my blossoming drug addictions and alcoholism, because I worked hard at keeping it from them.

CHAPTER SEVEN
NAVIGATING THE GULF

It was time for "cadet shipping," our first trip on a professional ship, which we took after the end of sophomore year. We would also be required to complete a "sea project," a hundred pages of navigation problems to solve, seamanship terms to learn, and diagrams to draw.

Cadets competed for shipping billets. My aspiration was to pilot huge supertankers, so I zeroed in on the big oil companies. I lobbied for and obtained a shipping billet with Texaco. At the time they operated more than a dozen large ships, and I envisioned someday being a captain with them.

I packed my sea bag with work clothes, khaki uniforms, and toiletries. My sea project was in my briefcase along with my academy-issued sextant for taking navigational sights of the sun, moon, and stars.

For the sea project, we were expected to identify everything on board, trace out all the systems, and then diagram how they worked and tied in together. The sea project was a daunting task that I'd have to work on after my daily work on deck with the sailors and after I stood watch on the bridge with the officers.

I flew to Texas, very much a wet-behind-the-ears cadet, to join the SS Texaco New York, a 700-foot stemwinder, meaning there was only one house (living and working quarters) on the stern. The ship carried diesel oil, gasoline, and other clean oils between Texas and Florida.

The captain picked me up in Beaumont. He was a nice old guy who sensed I was a scared young kid. I'd never been on a professional oil tanker, and I found the idea intimidating. We boarded, and he showed me to a nice stateroom with a bunk, desk, bureau, recliner, and a private head.

I looked out the porthole and saw men on deck tending mooring lines, turning valves, and working hard in the Texas sun, so I threw on a boiler suit and went to meet the chief mate, the other mates, and some of the crew. I noticed that all the officers were white, but the crew was multi-national, though several were Southerners from places like Mobile, Alabama, and Houston.

On my first day, the chief mate was busy wrapping up his duties so he could sign off. He gave me a list of nautical terms to define and sent me to the bridge to look them up. I pulled out Bowditch, a.k.a. *American Practical Navigator*, the nautical navigation "Bible." I was facing the chart table, leaning over as I was writing, when I heard the bridge door open behind me.

A voice said, "You must be the deck cadet. I'm the new chief mate."

My heart suddenly jumped as I felt something strange. I thought, *Did this guy just slap me on the ass?*

Stunned, I shook hands and introduced myself to a tall, mustached, deep-voiced, rugged-looking sailor.

"Hi, Darryl. How are things going? How do you like the Texaco New York?"

"Things are fine. I like this ship, and I'm learning a lot," I said, trying to sound normal.

"Good for you. We'll catch up later," he said and left.

My mind was whirling. *Is this guy trying to send me a message? Maybe he was slapping me on the back and missed. I'll give him the benefit of the doubt, but I'll keep an eye on him.*

The engine cadet, Mike Hurly, was also from Maine Maritime Academy, making us partners in crime, since we spent all our leisure time together. Really, we were just scared, inexperienced kids together on a big ship with a bunch of wizened, grizzled sailors.

I ran into Hurly in the mess hall the next night. Nobody else was around, so I said, "I had the weirdest thing happen to me yesterday. . ." and told him what happened.

Mike laughed. "He did the same thing to me this morning outside the mess hall. Think we've got a gay chief mate?"

"He better not touch me again, or I'm reporting him to the captain," I said, ticked off. "I've got enough to worry about without having my boss trying to get in my pants."

But the chief mate never laid another hand on either of us. He'd obviously been fishing around for takers. When we didn't respond, he left us alone.

Throughout my time on board the Texaco New York, I was always on the bridge when the ship arrived or departed port, which gave me a good feel for how things operated. In those days, cadets were treated differently. One time we were leaving port and I was on the bridge assisting the third mate with the pre-departure gear test. We tested all the equipment to make sure all systems were working properly.

At that time, the captain came up to the bridge and asked the third mate if all the gear was tested and fully operational. The third mate said it was and the only thing left to do was to wait for the pilot and tugs. Then the captain told me, "You stand in the corner and be quiet. I don't want to hear a word out of you!"

That's how cadets were treated in 1983. As ship's officers years later, we gave cadets full control over the watch at sea or in port handling the cargo. We shadowed them and assisted when necessary. The cadets made mistakes, but we never let things get out of hand. By allowing them the responsibilities involved in taking control of the vessel, they learned how to be competent officers at a much younger age than I did. When I did my cadet shipping, we were mainly there to observe.

After I had sailed on the Texaco New York for about a month, she laid up in Port Arthur on the Gulf of Mexico for lack of work. I then boarded the SS Texaco Montana, a mid-ship house tanker, meaning there were two houses, one amidships and another astern. The captain, mates, and cadets slept in the mid-ship house, with the bridge located at the top. The chief engineer, assistant engineers, and the remaining crew resided in the afterhouse, where the galley was one deck above the main deck.

The mates on the Montana asked me about the chief mate on the Texaco New York. Just as I suspected, they had stories about when he was captain and asked the third mate to model a pair of Speedos. I realized then that there were strange people on these ships.

Another odd one was the survivor of a supertanker accident. Three years earlier, the SS North Dakota had struck a Chevron oil rig in the Gulf of Mexico, resulting in an explosion and fire. The man aboard our ship who survived that tragic night seemed close to a nervous breakdown. He wouldn't go in any room without tying the door open and was always on the verge of crying. I found it unbelievable that he continued to go to sea.

Then there was our Greek captain, a germophobe who went around opening doors with a handkerchief. He had a CPR mouth insert for giving an unconscious person mouth-to-mouth without touching lips and carried it with him 24/7. He was an intense, quirky, nervous man who I thought was a bit insane, and he intimidated me.

Nobody had warned me of this aspect of the Merchant Marine, and I wondered what kind of person I would turn out to be after years of going to sea. Would I have a nervous breakdown? Become a person who lived only to go to sea?

There was also plenty of drinking on duty in those days. One night we were steaming through hundreds of oil rigs in the Gulf of Mexico. I was standing watch with an able-bodied seaman nicknamed Pee Wee, a thirty-year veteran of the Merchant Marine, about five-foot tall, and one of the nicest men in the world. We stood outside on the bridge wings acting as lookouts, and in our four hours on watch he periodically asked the third mate if he could step down to his room to get a coat, take some aspirin, use the bathroom, etc.

What I didn't know at the time was that Pee Wee was hitting the booze—thus the need to keep stepping below. I had no idea that kind of thing even happened on tankers. We were navigating a huge supertanker through crowded waters, and the thought of someone drinking on duty never crossed my mind.

CHAPTER EIGHT
PAIN LIKE I NEVER KNEW

Cadet shipping was quite the experience for this country boy from Maine. It was the first time I'd ever flown on a plane, the first time I'd ever traveled around the United States, and the first time I'd ever helped navigate 700-foot oil tankers. I was looking forward to some time off from the pressures of training.

The rest of my summer that year was work, drink, smoke, and chase girls. I got a job painting houses; it was hard work but there was money to drink on and buy a bag of weed once in awhile, so I was happy. I worked all day, partied all night, and most of my sleeping was done passed out from partying. If I couldn't drive home, I crashed a buddy's house, and it wasn't unusual for me to wake up on some stranger's couch.

At that time, my dad was still recuperating from back surgery. He didn't receive any kind of help from his employer, and that was tough on him mentally. Adding to the strain, my mom began to press him to get back to work. He wasn't healing as fast as the doctors and our family had hoped, and she was stressed by the mounting bills.

No one in our family realized Dad was dealing with depression, although I now believe I may have inherited the condition from him. At the time, we didn't understand the serious nature of depression as a mental illness.

I went back to school in the fall of 1983, a junior midshipman. As I said goodbye to my mom, I gave her a hug and kiss. I shook my dad's hand and knew he was proud of me; I could see it in his eyes. I was growing into a man, and he loved me. I assumed my father would eventually get stronger, get back to work, and our family would survive these tough times.

I quickly got caught up in the new school year. I took seventeen credits, as easy as it got at the academy—all maritime classes: Problems in Transportation, Ship's Stability, Seamanship, Celestial Navigation, Merchant Marine Officer, and International Law and Organization.

I began running cross country again. Though I'd smoked a lot of weed that summer, I had a natural ability and got in shape quickly. I was the team's best runner, as I'd been the past two years, and the coach looked to me for leadership. We ran every night after school. Eventually we were up to sixty miles a week, and I was back in peak form, running ten miles in about sixty-five minutes. I was not smoking any marijuana.

We were running in meets most weekends, but I had a few weekends off when I went home. My parents' home was in the tiny town of Nobleboro, but since Damariscotta was the center of Lincoln County—with the movie theater and all the main stores and banks—everyone in the area claimed they were from Damariscotta. Lincoln County was populated by about a dozen small towns with populations of eight hundred to three thousand people. Most people knew and cared about each other. It's still that way today.

I went home one Friday afternoon and greeted Mom and Dad at the door. They gave me hugs, and my father shook my hand warmly. They soon told me some troubling news: One of the town's leaders had committed suicide, a man we all called "Grampa Ralph." Ralph was elderly, sickly, and didn't want to wait to die. His suicide had shocked the entire community.

My father wasn't an outwardly emotional man and didn't talk about sensitive issues, but I could tell he was deeply troubled by Ralph's passing. Yet I was paying little attention to my father's emotional stability and had no idea the incident would cause some dark reflections regarding his own situation. I still can't help wishing I'd known what was going through my dad's mind.

The weekend at home passed, and my buddies arrived to take me back to Castine. I grabbed my books and sea bag and ran out to the car. As we pulled out, one of my brothers came outside to speak to me.

"Darryl, you forgot to shake Dad's hand. He sent me out here to say goodbye."

"Oops. Tell him I said goodbye, and I'll see him in a couple of weeks when I come home."

"Okay, Darryl. I'll tell him. See ya later, man."

The next couple of weeks of school progressed normally. I studied every night, ran cross country, and tried to get good grades—and not too many demerits. It was challenging, but I attended everything I was supposed to; up to that point I hadn't received too many demerits.

One afternoon we were playing intramural softball on a hill overgrown with grass inside Fort George, built in the Revolutionary War era, when an on-duty midshipman came up to me. He was in uniform, and I noticed by his nametag that he was a freshman.

"Are you Second Class Hagar?" he asked breathlessly. "The commander wants to see you in his office immediately."

Surprised and concerned, I asked, "What for? What's the problem?"

"You have a family emergency, sir. He wants to see you right now."

I ran over the hill and across campus. As soon as I opened the door to the commander's office, I saw my mother's sisters, Aunt Polly and Aunt Linda. They had both been crying.

"What's going on? What's happening?" I cried out.

Aunt Polly blurted out, "Darryl, there's been an accident. Your father shot and killed himself this morning."

"What?! No, it can't be. I just saw him a few weeks ago. He was okay." I was in shock and didn't know how to process what I'd just been told. I sat down and put my face in my hands, stunned and confused. I tried to cry, but I couldn't.

"Your mother sent us up here to get you. All three of your brothers and your sister are with her now. She wants you to come home," Aunt Polly said.

I looked at Commander Kropp. He was a disciplinarian, a tough drill-sergeant type, but he had tears in his eyes.

"Go home to your family, son. We'll be here for you when you get back." I could hear the compassion and sadness in his voice.

I looked directly at him and said, "Thank you, sir. I'll be back as soon as I can."

As I walked to my dorm room to get my things, my head was whirling. What the hell was going on? My dad had killed himself? I couldn't process the information. I couldn't believe it was really happening.

During the two-hour drive down U.S. Route 1 toward my boyhood home, I was quiet for some time. Then I started asking questions. I started with Aunt Linda, who was the Sheriff's personal secretary.

"A neighbor close to the Upper Cross Road heard a gunshot and called the Lincoln County Sheriff's Department," she said. "A deputy went to investigate and reported a suicide. They informed the sheriff, and your brother Mark went and identified the body."

Aunt Polly added, "It happened right out of the blue, Darryl. He drove there this morning and shot himself. Nobody knows why. Nobody knew it was going to happen."

"Where's Mom? Is she all right?" I asked.

"She's pretty shook up. She was down at Uncle Winty's pharmacy, crying. He's taking care of her for now." Aunt Linda explained that Winton would drive my mother home. All of my siblings were already there, waiting for me.

I sat in the car, dazed. This couldn't be real. This kind of thing didn't happen to normal families like ours. How did I fail to realize he was in that much pain? How could I be so caught up in my own self-absorbed little world that I couldn't see that my dad was preparing to end his life? I relived the last time I'd seen him, and guilt and shame flooded in. I'd forgotten to shake his hand, and when my brother had come out to tell me, I hadn't even gotten out of the car. What a considerate and loving son I was.

I began to weep quietly. My aunts knew I was in a lot of pain, and we drove the rest of the way home in silence. At home, the unreality of the experience continued. There were cars parked everywhere, and people milled around inside and outside of the house. One of my mother's best friends ran up to me and wrapped her arms around me.

She was crying. "Darryl, I am so sorry."

I walked toward the front door, and my oldest brother Mark came up to me. He was crying, and we hugged.

"Mark, you have to stop crying, or you're going to get me crying," I told him quietly.

"I can't help it," he said, sobbing.

God help me, my hardened heart was already being inconsiderate. Selfishly, I didn't want to come unglued in front of everyone. Sometimes I wonder what happened to my soul back then. Here I was, telling my brother, the one who had identified our father's body, not to cry. I couldn't even let him grieve properly.

I walked inside and hugged and kissed my mother and sister. I hugged my brothers Randy and Chris. My mother has always been strong, and she had been smart to send her sisters to collect her children. We would get through this together. We no longer had a father, but we still had a mother. We might be dysfunctional, but we'd be okay.

I went around and hugged everyone there. I didn't talk about my father's death; I just thanked them for supporting our family. I felt like I was in the twilight zone or having a bad dream—I wanted to wake up and realize none of it was true. After about thirty minutes I suddenly decided I needed to get away from all of the weirdness.

I looked at my younger brother Chris. "Want to go drink some beer?"

"Darryl, this is no time to go partying."

"Okay. Do what you gotta do, and I'll do what I gotta do."

It wasn't something I wanted to do, it was something I *needed* to do, and fast. At the time I didn't care what my family thought if I split to be alone and drink beer. I needed to process what had happened, and

I wasn't comfortable around all the grieving friends and family. I loved them all, but being there wasn't working for me. If they didn't understand, oh well. I was in self-preservation mode, and there was no stopping me. Only booze would give me some comfort.

My mother's friend Carol said I could go to her house. On the way, I stopped at the store for some beer. The road to her house went past Upper Cross Road, where my dad had shot himself. I don't remember that ride to Carol's house. I don't remember looking down that road as I passed by, but I know that I did. I didn't drive down that road that day, but I did many times in the years to come.

At Carol's house I started shooting down beers. They tasted good. I couldn't understand how the rest of my family could stay sober through something like this. I needed to escape reality, and I didn't want to go back to it for a very long time. I sat there and drank and drank and drank.

I wondered how my life was going to change. I didn't have a dad anymore. No one to go hunting and fishing with. No one to watch the Boston Red Sox with every year.

Carol showed up later and said my mother wanted me back home. I was already tipsy, so I agreed to let Carol drive me. I thanked her and went back into the house. The crowd had thinned out, so I sat down alone in the living room and finished my beer.

I thought about asking Mark what he'd seen when he identified our father's body. I didn't know any of the details except that he'd used a shotgun. I didn't know if he had put the gun in his mouth, against his temple, or at his chest. I figured he must have shot himself in the old blue Ford 150 pickup; I envisioned a bloody, gory mess.

I wondered about those things for many years, but couldn't bring myself to ask Mark about them. He had gone to the scene, and I didn't want him to have to relive it. I can only imagine how bad that messed with his head, and I figured it wasn't that important that he tell me. It wouldn't change anything.

I didn't talk about my father's tragic death for twenty three years. I stuffed my emotions down so deeply that nobody could have pulled them out. I then filled my body with alcohol and drugs to mask my pain, all the while telling the world—in deeds and sometimes in words—to leave me the fuck alone.

I believe now that I was born with a genetic predisposition toward addiction. If I had chosen not to feed those addictions, they would have lain dormant. But when I went to Maine Maritime Academy, and even before then as a teenager, I began to awaken those addictions, although for some time they were not fully engaged.

After my father killed himself, a switch was turned on, and I quickly became a full-fledged alcoholic and drug abuser. I drank whenever I could, smoked weed continually, and scored any other drug that was available as often as I was able. I self-medicated myself almost into oblivion. I didn't want to deal with anything other than getting through the academy without self-destructing. And because I refused to get professional help, I tormented my family, myself, and everyone whose lives I touched for many, many years.

The Man Overboard had been born.

It came time for the wake and the funeral. Meanwhile, I was most comfortable all liquored up, but nobody said a word to me about it. Everyone in the family was dealing with the pain of my father's death in his or her own way.

My heart had been hardened by attending the academy and being around men all the time. Crying was for the weak. After that first small show of emotion the day I came home, I didn't cry about my father, even when I was alone. I was hurting, but I put on a facade to show how strong I was. There was enough crying going on around me; no one needed me to add to the sadness.

The phone calls came in day and night, and friends and neighbors brought us more homemade food than we knew what to do with. The first flowers that had arrived were going bad, but new arrangements kept arriving. Our mailbox was full of sympathy cards.

My mother hired a local funeral home and undertaker, who was to perform plastic surgery on my father's face. I never asked where he shot himself, so I didn't know what needed to be done. The undertaker assured my mother that my dad would look natural, and if she wanted an open casket, he didn't see a problem with that. He told her that the family could view the body before the wake and decide then.

It had been about five days since the death, and my father's body had been worked on extensively. The family met and drove down to the funeral home together for the wake. When we got there, I was right back in the twilight zone. I felt like I was in a movie, and it was all make-believe. Mom, Mark, Randy, Chris, Karen Ann, and I shook hands with the undertaker, who led us to a private room.

There in the middle of the room was my father, dressed in a suit and tie, lying in a coffin. It was just too much. I couldn't believe we had to go through the ritual, but it was necessary to the grieving process. Seeing him made me wake up to the truth. Any doubt about the reality of the nightmare we were living quickly vanished.

We approached, and I looked down on my old man. His face was heavily made up and pale, but he resembled himself when he was alive. The funeral home had done an exceptional job. My mother was weeping, and my sister was holding her, also crying. My older brothers stood there, stunned. Chris was like me; he looked as if he were in disbelief about the whole strange event.

We had been told we each could put something in the coffin that had a special meaning. Karen Ann had written a letter to my dad, saying how she would miss him and that she knew he was now in heaven. She was the smart one to think of doing that. I didn't put anything in.

Karen was upset. She'd always been "Daddy's little girl." She used to sit with him in his recliner and they'd watch TV together. It was probably one way he comforted his inner demons; it was a chance to love and be loved and get out of his own head.

I got up close to my father's body and touched his hand. It was stiff and cold. There was no expression on his face.

I bowed my head and prayed, *God, I'm not sure why you took him at such a young age. Please take care of him in heaven and tell him we're okay. We forgive his decision, and we all love him very much. We'll be a whole family again when you call for all of us. Put his mind at peace and be with him every day. Amen.*

I raised my head. My father lay there, very still. I would see him one more time at the funeral, and then I knew I'd have to wait until heaven. That is, if God let me in. I was sure we'd be reunited one day, and that would be the sweetest day. That was my only positive thought about the whole mess, and I will hold onto that sentimental wish for the rest of my days.

The following day the family went to the funeral home in a limousine. Once again the whole scene seemed unreal. My mother, brothers, and sister were somber.

I was quiet and reflective during that ride. I thought about my dad playing baseball with his boys when we were young. Of the camping trips to Canada Falls and Baxter State Park. Of the times we went fishing on Damariscotta Lake, getting in the middle of a school of white perch, catching one fish right after another, and laughing uncontrollably all the while.

I thought back on the moments he and I spent together. In 1975, it was the two of us watching the Red Sox. My dad had let me stay up late that night to watch the game. I'll never forget that World Series, when Carlton Fisk hit the game-winning homerun in the ninth inning of game six—what it meant to me then, and what it means to me now. We were two peas in a pod, father and son, bonded by our love for each other and for the Boston Red Sox.

The eventuality that my father would be gone forever started to sink in. We would have the funeral, and afterward we'd bury him in the old Borland Hill Cemetery, his final resting place. It's where I intend to be buried one day.

At the funeral home, there were cars parked as far as the eye could see. The hall was overflowing with family and friends. My father had been well-loved; you would have been hard-pressed to find one person in town who didn't like him.

People's heads turned and watched us intently as we got out of the limo. I could feel their eyes on us and understood their curiosity and sympathy. People sincerely felt for our family and were wondering how we were holding up.

I wasn't much for crying and hadn't planned on starting, but I was surprised how strong my emotions were at seeing all the supportive faces. Tears welled up in my eyes and rolled down my face.

We walked into the funeral home to people's handshakes, hugs, and kisses. Some of my high school friends were there, all of the town's leaders, all of our friends, and all of our family. There were people there I hadn't seen in years that had been important in both my life and my family's.

The pastor of Damariscotta Baptist Church, Don Harrington, was to perform the service. I shook his hand and thanked him. He looked in my eyes, and I could feel his love for our family. He would say some kind words and give my father the respect that he deserved. He understood our family's pain, and I loved him as an individual and as a pastor. His family had long been friends with mine, and his wife and kids were good people.

We sat in the front row, close to my father's coffin. There were a lot of flowers, and I noticed that some of my high school buddies and MMA classmates had sent some of them. That was comforting, and I appreciated the thoughts and prayers. The funeral home continued to fill up, and soon there were no seats left. The doors were left open for people to stand outside.

Pastor Harrington started the service and spoke of my father being a good man in the community, a veteran, and a good family man. As he continued, my Auntie Linda ran out of the funeral home, screaming and sobbing. Everyone in the place understood; it all had been a lot to swallow. My dad had a wife and five kids, was a well-liked member of the community, and had decided to kill himself. It was an unusual, sad situation.

I felt the tears coming again. This time, I wept openly and didn't let my embarrassment get in the way. In truth, I had no control over it. I buried my face in my hands and wept, and I remained that way until the funeral was over. Later, Pastor Harrington told my mother he had seen and heard me crying and felt it was good that I had finally broken down.

My dad was gone, and suddenly I felt more alone than I'd ever felt in my life. Yet I didn't mention my father, the funeral, or the suicide to anyone. As far as I was concerned, there was nothing to say.

Nobody asked me if I needed help. Not the family. Not Maine Maritime Academy. Not our pastor, our friends, or professional therapists. The pervading belief at the time was: If it's too ugly a subject, better not talk about it. Sweep it under the rug and move forward. And I was too "strong" to ask for help, so I dealt with the pain my own way.

Such was the way of the world then. In the end, I hurt a lot of people because of that miscalculation. The people around me were saddled with a drunken, drug-riddled madman for many, many years. I take full responsibility for all of my subsequent actions, but because of what happened to me, I pray that in the future this society learns to handle these situations with greater wisdom and intervention.

Of course, hindsight is 20/20; I should have asked God to help me get through a confusing and emotional time. When I should have been talking to my minister, a therapist, and my family, I instead turned to the bottle and to drugs.

It took many very dark years before my faith finally resurfaced.

GLENN CHADBOURNE

CHAPTER NINE
SINKING LOWER EVERY YEAR

I stayed home for a week after the funeral. Our family grieved, cried, put up a good front—and had no other choice but to get on with our lives.

Despite it all, my mother urged me to go back to the academy before I got too far behind. I called my buddies, and they showed up on Sunday night to give me a lift.

"Mom, I'm sorry I have to leave. I'm coming home next weekend."

"It's up to you," she said. "We'll be all right. Stay and study if you need to." She reminded me that I'd be busy with cross country meets on the weekends.

I told her I was thinking about resigning from the team so I could come home every weekend to be with the family.

"Whatever you think is best, Darryl. I want you to go back up there and not worry about a thing besides your studies. Your father would have wanted it that way." She kissed me goodbye.

It was a quiet ride to Castine. Normally the four of us would be laughing and joking. The guys told me how sorry they were and asked if I was okay. After that we rode in silence for two hours.

Everyone at MMA was empathetic yet distant. Nobody really knew how to respond to the suicide. A lot of people asked, "Are you doing okay?" or said, "I'm really sorry," but no one pulled me aside and said what I really needed to hear: "Darryl, if you need to talk, I'm here for you, day or night." Nobody in the academy administration, in the commandant's office—not even any of my closest friends.

I continued to receive words of encouragement and expressions of sympathy from friends and acquaintances. I decided to tell the cross country coach I was resigning from the team. He accepted my resignation with sadness.

I found someone selling weed for $7 a gram and bought two. If I used it sparingly, that much weed would normally last me a week, but not this time. I found Itchy, Moil, Cool, HoJo, and a few others, and we got out the bong and started doing hits. Then we started to talk. They were the first ones to ask me about what had happened.

"What happened to him, Darryl? Why did he do it?" Itchy asked.

"I don't know, man. He was recovering from back surgery. He must have been depressed and freaking out about it somehow. The funeral was so weird; I thought I was going to have a nervous breakdown."

The weed kicked in, and I felt better immediately. Finally, my mind was medicated again. I was around my boys. I would be all right.

I said, "I had a hard time with it, you guys, but I'm better now." I expressed how relieved I was that I hadn't missed too much school and how I was anxious to get caught up.

HoJo explained that all my instructors had said they would allow me time to get back up to speed. My buddies had told them the details of my dad's death. What a tremendous feeling it was to hear that they were watching my back. True to my word, I quickly caught up with my schoolwork. The strong work ethic instilled in me by my parents kicked right in.

My work ethic may have been over the top, but so was my brain. My mind worked 24/7. The only thing that soothed it was drinking and using drugs, which allowed me to escape reality and my mental overactivity. Because alcohol was hard to sneak into the dorm, marijuana was my drug of choice. Smoking weed was an effective way to get out of my head, but it was also expensive. At $7 a gram and with my big-time habit, I needed a change of plan.

I figured the only way I could afford to get high all the time was to sell it. I could pick up a quarter pound a week, break it into grams, and make a nice profit. I thought I'd gain a few grams of free weed for myself and still have $100 left over. Nope. All the profits went into buying more homegrown.

When I brought weed back on Sunday night, the boys would be looking for me. We'd do a few hits and then I'd clear the room except for Itchy. We locked the door and stuffed a towel at the bottom. When we brought out the weed, the scent was as strong as if a skunk had crawled behind the bunk beds and died.

Itchy and I weighed out grams of bud and placed each in a baggie. Four ounces yielded 112 one-gram bags, and it took several hours to complete the operation. Of course, we had to take a bong hit every fifteen minutes or so. Itchy was paid handsomely every week in free smoke. I sold about a hundred grams and smoked the rest.

Every week for two years I took the profits and bought another quarter pound. It was the only time in my life I was a true pothead. I needed to be high after my father's suicide, so I self-medicated and brought a lot of my friends along with me. I often did bong hits all night, night after night.

Of course, we were professional drug users and knew what we were doing. We used blow rags and sprayed Lysol to cover up the scent. We also changed the locks on the dormitory room doors. The steel doors had heavy-duty steel locks with key tumblers inside. One side of the tumbler could be opened with the individual keys given to each roommate. The other side could be opened by academy officials and security officers with a passkey.

We took out the tumblers and rearranged the passkey side. If one of the duty officers grew suspicious and wanted to let himself in, his passkey would no longer open the door, and he would have to go back to the duty office and get a copy of the individual room key. By the time he got back with the key, we would have hidden anything illegal or incriminating.

We were getting a room inspection one day when one of the duty officers asked, "Do you men have a problem opening the door with your room keys?" The lieutenant fumbled with his keys at the door. "For some reason, this is the only door on the whole floor that my passkey won't open."

"My key works fine," Itchy said, glancing at me.

I walked over to the door and pulled out my keychain. I stuck the key in the lock and turned the deadbolt easily.

"My key works just fine, lieutenant. Maybe there's a burr in your passkey that makes it not work—did you try another passkey?" I asked innocently.

"If I remember correctly I've had this problem with this door before. As a matter of fact, there are several doors in this block that my passkey won't work on. I'll have to talk to maintenance," the lieutenant said.

He looked over the room. Everything was in order. All blow rags had been put away in the gang head next to the bong. All clothes were folded, beds made, shoes and brass belt buckles shined.

"Good job, men. Keep up the good work." He walked out, pausing to look at the door lock and muttering about how maintenance didn't keep things maintained properly.

That year I began to act up. I hadn't had any problem the two previous years, but neither had I ever smoked so much weed. My classes weren't a problem. Even though we were staying up late and getting high, I still studied for hours. But I started to blow off morning colors—at nine demerits for each unexcused absence. It would take a dozen infractions before I was expelled, but I was also nailed a few times for being out of uniform, for wearing orange boot socks instead of black military issue, and that boosted my demerit total. Before I knew it, I reached a danger point, and a letter was mailed home.

I then became careful about what I did, about how late I stayed up, and about wearing my uniform correctly every day. But one Friday afternoon I barely dodged a bullet. One of my hometown carpooling buddies sneaked an expired emergency smoke signal off the training ship. When activated, the smoke signals last thirty minutes and leave a cloud of orange smoke that can be seen for miles. They're designed to be used if a ship sinks or to make a lifeboat visible to search planes.

My traveling buddies and I left MMA and made our usual beer stop in Castine. The store had a reputation for being one of the top beer sellers in the state. Not hard to believe, considering its main customer base was six hundred thirsty midshipmen. We headed down the Castine

Demerits letter, Maine Maritime Academy.

Road toward Bucksport. I sat in back with my buddy and the orange smoke signal.

"What are you gonna do with that thing, man?" I asked.

"Light it on the Bucksport Bridge."

"Better be careful. I already have a ton of demerits. That would seal the deal for MMA to toss me out."

"They won't even know. Bucksport is twenty miles from the academy."

We drove on, drinking beer, and the anticipation began to build. Swiping an orange smoke signal, expired or not, would get us all tossed out of school if we were caught lighting it. But our renegade natures took over.

The Bucksport Bridge, connecting Waldo and Hancock counties, is 2,000 feet long and 135 feet above the Penobscot River. It's lower on both ends and highest in the middle of the span. You can only see half of the bridge at a time, except at the highest point.

We drove onto the bridge and were about a third of the way over when my classmate pulled the pin on the smoke signal. Heavy orange smoke immediately filled the car, making it impossible to see.

"Throw it out! Throw it out! I can't see to drive. Throw it out!" our driver yelled.

The smoke signal went out the window, and the inside of the car started to clear. By then the thick smoke had encompassed a third of the bridge, and both lanes of traffic had stopped.

"Drive off, drive off! We've got to get out of here!" I yelled.

I was sure only the guy in the blue van behind us knew what had happened. The traffic on the other side of the bridge, over the hump in the middle, couldn't have seen what we did. As we got to the middle of the bridge and started going downhill, we saw a Maine State Police cruiser coming onto the bridge. He saw the orange smoke and sped up to investigate. As we passed him, utter panic set in. Then the blue van suddenly tried to force us off the road. We gave him the finger and sped off, leaving him behind to tell the police it was us.

"Faster, man! Drive fast! We gotta get out of here before that trooper figures it out!"

I was freaking out. My heart was pounding. I thought for sure I'd get kicked out of the academy.

I wish I'd had a camera that day. All you could see were the ends of the bridge; nearly two-thirds was covered in a cloud of orange smoke. Traffic was backed up in both directions. No one knew what had happened or what to do. It wasn't a car on fire, it wasn't an explosion—what was that bright orange smoke?

We sped off and drove for about five miles to an old logging road, where we laughed and finished our beer. After forty-five minutes, we drove back onto the highway. We weren't pulled over during the ninety-minute ride home.

The spring semester of 1984 began, and my classes were again all maritime-related, including Ship's Medicine, Great Lakes Shipping Industry, Cargo, Celestial Navigation, Electronic Navigation, and Admiralty Law. If I hadn't been smoking so much pot and drinking so much, my grades would have been better.

Somehow I managed to make it through junior year without getting thrown out, and we celebrated at the annual Junior Ring Dance. The young women they bused to campus weren't allowed to spend the night with us in the dorms. Some of the women and midshipmen followed the rules, some didn't. Some of the young women were looking for dancing and fun, some for future husbands. Some intended to sleep in their assigned accommodations on our 500-foot training ship, and others didn't.

I was more interested in getting twisted than in meeting a girl. In the dorm, a bunch of us started doing shots of 151-proof rum, and after a few bong hits I went into a blackout. I somehow managed to make it back to my room and sat down in my old recliner. I had the feeling I was going to vomit, but I couldn't keep my eyes open or my head up. I passed out slumped over in my chair.

The next thing I remember, vaguely, is when my roommate came into the room and let out a shriek.

"Oh, my God, it stinks in here! What the hell, man? You threw up all over yourself, Darryl!"

I looked up at him through bloodshot eyes and tried to comprehend what was happening. "What's going on? What's the matter?"

"Oh, man," he said. "You shit and pissed yourself too. I can smell it. Darryl, you gotta go take a shower and clean up this mess. I need a gas mask just to be in the room with you. It's bad, Darryl, really bad."

"Okay, man, okay! Get off my case, will ya? I'll go wash up in the shower." I just wanted him to leave me alone. My head was screaming, my throat was dry, and there were foul odors coming from various parts of my body.

I stumbled out of the room and into the gang head. I thought about getting undressed, but thought, *What's the sense?* Still in a daze, I soaked my body for ten minutes. Piece by piece, I took off my wet clothes and threw them in the trash. I wanted no memories of that nightmare. I had reached a new low.

I was no longer just a potential alcoholic; my alcoholism was a sure thing, and I was sinking lower every year.

STATE OF MAINE

GLENN CHADBOURNE

CHAPTER TEN
ZERO DEGREES LATITUDE

In the summer after my junior year at MMA, it came time for our second cruise on the training ship State of Maine. We set sail from Castine and headed south. My fellow juniors and I were in charge of the vessel with licensed officers overseeing us. We finally got to run the watch on our own—navigating, avoiding other vessels, and talking on the VHF radio to the Coast Guard and other ships.

Our duties were broken into four segments just as they had been on our freshmen training cruise. There were 150 juniors, and this time we were in charge of the 150 freshmen on board. We stood watch with them, ate with them, performed maintenance with them, and kept an eye on them to ensure they learned and were safe. We also had daily training in shipboard classrooms that included lessons in seamanship, navigation, meteorology, and ship's stability.

On this voyage, there was a feeling of control that was hard to match, especially when we had "the con," when we were making the decisions directly affecting the ship's position, course, and how we passed other vessels. We could tell the freshman who was steering to bring the ship right or left to a new course, and he would follow our directions. There was always a licensed officer watching us perform our duties to ensure we followed safe practices.

We steamed for three days and stopped for a port stay near Norfolk Naval Base, where we again participated in firefighting training. After several days we got underway again heading south toward Brazil. But first we would cross the equator. It took about four days to reach Latitude 000 degrees, Longitude 040 degrees 26' West. The date was May 30, 1984.

The academy had planned quite an initiation party for those crossing the equator for the first time. We were dubbed "pollywogs" and were blindfolded, made to wear our underwear outside our pants, and put through an obstacle course. We were pushed and pulled, sprayed with a fire hose, had slime put in our mouths to mirror the feel of jellyfish, were made to swim through a "garbage" trough (filled with corn husks and seawater), and thrown into a rubber pool of cold seawater. We laughed and had a grand time. We had fantastic feasts that day and a big party at night. No alcohol was allowed.

After our first time crossing zero degrees latitude we earned the right to be called "shellbacks." The rite dates back to the Vikings and was designed to bring us into a worldwide fraternity of experienced mariners, and it unified us. The ritual is typical on both merchant and military vessels, though in recent years has garnered controversy with some reports of injury and harassment. That wasn't true on the State of Maine; for us, the ceremony was boisterous, but safe, fun and games. The initiation remains one of my fondest memories from MMA.

We steamed for another week and upon entering the coastal waters of South America were ordered to wear our dress white uniforms. As the ship docked at Fortaleza, Brazil, I was on watch at the quarterdeck in charge of checking the gangway for proper placement and operation, making me the first midshipman to step ashore. Coming down the gangway, I noticed a construction crew in hardhats working in a trench. Overseeing these men was a Brazilian beauty in a white hardhat. Our eyes met, and I could feel my heart racing.

I was mesmerized by this beautiful, exotic woman with dark blonde hair, a perfectly toned body, and bronze skin. Of course, in those days I was nothing to sneeze at. I was in good shape, slim, and tall. I'd been lifting weights and tanning on the upper decks on my off time, preparing specifically for moments like this. She looked at me in my dress whites with my officer's stripes and high pressure hat with its officer's

In my dress white uniform, sober.

gold band. We connected immediately. I walked up to her, stuck out my hand, and introduced myself.

She answered, "Welcome to Brazil. My name is Ana. How long will you stay?"

I explained that the ship would be there four days. I was psyched; she was showing interest in me. On board behind me, midshipmen were whistling and yelling, wishing they were me on the dock talking to the Brazilian beauty.

I blurted, "Would you like to go to dinner with me?"

"Yes, I would like that very much," Ana said, smiling.

We made arrangements to meet the next day, and I went back on watch.

My fellow midshipmen were excited to go out and play in Fortaleza with its beautiful beaches, bikini-clad women, and cold beer. When three hundred college-age men are released in that kind of environment, they're looking for fun and the chance to create memorable stories to regale their buddies with later. Relationships were established, pictures taken, and I suspect a few families were started unknowingly. Later on, my friends sometimes asked if I had any children around the world. To the best of my knowledge, I don't.

While dozens of other young American guys were running around the beaches of Brazil, I settled in with Ana. I was smitten. We met at a coffee shop and talked for hours. We walked the beaches and stopped at little huts to drink beer. She wasn't a drinker, but I drank enough for the both of us. We went out for dinner, and afterward Ana found a place for us to park in her car, tucked away off the road near a park.

We started kissing, and before I knew it we were ravaging each other. I had her shirt and bra off, when I noticed a small white light getting closer to the car. In the heat of the moment, I continued kissing and caressing Ana. Suddenly the white light was upon us. We were half naked when a Brazilian police officer began banging on the window.

"No! No! No!" the police officer yelled.

Ana pulled her shirt on and started the car. She sped off, leaving the police officer behind. We began laughing.

"The last thing I need is to get arrested in a foreign country!"

"It's okay now," she assured me. "This thing happens all the time in Brazil. Do not worry."

"I'm not worried, but I'd better get back to the ship. It's getting late."

Ana drove me back to the vessel, where we kissed and made plans to meet the next day. But once I was sober, I got cold feet and didn't go ashore again. She was a little older and more aggressive than I could handle, unless I had some liquid courage in me. One of the midshipmen brought word back that she was looking for me, and I caught a glimpse of her when we were undocking. But I was embarrassed and ducked belowdecks. To this day I wonder what would have happened with Ana. She was a beautiful, sweet person, but I was just a younger version of The Man Overboard, and I didn't have time for a serious relationship.

From Brazil we sailed north and east to the Canary Islands off the coast of Africa. We stayed a few days and then headed back across the Atlantic to Castine. It was a good experience going to foreign countries when we were young. I didn't get in any trouble or do anything too out of hand, although that would soon change.

GLENN CHADBOURNE

CHAPTER ELEVEN
PASSING OUT COLD

I spent the next two months at home partying; then it was time to go back for one more year at our stringent maritime academy. I was a senior and at the top of the food chain. That meant the officers knew we'd be busy with our studies. They left us alone as long as we wore our uniforms and showed up for morning colors and inspections. That year I roomed with my friend Cool. We had the same two groups of friends; we studied and partied with the deckies and played sports and partied with the engineers.

My maritime classes that fall included Marketing Management, Communications, Cargo, Rules and Regulations, Navigation Rules, General Navigation, and Electronics. Plus, I had two main hurdles to overcome, and both required me to buckle down and study.

The first was the test required to obtain my U.S. Coast Guard third mate's license, a difficult four-day examination scheduled in April, meaning I had eight months to prepare. The license would allow me to navigate ships of any size anywhere in the world under the watch of a captain. I would be in charge of the vessel while the captain and other officers were sleeping. The idea was daunting, but that's what MMA was training us to do.

The second hurdle was to earn a bachelor of nautical science degree, allowing me to obtain employment ashore if I grew tired of going to sea.

I stayed busy studying, but I was also smoking a lot of weed. I was trying to run a life full of intensity and confusion—along with depression I wasn't even aware of. I was so busy surviving, I couldn't see the turmoil around or within me.

In November, my buddy Itchy invited me up to the Moosehead Lake region to go deer hunting with the boys. We packed our stuff and drove up to Greenville. On Friday we partied most of the night, drinking beer and smoking joints. After just a few hours sleep, we got up at 4:30 a.m. and went out into the woods while it was still dark. Lucky for me, none of the guys ever got high that early in the morning, so I didn't have to worry about making that decision. It was cold outside, and I was still slightly intoxicated and very hung over, so I wasn't all that excited about hunting. But I didn't want my buddies to think I was a pansy, so I toughed it out.

I rode with Howie, Itchy, and one of their Greenville buddies to the hunting site. We got out of the car and loaded our guns. I had a light-weight 32 Special hunting rifle with a lever action. It looked like the rifles cowboys pulled from their saddles in old Westerns. Itchy had a powerful semi-automatic 30-06 with a scope.

We walked down a logging road. To my surprise, after two miles Itchy stopped, pointed into the thick woods, and said, "There's a knoll on a hill where deer run by all the time about three-quarters of a mile that way."

"Am I going by myself? I don't want to get lost."

"You won't get lost. Just head due west for a little less than a mile, and you'll run right into the knoll. Use your compass. To get back to the road, just head due east. Let's meet back here at 10:30."

I agreed and walked into the woods, keeping a small flashlight on until the sun rose. I walked for awhile and then stopped to rest and look around. I found a log, sat down, and listened for the rustling noises that meant a deer was coming. By that time the sun was above the horizon, and my anxiety about hunting alone in the big woods of northern Maine completely disappeared. I was enjoying myself.

I started walking again, and my mood darkened: I had to go the bathroom, and it was going to have to be done squatting on a log. I looked around and spotted a fallen tree. I unbuckled my belt, pulled down my pants, and suddenly I heard:

CRASH! THUMP, THUMP, THUMP, THUMP!

What the hell is happening! The crashing noise was headed right for me. I jumped up, pulled up my pants, and grabbed my rifle. I aimed it toward the oncoming ruckus, when a huge female moose appeared through the trees, running straight at me with her three-hundred-pound baby running behind. She didn't know I was there.

I normally hunt in mid-coast Maine, where moose are few and far between, so I was completely taken by surprise. I aimed my rifle, thinking that if she kept coming I'd have to drop her. I wasn't about to be run over by a thousand-pound beast. But if you shoot a moose out of season without a permit there's a heavy fine, and the government can seize your vehicle and your gun. Just the same, my gun was pointed right at the mother moose in case she charged me.

"Hey, what are you doing?!" I shouted as they got closer.

The mother moose and her baby were startled by my yell and immediately turned and ran away. At that moment, I had visions of pulling the trigger and having lots of moose meat in my freezer at home, but decided against it. As the animals scurried away, I pulled up my pants, which had slipped back down during the ordeal.

Nobody's gonna believe this, I thought.

After my heart returned to a normal rhythm, I headed west, and reached Itchy's knoll. I sat down to wait, and nodded off a few times. But there were no deer to be seen. At 10:00 a.m. I looked at my compass, headed east, and walked out of the woods where I entered. After a few minutes, the others came walking down the road.

I told them about the moose and her calf and what I was doing when it happened, and they laughed. They weren't surprised; they saw moose every time they hunted. The woods of northern Maine are home to a healthy, vibrant herd.

We headed to camp for an early lunch so we could go hunting again in the afternoon. As soon as we arrived, everyone cracked open a late-morning beer. We made sandwiches and laughed some more about my moose story. One beer led to another, and soon we were passing around the pot pipe. I hesitated; my dad would have been extremely disappointed in me for drinking and smoking marijuana before hunting. He had taught me hunter safety when I was about twelve. I immediately felt guilty.

But drinking and drugs ruled all my decisions, and soon I was stoned and a little drunk. Soon the guys wanted to hit the woods again. My friends were hardcore partiers and hardcore hunters, and it didn't matter if we had a little buzz on—there were deer to be shot. We drove to a big patch of woods encompassed by a single-file path. My buddies assured me this was where the deer would be.

"Darryl, I've got an idea. Let's switch rifles for the afternoon. You take my 30-06, and I'll try your 32 Special," Itchy said, taking me by surprise.

I agreed, hesitantly. Because I was stoned and tipsy, I didn't insist on using the rifle I was familiar with, as I should have. I took Itchy's powerful semi-automatic; he took my smaller rifle. The others headed to the left, and Itchy and I headed to the right. We would walk the entire circle of the woods until we met up, with the aim of stirring the deer toward the two hunters on the opposite side.

The path was narrow, so Itchy went first and I followed. It was a sunny day, but the weed started to kick in. I was walking with red, half-shut eyes, holding a gun I'd never shot. I checked the safety frequently, trying to be extra careful, since I'd never hunted stoned before.

After awhile, Itchy stopped. Over his shoulder, I could see a large doe. She had heard us coming, stood up, and froze. The doe was about a hundred feet directly in front of us—the easiest shot in the world. That is, if you're not stoned.

Itchy raised the 32 Special and fired two shots. After the second shot, we couldn't believe he had missed. The doe was in shock and hadn't moved an inch. I raised the 30-06 and let her rip—kabaam!—right over Itchy's right shoulder. Itchy threw down the 32 Special and grabbed his ears. At first I thought I nicked him, but it was the gun firing so close to his head that shook him up. I'm glad I didn't blow out his eardrum.

The doe was still frozen in place, watching our clown show. Itchy grabbed the 30-06 and emptied it at the doe. She turned and ran. I grabbed the 32 Special off the ground and fired a few shots at the escaping deer. We both got off several more shots.

We ran to where the doe had been standing, but after our barrage of bullets we didn't find any deer hair or one drop of blood. We hadn't touched her. The other guys came running and asked how many deer we dropped. From all the gunfire, they expected us to have two or three. They started laughing when they heard our story.

I thought Itchy was going to lose it. He decided to track the doe and took off deep into the woods. We didn't see him again until later that night. He got turned around, came out of the woods miles away from where we started, and had to hitch a ride back to camp.

I went back to MMA, where I was partying too much as always, which led me to fail my first class ever: Marketing, the subject I was least interested in. I was concentrating far more on classes that would help me pass my Coast Guard test in the spring. Despite my excesses, I passed my other classes and studied hard for the upcoming exams.

Things were slow in the middle of winter at MMA, so one weekend I decided to go to Moosehead Lake with Itchy, Howie, Moil, and Cool. All my buddies from the area would be partying with us. I started getting drunk on the ride up. We also got stoned.

"Slow down, Hagar," Itchy warned me. "We've got a long night up there."

"I'm fine, man. I'm just chilling out. As long as we eat, I'll be good."

We arrived at 5:00 p.m., just in time for our first happy hour. At 6:00 we headed to the bar next door for a second happy hour. At 7:00, we walked across the street to a third happy hour. By the time we got to the third bar, I was already blacking out. I have no memory of what happened next other than what Itchy told me later. While we were in the third bar, a married couple came in and started talking to Itchy. He introduced me, and as they were talking, I leaned over and started kissing the man's wife and sticking my tongue in her ear.

"Itchy, what's this dude's deal?" the man asked as I slobbered on his wife.

"Darryl, cut it out, man!" Itchy said. "Don't worry about him. He's harmless. We'll take him home. He's wrecked." Itchy hauled me outside, where we caught up with the others.

Itchy suggested, "Let's jump in the car and drink the rest of our beer. There's still a twelve-pack in the front and a case in the back."

"Okay. Darryl is pretty drunk, so that's probably best," Cool answered.

We went to Itchy's mother's house. After drinking for a little while, Itchy laughed and said, "Darryl, take Cool's keys and go get that last case of beer in the trunk."

I'm told I took that as a challenge because they were laughing at me. I put on my jacket and hat. It was snowy, windy, and very cold. I stumbled out the door and made my way to the end of the snowy driveway. I somehow found the right car and fumbled with the keys, finally managing to open the trunk. I saw the beer and leaned over to grab it, but instead decided to climb in the trunk for a nap. I don't remember doing that, but from the aftermath I know that it happened.

After awhile the guys were running out of beer, and I hadn't come back.

"We better check on Darryl and make sure he's not passed out in a snow bank," Itchy said.

"I'll go," Cool said, putting his coat on.

Cool got out to his car and couldn't believe his eyes.

He shook me. "Darryl! Darryl! Wake up, man!"

"What's going on?"

"You're going to freeze to death!" Cool yelled. "You passed out in the trunk, man. Get out of there!"

Cool later told me that I said, "Go find your own place to sleep, asshole."

"Darryl, you're out of your mind." Cool helped me back into the house. Between the three of them, they got me dried off and put me to bed. Cool told me later he'd felt like smacking me, but he didn't because I couldn't stand up.

I barely remember being there that night. When I got up and went downstairs, Itchy's mother said good morning and poured me some orange juice.

"You feeling okay?" she asked.

I was embarrassed. "Not too good. I don't remember much. Sorry for any inconvenience."

"That's okay. Nobody got hurt. Just your pride."

I realize now what I should have known then, but didn't because I was in denial about my mixed-up life: I was an alcoholic and a drug addict. I was smoking pot daily, but because I couldn't afford to drink much, I didn't see the severity of my problem with alcohol. Everybody recognized my alcoholic behavior—everybody but me.

GLENN CHADBOURNE

CHAPTER TWELVE
DEMOLITION MAN

Looming ahead was the milestone of the third mate's licensing test, consisting of eight segments, all difficult. Two-thirds of the test required a 90 percent to pass, providing little room for error. I was studying my brains out and putting a lot of pressure on myself to succeed.

At the same time, I was partying often. I was drinking too much and had added cocaine to the mix. In those days there was no drug testing at the academy. It was still four years before the Exxon Valdez changed all that.

At the time I was young and still in the beginning stages of my addictions, and I had a tolerance for drugs. Later in life, I'd do half as much cocaine with twice the effect, along with a whole new set of reactions—paranoia, sweating, and anxiety. But in the beginning, I snorted line after line so I could stay up all night studying, never realizing I was risking an overdose or an early death. In my drug-induced, twisted logic it made sense to me. I had a lot of work to do, I had a "cool" roommate who snorted with me, and I was still young. I figured my body could handle it.

Still, the stress of studying, classes, partying, and the upcoming Coast Guard tests finally caused me to boil over. I had stayed at the academy many weekends in a row to concentrate on studying, and it was time to air myself out. So I left MMA on a Friday and headed home. During the drive, my friends and I drank beer and smoked joints.

I borrowed my mother's one-year-old Subaru and headed to Damariscotta, where all the young people drove around on the weekends partying. That night I bought a fifth of Allen's Coffee Brandy, which is so popular in the state that they call it "the champagne of Maine." I drank the entire bottle. It relaxed me, easing my fears about the upcoming exam.

That night several girls I'd gone to high school with saw me go into a store, obviously drunk, and talked me into handing over my keys and riding around with them. To this day, I don't remember going home that night, but one of the girls dropped me off.

I awoke to my mother's voice and pried open my eyes. She was standing in my bedroom doorway. I could tell she was upset.

"Darryl, where's my car?"

"It's not in the driveway?"

"No."

"I don't know where it is. Let me think for a minute." I paused. "I can't remember. Check the high school parking lot."

"That's cute. You can't even remember where you left my car?!"

"No, I can't. I think I was too messed up to drive and left it somewhere. Try the high school. Sorry about that."

She stomped off and went looking for her car. My brother Chris gave her a ride, but they quickly discovered the Subaru wasn't at the high school in Newcastle. They then went into Damariscotta and found the car outside the beer store where I'd left it. My mother got out and tried the door, but it was locked. She came back to the house, even angrier than before.

I had fallen back into a drunken stupor. My mother woke me and told me I was irresponsible. She asked where her car keys were. I checked the pockets of my jeans. At least I'd undressed myself the night before; through the years, my mother had undressed me more than once when I was too drunk to do it myself. The keys weren't in my pockets. Then I remembered the girls; they probably had my keys.

Mom was pissed; she said to get up, find the keys, and bring home her car. Chris gave me a ride. When we found them, the girls said I'd been really messed up, and I thanked them for taking my keys. Then, knowing our only mission was supposed to be getting Mom's car home, Chris and I made a detour to get a half gallon of coffee brandy.

I was demonstrating four things at that moment: One, that not all college kids are smart all the time. Two, that not everybody listens to his mother, even when she is really, really upset at him. Justifiably upset, I might add. Three, that I was at a reckless point in my life when I had little regard for what others thought of me. And four, that I was showing my true colors . . . by acting like a raging alcoholic.

Chris and I started drinking the coffee brandy and decided to continue our detour by heading to Pemaquid Point, a peninsula on the coast about fifteen miles from Damariscotta. We met some friends at their oceanfront cottage and partied with them into the evening. I was already alcohol-saturated from the night before, and my little brother was also drinking. Neither of us had eaten much that day.

We finished the half gallon and numerous beers. I then bugged Chris to take me to The Homestead, a happening local nightclub with great rock 'n' roll, full of women who wanted to party and dance. Chris, wanting me to forget about our original mission, agreed to go.

The bouncer gave me the eyeball. At that time I was going through a tough-guy phase and had on my academy-issued combat boots, a heavy leather biker jacket, and was sporting a crew cut. But I tried to look sober and got in. We partied for a few hours. I was getting a tremendous buzz, but I wanted to get higher. I ordered two kamikazes and a Pearl Harbor. The bartender looked at me as if I were nuts, but got the drinks. I turned to my left and was surprised to see my auto insurance agent.

She asked, "Darryl, are you planning to go to war or something?"

I laughed and downed the drinks. A short time later the bouncer approached me and told me I had to leave. But I was a mean, obnoxious drunk and told him to fuck off. There was a scrap, and I got pushed out the door.

My brother yelled, "Get in the fucking truck!" He was two years younger, but he was heavier. In a fight, he could give me a run for my money.

"I didn't start it! That bouncer doesn't like me!"

"You're really drunk, Darryl. We're going home."

We jumped in his truck and headed down the highway.

"We're picking up Mom's car, right?"

Chris said, "You can't drive. We're going home."

I grabbed him by the throat and said, "We're picking up Mom's car, Chris. It's the only thing we were supposed to do today, and I'm doing it."

Chris knew it didn't make sense to argue with me when I was that drunk, so he drove to the beer store. Before I realized his intent, he blocked Mom's car with his truck, parking it with my passenger door even with the front end of the Subaru, so I couldn't get out of my door. As I was yelling at him, he got out and headed for a payphone to call Mom.

My drunken insanity took over. I climbed out of the truck, got in the front-wheel drive Subaru, slammed on the gas, and pushed the pickup ten feet until it was up against the gas pumps.

My brother and mother later told me they had this conversation:

"Mom, Darryl is really drunk and says he's going to drive your car. I blocked him in." Chris then turned back to look at me. "Mom, he just got in your car and plowed my truck over!"

"What's he doing now?"

"He took off on the street up Academy Hill toward the high school."

"Call the police on him, quick."

My brother didn't call the police, but somebody did. There were several witnesses to what I'd just done. Chris ran out onto the road and looked, but I was gone.

At the top of Academy Hill on a sharp, 90-degree corner about fifteen feet off the road sits Carroll Dinsmore's house, with its large picture window in the front. Mr. Dinsmore had parked three vehicles side by side in his driveway, and when I missed the corner I nailed them all. I don't remember any of it.

My mother later said she heard over the police scanner: "He hit another one" and another, one after the other, like tipping a line of dominoes. I then backed up and took off again.

I'm relatively sure that at that point I had a flat rear tire that made the car harder to drive. I went about a half mile back down Academy Hill to a four-way intersection near Wright's Store, about a quarter mile from where I'd left Chris. Mrs. Wright was a nice old lady who knew my family well. I tried to take a sharp left at that intersection, intending to head toward Mom's house, but I was going too fast. I rolled the Subaru several times. Mrs. Wright heard the crash, got out of bed, and came outside.

My brother was back on the phone with my mother when he heard a loud crash. He told her he was going to see if I was all right. Chris ran up to the car and saw me climbing out.

My memory starts to work again at that point. I don't remember anything after grabbing my brother's throat, but I vaguely remember climbing out of the overturned car, yelling at the top of my lungs, "O—U—I, I'm fucked!" and running down the road away from the scene. In Maine, OUI stands for "Operating Under the Influence."

Chris chased me, yelling, "You fucking pussy!"

I still have a hard time believing what I did next. I stopped, turned around, and said, "Who you calling a pussy?"

At that point the chase turned around, and I pursued Chris right into the arms of the police officers arriving on the scene. Mrs. Wright later told my mother, "I didn't know if Chris was chasing Darryl or if Darryl was chasing Chris." The cops wrestled me to the ground and handcuffed me. My blood alcohol content was later measured at .22, more than double the legal limit.

Once I was in the police cruiser, I was aware enough to know I had messed up big time, and I sobbed quietly to myself. I was worried foremost about getting kicked out of MMA just two weeks before graduation.

I asked the cops to call my mother, but she told them to leave me in jail—that was a good place for me. During the night, I kept getting out of bed, rattling the cell bars, and then lying back down pretending to sleep. Whenever I did that, a deputy came in, observed me for a minute or two, and then left, only for me to get up and rattle the bars again and again. I was still really drunk, and my mind was obviously twisted.

After a few hours, my mother called my older brother and asked him to bail me out. Mark told me to shut my mouth and not wake his family when we got to his house. I slept on his couch, and when I woke up in the morning I couldn't believe what I'd done. I had totaled my mother's one-year-old Subaru, damaged my little brother's brand new pickup, damaged Mr. Dinsmore's vehicles, and had ruined my reputation in my small hometown.

Mark gave me a ride home. I was thankful Mom wasn't around. I figured she'd go off the deep end on me. I went to my room and slept it off.

After awhile, she came in and asked, "Are you all right?"

I said, "I'm really sorry, Mom, for rolling your car over."

In reality I only vaguely remembered rolling the car, but the evidence was irrefutable. My body was banged up and bruised. But what was hurt most was my pride—I was embarrassed at having gone on a rampage like that in a small community where everyone knows everyone. The story of my wild ride was repeated often for many years afterward from the stools at the local soda fountain to the tables of the local diners.

The next day, someone bought Mom's car for $100 to salvage the bucket seats, the only part of the car that wasn't damaged. The insurance company called it a total loss.

I wasn't man enough to talk to Mr. Dinsmore about what I'd done until August of 2006, twenty-one years later, when I finally called him to make amends. He remembered the incident like it was yesterday. He had heard the crashes and got out of bed. His son ran outside, but I had already driven off. Shortly afterward, Mr. Dinsmore put concrete-filled barrels around his yard to protect his family from anyone else who might run a car off the road.

All those years later, he still remembered how much it cost him to make the repairs. After apologizing to him and his family, I wrote a check and mailed it to him. He insisted I shouldn't pay him because it was so long ago, but being in a twelve-step program, I knew I needed to make amends.

I later ran into Mr. Dinsmore's son, who told me his father had terminal brain cancer. I told him how sorry I was. He thanked me and told me that his dad had been touched when I called and sent the check.

God works in amazing ways. I had called a dying man and had paid him for what I'd done in 1985, not knowing of his illness. It felt good knowing that Mr. Dinsmore spoke positively of me, even with all his medical worries. I made my amends to him just in time. Incidents like that give me even greater assurance that there is a God.

Every cause has an effect. I had come home that weekend to blow off steam and relieve my worries. I had no idea I'd go off the deep end. Later, one of my buddies at MMA advised me to plead "temporary insanity" in court. I said, "No way. They'll think I'm nuts and never let me out."

In reality, I *was* nuts. But I wouldn't seek treatment for twenty more years, despite many more irrational and bizarre events in my life.

CHAPTER THIRTEEN
DOZING AT THE ZENITH

Because of the rampage with my mother's car, my life had taken an unexpected turn. I hadn't seen it coming, nor did I ever dream how much worse it would soon get. I was about to enter one of the most dangerous phases of my life. In hindsight, it seems especially reckless, out of control, and disturbing. In a way, I'm glad I didn't know it was going to happen. If I'd known, I would have died from fear of the future.

My car wreck was kept out of the local press by some influential people. As a result, the academy never found out about my OUI, and the Coast Guard didn't find out until after I'd already obtained my third mate's license. When I sat for my test two weeks after my arrest, I had not yet been convicted and still had a driver's license, so I could honestly answer "no" to the question on the application: "Have you ever been convicted of operating a motor vehicle under the influence of drugs or alcohol?"

I headed back to the academy, beat up and bruised physically and mentally, especially my ego. At that point it should have been hard for me to ignore that I'd hit four cars, one deliberately, and rolled the vehicle I was driving, but I soon continued on as if nothing had happened. It took all of a week after my demolition derby for my bruised ego to recover. Even doing extensive damage to five cars couldn't rein in my blossoming drug and alcohol addictions. In retrospect I was showing definite signs of denial, and like any good addict/alcoholic, I was hiding my disease.

Someone brought two ounces of cocaine to school. My buddies and I had made plans to have a class party near Moosehead Lake after graduation, and I was tempted to buy the entire two ounces to sell and use at the party. Instead, I bought the entire two ounces and went on like one possessed. We were finished with finals, and our regimental duties had been handed over to the juniors. Since we only had the Coast Guard tests to worry about, my partying didn't stop. It was one sick way to prepare for the biggest test of my life.

Every day for a week, my days started something like this:

"What time did we go to bed, Itchy?"

"We didn't go to bed, Darryl. You passed out at 5:30 a.m. You had a Bowditch navigation manual out, and you were snorting lines like they were going out of style. A regular Einstein."

"What time is it now?"

"It's 1:00 p.m. Let's get something to eat."

Every day we got up, made coffee, got high on some weed, and went into Castine to buy a sandwich. We couldn't eat at the mess hall; it shut down before we got up. Then we'd start all over again. First just a small line of cocaine to wake up and get motivated to study.

"C'mon, Hagar, lay out one bigger than that," Itchy would beg.

"C'mon, man, take it easy. We got all day and night." Then I would laugh and say, "All right. All right. Put this big fat line into you, and leave me alone for awhile, will ya?"

I look back on that time with deep regret. Buying those two ounces was among the stupidest things I've done in life. I had no control over myself. I was concerned only about partying, staying high to block reality, and my reputation as a renegade. Guys stopped by my room at all hours to buy cocaine. I stayed up every night the week before the exam coked out of my mind and slept during the day. It was complete insanity.

Several times, people implied that I was partying too much, at which point I told them to go screw. Some people were subtle, others more forceful. Either way, I told them to mind their own business. In fact, all that week I felt strong and able to pull off the madness.

On Monday the Coast Guard arrived to give the tests. Nervous midshipmen spread out in the gym, including a hundred engineers at regular size desks. The fifty deckies had larger tables so we could plot chart navigations. We started at 8:00 a.m. and finished around 4:00 p.m. each of the four days.

I had gotten a good night's sleep on Sunday for a change, and the first day's testing went well. I was euphoric after passing Monday's tests, and we celebrated by snorting cocaine that night. On Tuesday I received two more passing grades, and we again partied over Tuesday's success. When I look back on it now, it all seems sick.

Wednesday came, and I again passed both tests. I had a difficult test Thursday morning that required a 90 percent to pass and then an easier "Navigation General" on Thursday afternoon that required just 70 percent to pass. But I was six for six; I figured I just might pull this off. So we partied and studied all night, meaning zero sleep for me and several of my buddies. We did line after line of cocaine, studying hour after hour, thinking we were absorbing the information. Then the sun rose, and I realized I was out of my mind.

"Man, Itchy, I'm all messed up," I told him.

"I am too, Darryl. We can do it, man. It's the last day, and we're out of this prison."

We cleaned ourselves up and put on our uniforms. We snorted one last big line of cocaine and headed down to the gym to take our final two tests. I was a bit edgy, but not scared. I was young, and fear wasn't even in my vocabulary.

Itchy and I walked into the gym and sat down. An engineer that I played intramural basketball with had drawn the seat next to me. He didn't party like I did, but I thought he was a cool guy.

"Darryl, you all right?" he asked.

"Just barely," I said, laughing.

He laughed at me. What else could he do? He knew I was hardcore and probably sensed I'd been partying all week.

The tests were handed out. I was exhausted, but determined to obtain my third mate's license. I called it "steam-boating." I would steam full speed ahead and get through this storm. I went to work on the test, and before I knew it, I was finished. I again passed with flying colors. Just one more test, and I was going to pull this off.

Except that I was getting very sleepy. My brain was confused, and my body was tired. I snorted a big line of cocaine and decided to take a walk. I headed out of the dorm and walked around the football field and down to the waterfront. I continued my walk on the side streets of Castine, all the while reflecting on my life. I felt like a restless animal— or a pirate ready to go to sea. *What a trip I'm on. One more test. And if I pass, I'll go sail big ships around the world and make some serious money.*

I headed back to the dorms to do a little more cocaine in an attempt to stay awake for the last test. Itchy was there.

"There you are. I was worried you might have passed out somewhere," he said. "You're starting to look a little rough, Darryl."

"I'm feeling even worse. That's why I took a walk to wake up. You ready to do a big fat line and go take that last test?"

I handed him a little plate with a line of cocaine and a straw on it.

In the gym, my engineering friend sat next to me again. He shook his head, smiling; he didn't know I was doing cocaine, but he knew I was in rough shape. Apparently I looked worse than I thought, because several people expressed worry about me.

I soon had the Navigation General test in front of me, and the Coast Guard officers said we could start. I thumbed through the test just to see what it looked like:

1.   The Zenith is the point on the celestial sphere that is _____.

   A.   90 degrees away from the poles
   B.   Directly over the observer
   C.   On the eastern horizon
   D.   Over Greenwich

There were fifty dry, boring, and difficult questions.

As I started answering them, I started to crash. I caught myself dozing off, so I read the first few questions quickly and circled the right answers.

Suddenly I realized somebody was kicking me. It was the classmate next to me. *Oh God, I fell asleep.* My body was succumbing to all the madness I had put it through. I mentally wiped out the cobwebs and started answering more questions. I didn't need the coastguardsmen or my professors seeing me sleeping.

I answered questions one after the other, and suddenly my engineer friend, laughing quietly to himself, was kicking me again. I struggled to stay awake throughout the rest of the test. I answered questions quickly, dozed off, woke up, answered a few more as fast as I could, and fell asleep again. It was pure torture. Finally, I finished.

I shook myself awake one last time. Trying to appear normal, I held my breath, walked up to the front, and turned in the test. I could miss fifteen out of fifty questions, and I was pretty sure I could do that in my sleep. The coastguardsman graded my test, went through and counted, and looked at me. He rechecked it and counted again.

"I'm sorry, Mr. Hagar. You got a 68 percent. You'll have to come to Boston and take this section over in a month," he told me sadly.

"Are you sure, sir? Can you check it again?"

"I checked it three times already, Mr. Hagar. But it's all right. You passed the other tests. Go home and study Navigation General for a month, and I'm sure next month you'll get your third mate's license."

I asked him to sign me up for the test in Boston and walked away dejected.

My engineer friend came up to me smiling and asked, "Did you pass?"

"I failed by one question, man."

"Man, I kept trying to wake you up. I didn't know what to do!"

I thanked him and explained I could take the test again in a month. If he'd known why I kept falling asleep, he wouldn't have felt so sorry for me.

The big Coast Guard tests were over. I'd been relatively successful, considering I was under the influence of drugs and alcohol during all of them. You'd think failing the last test would slow me down, especially knowing that passing had been one of my main goals for four years. But once exams were over, I really started partying.

I had an ounce and a half of cocaine to get rid of. I had planned to take it to the class party, but a bunch of us started snorting it. We partied for twenty-four hours, right up to our graduation ceremony on April 13, 1985.

I had told my brother Mark and his wife Cindy they could crash in my room the night before graduation. By the time they arrived, I'd already been snorting cocaine and drinking, but I was an expert at covering it up. I gave them my room key and said good night.

That night the senior class erupted, destroying the dorms and causing thousands of dollars in damage. The dorms were made of concrete, but some of the senior classmen took recliners out of their rooms and threw them through the large picture windows.

I didn't break a single window. A bunch of us were holed up in a room partying and didn't need any heat. It sounded like a combat zone outside our locked steel door. I knew the security officers must be busy chasing after the drunken midshipmen who were causing the mayhem. Several of them got caught and weren't allowed to graduate with my class the following day.

My poor brother and sister-in-law. Here I thought I was doing them a favor saving them on a hotel room. Not only had the dormitory become a war zone—with them locked inside a room at the center of the battle—I had forgotten that people would also be knocking on my door all night wanting to score some coke.

Early the next morning, I went to check on Mark and Cindy. There were books, furniture, laundry powder, pillows, blankets, toilet paper, and papers strewn throughout the hallways—a foot-high level of destruction everywhere I looked. I knocked on my door. No answer. I knocked again, louder.

"Mark, it's your brother, Darryl. You in there?" I yelled.

The door opened. My brother's eyes were wide as saucers.

"What the hell happened last night?" he asked.

"My class went ballistic and destroyed the dorms. It happened four years ago when we were freshmen. I guess monkey see, monkey do, man. It wasn't me, and I had no idea it was going to happen. Did you guys get any sleep?"

"Not really. People were knocking on your door all night, and I could hear guys breaking windows, so we decided not to open the door."

"I don't blame you, man. Sorry about that. If I'd known, I would have reserved a hotel room for you."

They left to get something to eat. I decided to do a couple of lines of cocaine to wake up. I locked the door and chopped out some cocaine, though I was to graduate in three hours in dress whites with five hundred or so of our family, friends, and officials in attendance. Joe Brennan, the governor of Maine, was our commencement speaker. The admiral and other academy officials would see us off. Little did they know that about twenty of us would be snorting cocaine shortly before shaking their hands.

A little later, a bunch of us got together and snorted more cocaine. I was a runaway freight train; there was no stopping me. I needed help, but I didn't see it. My family had no idea what I was doing. I was good at hiding it. None of them found out how bad my drug use was back then.

My mom and family arrived, and I walked them down to the gym. My class was assembled, all in dress whites. A few of us sneaked away to snort a few more lines. I was flying high on cocaine as we marched into the gym through a wedge of midshipmen with drawn swords. It was a magnificent ceremony. One by one our names were called. We each marched across the stage to accept our diplomas and to shake the hands of the admiral and the governor of the State of Maine.

The admiral announced the graduation of the Maine Maritime Academy Class of 1985, and we hooted and howled and threw our high pressure caps in the air. I shook hands with all my classmates, gave hugs and kisses to my family, and then away from the academy I went to the class party at Moosehead Lake.

MMA was and still is a great institution, but to someone of my youth and temperament it seemed more like a prison. There were few women on campus, the rules made partying off limits, uniforms were mandatory, and there was always someone telling us what to do. My attitude at the time was, *Adios Maine Maritime, hello Merchant Marine.*

After graduation I straightened out and studied for a month. I retook the section of the Coast Guard exam I had failed and passed this time. But there were no opportunities to ship out right away because of a lack of jobs in the Merchant Marine in the summer of 1985. I decided to work on a herring boat that fished off the coast of Maine and New Hampshire. I figured I'd make a few bucks, get more seamanship and navigational experience, and in the meantime send my resume to various shipping companies.

I also had my OUI to worry about. I came up with a plan for minimizing the damage to my life caused by my drunken fracas. I decided to represent myself and asked my brother Mark and one of my father's old military buddies, Rod Weaver, to accompany me to court.

I decided to wear my military dress blues in an attempt to sway the judge toward leniency. As we walked into the courtroom, all eyes were on me. My full dress military uniform included a white shirt, black tie, shiny dress shoes, and high pressure cap with its officer's gold band. I was embarrassed because I felt people would think I was kissing up, though that's exactly what I was doing. I was worried about how an OUI conviction would be viewed by the Coast Guard and the negative effect it might have on my career. I wondered if a conviction might prevent me from shipping out altogether.

The judge called my name, and I bent over and arrogantly whispered in my brother's ear, "Watch this."

Surprised, he said, "What you are going to do?"

"Just watch."

I was sworn in, and the judge looked me over. I looked back over my shoulder. My brother was slumped down in his seat, his hand on his forehead.

"Mr. Hagar, you have been charged with operating a motor vehicle under the influence of alcohol. It also says here you left the scene of several accidents. Do you understand the charges, Mr. Hagar?"

Pleading my case.

"Yes, sir, Your Honor, I do."

"Let's take the charge of operating a motor vehicle while under the influence of alcohol. How do you plead?"

"Guilty as charged, Your Honor."

He looked at me, surprised. "Guilty?"

I said, "Guilty, Your Honor, no doubt about it."

He seemed astonished. "All right, then. I find you guilty of operating a motor vehicle under the influence of alcohol. Now, how do you plead to these other charges of leaving the scene of several accidents?"

"Not guilty, Your Honor."

I looked back at Mark and Rod. They were looking at me in disbelief.

"Your Honor, I was so intoxicated that night I don't remember, even to this day, being in any accidents. How could I leave the scene of several accidents if I didn't know I was even in one?"

Now it was the judge who was looking at me in disbelief.

"Your Honor, if I hadn't been drinking alcohol that night, I certainly would have stopped, gotten out of my car, exchanged insurance and driver's license information, and called the police. I'm like any other law-abiding citizen. The point is, Your Honor, that I was so intoxicated that I didn't know I was in any accidents. How could I leave the scene of an accident I didn't know I was in?"

The judge thought about it for a minute, imposed a $100 fine, dismissed the charge, and said, "Not guilty of leaving the scene of an accident. Next case."

Of course, my OUI case took place in 1985, several years before drunk-driving laws became stricter after the efforts of grassroots organizations such as Mother's Against Drunk Driving (MADD).

We left the courthouse, and I asked Mark and Rod what they thought of my defense. They said they couldn't believe I had the nerve to say that to a judge, that I was lucky, and that I'd better learn from it.

I didn't. Not even when I took a lot of ribbing from the townsfolk in Damariscotta. One of the town's leaders asked if I'd thought I was in a NASCAR race and said he hoped I'd learned my lesson: Don't drink and drive.

But denial is very strong and very complicated. Not only did I deny I had a problem to myself, my family, and my friends, I didn't believe that my chaotic behavior would influence my life, my health, or the people around me.

In order to get my suspended driver's license back I had to complete a state-mandated program about the dangers of drinking and driving. The speaker told the horrific story of his alcoholic life and how he finally was able to get sober. As I listened I was both inspired and confused.

I thought, *My life will go in one of two directions. Either I'm going to screw up and die from my crazy drinking or someday I'll become a great speaker and teacher just like this man and impact millions of struggling alcoholics.*

I realized either option was possible. One could be my fate from going overboard, and the other could be my God-given destiny. Only time would tell.

CHAPTER FOURTEEN
MILITARY SEALIFT COMMAND

I sent out dozens of resumes, but the shipping industry was tight; there were no third mate's jobs available anywhere. In the mid-eighties the industry was at the lean end of the pendulum swing. So, in the fall of 1985 I was working on a herring boat off the coast of Maine and New Hampshire.

I'd been off the fishing boat for a few days when the phone rang. Right away I could tell this call was different; I had an uncanny feeling this was the day I'd been waiting for.

"This is Susan Millhouse from the Military Sealift Command. We received your resume, and if you take a drug test and physical and go through our pre-employment training, we'll put you on a ship as an able-bodied seaman."

"What about a third mate's job?" I asked. "That's what I'm qualified for."

"To be honest, you're lucky that we need you for this position. Somebody just got fired, and we need someone right now. If you do a good job, you'll be considered for a promotion and a permanent position."

My heart was racing. It wasn't what I was looking for, but I would take it. I could get my feet wet, work hard, and get promoted. As I asked about where to take the drug test and physical, I tried to count the days from when I'd last smoked any pot. It had been a few weeks, and I figured I'd be okay.

She explained that I'd have to drive to Boston to take the physical and the drug and alcohol screen. After I got the results, they would fly me to Newark. From there I'd go to Bayonne, New Jersey, the headquarters for the Atlantic fleet, to take classes in hazardous materials, helicopter evacuations, and damage control. Then I'd be assigned to a ship.

Flying to Newark was the first time I'd ever gone off on my own, and I was scared. Naturally I decided to have a few drinks on the plane to calm my nerves. When I arrived, I took a cab to Military Sealift Command Atlantic headquarters. It was after 5:00 p.m., and everything was closed.

I still had a little buzz going as I walked into the bunkhouse. I looked around. The room was filled with a bunch of rough, dangerous-looking guys. I picked an empty bed and threw my sea bag on the top bunk. I felt uneasy and decided to get out of there until bedtime. I figured I'd go drinking.

I had half a dozen beers and some dinner and decided to sleep it off. Back at the bunkhouse I quickly discovered that my sea bag was lying on the floor, and a big dude was lying on the top bunk.

I looked up at him and said, "You took my stuff off my bunk, man."

"What are you talking about? This is my bunk. There wasn't any stuff on here."

"This green sea bag was on the bunk you're on," I insisted.

He got off the bunk, and I was still looking up at him. He was about seven inches taller and about seventy-five pounds heavier than I was. Another guy came over and told me to forget about it.

I looked at the alleged bunk-stealer, pissed off. There were no other empty beds.

"Fuck you, man!" I picked up my sea bag and walked out of the bunkhouse. I hailed a cab and rode to the nearest cheap hotel and checked in.

The next day I called Susan Millhouse and explained the situation. She told me to stay in the hotel while I completed the training and they would reimburse me. She didn't sound at all surprised by the bunkhouse story. *Jeez, what kind of men will I be sailing with?*

I completed the training and was assigned to the USNS Waccamaw, an underway replenishment ("unrep") oil tanker transporting DFM, diesel oil for ship engines, and JP5, aviation gasoline for jet fighters. I joined the vessel and met the captain, who referred to himself as an "Ecuadorian aristocrat." The crew told me he was a difficult captain who didn't care for people much.

I was taken aback at the size and age of the vessel. At 700 feet, the Waccamaw was bigger than I expected. It was also one of the oldest ships in the American Merchant Marine; the guys on board said it had experienced more collisions than any other vessel afloat. But it sounded worse than it was; the collisions occurred because the Waccamaw always worked closely alongside other vessels as they were underway.

A replenishing ship comes alongside a Navy warship at sea and shoots a line over in preparation to transfer fuel. The two ships steer the same course at the same speed while pumping fuel and passing supplies. It was my job to run the winch for the high tension wire that connected the two ships. If the ships started drifting apart, I'd slack the wire so it wouldn't split in two. If the ships drifted closer, I'd take up the slack so the fuel hoses wouldn't dip into the water.

The operation allows Navy warships and aircraft carriers to stay at sea and patrol without having to refuel in dock. An unrep ship refuels many warships until she's empty, at which point the captain and crew navigate to a fuel depot to fill up and do it all over again.

The Waccamaw had a crew of about 150 men. The officers had their own staterooms, but I had signed on as an able-bodied seaman (AB). I shared a small room with double bunk beds, a sink, closets, and a bathroom.

The older of my roommates was an able-bodied seaman from Maine, in his forties, and a big-time hunter in his time off. The other was in his twenties, from Florida, married with children, an ordinary seaman—a sailor just starting out, with no experience. The three of us got along fine. We worked similar schedules on deck.

In late 1985 and early 1986, Libyan dictator Colonel Gadhafi was still taunting the United States. Consequently, the U.S. military had battle groups in the Mediterranean keeping him in line. I found out the Waccamaw would be conducting unrep operations with the John F. Kennedy carrier group before it relieved another aircraft carrier on station in the Med. We were called out early one morning, all hands on deck, to prepare to refuel the Kennedy carrier group at a prearranged top secret time and location. We set up two refueling rigs that morning and rendezvoused at the chosen coordinates.

It was quite an operation. There were ten men at each of two stations, one at port and one at starboard. We wore hard hats of different colors, depending on our jobs. The rig leader supervised a team that included line handlers, a paddle signal man, a sound-powered phone communications man, a boatswain to fix any mistakes or malfunctions, a deck engineer to oversee mechanics, and a deck officer to communicate with the cargo mate and the captain.

There were two winch drivers per station, both standing on an elevated platform at the controls. I worked on the starboard side aft running the high tension wire. My partner ran the winch for the fuel hoses. There were two eight-inch hoses rigged up on wires and pulleys. The pulleys rode on the high tension wire I was controlling.

When the time came, the captain had our ship on station and on a steady course. A destroyer pulled alongside my station, and one of our men shot the rifle that fired the small heaving line over to the other vessel. The destroyer's crew pulled it over and attached it to a bigger messenger line. They began to winch the line over, which finally started to pull on the high tension wire I controlled. I slacked it away through the air, taking care not to let it dip into the water. When the destroyer signaled they were connected, I heaved mightily, taking all slack out, rigidly connecting the two ships. I had to pay close attention every second after that. The fuel hoses were pulled over and connected, and once they were tested for tightness, we began pumping diesel oil into the destroyer's fuel tanks.

I then glanced back over my left shoulder. At first all I could see was the gray afterhouse of our ship standing six stories tall. Suddenly a monster of a vessel, taller by five stories, overshadowed our ship: the John F. Kennedy aircraft carrier, steering the same course seventy-five feet off our port side. Of all the ships at sea, the USS Kennedy was the most incredible marvel I have ever encountered. Its awe-inspiring presence communicated an incredible feeling of power. *Man, what a trip this is, refueling the Navy!*

We continued refueling both ships at once, filling up the carrier with diesel for her engines and jet fuel for her jet fighters. Then the captain came over the intercom with an announcement: "Attention on deck! In approximately three minutes we will be flown over by a Russian Bear spy plane escorted by two U.S. Navy F-14s. They're doing surveillance in international waters, and there is no need for concern."

After a few minutes I heard the roar of the Bear then saw it as it flew overhead accompanied by the two smaller Tomcats, one on each side. I learned later that it was normal during the Cold War for the Soviets and the United States to spy on each other during these kinds of operations.

We finished refueling and disconnected. The other ships unfurled their flags, and the destroyer played the whistling song from *The Good, the Bad, and the Ugly* over its intercom. Our crew pumped our fists in an incredible moment of solidarity and patriotism I'll never forget.

We still had fuel left over on that voyage and continued with more unreps. We refueled many different types of destroyers, frigates, and tankers during my time with MSC, but I never refueled a carrier again.

Only once during that time at sea did I mess up with my drinking. My friend Joseph smuggled a couple of fifths of vodka aboard in his sea bag. We saved it for after our scheduled operations, so there'd be no chance of getting called out unexpectedly in the middle of the night to work. There could have been an emergency, but I wasn't worrying about the "what ifs."

Joseph and I didn't have to go on watch for eight hours. After dinner we started drinking the vodka and having a grand old time. There we were in the Caribbean, up on the smoke stack deck on a couple of lawn chairs, completely isolated with nobody to bother us. We drank until we were both very drunk. I suddenly realized we'd been drinking for four hours.

"Man, Joe, I only have an hour and a half to sober up! I'm on watch at 0400."

"There ain't any sense sleeping now," he said. "Just slow down on the drinking and stand your watch. Then instead of working overtime, go to bed at 0800."

"That makes sense to me. I'll drink more slowly," I said.

By the time 0400 rolled around, I was completely loaded. I jumped into a cold shower to try to sober up and went up to the bridge.

There were four of us on watch; the second mate was in charge of three men. One of three steered the ship for an hour. One was the look-out, standing outside on one of the bridge wings watching for other ships and hazards. The third man went on a fire and security round, looking for any problems within the ship's passageways, galleys, storage rooms, and machinery spaces. It was a serious job, no matter which duties were assigned; being drunk was not recommended.

I walked up to the dark bridge, the radars causing the only visible light, and said hello to the men talking there.

"Good evening, guys," I said meekly.

The second mate greeted me. Trying not to breathe on him, I asked where he wanted me to go. His instructions were: "You have fire and security rounds. Take the Detex clock and go around all the stations and make sure everything is all right."

"Okay, Mate, will do." Walking off the bridge, I breathed a big sigh of relief. Maybe I could pull this off after all. As drunk as I was, I went around to all the stations because the Detex clock recorded what time you were at each station throughout the vessel. After my round, I was tired. I had a few minutes to spare, so I figured I'd sit down for a cat-nap to sober up a little. It was 0440, and I didn't have to be back on the bridge until 0500. I sat down in a dark corner where nobody would see me and closed my eyes.

I woke up, looked at my watch, and jumped to my feet. It was 0530—I had dozed off for fifty minutes! I was going to get into trouble if I didn't think fast. I ran back up to the bridge. The second mate looked pissed off.

"Where have you been Darryl, drinking?"

"No, Mate, I did my rounds. Here's the Detex clock. One of the laundry rooms was flooded. The gasket on a washer was worn off, and it leaked all over the floor. I had to mop it up."

He had to know I was drunk. I'm sure I smelled like booze, and I was probably slurring my words. He told my watch partner to do the next fire and security round and told me to steer the vessel even though at sea we left it in automatic pilot. The ship could steer itself with the proper course pre-programmed, thus a sailor didn't have to stand in one spot for hours steering the vessel.

"Put it in hand steering, Darryl!" the second mate barked.

"Hand steering. Aye." I repeated.

"Right twenty-five helm," he barked again.

"Right twenty-five. Aye," I repeated and put the rudder twenty-five degrees to the right. The vessel swerved sharply to the right.

"Midship!" the mate yelled.

"Midship. Aye," I said, bringing the rudder back to zero. The ship slowed its swing.

"Left thirty!" the second mate yelled.

"Left thirty. Aye," I answered. The vessel shook and started turning to port.

"Midship. Steady on 230 degrees. I don't mean 231 or 229 either, Darryl. Steady on 230, and stay in hand steering. You could have at least told me the truth!" he yelled, walking away.

He was penalizing me. He knew I was drunk and exhausted. I could hardly keep my arms up to steer the vessel. My eyes kept trying to close of their own accord. Every fifteen minutes he made me steer a new course and yelled at any mistakes. He was teaching me a lesson. He kept me in hand steering for more than two hours until the end of watch. It was torture. I was relieved by another sailor at 0800.

I needed food, then sleep. I also wanted to avoid the second mate, so I got off the bridge before he did. The bridge and my sleeping quarters were in the house amidships. The galley and other quarters were in the aft house, and I had to go outside to walk there.

After breakfast I thought I had dodged a bullet. I hadn't been further reprimanded or sent to the captain. I sneaked out of the galley and back on deck, heading toward my room, when I came across the second mate heading to breakfast. It was full daylight as we approached each other.

"Now you can go back and sleep in your room instead of on watch, Darryl."

I hung my head and kept walking. I had made a mistake and drank before going on duty, and it had caught up with me. I would do my best to avoid doing so in the future. When I got to my room, I slept all day. Later, I apologized to the second mate. He knew I felt bad and didn't rub it in. He told me to be careful with drinking on the ship, because I could get fired and lose my Coast Guard license. I thanked him and became determined to do my best to contain the beast within.

When our tanks were empty, we pulled into the Roosevelt Roads Naval Station in Puerto Rico. We'd been at sea for a month, and it was time to take on food stores, do maintenance on the engines and refueling rigs, make crew changes, and let the crew get some R&R.

Ironically, the strict, straight-laced second mate turned into a big lush bucket when the ship was in dock. He went out night after night, often staggering back to the ship afterward. One night he laughed and said, "The captain put this in my Sea Officer's Evaluation: 'The second mate is a good worker at sea but needs guidance in port.'" It seems we were made from the same mold after all; later in my career more than one captain said the same thing to me.

While we were in Puerto Rico, I planned to go ashore to celebrate New Year's Eve with friends. John, a liberal-minded sailor from New York City, was in his thirties. He was a cool guy who was always joking around. The other was a Mr. T look-alike, muscular with a black Mohawk, sleeveless camouflage jacket, gold chains, and earrings. Whenever our "T" walked around Puerto Rico, kids swarmed him asking for autographs.

I was a surprised when Leo, my roommate from Florida, wanted to join us; he was a family man with a wife and kids he often spoke to via telephone. He knew we planned to visit a local brothel.

Though many people understand intellectually what a sailor goes through being isolated on a ship with a bunch of men, they don't live

it. We worked day and night, were often lonely, and missed the female population. There were no women to talk to or even look at. It's not a normal environment. That's no excuse to visit a brothel, but it was reality.

I had no plans to hook up with a prostitute, though the Black Angus was legendary in the Caribbean. We arrived in the late afternoon. A scantily clad waitress wished us "Happy New Year" and brought us a pitcher of beer. Within minutes we were swarmed by ladies.

Refueling the aircraft carrier USS John F. Kennedy at sea.

We drink several pitchers of beer. Leo, John, and T were laughing, talking to the women, and having fun. None of us had succumbed to the temptation to go upstairs. And then I noticed Leo get up. Only one of us was married, and he was the one leading a girl upstairs. But it wasn't really any of my business.

The rest of us were still pounding down beers and telling jokes, when Leo came back with guilt written all over his face. I knew he loved his wife and kids; he called them all the time.

"I can't believe I got weak and let her talk me into that," Leo said, sadly.

"Don't worry about it, man. Hopefully, you wrapped it up," I said.

"I did, but now I feel guilty," he said, tears sliding down his cheeks.

"It's okay, brother. We're all guilty for being here. Don't beat yourself up. Forget about it." I poured him a beer, trying to calm him down.

Fifteen minutes later I witnessed something I would have bet my life I'd never see: Leo was going back upstairs with a different woman! Apparently his guilt trip had subsided. He came back after half an hour.

The tears started flowing again. "I can't believe I did it again. Darryl, what should I do?"

"First thing you should do is get away from me with that 'sorry' talk," I said. "Then I suggest you go back to the ship. Man, you're too much!"

He got up and left. John, T, and I decided to celebrate somewhere else. We'd been there for several hours and needed some air. We said our goodbyes to the girls and left them a tip. We walked the streets of old San Juan, thinking about getting some grub. We stopped at an outside bar to ask a lady to recommend a good place to eat. Her name was Maria.

"My brother owns a restaurant and bar," she said. "He's having a New Year's Eve party tonight with a buffet. There will be tons of girls there, good drinks, and free food. How does that sound?"

"Sounds like a good deal to me," John said.

"You want to smoke a joint with me first, and then we'll walk over?" she asked.

I was floored. I hadn't smoked for six months, since I started sending out resumes and knew I'd have to take a pre-employment drug test.

"Hell, yeah!" I said enthusiastically. "Let's get stoned and go to your brother's place."

The brother's bar was surrounded by a tall cast iron fence. When Maria let us in, the gate clanged shut behind us. I had the creepiest feeling we'd just been locked inside. But I didn't want to offend Maria, so I kept my mouth shut.

My fears were put to rest when I saw beautiful women everywhere. The ladies outnumbered the men three to one, and I had a good feeling I was going to get lucky. Maria ordered drinks and plates of food for us, and the women started coming over to introduce themselves. My heart sank after meeting the fourth woman.

"What's the matter, Darryl?" John asked, looking worried.

"Did you notice the strong grip that last chick had?" I said as another woman approached us.

"Hi, guys. Welcome to our place. I hope we can all dance later and have some fun," she said, shaking our hands.

I realized my suspicions were valid. All these women were dressed to the hilt in evening gowns, make-up, and high heels. There was just one problem: They were all male.

"John, this is a transvestite bar, man. Let's get out of here!" I shouted.

"Take it easy, man. You don't want to piss these people off. We'll leave in a little while." John was from New York City and didn't seem upset. But I was a small-town Maine boy, and I needed to get out of that creepy place. If anyone was teaching young people political correctness back then, I certainly hadn't heard of it.

I really lost it when Maria's brother walked out onto the stage in a red evening dress and big black wig and started singing "The Big Bamboo." All I could think of was being tied up by a couple of these guys and them having their way with me. I took my chair and turned it around so I wasn't facing the stage. Mr. T just sat there, not knowing what to do.

"Let's get out of here!" I said even more forcefully.

Thankfully the iron gate opened, and we walked out.

"I've never been so scared in my whole life!" I said.

John laughed. "That was no big deal. I've seen crazier stuff than that in New York."

"You can have it! This is the last time I go ashore with you. You're a freak, man!"

"I didn't know it was a transvestite bar—take it easy!" John turned to T and asked, "What did you think?"

"I don't know what to think of what I just saw," T said, shaking his head.

We went back to sea and continued refueling the Navy. I started looking for another job that wasn't so military-oriented. I'd been on board just four months and was already going out of my mind. The crew was nuts, with its mix of alcoholics, misfits, and—I suspected—ex-criminals.

One of the most notable crazies was a messman, whose duties included taking our food orders, serving food, and cleaning up afterward. He had asked to get off the vessel and had been refused. Everyone knew he was a ticking time bomb.

One morning that messman was on duty at breakfast. I knew he was half nuts and kept my eye on him.

"What are you having?" he asked.

"Good morning. I'll have two eggs over easy, bacon, and home fries, please."

He came back a few minutes later with my breakfast. I decided to make some toast. I found some bread and went over to the toaster. When I got back to my seat my plate was gone, and the messman was looking at me.

"What happened to my eggs?" I asked aggressively.

"You got up, so I threw them away. I thought you were done."

"I just ordered them, asshole!" I yelled.

We were soon involved in a fistfight and wrestling on the floor. Other crewmembers broke it up, and the chief steward came running.

"What's going on here?" he yelled.

"Your messman threw away my breakfast before I had one bite!"

"He got up from the table. I thought he wasn't going to eat it," the messman yelled back.

"You're full of shit, man! You just wanted to fight so they'd toss your ass off this ship."

The messman was fired the next time we pulled into port.

I was stressed out from being on the ship, so I made some phone calls. God must have been looking out for me. I'd been bugging Crest Oil Tankers for a job; this time when I called the man in personnel said if I flew to Egypt that day he'd hire me. I couldn't believe what I was hearing.

I jumped in the air. Finally, a *normal* ship—or so I thought. I was signing on as an able-bodied seaman again. *At least I'll be away from all the freaks!*

I ran up to the captain's office. The "Ecuadorian aristocrat" signed my paperwork and angrily proclaimed that because I hadn't given notice, I'd never work with MSC again.

But I had my signed Certificate of Discharge for Merchant Seaman, an official U.S. Coast Guard document. Every time anyone gets on a ship in the Merchant Marine he signs a form indicating the date, the port of signing on, the captain's name, and the vessel's name, number, size, and trade. When a sailor gets off a vessel for any reason—vacation, being fired, quitting—he receives the discharge form with the date, port, and the captain's signature verifying sea time on the vessel.

I took my first discharge paperwork, payoff money, and sea bags and headed to Port Said, Egypt, to board a 900-foot supertanker discharging grain for the U.S. foreign aid program.

CHAPTER FIFTEEN

EGYPTIAN TOPAZ AND THE BOSTON MASSACRE

I was happy that a professional tanker company finally wanted me, even with the horrendously long, cramped flight to Cairo. I was met by a ship's agent, taken through customs and immigration, then driven to Port Said to board the M/V Copper Mountain.

On the massive vessel, hundreds of men were unloading and bagging grain using grain excavators. The surrounding air was so full of grain dust that I gagged walking up the gangway. No wonder all the workers were wearing dust masks.

I signed on with the captain, who assigned me a room and a watch. The next day I met the officers and crew. I soon discovered that both Egypt and our ship were full of colorful characters. A lot of old professional sailors worked for Crest Oil Tankers, leftovers from the old tanker companies: Gulf Oil, Texaco, Getty Oil, Sunoco, and City Service.

My duties on the Copper Mountain included unloading grain and providing support where needed. I stood the four to eight watch with eight hours off between. Some days I worked overtime, took an afternoon nap, and went back to work again after only four hours.

On other days I went ashore at 8:00 a.m. to shop and see the sights. What a culture shock it was walking the streets of Port Said. The women wore veils with just their eyes showing, and Muslim tradition meant they didn't look into the eyes of men on the street. I found it strange. Women looked down at their feet while walking to the shops where they worked, but as soon as they were inside they took off the veil and could talk openly to both males and females.

Among the crew, I got to know our old boatswain, Ben, a red-haired, pony-tailed bona fide Harley Davidson hippie with tattoos all over his body. He knew I was green and looked out for me the whole time I was aboard.

One time, I went ashore with him. We walked around, and I bought a couple of Persian rugs. Ben and I were having fun, although we couldn't drink, because alcohol is forbidden in the Islamic religion. We didn't want any hassles with the local people or authorities over alcohol. Yet somehow we managed to find some hashish sold by some guy on the street. True stoners at heart, Ben and I were willing to take the risk.

Ben said, "Darryl, you have a lot to lose. I'll hang on to this until we're inside the ship. Let's finish our shopping."

I looked longingly at the seven grams of beautiful blond Egyptian hash that Ben wouldn't let me carry. "You have a lot to lose too, Ben."

"They won't mess with an old guy like me. And it's better if only one of us got caught. Let's get something to eat."

We found an outside cafe and ordered lunch, water, and coffee. If it had been allowed, I would have been drinking some kind of alcoholic beverage. We finished lunch and started shopping again. We were in a foreign culture with amazing sights, sounds, and smells—and interesting things to buy. We passed a jewelry store with its doors open to the street.

"Come in, my friend," the Egyptian jeweler said. "We have many sales today and precious stones you cannot find anywhere else in the world."

"Okay, I'll check out your store," I said naively.

There were diamonds, gold, jewels, necklaces, bracelets, earrings, and rings of all kinds. It looked like a nice store, and I figured it must be an honest business.

"Where are you from, sir?" the businessman asked.

"We're from the USA. We're here in Port Said on a ship," I said proudly.

"Oh, I see. You cannot find these precious stones in the United States. You could buy these beautiful topaz jewels and get ten times your money in the USA, guaranteed."

"Wow, they sure are beautiful. How much for this one?"

"That is twenty American dollars. You would get $200 for this topaz in the USA," he assured me.

My young mind starting racing. If I bought that stone and made $200, wow. Maybe I should buy three or four.

"How much for three of them?"

"Sir, these are precious stones. It would be $60 for three. It doesn't matter how many you buy, the price is the same. They are all basically the same size and value. Would you like three?"

I looked over the stones. They were a beautiful light brown and looked like they'd bring some money from a jeweler in the United States, who could turn them into beautiful rings or necklaces.

"I'll take ten of those," my twenty-three-year-old self said. "Please give me the best ten, and I'll pay you in cash." I turned to Ben. "What do you think? Am I doing the right thing? Do you think they're real?"

"It's hard to tell, Darryl. I wouldn't buy them, but they *are* pretty. Who knows, maybe you'll make some money in Pascagoula when we get back."

I bought the gems, and we went back to the ship. We went down to Ben's room, and he gave me my quarter ounce of hash. We smoked some out of a pipe Ben had. I figured if the jewels weren't worth anything, at least the hash was a good deal.

We stayed in Port Said for another week. A signup sheet was posted for a visit to the Great Pyramids and tours on camel-back to all the historical sites. The captain encouraged the crew to sign up early so he could plan his workforce from those not making the trip. I ended up doing neither. There were adequate personnel for me to take a day off, so I blew off the tour. I wanted to find more hash.

The decision to try to score drugs rather than see the Great Pyramids has haunted me ever since. I joked about it with all my drug buddies back home, but later, in my sobriety, I finally understood the opportunity I'd missed. At the time, my addictions took priority over everything: my job, my life, even the opportunity of a lifetime to see one of the ancient wonders of the world.

In my sobriety, I've often looked closely at that decision, because it tells me how bad off I really was. I was blind to the true nature of my addictions. At the time, I thought my decision showed how cool a partier I was. In reality, I was a sick young man who stayed in denial for another nineteen years.

The M/V Copper Mountain was finally empty of grain. We sailed the Mediterranean, through the straits of Gibraltar, across the Atlantic, to the Gulf of Mexico and finally to Pascagoula, Mississippi. It took less than two weeks to make the voyage, and we had a lot of work to do. The 90,000-ton vessel had twelve cargo tanks, each large enough to hold a five-story apartment building. It was our job to clean them.

A souvenir photo of the 900-foot M/V Copper Mountain, Port Said, Egypt.

It was 1986, and drinking on ships was not yet taboo. In fact, the shipping companies allowed alcohol to be sold out of "the slop chest," the ship's store where sailors bought snacks and sundries. At the time the weekly ration was a case of beer or a fifth of booze.

The non-drinkers bought their allotment of alcohol and sold it to the highest bidder, allowing the real alcoholics to have extra spirits. Anyone who wanted to pay the price, which we always did, or who was friendly with the right people could have more than his share.

If the captain noticed someone was a problem drinker, he withheld the right to buy alcohol. It happened frequently. Typically, a sailor lost the privilege for a few weeks, but would have it restored if he caused no further problems.

In those pre-drug-test days, many of us also spent our time getting high. It wasn't unusual to smell marijuana smoke wafting through the ship's passageways. It was frowned upon, but we smoked quietly. As long as we did our jobs and didn't cause problems, most merchant captains left the crew alone.

We frequently had big parties on the stern with barrels full of ice, beer, and soda. The chief steward barbecued ribs and chicken, and there was potato salad, corn on the cob, and potato chips. The men on watch were not allowed to drink, but the off-duty men could enjoy as long as they didn't overindulge. Of course, many of us pushed the envelope. After the barbecue we'd continue the festivities in our rooms.

Ironically, most of Crest's oil tankers were named after wines. There was the Beaujolais, the St. Emilion, the Chablis, the Pomerol. Only the Copper Mountain was different, having been named for a Colorado ski resort. Yet I don't recall ever seeing a bottle of wine on any of these ships; we weren't refined enough for that. We drank beer, rum, whiskey, or vodka every night, smoked hash, and worked long hours day after day.

After arriving in Mississippi, we pulled into a terminal to load grain. I went ashore the next day, expecting to make some quick cash off my exotic topaz.

I found a jewelry store and said to gentleman behind the counter, "I'd like to sell some precious jewels. The jeweler in Egypt told me they'd be worth a lot of money in the States."

I handed him the ten gems. He looked at one. Then another. Then a third.

"How much did you pay for them?" he asked.

"I paid $20 each. How much do you think they're worth?" I held my breath, hoping for a big number.

"I would say that's about right, $20 each," he said, smiling. "They're pretty, but they're synthetic—and worth just about what you paid for them."

I saw my naïve money-making scheme quickly go up in smoke. I thanked him, hung my head in disappointment, and walked out. I kept those gems for years, although I don't know what eventually happened to them.

I stayed on the Copper Mountain for another month and then flew home from New Orleans. It had been a good trip, and it was time to unwind.

At that time I was living with my grandfather. We loved each other, and in the beginning there were no problems living together. I had the entire upstairs to myself, including three bedrooms, a bath-room, and a library. I had it good. I hung out with him during the day and did the chores: cooking, cleaning, filling the wood box, taking him for rides.

My grandfather was in his eighties and hard of hearing, but his mind was sharp and he knew I was partying. He was proud of me, but knew I was struggling with alcohol. He may have guessed about the drugs. At night he went to bed, sometimes listening to the Red Sox, and I went out and got screwed up. The next morning I'd drag myself out of bed, only to do it all over again the next night. I wasted a lot of my life on my vacations drinking, drugging, and sleeping. Grampa used to tell me someday I'd get in trouble at work for drinking too much; he was right. Some of the memories from that time haunt me today, because that was the way my grandfather knew me in the last years of his life.

At some point, I met Carolyn, a woman in her forties who was pretty, petite, sexy, and very much an alcoholic and cocaine addict. Together we were a dangerous pair. Carolyn adored me; I was her young stud. After snorting cocaine and drinking, we'd make mad, passionate love.

One night I snuck Carolyn upstairs, and we snorted lines and drank. I was very drunk and after her to have sex with me. I wasn't taking no for an answer.

"C'mon, baby, come over here and show me you love me."

"Darryl, snort that line and be good, will ya?"

I snorted the line. Then another. Then another one with her. I continued to make passes at her, kissing her and getting her all worked up. She wanted me, I knew it, but for some reason she wasn't going any further. I couldn't figure it out, because I was so insanely drunk, but I dragged her into bed, and we got naked.

"C'mon Carolyn, why are you fighting me off?"

"It's not a good time, Darryl. Believe me, you don't want to."

"Yes, I do. I want you right now," I insisted, kissing her.

I started kissing her body and moving down lower. I was licking her belly button and started going lower.

She grabbed me by the hair. "No, Darryl! No! Stop, I'm telling you. It's the wrong time!"

But I was oblivious. She tried to stop me, but couldn't, and after awhile she let me do what I wanted. Eventually I passed out.

I woke up in the morning with my head pounding. I pried open my eyes and couldn't believe my eyes. Carolyn was gone, and the whole bed was red with blood. The sheets were covered; my hands had blood all over them; my face was sticky. What had happened? It looked like the Boston Massacre in my bed. *Oh, my God, I killed her!*

I started to remember bits and pieces and finally put it all together. *Oh, my God, she was on her period.* Carolyn had told me to stop, and I wouldn't listen. How stupid could I be? I walked to the bathroom and looked in the mirror. My face, neck, chest, and hands were covered in blood.

I washed my hands and rinsed my mouth. I felt like throwing up. I sneaked downstairs while my grandfather was still sleeping and showered. The water turned pink as I washed my body. My God, was I losing my mind? *You're frigging nuts*, I told myself. Then I laughed, knowing how crazy I was becoming. I knew this wouldn't kill me. It was disgusting, but it wouldn't hurt me. My drinking was so out of control that having oral sex with a woman having her period was no big deal. I never pondered how screwed up that thinking was until I got sober twenty years later.

It should have been enough to make a person quit drinking. But that wasn't even an option. A true alcoholic, I wrote it off as just another mistake that could happen to anybody. I'd smarten up and be more careful in the future, or so I thought. In truth, the same kinds of crazy alcoholic behavior would happen over and over. I was becoming a dangerous man.

At that time I was spending time with a buddy from high school we called "Hop Sing," who was the cocaine connection between Coconut Grove, Florida, and the boys in Maine. I bought a lot and divided it into half-gram packs, but I hardly ever sold any. I snorted most of it. Looking back, I wonder why I fooled myself into cutting out magazine pages to make cocaine packages, when I continually broke into them with my friends.

Hop Sing and I partied most of that vacation. When it came time to go back to work, he gave me a ride to the airport, and as we got closer he laid out a huge line of cocaine and said, "Hagar, this is the last line of your vacation. I'm not giving you another one. This is it."

I snorted the line, and he dropped me off at Portland International Jetport. I stumbled up to the ticketing line. I don't have a clear memory of the experience, but they let me board the aircraft. I sat next to a very large woman, and as soon as I sat down, I passed out from exhaustion.

I woke up later drooling on the large lady's sweater.

My head popped up. "I'm very sorry. I'm really tired."

"That's okay. I really don't mind at all."

That's all I needed to hear. I put my head back on her shoulder and passed out again until we landed in Florida a few hours later.

I again signed on as an AB with Crest Oil Tankers, but joined a different ship headed to Coatzacoalcos, Mexico, to load crude oil at the Pemex terminal owned by the Mexican government. There I went ashore with a few guys from the ship to visit some dive in search of cold beer and hot Mexican girls. At the time we left, the sailing board hadn't been set.

The sailing board, usually a chalkboard located near the gangway indicating the date and time of the next sailing, must by law (and according to union rules) be posted so the crew won't miss the ship when it sails. Sometimes a captain will set it early, so he doesn't sail short-handed.

The ship would only be in port about fifteen hours, so my intent was only to visit the bar. I didn't plan on a cute Mexican girl taking me home and doing things to me I can't write about here. At her place we partied and made love all night. I was quite drunk, and we had also smoked some pot. I wasn't worried about a thing until I suddenly woke up in the morning and looked at my watch. It was 6:00 a.m.

I don't know what time the ship is sailing! I woke Rosie up and told her I needed a cab right away. She started kissing me, and I decided fifteen more minutes was a risk worth taking. After our morning love-making, Rosie called the cab. I started to worry—would the ship still be there? Who would I call to wire me money or an airline ticket if it wasn't?

I said my goodbyes to Rosie and asked the cabbie to hurry. He peeled out and drove like a madman. We reached a gate near the terminal, and he could drive no farther. I still couldn't see if the ship was there. I'd have to sprint down to the dock.

"How much do I owe you?"

"Twenty dollars, señor."

"Can you break a fifty? It's all I have."

"No, señor. No change. I'm sorry," he said, smiling.

"Take it!" I said, more than a little pissed off.

I ran as fast as I could down to the dock and around a warehouse. As I went around the corner, I held my breath—and there it was. The ship was hooked up to tugboats, and the crew was releasing the mooring lines. I ran forward, yelling and pumping my arms in the air in a good imitation of a Rocky Balboa victory dance. I knew they'd let me on. My shipmates saw me and started cheering, whistling, and applauding. I was laughing—until I looked up at the bridge wing where the captain and the Mexican pilot were looking down, observing the madness.

The captain didn't talk to me for an entire day. When he did finally speak to me, it was to lecture me about how it was my duty to be back on board in a timely, sober fashion. He reminded me that the crew was his responsibility, but that he would have left me in Mexico to fend for myself if I hadn't shown up. He pointed out that merchant ships are chartered at a cost of tens of thousands of dollars per day—every hour of delay can mean a loss of thousands of dollars. The captain didn't like me for the rest of that trip.

I tried not to screw up again. If I refrained from drinking, I was an excellent worker and a smart guy. But I always found myself getting into some kind of trouble when I drank.

That ship had a basketball hoop set up, and I exercised by running laps around the deck, shooting hoops, or lifting weights. I figured if I got back into shape and away from the partying I could keep myself out of trouble.

The rest of the trip was uneventful, and I finished the work tour and flew home from Houston in September of 1986.

During the vacation that followed, I was my usual renegade self. At that time I was still riding my motorcycle and looked like something out of *Easy Rider*, roaring down the highway with the wind blowing in my face. I loved the idea of being a rebel without a cause.

A guy named Louie in Waldoboro had tuned up and fixed my bike. My mom and sister gave me a ride to Louie's, and I told Mom we'd stop for lunch afterward to thank her for helping me out.

Playing basketball at sea, 1986.

After our meal, I was being flip and joked, "You might as well let me leave first, that way I won't have to pass you on the road."

My mother didn't think I was funny and gave me a scornful look. I jumped on my 650 Yamaha Special and roared away. The speed limit was 55 mph then, and the bike's speedometer only went up to 85. Once I hit top speed, I didn't know how fast I was actually going.

I had traveled about five miles when I came upon Snowball Hill in Nobleboro, where the road is straight and you can see downhill quite a ways ahead. I got on the accelerator and started going really fast. That's when I saw blue lights flashing.

I'm screwed this time. I pulled over, and as soon as the trooper got out, I recognized him. It was Dale York, the local statie. He knew who I was.

"Where are you going so fast? You were going way over a hundred."

I handed him my license and registration. "Mr. York, my bike only goes up to eighty-five. Look at the speedometer. I'm sure I wasn't going anywhere near a hundred."

"Mr. Hagar, I had you on radar. It took me several minutes to catch up to you. Also—in case you don't know—your registration has expired." He instructed me to stay put and went back to his cruiser to run my record.

I had forgotten all about my mother and sister. After several minutes, along they came. I could see them looking at the flashing blue lights, my pulled-over motorcycle, and me standing outside. They didn't slow down. They probably thought I deserved it.

Trooper York came back, agitated. "Mr. Hagar, I just called for a flat bed tow truck to pick up your motorcycle. Your registration is expired. I should arrest you and take you to jail."

"I really don't think I was going that fast. Show me the radar," I demanded arrogantly.

"I don't need to show you anything. You'll be going to court for 'imprudent speed.' And don't even think about riding this bike again until it's properly registered."

I rode with the motorcycle to the towing yard. The driver asked, "Why didn't you outrun him?"

"I thought about it," I admitted, "but I didn't have a helmet on. If I wiped out at that speed, I'd be dead. So I pulled over."

My wild behavior continued for another month. I was partying with a beautiful redhead named Julie the day before I was to fly to the Bahamas to catch the SS Beaujolais. We went barhopping and spent the night together. Julie had agreed to give me a ride to the airport the following morning. But we'd been drinking all night, and we didn't wake up on time.

"Julie, wake up!" I shook her as she lay sleeping. "We're late. My plane leaves in an hour, and it takes an hour to get to the airport. I'm gonna try to make it. I can't miss my flight."

I don't know what I was thinking. It took an hour at 55 mph; I'd have to drive 90 mph—a bad plan. It was winter, but there was no snow on the roads, and my studded tires threw sparks going down the highway. I sometimes drove more than 90 mph, darting in and out of traffic.

"Darryl, you're scaring me! You're driving really crazy. We're gonna get in an accident!" Julie yelled.

"No, we're not. We're making good time. We might make it."

People in the cars we passed looked at me in disbelief. I was passing on the right and speeding like a madman with sparks flying. We got as far as Yarmouth, about fifteen minutes from the airport, when a State Police cruiser heading in the opposite direction turned on his blue lights. I looked in the rearview mirror and saw the trooper barreling down the meridian dividing the northbound and southbound lanes. I didn't slow down.

"He's coming after us! Pull it over! Pull it over!" Julie screamed.

"Maybe he's not coming after us. He's got another call."

"Darryl, please pull it over!" Julie begged.

I gave up and decided to pull over before I got arrested. I knew I'd miss the flight. The trooper pulled up behind me, got out of his cruiser, and walked up to my rolled-down window.

"Where are you going that requires you to go over 90 mph?" he said angrily.

'I'm trying to make a flight to the Bahamas to join a ship, Officer, and I overslept."

"You people going to the airport think you can drive any way you want. License and registration, please." He looked at my license closely. "Oh, I see. A one star general," he said sarcastically. "When did you get the operating under the influence charge?"

My license had a star on it to inform police officers I'd been convicted of drinking and driving. In Maine, each OUI conviction gets you a star on your driver's license. At least I only had one.

"I got that OUI in 1985. Over a year ago."

He looked at me. Looked inside at Julie. Looked at me again. "You were probably drinking last night. That's why you're late. Give me one reason why I shouldn't arrest you, Mr. Hagar. I have you on radar driving 92 mph in a 55 mph zone."

"Officer, I'm just trying to get to my ship," I said quietly.

"I said give me a good reason why I shouldn't arrest you right now!" he yelled.

"Officer, it won't happen again. I can assure you, sir." I was worried I was about to get thrown in jail—and lose my job.

The trooper went back to his car and ran my record. My license had only been restored a week from the motorcycle incident. He came back to the car.

"Mr. Hagar, I suggest you take a closer look at how fast you drive and at your lifestyle. You're lucky that I'm not going to arrest you. I'm sure you'll have your driver's license suspended again. So don't even try to make your flight. Book another flight—and *slow down*."

The trooper wrote up a speeding ticket and walked away.

"Holy shit!" Julie said, laughing.

"I guess I'll have to book another flight," I said, pulling onto the highway again.

After speeding a little bit, I pulled up to the jetport—just as my original flight was taking off. I had to wait a few hours, but I finally got another flight to Miami. I had a few drinks on the plane to calm my nerves. In the mornings I always drank a Bloody Mary—to hide that I was drinking alcohol so early in the day.

I arrived in Miami and caught the connecting flight to Freeport, Bahamas. After arriving, I waited for an hour in baggage claim for my sea bag to show up. *Oh, no—another casualty of my excessive drinking*. I had tested the limits of irresponsibility, had almost been arrested for speeding, had missed a flight, and now had no work gear.

I spent two days on board ship without my luggage. I borrowed socks and T-shirts, but wasn't going to wear anyone else's underwear. My jeans were dirty, and I had on the same underwear I'd been wearing for two days.

I spoke rather loudly to the captain about my missing luggage. "I'm not sailing with this ship if they don't find my luggage. I'll throw the mooring lines off the bollards on the shore for you and save you some money on line handlers," I said sarcastically.

"Let me check in Miami," the captain said politely. "I'll get back to you today." He needed every crewmember and knew I was serious about not leaving port without work gear.

The captain called the shipping agent and raised his voice. Someone found my bag tucked in a closet in the Miami airport. We sailed the next day. I had my gear, but I'm not sure I had my sanity.

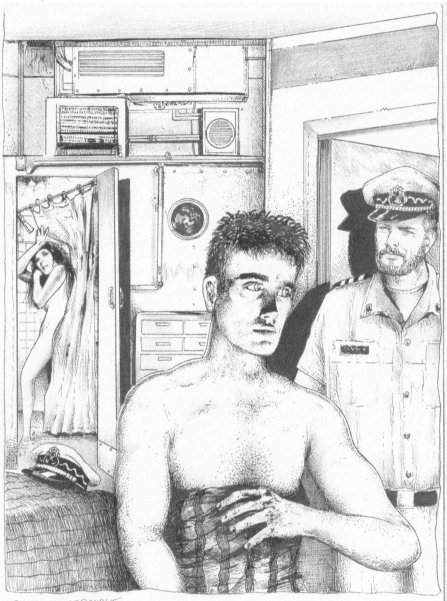

GLENN CHADBOURNE

CHAPTER SIXTEEN
IT'S ALL JUST PIRATE'S BOOTY

Shipping jobs were still tight, but I had some good contacts and in September of 1987 I was asked by Maritime Overseas Corporation (MOC) if I wanted my first job as a third mate. I was eager to accept. After two years of sailing as an able-bodied seaman, I'd finally be sailing as a ship's officer.

I was told to fly to Houston to join the S/T Overseas Valdez, a 700-foot, 37,000-ton clean oil tanker on hire to the U.S. military. It was normal for her to carry four or five different types of fuel to military depots and bases around the world.

The captain of the Overseas Valdez was a stout, jolly old man who had worked for ARCO and had more than forty years of seagoing experience. He was the perfect captain to work under as I was breaking in. He wasn't uptight and watched me closely in the beginning, which gave me great comfort. It takes courage to walk up the gangway of one of those behemoths, let alone be in charge of it. It was what I trained for, but I was anxious the first time I took the con.

We loaded the ship and headed down the narrow Houston Ship Channel, where vessels passed very close to each other, meaning there was no room for error. We made it safely through to the Gulf of Mexico into a field of hundreds of oil rigs. I had sailed between those rigs with Crest Oil Tankers, but it was totally different being in charge. I had the daunting responsibility of navigating the ship between the tall oil rigs and safely passing oncoming ships, work boats, fishing boats, and potential hazards.

It was night, and the Gulf glittered with the white lights of the oil rigs and the work vessels around them. I stood the eight to twelve watch, and the captain stayed on the bridge with me, letting me navigate. It was nerve-wracking at first, but I quickly got the hang of continually watching the radars, looking with the binoculars through the bridge windows, and taking fixes every few minutes to make sure we were on course. I told the able-bodied seaman what course to steer, and he did whatever I asked. A lookout reported to me any vessels, moving targets, and anything else that came close to the ship.

I finished the watch that night with an incredible sense of accomplishment. I was finally doing what I'd been trained for, and I was good at it. After I was on the job for awhile and as he felt more comfortable with my abilities, the captain no longer stayed on the bridge the entire watch. He later told Maritime Overseas Corporation they had found a good man.

Third mate on the Overseas Valdez (this was NOT the Exxon Valdez, which was a different ship).

The ship had orders to go to Europe to transfer oil between different U.S. military installations. There was an AB on my regular watch,

Larry, who became a close friend. He was an experienced sailor and good helmsman, a valuable man to have working with me, but he also liked to smoke grass and drink.

When it came to my addictions I didn't have any common sense regarding what was acceptable or unacceptable behavior. Larry wanted me, his watch officer, to party with him. I was too easily convinced it was okay. Many times we got together at midnight to drink and smoke hash and marijuana, and he'd tell me his sea stories.

We crossed the Atlantic on our way to Gaeta, Italy. It was especially interesting going through the Straits of Gibraltar, where there were many ships, ferries, and fishing boats. If we came across a traffic situation we could put the vessel in hand steering with the click of a button, but otherwise the ship steered itself according to the courses I set. But Larry and I still had to be on our toes on watch, and as an experienced sailor Larry was always close to the helm. The captain was on the bridge through the Straits, but once we hit the Mediterranean he went below to work on port preparations.

We hit a patch where as far as we could tell there wasn't any traffic. Larry was leaning against the console, smoking his pipe. I was in front of the radars, looking through the bridge windows. We were having a conversation about what we'd do in Italy. It was windy, and we hit big seas. Perfect conditions for a fishing boat to be hidden in the troughs of long, deep-rolling swells. As we were steaming through the water, I suddenly saw it.

"Larry, put it in hand steering, and hard right rudder!" I yelled.

"I already am, Mate!"

The ship turned to the right, and a fishing vessel, camouflaged by its purple color against the deep seas, passed close by on the port side. We had just missed it. If we hadn't changed course, we probably would have sunk it. Larry and I looked at each other and burst out laughing. As we were laughing, the radio officer came up to the bridge.

"What's so funny?" Sparky asked.

"See that purple fishing boat right there?" I said, pointing through one of the after-facing windows. "We almost ran over her and sent her to Davey Jones' locker." I laughed again.

Sparky looked out the windows for a minute and then went below.

A few minutes later, the captain came up to the bridge and said nonchalantly, "Any vessels around?"

"Actually, Captain, we just came very close to a fishing vessel. It's purple and blended into the seas in these rough waters. He didn't show up on radar, but Larry and I saw him at the last minute and avoided him. Other than that, nothing around," I said.

"Okay. Just keep a close eye out. Sometimes they can sneak up on you, and it's your responsibility to always be on the lookout."

"Yes, sir, Captain. It happened quickly. We'll both pay close attention," I assured him.

He went back down below.

I turned around and looked at Larry.

"That was kind of weird that he came up right after that happened," I said, scratching my head.

"Are you kidding me? That radio operator went down and snitched on us. He went down and told the old man we were up here laughing. I guarantee it."

"Oh, well. It was a good lesson learned. No harm done."

That near miss was one of the closest I had in my entire twenty-year career. There were several others—a few ships, a few boats—but that's one I'll never forget.

We stopped at Gaeta and then got orders for St. Theodore, Greece. I didn't go ashore much in Italy, but I did go out in Greece to an outdoor café where I drank a few Heinekens and watched the locals walk by. That time, I stayed in control of myself and went back to the ship to rest before I stood cargo watch. On cargo watch I walked up and down the deck of our 700-foot vessel, opening and closing valves and measuring oil levels as we discharged the oil ashore.

On that trip we also went to Rota, Spain. The crew had bonded by that time, and six of us went ashore to a Spanish bar to drink beer. After awhile one of the guys suggested we go find some women. We talked to the locals, who sent us to a Spanish brothel.

We took a cab to a hotel, where we were greeted by a roomful of women. Someone was sent to retrieve a case of beer for the drunken American sailors. While we waited in the lobby, the women started flirting with us. I was the young one of the group and attracted the attention of several hot-looking women. I was now open to the idea of sleeping with a lady of the evening. It was like a rite of passage, and none of us wanted to look like a wimp in front of our fellow sailors.

I paired up with a buxom brunette, who was all over me. I was just a young skipper, and I had a feeling I was in for a wild ride. I grabbed a couple of beers and took her to a private room. As always, alcohol was a part of everything I did outside of work. At one point we were going at it—me with a beer in one hand as the brunette kept saying, "Mucho grande, señor!" It was my first time with a prostitute, making it one of those moments I'll always remember no matter how much I was drinking. Even then I knew my behavior wasn't good, but I couldn't say no when I was under the influence. Alcohol ruled my decision-making. It owned me.

We sailed east from Spain through the Mediterranean. We stopped to pick up a pilot, and I transited the Suez Canal for the first time. We proceeded into the Red Sea. I stood watch as we reached the narrow opening at its southern end near Djibouti.

We entered the Indian Ocean en route to Diego Garcia, the largest atoll in the British-controlled Chagos archipelago. The United States has a big military base there housing B-52 bombers and nuclear weapons, stored and ready. Nobody was supposed to know they were there, but it somehow became common knowledge. Also housed there is a maritime pre-position fleet of civilian manned merchant ships of all types, usually twelve or thirteen vessels.

There were four 900-foot roll-on/roll-off ships full of brand new Abraham tanks and U.S. Marines. There were ships full of ammunition, medical ships, barges, and ships full of jeeps, construction equipment, trailer trucks, etc. We were stationed there periodically as the second tanker that could refuel the Navy at sea. These huge vessels— all grouped together about a week's steaming time away from the Persian Gulf—were an awesome sight. The United States maintains a half dozen pre-positioned fleets across the world designed to support U.S. military operations. The ships are anchored and stay on station in case of emergencies or war.

In my time in the Merchant Marine, I spent months on Diego Garcia where the ships sat at anchor. It was not a good place for someone trying not to screw up by drinking too much. One time I filled my locker with beer. I was able to keep it hidden, even when we got surprise orders to go to the Persian Gulf to refuel the Navy. The chief mate also had a drinking problem and showed up at my door every afternoon when he found out I had stashed away seven cases of beer.

The Coast Guard had rules, but we made up our own minds about drinking. And it was still more than eighteen months before the Exxon Valdez oil spill, the biggest in U.S. history. Of course the captain of the Exxon Valdez had the same kind of drinking problem many of us had, which played a role in that accident.

We were in Diego Garcia for several weeks, and the crew was working all day and drinking all night. Since all the pre-position ships were anchored, the only way to get ashore was to climb down a pilot ladder on the side of the ship onto a launch boat. The problem wasn't going ashore, it was sailors climbing back up the ladder late at night all liquored up.

There were a lot of guys screwing up by drinking too much and causing problems both on the launch boats and on the ships. The men acted out because they knew it was expensive for the companies to replace them halfway around the world; it was difficult to get fired unless you did something really bad.

The mates on watch met the launch boats every four hours to make sure everybody got on board safely and behaved themselves. Since the guys were becoming more unruly, the captain instructed the ship's officers to inspect their bags and confiscate any alcohol. One time I had a conversation with a pumpman, an older man known to be a bad alcoholic, before he went ashore.

"Hi, Pumps, how are you?" I said politely.

"Hi, Mate, how's it going?"

"You know the captain says no more booze on board, Pumps. If you bring any back I have to take it, so please don't. Have some drinks over there, but don't bring any back"

"I'm going ashore for a haircut, Mate. I might have a beer or two, but that's it," he insisted.

He didn't come back that night. We figured he had passed out and would show up in the morning, but he didn't show up the next day either. The captain was anxious, concerned, and angry. We were about to send out a search party, when he finally showed up. He climbed the pilot ladder, and I could immediately tell he'd been drinking.

I stopped him. "Pumpman, the captain's been worried about you. I need to search your bag."

I found a fifth of whiskey and a fifth of rum, unscrewed the caps, reached over the railing, and poured the alcohol into the harbor.

"Who's going to pay for that?" the old pumpman cried out.

"I told you not to bring any booze back. The captain wants to see you in his office."

He stumbled off. After about twenty minutes the captain called me on my walkie talkie.

"Third mate, this is the captain. What did you do with the alcohol you confiscated from the pumpman?"

"I poured it over the side, Captain."

"Mr. Hagar, next time I want you to bring the evidence up to my office."

"Roger that, Captain," I said, confused by the request.

Did he really want to keep the evidence—or drink it himself? The captain wasn't a drunk, but I suspected he wanted a supply for his room. The pumpman got fired, so maybe the captain really did want the evidence, but I never asked him about it.

It wasn't long before we received orders to go to the Persian Gulf. The main reason for the pre-position fleet in Diego Garcia was to protect U.S. interests in the Middle East and to keep crude oil flowing to the Western world. The Iran/Iraq war was raging at the time, and the U.S. Navy needed refueling support.

I was looking forward to seeing our military might again. I believed my experience in refueling the Navy with Military Sealift Command would prove invaluable, and it did.

The plan was to refuel several ships and fill up the fleet oilers. We took on food stores, supplies, and bunkers (fuel for the engines) and proceeded north to the Gulf of Oman at the northern end of the Indian Ocean, the entrance to the Persian Gulf. We discharged the last of our cargo and proceeded in a convoy with U.S. Navy vessels to Jebel Ali, United Arab Emirates, to refill the tanker. We went back out and refueled more Navy ships until we were empty. We came back again and refilled in Bahrain.

Then we were assigned to drift in a ten-square-mile "box" at sea, waiting for our next refueling orders. Sometimes we'd go several weeks before the next operation, and we would get bored. We often stayed at sea for more than a month without seeing land, and the guys got squirrelly. But I had filled my locker with San Miguel beer and was drinking every day on my off time.

We left the Persian Gulf with orders to go to Sasebo, Japan, via the Singapore Straits. We were warned by the Navy and the Coast Guard that we might encounter pirates. Many ships had been robbed by small boats full of armed men who came up behind them at night, threw a grappling hook over the side, and climbed on board. The pirates were armed with machine guns and stole money out of the ship's safe.

It wasn't unusual for our captain to have $100,000 in the safe. Most American ships have a lot of cash on hand; all ships in the Merchant Marine keep at least $50,000 for emergency repairs. Pirates know this. Most merchant ships carry no weapons and therefore are easy targets. But we were on a government charter and were armed. We had two M16 semiautomatic rifles, one sawed-off 12-gauge shotgun, several pistols, and plenty of ammunition.

The chances of encountering pirates were minimal, but the captain took the threat seriously. He made up a security bill with assignments for weapons, extra patrols, and extra security duty. I thought it was both fun and funny when we participated in drills as if we were being boarded by pirates. We were assigned numbers; I was "Agent 10." We felt the captain was going off the deep end with the pirate preparations, but I did what I was told. The officers had walkie talkies and could communicate with the captain, "Agent 1."

The number one line of defense against pirates was to run at night with the deck floodlights lit up like a Christmas tree. Pirates were known to stay away from well lit vessels, where they could easily be seen. Fire hoses were let out and pressurized; we could spray the pirates so they couldn't scale the side of the ship. Of course, a man could get shot using a fire hose, but it was part of our defense strategy. The ship also steamed at full speed through pilotage waters (where a pilot comes aboard as a guide) so small boats would have a difficult time coming alongside. Armed security personnel made rounds on the vessel in highly visible places.

After practicing our piracy drills and issuing weapons, we finally arrived in pirate waters. The chief mate was on the bow with one of the M16s. The other M16 was on the bridge with the captain. The shotgun was on the stern.

I started my watch on the bridge, and when I got off I would take over for the third engineer, an old man who'd been through it all before. He was astern with the shotgun accompanied by an able-bodied seaman holding a night stick and a can of mace. I thought that was

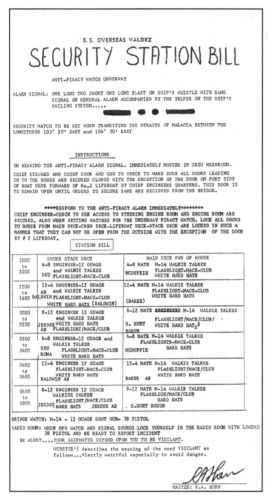

Anti-piracy station bill for the S/S Overseas Valdez. (Note the weapons used!)

pretty funny: Spray a pirate holding a machine gun with a can of mace. I said good night to the third engineer, got out my walkie talkie, and decided to have a little fun with the captain.

"Agent 1, Agent 1, this is Agent 69 checking in from the stern," I reported.

I could hear Larry, who was on the wheel at the time, laughing in the background. But the captain wasn't amused.

"Mr. Hagar, there isn't any Agent 69 on this vessel!" he called back.

"Oh, excuse me Agent 1, this is Agent 10. My mistake. Agent 10 on the stern, armed and ready, Agent 1."

"Roger that, Agent 10. Over and out."

I started laughing. He was a good old guy and knew I was kidding. He wouldn't be angry for long.

He never mentioned it to me, and I never worried about it.

We steamed through the Singapore Straits safely with no pirate attacks, steamed by Singapore without stopping, and headed for Japan to discharge our cargo.

When I'd been aboard the S/T Overseas Valdez for six months, I volunteered to stay two more. I was making almost $7,000 a month at the time and figured I was drinking less on board than I would at home. I called it "sea-hab"—*sea rehabilitation*. At eight months a complete crew change was due, and I'd finally get to go home and see my girlfriend.

Just before the crew change, the chief mate came up to the bridge to talk to me. "Darryl, we have good news and we have bad news."

"What's that, Mate?" I asked.

"The good news is everyone on board is going home tomorrow, except one guy." He paused and said, "The bad news is: You're the one guy."

"How can that be, Mate? I have eight months on board! I have the most time out of everyone!"

He smiled. "It's low man on the totem pole. They need at least one deck officer with underway refueling experience, and you were chosen. Look at it this way, Darryl. The company is happy with your work."

"I can't believe this," I said. "But whatever they want, Mate. Like I have any choice."

"Okay. I'll tell the captain you're willing to stay. Right?"

"Tell him they owe me one," I said as he left the bridge laughing.

I can't believe this. I'm about to do close to a year on my very first officer's job! I'd have a lot of money in the bank, but the more money I had the harder I drank and did drugs. Three months off with $75,000 dollars in the bank isn't a good thing when you're an alcoholic.

In Japan we boarded a new captain and chief mate. I was sad to see both the old guys go. The new pair turned out to be quite a trip. Both had vast experience on cargo ships, but were inexperienced as tanker men, and oil tankers are more difficult to handle. Plus, the captain was a hardcore alcoholic. He stayed sober every day until about 4:00 p.m. Then he drank . . . during convoys, during refueling, when we were steaming to the next port, whenever. It was my first experience working with an alcoholic higher up the food chain than I was.

I could always tell when the captain was screwed up. Every night I went up to the bridge for "supper relief." I was paid an hour of overtime for a half hour of standing the bridge watch while the second mate ate his dinner. By that time, the captain was into the gin bottle. He got nasty mean when I came down off the bridge to eat after supper relief. I used to joke that for twenty-three and half hours the captain told me how great I was. Then in that half hour during supper when he was drunk, he'd tell me how messed up I was. It got to the point where I skipped supper to avoid the torture.

When we got to Japan, I was a disappointed at not being able to see the country other than by sea, but I was too busy pumping oil and taking care of business to go ashore.

While we were there, I noticed that the captain was rude to the Japanese pilot. They were both in their sixties, and I think the captain was treating the old pilot as if he were personally responsible for Pearl Harbor. It was strange watching them interact. Nothing was ever said about World War II, but I sensed they both knew the source of the animosity. Sadly, the Japanese pilot acted as if he deserved to be treated badly by the old American sea captain. It was uncomfortable and embarrassing.

Just before we sailed from Sasebo, I walked the pilot to the ladder where he would disembark the vessel. I took the opportunity to apologize for my captain and explained that he was having a bad day. The pilot smiled, thanked me, and said, "No problem."

After leaving Japan we headed past China, Taiwan, and the Philippines and through the South China Sea past Vietnam. A pirate watch was set again as we passed through the straits. We anchored off Singapore, and hooked up to a fuel oil barge to take on bunkers for the engines. The boom (ship's crane) lifted aboard cargo nets full of necessary equipment and food. As we loaded stores, small boats came alongside and native Singaporeans scaled our accommodation ladder. We called them "bum boats," because the people came aboard to sell souvenirs and trinkets. And, of course, there were prostitutes.

I ignored the commotion and concentrated on my job. It wasn't my responsibility to ward off the natives trying to make a buck off wealthy American sailors. There were other officers around to deal with them, and I tried not to let them distract me. The chief mate had put me in charge of safely loading the stores, and I wasn't going to let him down.

Out of the corner of my eye I noticed a Singaporean woman checking me out. She walked up to me in her tiny dress with plenty of cleavage showing and said bluntly, "Hi. Would you like to take me to your room?"

"I can't, lady. I'm loading stores."

"I'll love you for a long time. C'mon, sailor, take me!"

She walked away, and the wheels in my brain started turning. I knew I shouldn't, but I was tempted. I tried to pay attention to loading the stores. She didn't give up, though, and came back over.

"C'mon, take me to your room," she said again. "Suckie, fuckie. Me love you long time."

I looked around. No other officers were watching. I decided to go for it.

"Listen; go up to the D deck four levels up." I held up four fingers. "Find the room that says 'Third Mate' and get undressed and into bed. I'll be up in five minutes."

After five minutes I walked up to the boatswain and said, "Bosun, I have to use the bathroom. Can you handle running the gang for a little while?"

He agreed, and I took off, admittedly excited. It was risky, but I was a risk-taker. I scaled the stairs to my stateroom, opened the door, and there she was, naked and waiting in my bunk. I locked the door behind me and stripped. I hadn't been with a woman in awhile. I jumped into bed and was going at it within seconds.

After just a few minutes there was a knock on my door, and a voice called out, "Third Mate, are you in there? This is the chief mate!"

I raised my index finger to my lips and said "Shhh! Get in the shower, quick!" I pushed her into the bathroom and into the shower. I closed the shower curtain and wrapped a towel around me as the chief mate knocked again.

I opened the door. The chief mate's eyes widened when he saw me undressed.

"Darryl, what are you doing in here?" he asked, looking over my shoulder.

"I spilled some paint on my clothes loading stores and I had to shower real quick," I lied convincingly. "I'm getting dressed and going back out to finish loading the stores with the bosun."

"Hurry up. Supposedly there's a bunch of hookers running around the ship, and I want you to round them all up and kick them all off ASAP."

I agreed to get on it and shut the door as he scurried away.

I got the woman out of the shower and climbed back into bed with her and finished what I started. I justified it by saying to myself that she was already there—I might as well finish. It was typical brazen behavior for me then.

As soon as I was done I jumped out of bed and said, "You have to get off the ship. Go find all the ladies and take them with you. Captain very angry!"

I gave her $40, and she told me she'd round up the ladies and leave the ship. I never saw her again. I quickly dressed, went out, and rounded up everyone foreign to the ship and kicked them off. Not one person on our ship ever knew I had a prostitute in my room; I kept that secret a long time.

We eventually reached Diego Garcia. I met a young officer from one of the roll on/roll off ships who got permission from his captain to give me a tour. The M/V Hague was a Maersk Line ship, 900 feet long and full of war equipment. It made our twenty-year-old oil tanker look plain next to its staterooms with wall-to-wall carpet, paneled walls, TVs, and recliners. The S/T Overseas Valdez was a steel walled, tile-decked, nuts-and-bolts working oil tanker.

My friend took me into the cargo holds. What a sight: rows of never-used Abraham tanks! I was awestruck as we walked around the armored vehicles and climbed into a tank and sat in it. The unbelievable might of the U.S. military right there on the island—more than many countries have in their entire arsenal—made me proud to be an American. Diego Garcia is still home to a fleet of pre-position vessels and B-52 bombers and a large contingent of U.S. Marines and Navy sailors as well as numbers of British armed forces.

Pre-position ship in Diego Garcia.

Periodically some of the ships went to Kuwait to unload tanks or supplies or the other oil tanker in port left to refuel the Navy. At times we formed various convoy patterns at sea in preparation for wartime. Then we zigzagged together according to orders sent out ahead of time.

We changed course by radio command, but we were supposed to follow a secret convoy manual. Some ships would zig when they were supposed to zag, and our old, alcoholic, nervous, angry captain would curse about how screwed up the Navy was.

Inevitably he waited for a break in the action and then came up with a reason to leave the bridge: "I've got to go throw my laundry in the washer. Keep an eye out," or "I've got to get my other jacket," or "I've got to throw my wash in the dryer," or "I've got to go use the head." It never stopped.

The captain did more laundry than a hotel maid. We all knew he was going down to his room to take a shot of gin or whiskey. He'd come back with a better attitude, until he eventually drank too much. Then he got mean. If I hadn't witnessed these things first hand, I wouldn't have believed them.

While we were in port, I met a female sailor stationed with the Navy at Diego Garcia. Females in the military were few and far between, and any guy who was lucky enough to find a girlfriend on the island was fortunate. But on my time off I was determined to catch a buzz, and having a girlfriend was not going to screw up my drinking. She gave me several chances, but finally told me to get lost. I don't blame her; she recognized the signs of early alcoholism. Looking back, I now realize I could have had a very special woman in my life. She was beautiful, smart, sexy, and really liked me, but she knew it would never work.

We got orders to go to the Persian Gulf again to refuel the Navy. The Iran/Iraq tanker war was raging, and hundreds of oil tankers had already been destroyed. The Iranians had Chinese Silkworm missiles set up five miles from the Strait of Hormuz, the only entrance and exit to the Persian Gulf, where 40 percent of the world's oil reserves are located. The Iranians also had small, fast speedboats carrying weapons used to terrorize ships. The Silkworms destroyed many tankers carrying oil out of Iraq.

The Iraqis had French Exocet missiles that could be fired from a seaborne vessel. These highly accurate and deadly missiles blew up many tankers carrying Iranian oil. In fact, many ships from many nations were blown up by missiles and mines laid by both countries in the Persian Gulf.

By that time, President Reagan had asked Kuwaiti oil tankers to fly U.S. flags for their protection. Both Iran and Iraq were blowing up tankers in the Strait of Hormuz they suspected of aiding the "enemy." We believed neither country would mess with the USA.

The U.S. Navy also conducted convoys. Merchant ships, including our vessel, met at the entrance to the Persian Gulf and proceeded north single file, accompanied by U.S. warships. It was surreal and dangerous. Our alcoholic captain joked that since the Silkworms had a range of fifty miles and we were only five miles away, the missiles would just fly right over our heads.

We arrived in the Gulf of Oman and refueled our fleet of Navy destroyers, frigates, and tankers so they could protect friendly ships and keep the Persian Gulf open. After refueling we again drifted at sea, waiting for the next operation. That time I didn't see land for forty-five days. I tried not to go crazy with loneliness and to be patient with the other unruly sailors. I did it in part by drinking from the store in my closet every day.

We got orders to do another refueling at sea with the rest of our cargo and then were told to anchor outside the port of Khor Fakkan to await convoy operations. This was all highly secret, as the U.S. Navy did not want the Iranians or Iraqis to know when the convoy operations took place. There were no satellite phone calls to give us an idea when we'd move, no radio messages telling us what would happen, nothing. Because of the secrecy, our alcoholic captain was going stir crazy. He was a nervous man as it was. I'm sure he tried to control his drinking, but the fear of the unknown seemed to drive him nuts.

Me, steering the ship.

He complained, "I can't believe they're not telling us what's going on. I can't believe we don't know what day we'll be forming a convoy. I can't believe they're doing this to me." Blah, blah, blah . . . he cried to us every day.

We sat at anchor day after day without hearing a word, and then without any notice at all, huge ships came one by one and anchored close to us. The first was the Bridgeton, a 300,000-ton Very Large Crude Carrier (VLCC), the most well known of the re-flagged Kuwaiti tankers. Other ships anchored as well, and then the destroyers and frigate showed up.

I was in charge on the bridge standing the anchor watch when I saw a military helicopter drop a wire down to the Bridgeton. A Navy officer in full camouflage was lowered onto the deck. The helicopter headed toward us and out came another Navy officer. I ran to the phone and dialed the captain's office.

Navy liaison officer landing on our deck from a helicopter.

"Captain, the convoy is starting. A Navy helicopter just lowered an officer onto our deck. He's coming up right now!"

"Holy shit! Talk about no notice, for godsakes!" he screamed into the phone.

I knew what was about to happen next. The captain ran up to the bridge. We observed the helicopter as it proceeded to another tanker to drop off another Navy officer. The bridge door opened, and in walked the officer in camouflage. He stuck out his hand and the captain shook it, looking dumbfounded.

"I'm your U.S. Navy liaison officer. We'll be leaving in two hours when it's dark. I'll be going over your navigation charts to show you what our course and track line will be so you can review them with your deck officers."

"You guys could have given us a little notice," the captain barked. "We've been sitting here for a week without a word from the Navy, and all of a sudden you tell me to be ready in two hours."

"Captain, you had orders to have your ship ready to move at any-time. We do not give advance notice to anyone. We wanted this to be a surprise, especially to the Iranians," he said sternly.

"Okay, okay. What do you want me to do?"

"Tell your engine room to get steam on the engines and be ready to get underway in two hours. Get your deck officers assembled on the bridge, and we'll go over the operation. Please have your crew fed and ready to move the ship."

The captain assembled the deck officers, and the Navy officer went over the track line. He noticed our charts were out of date and that we had the wrong edition. This was the second officer's responsibility as the officer in charge of navigation. We were still able to use the charts with minor adjustments. We penciled in new traffic lanes, and the second mate drew in the convoy course lines, where we would change course, and possible hazards—mine fields, missile placements, etc.

After two hours we heaved anchor and got underway. The convoy was given the operation name "The Little Big Horn." As the lead ship, we were "Reno." The vessel in charge, the destroyer, was "Crazy Horse." The other U.S. Navy ship was "Custer."

The Navy liaison officer on each ship had a super-encrypted radio. Neither the Iranians nor the Iraqis nor any other ships could understand the convoy's radio communications. By the time my watch rolled around, it was dark. Everyone was sleeping except those on watch and the Navy officer. I went up to the bridge and took the con from the mate on watch; the Navy officer observed the watch transfer.

First, I took a position, checked that all the men were in proper position as lookouts and that we were steering the right course, and then drank my coffee. The Navy officer was checking me out—I figured to see if I was nervous, but I thought it was all pretty exciting. After we got through the tight spots in the Strait of Hormuz and steamed for awhile, we broke out into the open waters of the Persian Gulf. A course change was coming up that the Navy officer had talked about, when the super-encrypted handheld radio I was holding went off.

"Reno, this is Crazy Horse. Over."

"Crazy Horse, this is Reno. I hear you loud and clear. Over," I said back, my heart racing with anticipation.

"Reno, this is Crazy Horse. In seven minutes we will be changing course to 335 degrees true and reducing speed to 12 knots. At that time we will be out of the Silkworm envelope. Over."

"Crazy Horse, this is Reno. Roger that. In seven minutes we will change course to 335 and reduce speed to 12 knots. I copy. Reno out."

I turned and looked at the Navy officer, who was smiling at me.

"Holy shit, I didn't even know we were in the Silkworm envelope," I said, laughing.

We changed course on time, and everything went smoothly for the rest of the night. We proceeded to Kuwait at the western end of the Persian Gulf and docked. That meant I was finally going home, ten and a half months after signing on for the first time as an officer in the Merchant Marine. I never met anyone who had done a longer trip as a ship's officer on an oil tanker.

We were to fly home on Kuwaiti Airlines, which served no alcohol. I felt it was a small sacrifice in order to finally go home. Our alcoholic captain made a big stink and came close to refusing to fly on that airline until a bunch of us got unruly; we wanted to go home, alcohol or not.

Like any good alcoholic, the captain improvised by sneaking aboard little airline-sized bottles of vodka and ordering soft drinks to put them in. That way he drank booze illegally in the back of the plane. Good thing for the United States he wasn't caught or we could have had an international incident on our hands.

We had a layover in Shannon, Ireland, where there was no prohibition against alcohol. Everyone got off the plane and headed straight for a bar as we waited for our connection: twenty-five guys drinking in the airport at 7:00 a.m.

Life was good. I had completed my first work tour as a ship's officer. I had earned good evaluations and had a permanent third mate's job with a prominent U.S. tanker company.

Except for one thing: I was sick and getting sicker every year . . . and didn't know it.

CHAPTER SEVENTEEN
SPILLOVER FROM THE EXXON VALDEZ

With a great sense of relief, I arrived home from my first job as third mate. I had been shanghaied into working almost eleven months on a ship traveling repeatedly through a war zone halfway across the world, but I had pocketed almost $70,000 and used the time as "sea-hab." Though I drank excessively at times, I got away from the chaos of constant drug use and had purged my body of cocaine. That didn't last long once I was home.

It wasn't long before Maritime Overseas Corporation flew me to Texas first class to testify in a deposition as a witness in a slip-and-fall case. What the company lawyers failed to tell me was to get a good night's sleep the night before testifying. I was twenty-six, and the temptation to go out and explore Houston was just too much.

I was in awe of my beautiful hotel room with all its amenities, including a full bar and gold bathroom fixtures. I was styling—and thought I was something special. I cracked a beer, and five hours later I was in Rick's, a high class gentlemen's club. Men were dressed in suits and ties, and the strippers were knockouts. The waitresses were dressed in little cocktail outfits with fishnet stockings. I was in my glory and started drinking like there was no tomorrow, completely forgetting why I was in Houston.

I got friendly with Debbie, a pretty, sexy waitress. It wasn't long before we were flirting. She asked what I was doing in Houston, and I told her. I was surprised when she asked where I was staying.

I whispered in her ear, "Do you want to stay with me tonight? I'll wait for you until closing."

"I think I'd like that."

Her answer was unexpected, and I was excited. I continued to drink until closing and took Debbie back to my hotel. I had to get up in a few hours, and we made love most of that time. I finally dozed off. When the alarm went off at 7:00 a.m., I realized I was still half drunk. *Oh, man, this is going to be rough.*

"Debbie, wake up, sweetie. I'm sorry, but I have to get ready," I said quietly.

She got dressed in her sexy little cocktail getup from the night before. I felt I had to be a gentleman and walk her downstairs. I was embarrassed when we hit the lobby. Her high heels clicked noisily on the marble floor, and everyone got an eyeful of the drunken sailor and the cocktail waitress who'd been up all night. We exchanged phone numbers, and I kissed her goodbye.

I scurried back to my room, showered, brushed my teeth, used mouthwash, and put on aftershave. I looked in the mirror and didn't like what I saw. My eyes were red, and I still stank like booze. I got out my suit and ironed the slacks, shirt, and tie. I wanted to look good.

I also wanted to get a good report from the lawyers, because I wanted a second mate's job after I sat for the license. I wanted the company to know I was a team player, and I certainly didn't want any reports of alcohol use.

I took a second shower with strong-scented soap. I could still smell the alcohol on my breath, although I'd already brushed my teeth twice. I brushed my teeth yet again and put on my suit and tie. I felt okay.

At the law firm, I shook hands with several attorneys and went into an office for an interview with the lead lawyer for Maritime Overseas Corporation. He didn't seem to notice that I'd had a rough night. I breathed a little easier. Soon the opposing attorneys showed up. I shook hands with everyone, including the court reporter. The deposition dragged on for several hours; then my lawyer asked for a bathroom break.

He grabbed me by the arm and whispered, "Darryl, I want to talk to you outside." I followed him into a hallway.

He seemed upset. He leaned over and asked quietly, "Darryl, have you been drinking this morning?"

I was taken aback, since the deposition had been underway for some time.

"If you're asking me if I had a drink this morning—no, I haven't. I stayed up later than planned, but I'm fine," I told him truthfully.

"I could smell alcohol coming from you, Darryl. I wanted to know what was going on in case the opposing attorney smelled booze and asked you under oath if you'd been drinking this morning."

"I met a woman last night and stayed up late with her, but I got a few hours sleep."

"Try to stay out of their faces, and don't breathe on anyone."

Nothing ever came of it. After the deposition, I flew back home thinking I had another good story to tell. In truth, what happened was typical irresponsible alcoholic behavior. I always had good intentions, but somehow I always made the wrong decisions at the wrong times. I never failed to fail.

At home I picked up right where I'd left off in Texas. I got extremely drunk in a hometown bar a few nights later. Janine, a woman I'd spent time with in the past, approached me.

She smiled and whispered, "Do you need a ride home?"

"Actually, I do. Want to leave?"

"Let's go find a place to get reacquainted." She grabbed my hand, and we walked out of the bar. "Where are you staying tonight?"

"I'm staying with my mom. We can't go there," I replied drunkenly.

As we drove around that summer night, we began getting frisky. It was late, and I was too drunk to get a hotel room.

"Pull over up here beside the road, Janine. There's a good spot on top of this hill on Lower Cross Road."

She pulled over, and we started ripping each other's clothes off. It was hot outside and even hotter in the car. We got out and went at it on the hill beside the road. It was after 1:00 a.m., and no cars or people were around. I thought I was pretty smart. I got a ride home, got laid, didn't have to pay for a hotel, and not a soul knew about the wild, late-night, outdoor sex.

Janine dropped me off at my mom's house. I stumbled inside and passed out in a spare bedroom. At about 9:00 a.m., my mother knocked on the bedroom door.

"Darryl, are you awake? Ernie Bowen just called. He wants you to call him when you get up."

My mind started racing. Ernie and his wife were old family friends, but he never called out of the blue. I started remembering Janine and the outdoor sex. *Oh, no!* I couldn't remember where we pulled over. Was it next to Ernie's house? Did I have sex on his front lawn? Had he had found something, or—even worse—had he heard or seen us?

I jumped up. This was a conversation I wanted to get behind me. I looked up Ernie's number and dialed.

Ernie asked, "Did you lose something last night?"

"I'm not sure what you're referring to," I said, fidgeting.

"Did you lose a wallet with a lot of money in it?"

I set down the phone and checked my clothes. No wallet.

"I'm missing my wallet. Where did you find it?"

"Why don't you come on down, and I'll talk to you about it."

When I hung up, Mom asked, "What did Ernie want?"

"Apparently my wallet fell out of my pants—maybe when I was driving my motorcycle," I lied, heading for the front door.

I imagined the worst as I sped the three miles to Ernie's house. Who knew what he'd seen . . . or found. When I pulled into his driveway, I saw Ernie's wife and another woman working in the flower gardens. They waved and walked toward the house, laughing to each other. *Oh, no, it's bad. They're obviously talking about me.*

Always the gentleman, Ernie shook my hand. "How have you been, young fella?"

"I'm good, Ernie. Where did you find my wallet?"

"I was driving across the Lower Cross Road, and I noticed something sticking up beside the road. I pulled over and saw it was a wallet. I opened it, and it had almost $50 in it and a card with your name on it."

"Oh," I said innocently. "I was wondering where I'd lost it."

Ernie smiled. "Were you having sex with some woman beside the road?"

I was surprised, but I didn't want to lie.

"As a matter of fact, a woman gave me a ride home from the bar to mom's house last night, and I didn't have anywhere to take her."

"That's what I figured."

"Why would you think that?"

"There was a used condom right next to the wallet," he said, laughing.

I turned three shades of red, took the wallet, thanked him, and left before the women walked back outside. To this day, I don't know if Ernie ever shared that story with my mother, and I never brought it up again.

My next work assignment was to join the S/T Overseas Ohio, one of four San Clemente supertankers owned by Maritime Overseas Corporation. In their day they were large ships—90,000 tons, 897 feet long, and 105 feet wide—known as Panamax vessels, the maximum size that could fit through the locks of the Panama Canal.

I went through the Panama Canal twice in my career. On the San Clementes, there's about a foot of clearance on each side. The ship must be handled delicately to prevent it striking the sides of the locks and opening a gash in the hull. The San Clementes held up to 640,000 barrels of crude oil—a big mess to clean up if one of the tanks ruptured.

Approaching the locks, Panama Canal.

Shore gang and me on deck, transiting the Panama Canal.

I joined the ship in Nederland, Texas. We discharged the load and headed to Chiriquí Grande, Panama, to fill her again.

The company had several large supertankers that hauled Alaskan North Slope crude oil (ANSCO), similar to what the Exxon Valdez carried. They were too big to go through the Panama Canal, so they steamed from Alaska to the west coast of Panama then pumped oil across the Trans-Panamanian Pipeline, built during World War II. Tankers on the east coast of Panama carried the oil to Texas refineries.

We steamed three days from Texas to Panama, around oil rigs in the Gulf of Mexico and through the Yucatan Channel, 135 miles of ocean between Cuba and the east coast of Mexico that connects the Gulf of Mexico and the Caribbean Sea.

One night as I stood my evening watch, I noticed a radar target twenty miles away. It was obviously a large steel vessel, because it was a strong blip on the screen. I picked up my binoculars to see if the running lights would show me what direction it was moving, so I could act early and avoid a collision. To my surprise, there were no lights; I assumed I was still too far away. I then noticed a smaller blip on the radar fifteen miles away and picked up that vessel's running lights.

To my surprise, I still could not see the larger vessel's running lights at fifteen miles. The target was right in my way, and I was confused about what was happening. I picked up the VHF radio.

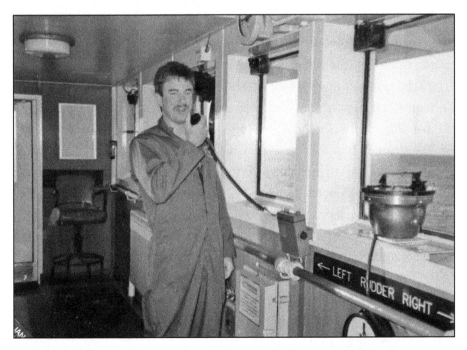

Calling another vessel on the VHF radio.

"Calling the large vessel with no running lights on, this is the south-bound tanker, Overseas Ohio, fifteen miles away from you. Come up on VHF Channel 16, please. Over."

No response.

"Calling the large vessel approaching the smaller vessel in the Yucatan Channel. Captain, this is the supertanker Overseas Ohio. Presently we are on a collision course, and you do not have identifying navigation lights. Come up on Channel 16, please. Over," I repeated.

The unlit vessel finally responded: "Overseas Ohio, Overseas Ohio, this is U.S. Naval Warship. Sir, we are conducting drug interdiction at this time and are preparing to board the small vessel. Please give us a wide berth so we can conduct our mission. Out."

Yikes, no wonder they weren't lit up. They were sneaking up on a vessel to see if it was drug running.

"U.S. Naval Warship, understood. I am altering course to port and will give you a five-mile CPA. Overseas Ohio, out."

I told the helmsman to come left twenty degrees, and we passed the two vessels at a closest point of approach (CPA) of five miles to starboard. I realized then that the Yucatan Channel was an entry point for drug smuggling to the United States from Central and South America. Though I had blown the Navy's cover for safety reasons, in the future I'd just change course and avoid large ships without running lights.

We steamed into the Caribbean, and I soon realized how rough it can get at sea even on a large ship. During the last leg of the trip to Chiriquí Grande, we kept a course at about 192 degrees true, or steady to the SSW. The prevailing swells were from the east, coming at us at almost 90 degrees to our port side, which caused the vessel to roll. That portion of the voyage took about twelve hours, and there wasn't any way to avoid the rolling.

Before long, the easy rolling motion built up to violent jerking. The captain warned the crew to tie everything down. Anything not secured would end up on the floor or could become a missile. I've seen a full-size refrigerator break free and slide across the deck, damaging tables and walls, and with the potential to damage unsuspecting people. Yet there were always people who didn't heed the captain's advice.

I was walking by the captain's office that night and paused to say hello. He was sitting at his typewriter. As he looked up, the ship heaved suddenly. The typewriter flew five feet through the air and smashed into pieces on the deck. As he let fly a string of blue language, I hurriedly left to secure items in the hallways that were banging around keeping people awake.

At night, if your bed was pointed in the wrong direction you'd roll side to side, making it impossible to get a good night's sleep. Sometimes I took my life preserver and propped it up on the outside edge of the mattress to make it sit higher, forcing my body into a tight corner. I wouldn't roll, but after several hours I'd get uncomfortable.

At other times I hauled my mattress onto the deck and arranged it so the rolling motion was from head to toe so I could at least get a little

Rough seas.

sleep. Still, the ship creaked, the wind howled, and sea spray slammed against the portholes. I had more than one nightmare in my career in which the ship broke in half.

In rough seas, mop buckets on wheels rolled around inside lockers. Unsecured doors slammed unexpectedly. People's personal items, even TVs, occasionally were thrown to the deck and ruined. That night I walked into the galley and saw ketchup, relish, syrup, pickles, silverware, cups, and plates all over the deck. It was one big smeared mess of broken glass and food. I took one look and beat feet to my room. I wasn't on watch, and it wasn't my responsibility. The steward department should have secured it better. The roving security watch would find the mess and wake them up to clean it.

I stepped into my stateroom and looked around. A few notebooks and magazines were on the deck, but other than that I had done a pretty good job of being ready for rough seas. Of course, the captain could have ordered the bridge to alter course to ease the rolling, but doing so would have lengthened our trip. So he remained on 192 degrees true, and we all paid the price.

Going to sea isn't as romantic as many landlubbers think. People often asked me, "How was your latest cruise?" I just laughed and replied, "Working on a ship for three months, eighty-four hours a week with no days off? I wouldn't call that a cruise."

I went home on February 9, 1989, for some much needed rest and recreation. But my three months of "recreation" came at the end of a straw and at the bottom of a bottle. I was a classic binge drinker. Once I started, I couldn't shut it down. I never drank just one or two beers, nor did I ever do one or two lines of cocaine. I kept going until the bag of cocaine was empty and only stopped drinking after the bars closed, when I ran out of booze, or when I passed out.

My life and the world of shipping changed drastically while I was on that vacation. Just a few weeks after I got home, Captain Joseph Hazelwood and his third mate Gregory Cousins drove the Exxon Valdez onto Bligh Reef in Prince William Sound, Alaska, causing the worst oil spill in U.S. history. It was later discovered that Captain Hazelwood had a severe drinking problem, had gone through rehab in 1985, had several DWIs, and was allegedly drunk at the time of the accident. Reportedly he drank eight double shot vodkas at a local bar before the ship sailed that night and tested at .24 percent blood alcohol content after the oil spill.

The American public and Alaska fishermen were outraged. Changes in Merchant Marine operations followed immediately. Sailors everywhere were heavily scrutinized regarding their alcohol use. Alcohol was banned by almost every company—especially on oil tankers—and a zero tolerance policy was adopted by Maritime Overseas Corporation and the entire seafaring industry.

We had to sign a form allowing the Coast Guard to periodically check our driving records, and they could look at our criminal records in the process. The shipping companies also kept a folder on each employee. There were three arms of enforcement: the police and courts, the U.S. Coast Guard, and the companies we worked for. The one thing they never did was share information, I suppose because of privacy issues. That gave sailors a chance to hide their screw ups.

Alcoholics are adept at hiding their problem. We justify our right to drink and are usually in denial that a problem exists. This was true in my case. In hindsight, I wish I'd woken up years earlier. But even after the Exxon Valdez, I continued to drink and use drugs. I knew I had a problem of some kind whenever I drank and got in trouble. But I honestly didn't think I had a drinking problem. Denial is a survival technique. By drinking, I masked my pain and was able to live life as normally as possible, though I just covered up one set of problems with another.

I've thought a lot about this thing called denial, and I believe I went through two phases. First, I didn't think I had a problem. I truly believed I drank too much because of my stressful job. Anyone who had to endure months at sea would drink too much when they got their feet back on dry land.

Then after ten years of alcoholism and drug addiction my denial changed. I realized I had a problem, but felt I could handle it. Everyone has problems in life; I thought mine were just bigger than most. I'd try to keep my drinking and drugging under control, work hard, and everything would be okay.

I often tell people, "For ten years I had fun with drugs and alcohol. Then they had fun with me." That statement is true for all alcoholics. In the beginning it was fun; then things changed. Drinking began to affect my health. I progressed into a different person, a different drinker, a different stage of alcoholism.

On April 11, 1989, I flew to Houston to join the O/S New York, a 900-foot supertanker with a seasoned captain, chief mate, and crew. I was still a young Merchant Marine officer and admittedly excitable. Yet I took my job seriously, just as I took my drinking and drugging seriously at home. I did everything to the max, and I worked as hard as anyone on the ship.

Because the Exxon Valdez accident had just occurred, the industry was in a state of hyper-alertness that felt like total insanity. The Coast Guard was inspecting ships. British Petroleum and the other oil majors were sending out safety and pollution alerts. The shipping companies were talking to the captains about safety, clamping down on drinking, and allowing zero tolerance for mistakes. The American public was outraged at the Exxon Valdez accident and the implication that alcohol was involved. Environmentalists were freaking out about the oil spill. And Alaskans were devastated by the ramifications to their beautiful coastline.

Pressure came from above to be extra vigilant, and along with that pressure came anxiety. Plus, drugs and alcohol take a toll on your mind, especially when you're young. As a result, my patience was next to zero, and if anyone tested it, I quickly became angry. There's a correlation between alcoholism and anger, and I had a severe problem with both. I also had little tolerance for anyone who did not do his job the way I saw fit.

The boatswain on the New York was older and experienced. He was an extremely hard worker who always gave 150 percent. In fact, he worked way too hard keeping the New York looking like a 900-foot Cadillac. It always had freshly painted bright "BP green" decks (British Petroleum's logo color) all the wires and valves were greased, all the storerooms neatly organized, and the ship was always ready to go into port to load or discharge oil. He was the best there was.

Sometimes that wasn't enough for the young alcoholic third mate. One night the boatswain was outside standing lookout. With the kind of responsibility he had, he was working too many hours and had fallen asleep on watch. I went out and barked at him, and he denied he'd been sleeping. Sadly, I had no compassion for the men who worked for me, with me, or above me. Alcoholism is an angry disease, and I had a full blown case of it.

A month later we were pulling into port, and I noticed that the scupper plugs were not in place. Scuppers are holes that allow for drainage when water comes onto the decks. In port, the scuppers are plugged with rubber fillers designed to contain accidental spills and prevent oil from getting into the harbor.

The boatswain is in charge of making sure everything is ready to load or discharge cargo, so I asked, "Bosun, are we ready to load cargo?"

"Yes, Mate. All set to start cargo operations."

"Why are the scupper plugs out, then?" I asked.

"I told the men to put them in!" He swore loudly and yelled to two men to go around and put them in.

"Bosun, it's your responsibility to check on these guys. What else isn't done that you haven't checked?!" I screamed.

"You know, Mate, when the men are gone, the ship will still be here," he responded.

I stomped off and thought about what he said. He was telling me not to let the oil business eat me up with worries and anxiety. The big money and high pressure had ruined many a man.

I made my rounds on deck and found everything else in order.

I walked up to one of the able-bodied seamen, Manny, who didn't get along well with the boatswain.

He laughed. "Man, you chewed on that bosun's ass."

"I have to calm down. He can't do everything. I have to be careful how I treat everyone," I said, looking for sympathy.

"You know what, Mate? You were right. The scupper plugs should have been in. That's important. You have a right to raise your voice sometimes," he said. "I know you mean well, but you're going to hurt an awful lot of people in your career."

I was taken aback. Was I that bad? Was I the only one really hard on the crew? As my career progressed I earned a reputation as a hard-nosed mate from Maine. People asked if I was coming to the ship months before I was due aboard—and not because they were looking forward to seeing me. I owe all those men an apology for my excessive worrying and unruly behavior. My intentions were in the right place, but my life was out of control. I was an alcoholic and drug abuser who had no control over my emotions—and I took no prisoners.

On July 14, 1989, I went home to study for my second mate's test. A second mate is the ship's navigator in charge of a vessel's navigation charts, plotting all the course lines, and making sure the electronic equipment on the bridge works properly. I badly wanted to be the ship's navigator. I applied myself to my studies and tried to keep my drinking and drug use to a minimum.

Studying for my second mate's license, 1989.

I did well for six weeks, and then went out partying one night to blow off steam. I took a twenty-five-minute drive on a strip of highway watched closely by the police for drunk driving between Nobleboro and Boothbay Harbor, a summer hot spot for tourists. I drank on the way, though I was still relatively sober. On the drive home I'd have to be careful. There were few times I didn't overindulge when I drank; getting home was always an issue.

I parked my blue Toyota pickup at the local post office and hid my keys under some wood boards in the back, thinking not only wouldn't I lose the keys but maybe I also wouldn't drink and drive. Sometimes when I drank I found a ride home and returned the next day to retrieve my vehicle. I had to plan my drinking so I wouldn't lose my driver's license. The cops were strict in Lincoln County—you didn't get any breaks if they pulled you over.

At Boothbay Harbor I kicked up my heels. I drank a lot of beer and mixed drinks and got out on the dance floor with the summer and local girls and had a great time. I forgot about ships, Coast Guard exams, oil companies, and the stress of going to sea.

I stumbled out of a bar after midnight and walked to my truck, out-of-my-mind drunk. The parking lot was dark, and I muttered to myself as I looked for my keys.

I vaguely remember a Boothbay Harbor police officer approaching me. "Can I help you? What are you looking for?" he said.

"What's it look like I'm looking for?" I said rudely. "I'm looking for the keys to my truck."

"You can't drive. You've been drinking. Is there someone I can call to pick you up?"

"No, it's late and everyone is sleeping. Can you give me a ride to Nobleboro?"

"No, I can't give you a ride. Why don't you get in the back of your truck and sleep for awhile and drive after you sober up? If you drive now, I'll arrest you for operating under the influence."

"Okay. I'll sleep for a few hours. I'll find my keys later."

He walked away. I knew he didn't believe me, and he was right not to. My judgment went out the window when I drank, and that night I had no intention of sleeping in my truck. I found my keys. My genius alcoholic mind told me if I didn't turn on the headlights I could sneak out of town undetected. I soon noticed the cops were following me, so I floored it. I got away from them a little bit.

The next thing I saw was blue lights flashing. I sped up again, but couldn't lose them. I pulled over, knowing I was about to get my second OUI.

The police officer I'd spoken to earlier approached and yelled, "Get out of the vehicle! You're under arrest for operating a motor vehicle while intoxicated!"

"I told you to give me a ride, and you wouldn't, you asshole. You fucking communist pig!" I yelled as he handcuffed me.

He smashed my face into the hood of my truck to shut me up.

"You just assaulted me!" I shouted. "Police brutality! You're a tough guy when someone's handcuffed!"

I was a nasty drunk. When I drank too much, all my bottled up emotions came out. I had never gotten over my father's death. I had begun to hate my job, because it stressed me out. I no longer liked going to sea. I had never met the right woman, because I was always drinking and drugging. I wasn't happy with my life, and yet I did nothing to change it.

The officer called for backup and tried to get me to take a breathalyzer. I told him to forget it; I wasn't blowing into any tube unless my lawyer was present. A sheriff's deputy showed up, put me in his cruiser, and transported me to the Lincoln County jail. I had a breakdown in the back of the cruiser. Tears began to fall for the first time in years.

"That cop just beat the shit out of me," I cried to the deputy.

"You're safe now with me," he assured me.

"I want to file a report of police brutality," I cried again.

"You can do that at the jail."

I was booked, fingerprinted, and held overnight. Once I sobered up, I decided not to press charges against the officer. I had screwed up again and probably deserved what I got. I'd get a lawyer and try to get out of the OUI. I wasn't worried about my driver's license; I could always find rides, take a cab, or walk.

What worried me was taking my second mate's test and whether the Coast Guard would take away my Merchant Marine license. Because the captain on the Exxon Valdez had three DWIs, the Coast Guard was clamping down on all of us. My profession was at stake because of my drinking. Even I could see that my dysfunctional life was spinning out of control.

Many in the Merchant Marine had problems with substance abuse; after the Exxon Valdez we had to learn how to hide it even more. I decided to fight the OUI and try to stall the process until after I sat the second mate's test.

I took the test without too much scrutiny. The Coast Guard knew of my 1985 OUI conviction, but I could truthfully say I didn't have another conviction because the pending charge had not gone to court. I filled out the application truthfully, with one exception. I checked the "No" box for the question: "Have you ever tried any illegal drugs, including marijuana?" I had also checked "No" when I sat for the third mate's test, although at the time I had stayed up for days doing cocaine.

Nobody ever checked "Yes" to that question, not military, federal employees, cops, firemen, lawyers, judges, or Merchant Marine officers. Who would admit to using drugs on an official government application? Not this alcoholic and addict. Admitting drug use meant rehab and a work stoppage. I wouldn't go along with that, because I hadn't reached bottom. I didn't even know what my bottom was. I just knew that after I earned my second mate's license and sailed on it for twelve months of sea time, I wouldn't have to deal with the Coast Guard again until I sat for my chief mate's license.

On August 18, Congress passed the Oil Pollution Act of 1990, which stated, "A company cannot ship oil into the United States until it presents a plan to prevent spills that may occur. It must also have a detailed containment and cleanup plan in case of an oil spill emergency." The effect of the legislation was to severely tighten the industry.

The law was enacted sixteen months after the Exxon Valdez incident. During that time all the alcoholics in the Merchant Marine scurried around getting our houses in order, taking exams and putting paperwork in order. The Alaska oil spill occurred in March 1989. I was arrested for my second OUI that August, and I passed the Second Mate Unlimited Tonnage, Any Oceans license exam in October. I wasn't convicted of my OUI until March 1990. I had dodged yet another bullet.

The Exxon Valdez made me think about being more careful with my drinking. It taught me to try to gain some control, because I didn't want to end up like Captain Hazelwood. But that's not how it works. Alcoholism is cunning, baffling, and powerful. My drinking only got worse, and in the days ahead I had to hide it even more.

CHAPTER EIGHTEEN
NORIEGA, HUSSEIN, AND ANOTHER BUDDING ADDICTION

While I was dealing with my legal difficulties and other issues, including a new diagnosis of high blood pressure from all the cocaine, alcohol abuse, and work stress, the entire country was dealing with much bigger problems brewing to the south.

On November 4, 1989, I flew to Nederland, Texas, to rejoin the Overseas New York. She was still loading Alaskan North Slope crude oil pumped through the Trans-Panamanian pipeline. There were probably a dozen ships like ours shuttling crude oil from Panama to Gulf Coast refineries. It was steady work and for the most part uneventful.

But turmoil was unfolding in Panama. President Reagan had already asked Panamanian dictator General Manuel Noriega to step down; Noriega was suspected of spying for Cuba and supporting illegal drug trafficking to the United States. In addition, the Panama Canal was due to be handed over to the Panamanians, with full control to be returned at the turn of the century. The United States, under President George H.W. Bush, wanted to ensure that the canal stayed under democratic control. It was too important to world commerce and too strategic militarily to risk it falling into the wrong hands.

On December 11, 1989, I was promoted to second mate/ship's navigator. It was a proud moment in my career. I was now in charge of the vessel's bridge operations, including charts and courses, radar, the electronic navigation charts system (ECDIS), emergency satellite communications, satellite navigation, fathometers, VHF radios, Loran-C, Global Positioning Satellite Navigation Systems, and Global Maritime Distress Satellite Systems.

At the time, we were hauling oil for British Petroleum, which had based a port captain in Panama to oversee operations. The U.S. government got word to BP that it intended to invade Panama and to get its people safely out of the country. The port captain and his wife secretly boarded a Maritime Overseas Corporation ship one night and traveled back to the United States.

On December 20, 1989, the U.S. Army, supported by the Air Force and the Navy, invaded Panama to remove Noriega from office. The operation, called "Just Cause," involved more than 57,000 troops; more than three hundred aircraft supported the ground invasion. The American military lost 23 troops, 325 Americans were wounded, and 516 Panamanian forces were killed. Noriega fled, eventually seeking refuge at the Vatican Embassy in Panama City, where he remained holed up until January 3, 1990, when he surrendered to American military forces. He was extradited to the United States, where he was tried, convicted of drug smuggling, and imprisoned. The Panamanians chose a new president, and the country became a democracy.

Sunrise at sea.

The O/S New York received two special guests while in port in Texas. BP Port Captain Mike Callander and his wife boarded our vessel for a ride back to Panama, since it was safe to return. At the time I was oblivious to all that was going on, and I didn't talk to them about the invasion. The evacuation had been kept quiet, and I didn't figure it all out until after the fact. We steamed south with our special guests, who frequented the bridge to watch us navigate the ship and ask questions about what we did and why. It was refreshing having them on board and made for interesting conversations and meals.

In Panama we took on a pilot, an American who told some amazing stories about the invasion. He was there during the initial onslaught, when the streets were filled with gunfire as the U.S. military rolled in and took control of Panama City. He owned a bar used by the Army and the Marines as a command center. They had flipped over all the tables and used them for shields and barricades.

I went home in February of 1990. In May I was asked to report to the Overseas Valdez at Diego Garcia. The Valdez was still chartered to the U.S. government, carrying aviation gas for warplanes and diesel oil for warships. I got orders to fly out of Philadelphia on a charter for military personnel and sailors reporting for duty on the island. The charters took off once every four months.

After a brutal twenty-hour flight, we still had to go through customs, which took more than two hours. When I finally boarded the vessel, it was obvious that the O/S Valdez was again headed to the Persian Gulf— they wanted people with experience on board to help with refueling the military at sea.

We remained anchored for some time, and I quickly fell into my old ways. I stood my anchor watch on the bridge, many times drunk. I went ashore on the launch boat at 4:00 p.m. after working all day, drank beer, and lost track of time and my common sense. It was a nightly ritual for the launch boat to ferry home a load of drunken sailors—singing, fighting, throwing up, being loud and unruly—me among them.

Countless times I climbed up the pilot ladder onto the Valdez to stand the midnight watch, still half drunk. Many times I passed out in the captain's chair, drunk on duty, supposedly watching to ensure the vessel remained safely anchored in the harbor, that a fire and security watch was done, and that everyone on board was safe.

I cared about my job, and I worked hard, but I underestimated my closest enemies: alcoholism and denial. It's pitiful to think back on. I had no control over my disease, nor did I realize I was an alcoholic. And yet my alcoholism had progressed into a more dangerous form. I could no longer pick the times and places I drank; they picked me. I didn't get in trouble every time I drank, but I was drinking *every* time I got in trouble. It got to the point where I stayed on board for fear of what I might do ashore. I look back and see an alcoholic out of control and a supremely irresponsible Merchant Marine officer.

Before long we got orders to head to the Gulf of Oman. As second mate, I planned our route and drew the course lines on the charts, and the captain approved them. He knew I was a good sailor when I was sober; it was when I was in port that he had to watch me. Once we got underway I was a better, more responsible worker.

Ship's navigational officer, second mate.

Yet when you take away the drink from an untreated alcoholic, you still have alcoholic behavior. When I was sober, I was irritable, angry, and discontent—a ticking time bomb. I still had untreated mental wounds from my father's suicide. And I had no clue just how sick I was.

The only way I knew how to deal with my inner demons and mental instability was to work, work, work. I worked harder and longer than anyone on board. I knew I had to make up for my shortcomings, and I did that through performing at a high level for months at a time. I didn't realize I was building up tremendous pressure that boiled over when we hit shore, making me unpredictable and even dangerous.

We steamed for a week to the Persian Gulf and refueled a Navy battle group at sea. It was rewarding, and I felt patriotic being one of the officers in charge of such an important duty. I felt proud to be an American, knowing that ship after ship was fueled and ready to protect American interests, ready to keep Persian Gulf oil flowing to the rest of the world.

While I was still on duty on the O/S Valdez, on August 2, 1990, Saddam Hussein mobilized Iraqi troops and invaded the neighboring oil-rich country of Kuwait. The two countries had long disputed territory. Though Saddam had been warned not to invade, he brazenly sent in hundreds of tanks and raised the Iraqi flag over Kuwait City. President George H.W. Bush quickly formed an international coalition of thirty-four countries and with the United Nations demanded that Iraq withdraw. The U.S.-led coalition began an operation initially called Desert Shield and quickly began building up forces in the Persian Gulf. At the time, many civilian-run merchant ships were used to ferry tanks, ammunition, war supplies, and troops to the region.

President Bush gave Iraq an ultimatum to withdraw by January 15, 1991, or the coalition would remove them by force. Saddam continued to occupy Kuwait, and Operation Desert Storm loomed on the Iraqi horizon. I wondered if I'd be involved. I was due to leave the O/S Valdez in October of 1990.

Of course we all know how the story ends . . . the January 15 deadline came and went. The world held its collective breath as war seemed inevitable. On January 17, U.S. warplanes attacked Baghdad, Kuwait, and military targets in Iraq. Initially more than a thousand sorties were launched each day. After five weeks of bombing, Saddam was given another ultimatum to withdraw. When he refused, Marines, Army, and Arab forces, tanks, and air support poured over the Kuwait/Iraq border in what later became known as the "100-Hour Ground War."

On February 27, President Bush declared a cease-fire. Kuwait had been liberated. Saddam signed a peace agreement and remained in power. U.S. military forces were permanently stationed in Kuwait and in other places in the region. No-fly zones were established over Iraq's northern and southern borders, and U.S. warships and warplanes stayed in the region to keep Saddam from threatening his peaceful neighbors.

My involvement occurred in the months after Saddam's initial invasion of Kuwait. We received orders to take a load of fuel to Djibouti, a French-owned territory outside the southern end of the Red Sea, where U.S. military personnel were stationed. I was warned by shipmates that prostitution was rampant, and I should be careful. I filed that piece of information away in my brain as useful but unnecessary and forgot it.

En route, my buddy Sean and I were lifting weights in the rec room when we heard on shortwave radio that Texas-born rock and blues guitarist Stevie Ray Vaughn had died in a helicopter crash. Never mind that the world's attention was on Kuwait, I was crushed by the news of the death of one of my heroes. I gave the captain the bad news. He was a cool guy and was just as bowled over as I was. It was one of those moments when I'll always remember where I was and what I was doing.

Stevie Ray Vaughn died August 26, 1990, after playing a concert with Eric Clapton and others. Vaughn had struggled with alcoholism and cocaine addiction. In the mid-eighties he had progressed to dissolving cocaine in whiskey. Doctors warned him that his stomach lining was being eaten up. He kicked alcohol and cocaine through rehab and a twelve-step program. But I learned no lessons from Vaughn's example. I admired him and his music, but didn't heed his message that alcohol and drug abuse were dangerous. I continued using with reckless abandon, thinking I was different, that alcohol and drugs wouldn't rule me, that I ruled them.

Sean and I went ashore in Djibouti. The French colony was a lively place with bars and restaurants lining the streets. All kinds of people were milling about, and the city had a seedy atmosphere. Everywhere we went women made a "pssst" noise, trying to get us to stop and talk.

Sean and I were drinking and ready for female companionship. We picked up two women who propositioned us, following them through back alleys and strange pathways to a one-room apartment. Inside, I looked around in disgust. We were in a concrete room with a mattress on the floor, a table with a lamp, and a separate bathroom with a shower and toilet but no door.

I looked at Sean and said, "I'm not doing this with both of us in the bedroom, and I'm not lying down in that bathroom."

"We'll go into the bathroom. You can have the mattress."

We separated. I lay down on the mattress with a stranger, and we started kissing and undressing. I somehow realized how drunk I was and how sick the situation was. The place was dirty, and there was no privacy. I thought, *I gotta get out of here and fast*! I reached for my clothes and yelled to Sean.

"Sean, I'm getting dressed!"

"What are you doing?" he called back.

The woman I was with asked, "You're not leaving already?"

"Yes, I'm leaving. I'm too drunk to have sex."

I yelled to Sean, "Let's go, man. I want to get out of here!"

"Okay. I'm getting dressed!"

My lady said, "You must pay us now. We need money for bringing you here."

"We didn't have sex. I'm not paying you!" I yelled drunkenly.

The other woman left the room; I quickly realized she was going for help.

"Sean, we gotta get out of here!" I grabbed him by the arm. We stepped into the hallway and saw three men and the other prostitute headed toward us.

"Run!" Sean yelled.

We sprinted down an alley and around a corner. The men chased us. We continued to dart around corners and through alleys, until we lost them.

"That was a close one!" Sean said, gasping for air.

"That was a mistake from the get-go," I said, trying to catch my breath.

We scurried back to the ship. I realized we were lucky we didn't get shot or stabbed. In that dark business of money for sex, if you don't pay, you might not live. It was a young, stupid, drunken mistake, and we were fortunate to escape without getting hurt. Most people would learn from their mistake and not dabble in prostitution anymore. But for me, this was just the beginning. The ships and my alcoholism would continue to take me around the globe to many strange places with many strange people.

I stayed on the O/S Valdez, serving my country, for almost five months. We refueled the Navy and carried oil wherever it was needed. But whenever I got off the ship, my alcoholic, sex-starved brain told me: "Go have fun chasing women and drinking. You deserve it."

Perhaps I had more problems than just alcohol and drugs. Sex was also beginning to rule my decision-making; it was becoming another addiction that I tuned out. There were plenty of warning signs, but I ignored them. And when I started drinking, *all* of my addictions consumed me.

GLENN CHADBOURNE

CHAPTER NINETEEN
AN ANGRY, INTOLERANT DRUNK

Though the Middle East was in turmoil in 1991, for me the year was relatively routine. I was transferred to the 894-foot, 125,000-ton Overseas Juneau, sailing as second mate. One thing had dramatically changed since I'd been in the Persian Gulf: The public outcry had continued over the Exxon Valdez oil spill, and Congress had responded. Mariners were thoroughly scrutinized by the Coast Guard, there were brand new oil spill recovery boats throughout the country, and the oil terminals conducted sobriety checks on crewmembers whenever they returned from shore leave.

On the Overseas Juneau, the captain was known to be eccentric, a bit "touched" from forty years at sea. My take was that he was living life just to screw with people. And it didn't matter if it was one of his officers, someone from the Coast Guard, or an oil terminal official, especially one from Alyeska Pipeline Service Company.

One day we came back from shore carrying several boxes of pizza for the crew. At the terminal security station in Valdez, an Alyeska official asked for the captain's ID and asked him to open each pizza box. In return, the captain demanded to see the guard's AIDS-free certificate before he touched our food. I was embarrassed. It took fifteen minutes of back-and-forth before we were allowed to pass through the gates with the pizza.

Alyeska—a subsidiary of the big oil companies, Exxon, British Petroleum, ConocoPhillips, and others—owns and maintains the 900-mile Trans-Alaska Pipeline. They're an excellent operation with highly skilled professionals. Both the production/pumping facility in Prudhoe Bay at the northern end of the pipeline and the Southern Loading

Terminal in Valdez (where 900-foot supertankers are filled with millions of barrels of crude oil) are closely watched and regulated.

Since the Exxon Valdez, Alyeska has been careful of public perception. The company changed its procedures after Captain Hazelwood came back to the ship intoxicated and passed through Alyeska security unhindered, causing the worst oil spill in U.S. history soon afterward. It clamped down on sailors going ashore and searched our bags to make sure no alcohol was brought on board. Alyeska officials often got very close to crewmembers physically; if they smelled alcohol or suspected alcohol use, the sailor was given a breathalyzer.

The new rules angered our crazy captain, and he messed with Alyeska officials every chance he got. Rumor was that he brought aboard empty liquor bottles when the ship was in California or Washington State where there was less scrutiny. In Alaska, he went outside and planted the bottles deep into snow banks near the three Valdez docks. When the snow melted in the spring, bottles were scattered everywhere, making it appear as though sailors on the tankers had consumed alcohol and had thrown the empties overboard.

The captain was known to make up false messages to the officers, supposedly from the company. I received one at the end of one trip stating that "due to a family emergency" the relieving second officer would not be coming. I would therefore be required to stay on the vessel longer, perhaps a significant amount of time, until they could get a replacement.

I didn't fall for the prank, but he did it to several other people who flipped out with rage and anxiety, running to phone booths when we hit the dock in Alaska to demand a relief officer. Of course, the company told the anxious, angry officers it didn't know what they were talking about.

The final clue for me of the captain's state of mind occurred when he sometimes looked out the windows on the bridge and said, "I like to come up here and look out over my kingdom." The guy was losing his mind—and everyone in our fleet knew it. Still, he survived in his job for many years, enjoying every second of notoriety.

I believe he illustrates what is known among merchant mariners as "tankeritis." Too many years on tankers away from normal society eventually makes a sailor half crazy. I also developed a full-blown case of "tankeritis" before I retired; it's something I'll live with for the rest of my life.

Despite the crazy captain's antics, a year passed relatively uneventfully. My second work tour on the Juneau began on March 3, 1992. We passed under the Golden Gate Bridge and pulled into San Francisco Bay. The ship was to discharge a partial load, but our designated berth was occupied, so we dropped anchor and waited. For me it was a brief respite. In those days, a ship at anchor was one of the few times we could get away with going out and throwing down a few beers.

Two engineering officers and me (center) on deck, arriving in San Francisco, California.

On the Overseas Juneau, San Francisco, California.

Everything was going well for me personally at the time, but the ship was in some confusion because there were four openly gay men among the crew. A person's sexuality wasn't usually a problem as long the person kept it private. But the gay men on this crew wanted it known that they were different.

Even that would have been fine if the chief cook hadn't joked about the sausages being shaped like dildos—as he was serving them. I yelled at him that I would complain of sexual harassment if he kept joking about the food.

Being the insensitive person I was at the time, I joked to the captain that if we weren't careful the Juneau would become known as the "fag ship" rather than the flagship of the fleet. In truth, it was disturbing to me at that point in my life. There recently had been other incidents with this crew—what would happen next?

That night the chief mate and I met one of his buddies in San Francisco. There were tons of women around, and we were having a lot of fun. It was unusual partying with the chief mate. He was one of four senior officers and usually stayed on board; typically there was no socializing with junior officers. But as second mate I was one step away from the chief mate position, and sometimes exceptions were made.

After five hours, I started to catch a pretty good buzz. The chief mate had never seen me in action and had no idea how bad an alcoholic I was. We were at "Lou's" on Fisherman's Wharf, when I got into the vodka bottle, always a bad idea for me. Like a good alcoholic, I tried to control it "this time." After all, I was drinking with influential people.

We left Lou's and hailed a cab. Wanting to make the others laugh, I unthinkingly jumped on the front bumper, twisted around in the air, and landed buttocks-first on the hood. I got up laughing—and there was a big dent. The guys had already hopped in the back seat, and I joined them. The cab driver, understandably upset, started cursing at us.

The chief mate looked at me, looked at his buddy, and said: "Run!"

We sprinted down the street, three guys running away from a crime scene, two of them serving on a supertanker anchored in the bay, where we could end up in the brig. After we were well away, I started laughing. The chief mate couldn't believe what I'd done. Yet by the end of the night that whole scene seemed incidental.

We continued to drink. The chief mate finally cautioned me to slow down. I tried, but soon went into a blackout. The next thing I remember was waiting for the launch boat at Pier 9. It was late, and I had to go on watch at 0400. Soon I'd be on the bridge making sure the ship stayed in position without dragging anchor. The main thing I worried about was passing out in the captain's chair.

While we were waiting, the chief cook and the pumpman came back from town. I was in a near blackout, and what I describe next is based on eyewitness accounts and the pumpman's written statements. I don't remember the events clearly.

"Hey, what are you two doing out this late together? Did you get any action?" I laughed drunkenly.

As a gay man, the pumpman knew exactly what I was implying. He came up to me, yelling at the top of his lungs: "What's your problem, Second Mate? You got a problem with us?"

"No, man, I don't. I'm just kidding. Listen, Pumps, I'm sorry, man. I didn't even mean it. I apologize. Now leave me alone."

I walked away, thinking he would leave me alone after that. I'm 6'1" and weighed 200 lbs. The pumpman was twenty, stood about 5'3" and weighed 140 lbs. I looked over my shoulder expecting to see him settling down. Instead, he was raging at the chief cook about harassment.

He ran over, stood an inch away from my face, and said, "You think you're funny—a ship's officer harassing us. You think I'm scared of you?"

I lost control. He had no idea who he was messing with. "I tell you what, Pumps!" I yelled. "This is your last warning to leave me alone! If you get in my face again, you know what I'm going to do with you?!"

"What are you going to do to me?!" he asked defiantly.

"I'll fuck you up the ass, break you in half, and throw you in San Francisco Bay. How do you think you'd like that?"

The pumpman looked at me in fear, turned around, and walked away.

Finally, he's gonna leave me alone. I was due to stand watch, and I didn't need anything more to worry about.

We all got on the launch to the Juneau. I didn't realize how drunk I was until I was stumbling up the accommodation ladder. On board, I hurried to my room, changed into work coveralls, and headed up to the bridge to take over from the third mate. The officer on watch has the responsibility to ensure that the relieving officer is in good condition to stand watch. But after seeing me go ashore and come back with the chief mate, the third mate was not about to make waves by questioning my sobriety. He turned over the watch.

I immediately tried to read the captain's night orders, which are left in a hardcover log giving specific instructions for the vessel and crew pertinent to the itinerary for that day and the next. I was barely able to get the information through my drunken mind. It was 0400, and I knew I had nothing to worry about for at least a few hours, so I looked at the radar. Yep, it was still there. The sailors on duty were on lookout. So I sat in the captain's chair and dozed off. It wasn't the first time a mate on watch had fallen asleep at anchor. At least the ship wasn't underway. I knew several guys who had nodded off at sea.

Every hour the sailors on duty called to tell me everything was all right. Each time, I nodded back off to sleep. I woke up at 0600 and looked around. My heart jumped; I should be calling someone. I ran over to the night orders and re-read them. At 0600, call San Francisco Pilots on VHF Channel 10 to see if we were shifting to berth at 0800.

I went over to the VHF and put it on Channel 14.

"San Francisco Traffic, San Francisco Traffic, this is the Overseas Juneau anchored in Anchorage No. 9, please come in. Over."

"Overseas Juneau, Overseas Juneau, this is San Francisco Traffic, come in, sir."

"San Francisco Traffic; Overseas Juneau. Um, do you know what time this vessel is supposed to shift to the berth?"

There was a short delay, as if San Francisco Traffic was surprised to hear from me.

"Overseas Juneau, this is San Francisco Traffic. Stand by, sir. I'll contact the San Francisco Pilots."

"Roger that, Traffic. Overseas Juneau standing by on Channel 14."

Oh, man. I had called the U.S. Coast Guard Vessel Traffic System instead of the San Francisco Pilots! Vessels only called San Francisco Traffic when they were underway. The Coast Guard was wondering why I had called them instead. They probably thought I was a rookie making an honest mistake, not a drunk messing up.

"Overseas Juneau, San Francisco Traffic. You aren't scheduled to get underway until later this morning. San Francisco Pilots will board you at that time, and you will proceed directly to the berth. Please stay in contact on VHF Channel 10 with San Francisco Pilots for updates. Over."

"Traffic, Overseas Juneau. I copy that. Pilots on board later this morning and proceed directly to the berth. We'll stay in touch on VHF Channel 10 with the pilots. Thank you, Traffic."

"Overseas Juneau, you're welcome, sir. San Francisco Traffic, out."

I was glad that was over. They didn't have a clue. Now to tell the captain and the engine room. I called the captain first.

"It's 0600, sir. I talked to the pilots, and we're not getting underway until later in the morning. I'll call the engine room right now."

"Okay, Darryl, good. I'll be up in a little while for coffee."

I made coffee and then called the engine room.

"Engine room, second assistant engineer. Morning, Darryl. What's up? When are we leaving?"

"Not until later in the morning so the eight to twelve watch can test the gear."

After a few minutes, the captain arrived on the bridge.

"Are we all set?"

"Yes, sir. I'm monitoring VHF Channel 10. The San Francisco Pilots said they would call us two hours before the shift so we could be ready."

"You look like you've had a long night. Why don't you get some rest? Go to bed, and I'll stay up here until the third mate shows up. I'm going home today."

"Thanks a lot, Captain," I said, gladly leaving the bridge.

I thought I'd gotten away with that one. I climbed into my rack, assuming I would get a nice long sleep, knowing they would wake me only when needed. After I nodded off, I was suddenly awakened by pounding on my stateroom door.

It was the chief mate. "Darryl, wake up! You've got to get up right now and talk to the pumpman."

"What's going on?"

"You told him you were going to fuck him up the ass and throw him in Fan Francisco Bay last night. He said he's going to write it all down and hand it in to the captain. Get up, man! Go try to talk him out of it."

"Oh, man. You gotta be kidding me!"

I dressed quickly and went to find the pumpman.

"Pumps, can I talk to you, please?"

"Get away from me, you crazy second mate."

"Please, Pumps, it wasn't intentional what I said last night. That was the booze talking. Can't you give me a break? Please, Pumps. I might lose my job."

"You're a foot taller than me and twice as heavy. Do you know how scary it is having a crazy drunken man telling you he's gonna fuck you up the ass, break you in half, and throw you overboard? I was scared for my life." He was nearly in tears.

"I'm asking you to give me a break, Pumps. It won't happen again."

I didn't know if he would report the incident or not. I knew if he did, I might get fired. But the captain was due to get off when we docked. If I was lucky, he'd leave before the pumpman reported the incident, and the new captain, not being around when it happened, wouldn't know what to do. That way I might just skate by.

The ship proceeded to the dock. Nobody asked about last night's horror show. Maybe this alcoholic had luck on his side after all. We tied up the ship and got ready to discharge the remaining crude oil. The new captain had come aboard, but I was still nervous about what might happen.

I saw the old captain come out on deck with his luggage. *If I can get him off the ship and into a taxi, I just might pull this off.* I walked up and asked if I could help him with his luggage. He said "sure" and thanked me.

Thank God. He would have said something if he'd received a complaint.

I grabbed the luggage and hurriedly carried it down the gangway. The sooner I got him off the ship, the better chance I had of saving my job. I'd been working for Maritime Overseas Corporation, hauling oil for British Petroleum, for years. It was an excellent, high-paying job, and I wanted to keep it.

I got the captain's bag in the van; he thanked me for all my hard work and left.

Thank God that's over.

I went back up on deck and prepared to do some crude oil washing. I started tinkering with one of the machines to ensure it was ready to go when we opened the valve to wash the cargo tanks. My back was to the house, and I was bent over. I didn't realize until he spoke that the new captain was standing over me.

"Darryl, what's this about you telling the pumpman last night you were gonna fuck him up the ass?"

My heart about jumped through my throat. I looked up and lied, "I don't know what you're talking about, Captain."

"The pumpman just came to me with a letter he wants me to send to headquarters saying you harassed him last night. He's dead serious, Darryl."

"I still don't know what you're talking about, Captain. I said a few things that were inappropriate. I was just joking, and then he exploded. I told him I was sorry, and he became even more upset. Things got out of hand, but I never told him I was gonna fuck him up the ass."

The captain shook his head in disgust. "I'm going to have to send this letter with an official complaint. It's my responsibility to keep the office informed."

He paused. "He also said you said his hair was nappy."

"I don't even know what 'nappy' means. This guy is trying to get me fired," I said truthfully. I figured the pumpman was so upset that he was sensationalizing the story to get me axed.

"I still have to send in this letter. We'll see what the company says," the captain said, walking off.

I couldn't believe all this was happening. My out-of-control drinking had brought me into chaos once again. Would I never learn? I still had two months left in the work tour, so I determined to lay low and study for the chief mate's exam I would take during vacation. There was nothing I could do about the situation with the pumpman, so I would look forward, keep my nose clean, stay on board when the ship was in port, and in my off time prepare for the upcoming tests.

I didn't hear anything more about the incident with the pumpman for the rest of that work tour, though I worried about it every day.

I stayed on the Juneau until June 10, 1992, when I signed off in Ferndale, Washington. After two months of working hard without a word from headquarters, I figured I had dodged another bullet. No, not a bullet, a nuclear-tipped missile.

GLENN CHADBOURNE

CHAPTER TWENTY
MILE HIGH CLUB

I hadn't touched alcohol for two months, and boy was I thirsty. I stressed out over my mistake with the pumpman every day for weeks, and that meant I deserved a drink. I got off the ship and made my way to the Seattle airport. There was nothing like having made $35,000 dollars in three months with three months to do as I pleased. I had to study for my chief mate's test, but first I needed to put out a fiery thirst.

At Sea-Tac I checked my luggage. I had four hours to kill and immediately headed to the nearest airport bar. There were a few people inside, including a sexy woman wearing a tube top and no bra, reading a book. I ordered a 22-ounce Budweiser and slugged it down in about five minutes. Boy, I needed that. I could feel the tension leaving my body.

I looked over my shoulder, and the sexy woman was looking up. "Can I buy you a drink?" I asked.

"Not right now, thanks. I'm trying to finish this book. Maybe in awhile."

The wheels started to turn in my brain. "Okay, let me know, and I'll set you right up."

I continued to drink beer and chat with other people, when I was happily interrupted.

"I'm ready for that drink, if you're still offering," the sexy woman told me. "I'm Laurie. How are you?"

"I'm Darryl. I'm doing a lot better now I'm having a drink with a pretty lady and I'm off the 900-foot oil tanker I've been on for three months." As I ordered her a drink, my self-serving mind was thinking if she felt sorry for me for working so hard I might get lucky later.

U.S. Coast Guard Discharge, June 10, 2002
Ferndale, Washington.

"Wow! What do you do on the ships?"

"I'm the second officer. Ship's navigator. We carry almost a million barrels of oil, and we're not allowed to drink on board. These beers are tasting real good."

We were both waiting for the flight to Chicago O'Hare, where I was connecting to Portland, she to New York. I bought her several drinks and had half a dozen more tall Budweisers. I wasn't overly concerned about drinking; the airlines wanted our business. As long as I behaved, they didn't say much.

When it came time to head to the gate, I said, "Maybe we can sit together."

"Sure, I'll sit next to you. You're a fun guy."

I asked the agent at the gate if the flight was full.

"No, sir. This plane is about half full. You can stretch out and sleep if you want."

I wasn't thinking about sleeping. I was thinking about Laurie's tube top and hoping this would be the flight where I'd join the "Mile High Club."

I led Laurie to the back of the plane, where we continued to flirt, touching each other's hands and legs. I was getting pretty excited. When the flight attendant came around, we ordered wine.

"Are you cold, Laurie?" I noticed she had her arms wrapped around herself.

"A little."

We wrapped ourselves in a blanket, and the flight attendant brought the wine. I started massaging Laurie's legs. The lights were out, and most people were sleeping. I leaned over and kissed her on the lips, and she responded. I reached my arms over and under the blanket and rubbed her body softly. She let out a drunken moan. I could tell she wanted more.

"Let's go in the bathroom, Laurie. I want you." I whispered, nibbling on her neck.

"I'd like to, but I don't think it's a good idea," she whispered.

Nobody was paying attention to us. I put up the arm rest that separated us, picked her up, and sat her in my lap facing me. I pulled the blanket up over her shoulders and pulled down her tube top.

"Let's go in the bathroom, Laurie. It's more private," I begged.

"I can't, Darryl. I just met you."

We must have been giggling and whispering too loudly, because the flight attendant approached. I quickly covered us up.

"You two are way out of control back here. Not only that, but there are children on this flight. You have to go back to your own seats."

"Sorry about that," I said contritely. "We're just excited to see each other, ma'am. It won't happen again."

The flight attendant walked away, and Laurie pulled her tube top back up. She got off my lap and sat down next to me.

"I told you we should have gone into the bathroom," I laughed.

We fell asleep holding hands and didn't wake up until we landed at O'Hare. We got off the plane, still a little drunk and tired. Since we had a few hours to kill, we found a bench and lay down. I held her in my arms, and we quickly fell asleep. I was awakened by the sound of jet engines, and as my eyes opened, an old man nearby met my gaze. I'll never forget the look he gave me. Maybe it was obvious that we were drunk and Laurie was scantily dressed; he glared at me in pure disgust.

I shook Laurie awake and told her it was almost time for her to leave. Then she told me about her boyfriend and said to e-mail, not to call, because he'd wig out. I told her I'd write soon, gave her a hug, and off she went. I never saw her again. The incident was just another in a long line of events that illustrate just how out of control I really was.

I arrived home and studied for the test that would earn me a Chief Mate's Unlimited Tonnage, Any Oceans License, allowing me to sail as the chief officer of any vessel of any size anywhere in the world. The only level above that is a master's license.

The chief mate is a busy man with many responsibilities. He's the number two man on board, something like Mr. Spock of *Star Trek*. People always laugh at that comparison, but they seem to understand the position better after I put it that way.

The chief mate is responsible for the vessel's cargo. Since cargo is the only reason for merchant ships to exist, the job is the most important on any vessel. On 900-foot supertankers, the chief mate is responsible for millions of barrels of oil as it's loaded and offloaded, or "discharged," and for the officers below him, to ensure all are capable, sober, and trained to handle cargo operations in his absence.

The chief mate oversees vessel maintenance and hands out specific jobs to the junior deck officers, the pumpman, the boatswain, and the deck crew, ensuring the vessel operates safely and efficiently. Machines need to be greased, the vessel chipped and painted, and safety equipment inspected. Cargo systems, inert gas systems, the crude oil wash system, pipelines, valves, and pumps need to be tested, documented in good working order, and repaired or replaced when defects are found. The chief mate is responsible for the ship's stability and usually is both the ship's safety officer and its security officer.

The chief mate's exam is challenging. The Coast Guard tests candidates on all the chief mate's responsibilities to ensure individuals are highly trained and competent. I planned to sit the four days of tests in August. Until then I tried to keep the drinking and cocaine use under control. I would drink some beer and smoke some pot after studying, but maintained pretty well.

Rolling a joint and drinking a beer on vacation.

I stayed home most nights and concentrated on studying, because any time I went out I drank, and my drinking usually culminated in late nights, hard drugs, and wild women. I partied so hard it took days for my body to detox and my mind to clear. But I was still young enough that hangovers only lasted a day. That changed as I got older, when hangovers sometimes lasted three days and I had to drink the morning after for fear my system would shut down.

The exam section that concerned me most was navigation chart work, a four-hour sit-down that required a 90 percent to pass. The Coast Guard had been testing Merchant Marine officers for generations, and they included common wrong answers among the multiple choice questions. If I missed just three questions, I'd earn an 88 per-cent—that meant retaking the test a month later. The rules of the road section also required a 90 percent grade. The rest of the test required 70 percent.

Each time before, I had to retake one section of the licensing tests. We were given three tries to pass each level. After three failures, an officer couldn't sit the test again for a year.

At the Coast Guard station in Boston I passed in my license application. I was fingerprinted and photographed. I indicated that I'd never used drugs, but I admitted the OUI arrest in March 1990. No OUI offenses were allowed within a year of sitting a test, but more than two years had passed and my lawyer said I should be fine. Just the same, I was nervous because of the drinking history of the captain of the Exxon Valdez. He had three DWIs on his record before the oil spill, and the American public was still outraged over the incident.

I waited nervously until my name was called. I stepped up to the counter and was told, "Mr. Hagar, a senior Coast Guard officer wants to talk to you in the back."

The senior officer explained how worried the Coast Guard was about its civilian merchant officers drinking too much and that any further offenses might jeopardize my career. I think they wanted to look me in the eyes to make sure I was fit to serve.

"I realize I made some mistakes," I said. "I've been working on my personal life, and I can assure you I will not repeat past mistakes. I don't drink on duty, and I won't drink and drive again. You have my word on it."

"The Coast Guard is cracking down on people with substance abuse problems. You'd better be very careful, Mr. Hagar. There's very little room for error. You could lose your privilege working as a ship's officer. I'm going to approve your application today, but I urge you not to repeat any drinking violations."

"I'll be vigilant. And careful. Thank you very much." I shook the officer's hand and left the station.

I could convince anyone, even myself, that I didn't have a problem. And at the time I meant everything I said. I intended to do my best to keep my drinking and drugging under control. I wouldn't drink and drive at all costs. Even if it cost me $100 for cab fare, I promised myself I'd pay it.

I returned to Boston in August and passed all my chief mate's tests, except the chart work.

GLENN CHADBOURNE

CHAPTER TWENTY-ONE
AN OUTRAGEOUS, AUDACIOUS HIGH

The telephone rang. It was my cousin Joe from Waltham, a suburb of Boston.

"Cousin Darryl, Cousin Joey!" He asked how I'd made out on the chief mate's tests.

I explained I'd be in Boston in September to retake one section. He said, "Why don't you come down the day before and stay with me? I'll get you up early and run you to the Coast Guard station, and we'll go out afterward and celebrate."

It sounded good. I wouldn't have to worry about a hotel and parking. In preparation, I stayed relatively clean and sober and studied the whole month. I arrived at my cousin's apartment the day before the test, and we spent some time getting caught up. It was just as I'd expected: a quiet old building perfect for studying. I'd cram that night and get up early to review.

Joey wasn't a partier like me and didn't have the drinking and drug problem I had. As long as I didn't start, I figured I was all set. But I didn't have a problem with drinking too much; I had a problem with drinking at all. Once I started, my thinking changed and my decision-making turned reckless. Common sense went out the window.

I started drinking beer that afternoon, thinking I had studied plenty. I would enjoy my cousin's company, relax with a couple of beers, look over my stuff one last time, and get a good night's rest.

After Joey and I had several beers, I jokingly said, "Man, a couple of nice fat lines of cocaine would be good right now."

"What about your test tomorrow? You don't want to be up all night."

"I don't mean all night, just a couple of hours. Can you score anything around here?"

He laughed. "Yeah. There's a coke dealer next door. Some young guy from Haiti. But I don't want you to mess up your test because of me. Why don't we wait until after?"

"C'mon, man, let me worry about my test!" I figured it was early afternoon, we could party, drink beer to take the edge off, and still get plenty of rest. It was typical dysfunctional, alcoholic, drug-addicted thinking.

"It's $200 for an eight ball, but it will knock your socks off," he warned.

I dug out some money, my mouth already watering. Joey came back holding a big rock of cocaine. We cut it up and started snorting lines.

At age twenty-nine, I could still do an eight ball or two with friends and go out to bars and socialize. In my late thirties I graduated to crack, which quickened my descent. In my forties, my body reached a cocaine and alcohol saturation point. After a couple of lines I turned into a paranoid nut, constantly peering out the window. But in 1992, I was fearless. I had no worries and plenty of money. And I never thought deeply about any of my actions.

We snorted the entire eight ball before 9:00 p.m. We still had time to get more without being up all night.

"Let's get some more, man."

"No way, Darryl. Relax and take it easy."

"C'mon, man. You don't have to snort any. I'll pass my test. We could do another eight ball and be in bed by midnight. I'll still get five or six hours of sleep."

"All right, but promise me you won't stay up all night."

"I promise. I'll be in bed by midnight. Don't worry about me, Cousin Joey. I'm a big boy," I said, my alcoholic arrogance fully unleashed.

Not once did I think about what I was actually doing: using cocaine the night before I entered a U.S. government building and brazenly taking an official Coast Guard examination under the influence of narcotics. I never considered the ramifications. Now I understand that an addict doesn't recognize the severity of his illness. Nor can an addict say no. It doesn't matter what the situation is. Your wife could be having a baby in the hospital. You could be taking an official government test in a government building. Alcoholism and drug addiction don't discriminate. The disease is ruthless.

My cousin scored another eight ball—3½ grams of cocaine. We immediately started snorting big fat lines.

"Man, you'd better be careful. You're gonna have a hard time sleeping," Joey warned me.

My arrogance was in full gear. "This is what they call steam-boating, man. I'll build up a good head of steam, and I'll steam right through that test."

But I was no longer steering the ship; it was steering me. I was a sick individual losing touch with reality. The downfall had started.

The hours slid by. At 1:00 a.m., Joey went to bed, guilt-ridden and no longer enjoying the ride. He encouraged me to go to bed and save the rest of the cocaine for the next day.

I stayed up. I was fearless and cocky. I was good at everything I did, including hiding my drug problem. I knew they didn't drug test before Coast Guard exams. Who would be crazy enough to go into the Coast Guard Station all messed up?

The cocaine was gone before morning. I lay down and tried to shut down my racing mind. I prayed God would forgive me and help me through the day, but I was making empty promises when I told God I'd stop using. I tossed and turned the rest of the night and finally gave up. The sun was coming up when I woke Joey.

"Hey, you gonna sleep all day, man?"

"What time is it?"

"I don't know; 6:30 or so."

"Did you get any sleep at all?"

"Not really, man. I just tossed and turned. I'll be all right."

"Did you finish it all?"

"It's gone, man. Seven grams of cocaine. Not what I had in mind, but I'll survive."

"I kept telling you to stop and go to bed, but you wouldn't listen."

"You didn't hold me down and put it up my nose," I reassured him. "Let's get going. I don't want to walk in late and raise any red flags."

We jumped on the Mass Pike and drove into Boston, never mind that neither of us was in any shape to drive. In hindsight, I suppose I could have called in sick. The Coast Guard would have excused me until the following month. But Maritime Overseas Corporation expected me to have a chief mate's license after that day, and by God I'd give it my best shot, messed up and all. The company hadn't read me the riot act after the incident with the pumpman, and I wouldn't let them down again.

At the Coast Guard Station, I could tell Joey was feeling guilty. "You gonna be alright, Cousin Darryl?"

"I'm tough, man."

I took a few deep breaths and walked in. I figured I'd keep contact with people to a minimum. I signed in without talking to anyone. A Coast Guard official called us into the exam room, and officers filed by him one by one. As I walked by, I took a deep breath and held it, wondering if anyone could smell the booze inside my body.

The morning test flew by. I was still under the influence of cocaine, wide awake and aware of everything around me. I finished with no one suspecting what I'd done the night before. After looking my test over again, I took it up to the Coast Guard examiner. He graded it and handed me the results.

"You passed. Just barely. I'll see you at 1:00 for the navigation chart work."

That was a trip. One down, one to go.

I went outside and sat on a park bench. I began to sweat and shake. I needed a few more lines to get through the afternoon, but there were none. I'd have to suck it up. I started to worry. What if I fell asleep? Maybe somebody would figure out what I'd been up to.

I walked back to the station and went into the bathroom. I sat down on the toilet and put my face in the palms of my hands. I started to have the dry heaves. I had nothing in my stomach except a little water and last night's beer. Finally I felt a little better. I washed my face and wiped myself down with wet paper towels. I looked in the mirror and decided I could pass muster. Good thing I was the only one who knew how bad off I was.

I sat down and got out my navigation tools: a mechanical pencil, calculator, leaded compass, and steel dividers to measure distances. The twenty-five question multiple choice test on navigating Block Island in New York would be a challenge. The Coast Guard had constructed the test as if we were on a ship approaching from sea.

Navigation is critical to ensure candidates are qualified, that they know where the ship is going at all times to avoid grounding, environmental pollution, loss of life, and protection of property—namely the $50 million ship I'd be driving around. Knowledge of rules of the road is also important so that the watch officer can safely pass other vessels without collisions. It all comes down to protecting human life, the safety of the vessel and crew, and protecting the environment. That's why a 90 percent is required to pass those sections.

The thing that was missing that day for me was 90 percent sobriety. I was smacked out of my mind and about to take the most difficult merchant officer's navigation test in the world.

The Coast Guard officer came around and handed each candidate a chart. I was pretty good at navigation. I forgot about my problems and went to work. I had studied hard, and I badly wanted my chief mate's license. I soon noticed my hands were shaking badly. That's what happens when you snort seven grams of coke the night before. But I'd gone through a lot tougher things—I'd get through this.

After working on the test for three hours, I was exhausted. I checked and rechecked the test. I knew Block Island like the back of my hand, and I felt confident my answers were right. I gathered my tools, rolled up the chart, and took the test up to the instructor.

He scanned through it, paused as if to speak to me, stopped, and checked it again.

I asked anxiously, "How did I do?"

"You got a hundred, Mr. Hagar. I don't see many of these. Congratulations."

I pumped my fist. "All right! I'm psyched!"

My company would be proud of me. I had passed an important milestone and redeemed myself. I'd be back in the good graces of Maritime Overseas Corporation.

I forgot all about my hangover. It was time to party. I had earned my chief mate's license. I could now become a first officer, one step below captain, on any vessel of any size in any body of water on the planet. Not bad for an alcoholic and drug addict.

U.S. Coast Guard Chief Mate's License.

My cousin was waiting for me in his car, looking like a dog with its tail between its legs. He still felt guilty and expected me to be crying about failing or angry at him.

I tried to keep my face expressionless.

"How'd you do?"

I broke into a smile. "I aced it! I threw up between tests and still got a hundred! Can you believe it? Take me to the beer store, Cousin Joey. I gotta calm my nerves."

"Okay. But let's not repeat last night's performance."

"Don't worry. I'm gonna drink a six-pack and sleep, man. I'm drained."

GLENN CHADBOURNE

CHAPTER TWENTY-TWO
SURVIVING THE PRINCE OF DARKNESS

A couple of days after the chief mate's license exam, the telephone rang. I looked at the caller ID.

Oh, man, it's Maritime Overseas Corporation. Maybe they'll just ask me if I passed my test.

"Darryl, this is Noel Capellini. How are you?"

"I'm fine, thanks. I passed my chief mate's test; I'm good to go back to sea."

"That's why I'm calling. Bob Johnston, the vice president of marine operations, would like to talk to you in person. He wants you to fly to New York headquarters as soon as possible."

"Um, okay. What's this all about?"

"I can't get into that. Just book a flight and let me know when you'll be here."

Oh, man! I'm gonna get reamed out.

Imagine a country boy from Maine flying to New York to meet one of the most powerful oil men on the planet. Maritime Overseas Corporation was operating sixteen vessels at the time, and its parent company, Overseas Shipholding Group, operated and owned hundreds of ships around the world. Johnston was a major player with the power to affect petroleum prices around the globe. We hauled a good part of our oil for British Petroleum, a company that didn't like controversy. I was more than just anxious. I didn't expect Johnston to congratulate me on passing my chief mate's test and tell me how bright my future looked with Maritime Oversea Corporation.

The company always paid for my flights to and from the vessels, but no one had offered to pay for this one. *Should I ask if they're going to pay for my flight? Hell, no, I'd better suck it up. Maybe if I still have a job after the meeting, they'll offer to reimburse me.* I didn't have the nerve to call and ask. I'd pay for the trip and try to save my job.

When the day rolled around, I was a mess. I got out of bed feeling like a train had run over me. I was not a pretty sight. In the shower I strategized about what I could do to positively influence the day. I pulled out my best suit, shined my dress shoes, put on a new white shirt and tie, and headed to the airport. I boarded the plane and sat nervously in my seat, thinking and rethinking what I'd say to Bob Johnston.

I chatted with the gentleman in the seat next to me. He asked, "What's going on in New York?"

Oh, nothing much, just defending my $80,000-a-year job. Telling the vice president of a major oil company that I never told the pumpman the nasty things I'm pretty sure I did say.

"I'm a Merchant Marine officer on oil tankers, and I'm going to headquarters for a business meeting," I said.

I closed my eyes. I didn't feel like making small talk. What I felt like was throwing up. My nerves were shot, my emotions were all over the place, and I was sweating bullets. What I wanted was a good stiff drink. But the last thing I needed was to have the bigwigs in New York smell alcohol on my breath. I was drunk when I got myself into this mess; I'd get myself out of it sober.

I dozed off and had bad dreams about ships. Nightmares weren't unusual for me; my mind worked overtime, even in sleep. As the plane landed, I rethought what I'd say. I would tell Johnston I'd had a serious lapse in judgment, that I'd been drinking, but that I never threatened the pumpman. I decided to deny the part of the story I was sure would give the company grounds to fire me. I had to do what I had to do.

I hailed a cab and started to sweat profusely. *It's a good thing I'm only twenty-nine, otherwise I'd probably have a stress-induced heart attack.*

We pulled up to the Grace Building at 43 W. 42nd Street, a typical New York City skyscraper, headquarters for both Maritime Overseas

Corporation and Overseas Shipholding Group. I took a few deep breaths, walked in, and took the elevator. I introduced myself to the receptionist. A few minutes later Noel Capellini, the marine personnel manager, came out and greeted me.

I said nervously, "Noel, can I ask you a question, please?"

"I don't know if I'll have the answer, but go ahead."

"Am I going to have a job at the end of the day?"

"I'm not sure, Darryl. We'll have to see how your meeting with Mr. Johnston goes."

Capellini asked me to wait, and I sat nervously for another ten minutes. I was sweating and my face was beet red. *I wish they'd hurry up and get this over with. Hell, if they fire me they fire me. I was looking for a job when I got this one.*

Another fifteen minutes passed. I thought they were messing with my mind. Here I was in suit and tie all nerved up with no place to go. Were they stalling intentionally to make me break down? I was getting extremely impatient by the time Senior Port Captain John Ripperger came out to speak with me.

"Hi, Darryl. We'll be a few more minutes," he apologized. "We've had an incident with one of the ships."

"Okay, Captain."

Again I wondered if they were dragging out the process to penalize me. Later, I found out the S/T Overseas Ohio had struck an iceberg that morning, creating a huge hole in the bulbous bow—more than $1 million in damage.

Noel finally came out and said they were ready for me. *THEY! I thought I was meeting with one person.*

Surely meeting with Bob Johnston was enough. I'd flown to New York alone in good faith, figuring if I took my lumps and didn't bring some bellicose lawyer, I could save my job. Noel led me to a door and wished me good luck. To my surprise, there were three men waiting for me. *Three against one. Maybe I should have brought my lawyer.*

Behind a big desk sat Bob Johnston, a respected leader in the oil shipping industry. Next to him was John Ripperger, known around the fleet as "the prince of darkness." As Johnston's hatchet man, when someone needed to be reprimanded, demoted, or fired, Ripperger was the man to do it. Yet he was a competent, fair man whose position was necessary for maintaining peaceful, mutiny-free vessels. He was aware of the nickname; I'd heard him laughing about it at a conference.

The third man was Port Captain Dave Balduc, who had a long, illustrious career as a sea captain and port captain. A port captain is typically in charge of four ships and answers to a senior port captain. They, in turn, answer to the vice president of marine operations—the position held by Bob Johnston.

I shook their hands and sat facing them. It looked like I was going on trial.

Johnston immediately said, "Darryl, the reason you're here is we'd like to hear what happened on the S/T Overseas Juneau. Apparently you had a confrontation with the pumpman and the chief cook. What happened?"

"I acted inappropriately that night," I answered. "I said something to the pumpman and the chief cook, but I was kidding. I apologized immediately, but the pumpman flipped out."

Johnston asked, "Darryl, did you tell the pumpman you were going to fuck him up the ass, break him in half, and throw him in San Francisco Bay?"

"No. We got in a heated argument, and I told the pumpman I was sorry, but he kept confronting me as I walked away."

"Were you drinking that night?" Johnston wanted to know.

"I was drinking a few beers that night. I'm not gonna lie to you. The whole thing was a mistake that spun out of control. I have nothing against the gay guys on board. There were four guys fucking around with each other on the Juneau, and the whole ship was upside down because of it. The chief cook was telling the crew that the sausages he was about to serve looked like dildos. Who knows what was happening to our food? The pumpman was putting some kind of wig extensions in his hair in the pump room. I've never been on a ship so crazy."

Balduc interrupted. "Darryl, if you have a drinking problem, we can send you to get professional help. Would you like to do that?"

"I don't have a drinking problem, and I don't need professional help," I said. "The whole thing was just a misunderstanding that spun out of control."

Johnston asked again, "Did you tell the pumpman you were going to fuck him up the ass?"

"No, sir. I never said that. There was some inappropriate language, but not that. I told you that once already, sir."

"In your defense, we've learned that the pumpman and the chief cook had been to a gay pride event that day, and we believe they may have been a little trigger-happy, that they overreacted," Johnston said.

That was the first time I'd heard that piece of information. Johnston asked me to wait outside while they made their decision.

"I'd just like to say that I apologize for this whole event," I said. "I've worked hard. I've given Maritime Overseas 125 percent each and every day. Everybody makes mistakes, and I made a bad one that night. I promise all three of you it won't happen again."

Ten minutes passed before they beckoned me back inside.

"What do you think, Captain Ripperger?" Johnston asked.

"I think he's still salvageable," Ripperger said with a slight smile.

The other men were also smiling. *Thank God.* I still had a job.

Balduc said, "Darryl, remember, if you ever need help with an alcohol problem, we won't hold it against you, and we'll make sure you get the help you need."

"I appreciate that, Captain Balduc. I'll keep that in mind. I promise you this will not happen again."

"Keep your nose clean and work hard. We won't hold you back. We know you just passed your chief mate's test, and we have plans for you. But don't repeat this type of behavior," Johnston warned me.

I thanked them and scurried out of the office. Noel Capellini met me in the hallway.

"How did it go in there?"

"Pretty stressful, Noel. But I still have a job. When am I leaving?"

"Go home and relax. I'll call you."

"Seems like they wanted to see me squirm, to teach me a lesson. Why didn't you tell me what I was up against?"

"Bob Johnston told me to get you down here and to not inform you of anything. Say, do you want to go out to lunch?"

"I don't have time, Noel. I've got a flight to catch," I lied.

I actually had plenty of time, but I wanted to go to a bar to celebrate still having a job. I couldn't drink in front of anyone from Maritime Overseas Corporation at lunch, and my nerves needed calming far more than I needed to schmooze the marine personnel manager.

I thought about asking for my travel reimbursement, but was afraid I'd look unappreciative. At least I learned one lesson: No drinking while on board ship. Zero. Nada. None. I had every intention of sticking to that decision.

Yet at home I did nothing to change my behavior; I drank all the time. One time I drove my IROC Z28 convertible to Old Orchard Beach and met a younger guy at a bar called SoHo's. I thought he was pretty cool, so we drove around looking for chicks. We scored some cocaine and went to my house.

The guy was from Peak's Island and to get home he'd have to catch a ferry. We were both messed up from drinking and drugging, so I told my new friend he could crash on my couch.

Far too early in the morning, I woke to pounding on my bedroom door. Then I heard someone scream, "Where's my money?! You ripped me off!"

Who the hell is that? I thought, confused.

"I know you have my money! Open the door before I break it down!"

The kid was clearly losing his mind. I unlocked the door and said loudly, "What the fuck, man? I don't have your money!"

"I looked all over your house. You took my money! I don't remember putting it anywhere!" He was close to tears and shaking violently.

"I didn't take your money! You probably hid it yourself, for godsakes! Let's go downstairs and look around," I said, trying to calm him down.

He bitched the whole time we looked. I searched the kitchen, the dining room, and where he slept. I finally lifted the toilet tank cover in the downstairs bathroom.

"Come here and see this, you bonehead!" I yelled.

He looked down at the roll of bills tucked between the float and lever.

"Take your money and get the fuck out of my house—and don't ever come back! I don't need that kind of stress from clowns like you!" I yelled in his face.

He grabbed his money and walked out the back door. I never saw him again, nor did I want to. That incident was typical of my insane life. Even if I wasn't the one being crazy, crazy people found me.

GLENN CHADBOURNE

CHAPTER TWENTY-THREE
12-GAUGE REVENGE

I flew to Los Angeles in September, returning to the Overseas Juneau as second mate. I felt lucky to still be in the company's good graces and was determined to clamp down and keep my nose clean. Better yet, I would start learning the chief mate's job and try to impress the captain with the new me. I would try to get a promotion. I had never failed at anything in my life, and I wouldn't fail now.

We hauled load after load—800,000 barrels at a time from Alaska to the West Coast and Hawaii. When we were at anchor in Alaska, we often fished and caught big halibut that the ship's cooks prepared deliciously in various ways.

I was careful and kept my nose clean for the rest of the trip. On January 15, 1993, I got off the ship in Long Beach, California, and flew home, having received a good evaluation from the captain. Things were looking up.

I went home to the house where I lived alone and started celebrating my accomplishments—with drugs and alcohol. It wasn't long before I was back to drinking daily and partying in the Old Port in downtown Portland with its cobblestones streets, gift and clothing stores, and numerous restaurants. This famous section of the city has more bars per square acre than anywhere else in Maine. I partied hard there for years. I've passed out in an alley and on a street bench, pissed and thrown up on the sidewalks, been bloodied—you name it, I did it in the Old Port.

It was in the Old Port Tavern, a historic basement bar, on one cold February night when I met her. A young guy from my hometown walked up to me and said hello, and after talking for a minute he introduced me to his friends. One of them was an eye-catching brunette named Jennifer. She was stunningly beautiful, sexy, and had the cutest way about her. I was immediately smitten.

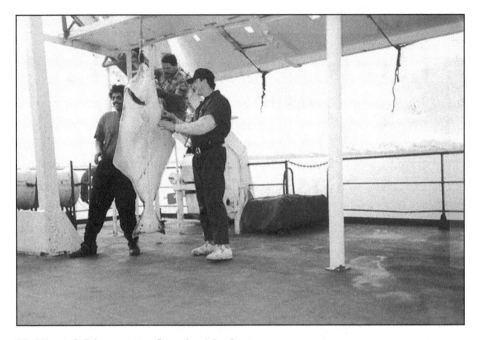

Halibut fishing at anchor in Alaska.

Reflecting back on that wintry Tuesday night in February 1993, even then the words he spoke were surreal, perhaps because in part they proved true: "I'm going to marry you, and you're going to have my babies some-day." My friends tried to convince me Darryl had a reputation with women. In other words, he was "full of it." Odds were he was just trying to pick me up.

We were in Portland's Old Port. I was twenty, and it was my first time in a bar. I was underage, but a friend somehow swept me through the door. That same person introduced us to Darryl, because we were all from Damariscotta. I remember dancing, drinking, and kissing Darryl in the bar. Darryl was twenty-nine.

That night foreshadowed what was to surface in coming years. Later that evening we gathered at our friends' apartment in the Old Port, where Darryl got into a violent physical altercation because he'd been asked to leave, more than likely because he was drunk. Darryl made it clear he wasn't leaving without me.

Darryl pursued me for a month before I returned his calls. I'm not sure why I was attracted to this man, but at twenty I was nervous about going out with him. Perhaps because I considered him an older man; he was probably experienced sexually, and I was not. Darryl told me he had a month left of vacation before returning to sea. He wanted to see me before he left.

Darryl was a charmer. I'll never forget our first date. He picked me up wearing the same L.L. Bean blue wool sweater with white specks he had on the night we met. The same sweater he wore when I fell in love with him. The sweater I now own and will forever have in my possession. It always smelled of his cologne. We dated consistently for more than a month. During that time Darryl did a masterful job of separating me from his crazy lifestyle.

I had absolutely no idea what this man was really like. I saw a handsome, caring man for whom I was falling fast. It was the first relationship I had that lasted more than a week. He swept me off my feet, showing up at my apartment with flowers and taking me places, including the Bostonian Hotel. We did much together in a short time. He told me he'd be back for me when he returned from sea, and you can bet I counted the days until his return. I longed for his phone calls. It was the most amazing feeling I'd ever experienced! I had no idea what would happen when he returned from sea. I had no suspicion, no indication. Why would I?

I picked Darryl up at the airport. The first two days were like a honeymoon. For years, it was like that every time he came home. We'd spend one to two days together, no one else around, and then I'd witness what I later realized was Darryl's regular pattern and normal way of life after returning from sea. The best way to put it is that Darryl came home from the ship, hit the ground running, and never stopped.

Where was the functional, loving man I'd met that night in February? I wasn't prepared for the mind-blowing experiences that inevitably

happened to someone as naive as I was, or for the culture shock that re-
vealed itself in the years to come. There was no warning, at least not that
I was aware enough to see. It didn't matter if there was. It was too late.
I was already in too deep with this man and couldn't walk away. —Jen-
nifer

When I met Jennifer, I still had a month at home before going back
to sea. That was good. I could concentrate on the new relationship, stay
sober, and hide my drug use. I planned to try to attract her and then lay
a good foundation for a potential loving relationship. I hoped by the
time I went back to work she'd be hooked and waiting when I returned
home.

Jennifer and me, 1993.

We went on daytrips, overnight trips, and did things together like
any normal couple. I still ran around and drank and drugged when I
wasn't with her. I was able to keep her from knowing the real me.

Jennifer and I fell in love, but the relationship never got a fair chance. Any relationship I was in was by definition dysfunctional. My alcoholism and drug use ruined all my relationships except with people I used with: a group of about twenty friends, both men and women. They were all decent people, but we partied too much. Some of us, especially me, were hardcore users.

I flew to Seattle on my thirtieth birthday, April 2, 1993, and rejoined the Overseas Juneau. I again enjoyed a successful work tour. I pressed forward, learning the chief mate's job. I worked at getting along with the people I worked under and the people who worked for me. I was also happy to have Jennifer in my life. It was a nice change to have someone to call from Alaska, Hawaii, or the West Coast. I was happier on board because my personal life was becoming more stable.

Soon it was June 30, and I was flying home. I again received excellent recommendations from the captains I worked under. I would be promoted to chief mate if I toed the line. At home, Jennifer and I became an item, but it wasn't long before she learned about the real me. I'll never forget the first time she saw me doing cocaine. She was so upset she called her mom and cried. At the time I couldn't believe she had involved her family in something that personal, but in hindsight I understand.

Jennifer and I were together for six years, on and off. During that time, not once did she try drugs. All my friends did drugs. I did drugs. She was around while my friends and I did drugs, but not once did she get sucked into our addictive behavior. I'm proud of her ability to not give in, although I never put any pressure on her. In fact, I was glad she didn't participate.

With Jen, my life took a turn for the better, but I didn't take full advantage of it. I had met a woman who really cared about me, and I put her on the back burner more than once in order to feed my alcohol and drug cravings. In truth, I wasn't ready for a serious relationship. I wasn't ready for much of anything serious in my life. I had my hands full with my job and my exploding addictions.

One night in the late summer of 1993, I went drinking with my close friend Woofie. We both loved the fast life and had the same issues: alcohol, women, marijuana, and lots and lots of cocaine.

Woofie and I went to the Old Port in my IROC Z-28 Camaro, a maroon convertible with a black ragtop, a head-turner boasting a 305 V8 engine. We ran into two guys at a bar who could set us up with some cocaine. Dean was a muscle-bound black guy. I knew he wasn't a cop; he was a bouncer at a local dance club, so I felt comfortable enough to make a drug deal with him. He was hanging out with Billy, a white guy who was a bit of a shady character, but I didn't care. I wanted to do some lines.

"You have cash for the coke, right?" Dean asked.

"I have plenty of money, man. No worries there," I assured him. Then I started to think. I didn't have enough cash on me, because I didn't know we were going to score, but I had thousands of dollars in the bank, a nice home, and a nice car outside. *He'll take my check if it's at my house.*

I bought us all drinks. Woofie and I always liked to get a good buzz going before we started snorting so we wouldn't get too wired. We ordered another round. *Life is good. I've got a good job, I'm partying with my buddy, and we're gonna get some white stuff. What could be better?*

"Hey, let's grab a twelve-pack and go to my house to party," I said.

"Sounds good," Woofie agreed.

I jumped behind the wheel, not caring that I was drinking and driving. Dean and Billy jumped in the back. I took off without a care in the world. We blasted music and drove around town like we owned it. We stopped at a store, and Dean and Billy jumped out to get a twelve-pack and cigarettes. While they were inside, I remembered I had only a little cash on me.

"Woofie, I only got about $30 on me. An eight ball is gonna cost at least $250. You got any cash, and I'll pay you with a check?"

"I don't have that kind of cash. Do you have your ATM card?"

"It's at home. I wonder if these guys will take a check."

"I don't know, man. People don't like checks."

Woofie became concerned; he really wanted to do some lines. I assumed everything would be okay. We drove to my house and went inside.

"Lay some lines out, man," I said, walking into my dining room. Dean and Billy followed.

"What do you want? An eight ball costs $250. Do you have that?" Dean asked.

"Dean, I only have a check. I don't have any cash on me."

"I'm not taking no check, man. You said you had the money, and we got all the way over here, and now you want to give me a fucking check! Who do you think I am, man?!"

"Hey, man, does it look like I don't have the money? I drove you in a nice convertible to this house that I own. Who do you think I am, man? I'm a Merchant Marine officer. I make $100,000 a year! There's plenty of money in my checking account. Just take the fucking check!" I yelled.

Woofie was outside getting the beer when he heard yelling and screaming: "Let me go. No! Don't hit my face! This is my house! Let me go! You guys are gonna pay for this!"

Billy had sneaked up behind me and pinned my arms back. Dean, the big, tough bar bouncer who knew karate, punched me in the face, splattering blood all over my dining room table and chairs. He then kicked me in the ribs and stomach.

I struggled as I was being pummeled and finally broke free. I ran upstairs and grabbed a 12-gauge shotgun. In my drunken rage, I was going to kill them. I grabbed some shotgun shells and loaded the gun, my hands shaking, blood all over the front of my face and shirt.

I heard Woofie yell: "You guys better get out of here! He's got a gun!"

I barreled down the stairs, ran out the front door, and aimed my shotgun at the drug dealers as they sprinted away. I stopped at the steps and let them go. I put the gun away, then went into the bathroom and looked in the mirror. My face was swollen and bloody. I would have at least one black eye, maybe two.

"Where the hell were you while those guys were pounding on my face?" I yelled at Woofie.

"I went out to get the beer and heard you screaming. By the time I came back you were upstairs, and they ran off!" my friend defended himself. "I'm getting out of here before the cops show up." He jumped in his vehicle and drove off.

I locked the doors, went into the living room, and lay down. My face and nose were throbbing, and my body was sore from being kicked. I was feeling sorry for myself for getting beaten up.

What the hell just happened? I didn't try to rip the guy off or anything. I just wanted to pay with a check. I never considered that I was a belligerent drunk giving them a hard time.

That night I woke up every few hours moaning in pain, bleeding onto my pillow, and feeling the need to throw up. My head throbbed and my ribs and stomach hurt. *How will I explain this one?* Black eyes are hard to hide—and embarrassing. It wasn't my first black eye, though, nor would it be my last.

Jen and me (with broken nose and two black eyes).

The next morning I was sore, and my face was still swollen. I could tell I'd have two black eyes, but at least they hadn't closed up. I'd had worse and knew they'd heal. I cleaned up the blood spatter, went upstairs, and jumped in the shower to wash away the remnants of the previous evening. Every time I took a shower after an "incident" I felt like the adventures—or problems—of the night before had been removed. That was my M.O., something I did for years.

The next night I had my friends Go-Go, Pusherman, and a couple over for a big turkey dinner. It was the latest thing to talk about what had happened among our group of friends. One of us, lots of times me, was always getting into a fix. We talked and laughed about the previous night, drank beer, and acted as if nothing unusual had happened. We were so caught up in our crazy, alcohol-and-drug-fueled lives that even a face-beating or an incident with a gun didn't seemed that far out of the normal.

The phone rang, and I took the call at the table. The voice was familiar; it was my neighbor, the college professor.

"This is your neighbor across the street. I wanted to speak to you about what happened at your house last night. My wife thought she saw you chase two men out of your house with a rifle."

"I wouldn't worry about it. I don't think they'll be back," I said abruptly.

He pressed on. "Who were they, Darryl? My wife is quite nervous about what happened over there."

"They were friends of friends. I didn't even know them, and I'm sorry about the ruckus. I can assure you it won't happen again. Some mistakes were made. They won't be repeated. That's all I have to say about it. Goodbye," I said firmly and hung up.

My friends laughed. Of course it wasn't funny. Of course I was out of control. I was in full alcoholic denial. I brushed off my neighbor's concern as if it was no big deal. Nobody got arrested or seriously hurt. I didn't get robbed. My pride was hurt, but I'd bounce back. It was typical alcoholic thinking that this was just normal life for a Merchant Marine officer who liked to drink. I believed my life was controlled chaos, when in fact it was out-of-control insanity.

A few months later, I realized just how scared of me my neighbors were. The day after an ice storm I got an ax out of the garage to chop ice from the roof and clear the gutters. As I walked around the corner of my house, the college professor's wife—who'd seen me chase the men with a shotgun—saw me, ax in hand. Her eyes got big as saucers, and she scurried back into her house.

Oh my God. They must think I'm going over the edge. I thought it was funny they were paranoid of me. If they were afraid, they might leave me alone and let me do what I wanted: drink, do drugs, and chase women.

When Darryl came home, the music got loud, the parties began, and the late-night cabs dropped off and picked up party-goers. The police showed up some nights, because the neighbors down the street had a nephew in the Portland Police Department, and they'd call him and complain. The married couple directly across the street from Darryl, the college professors, told other neighbors they once saw Darryl chasing two men down the street with a rifle. They finally decided it wasn't safe to live across from him and sold their house. The day they moved, they faced Darryl's house, gave him "the finger," and that was the last time we saw them. That attitude toward Darryl was far from isolated.
—Captain Hal Cozens, Jet Blue pilot and neighbor

I never realized how much hell I put my neighbors through. I've since made amends to them all, except for the couple across the street. I feel guilt and shame because of that. None of my current neighbors know their names or how to get in touch with them. Perhaps someday they'll contact me, and I can tell them how I sorry I am for my insane alcoholic behavior.

Though I had turned the corner by doing well at work, as my vacation continued that year, I continued to be an unstable, unpredictable person. Then I flew to San Francisco to rejoin the Overseas Juneau as second mate. I somehow managed to clean up my act enough to have a decent work tour, but the pressure in the cooker was building.

It was December 14, 1993, and I'd been on board the Juneau for seventy-three days. We were in Hawaii. I was almost done with my work tour and about ready to uncoil. I really wanted to drink. I thought about going ashore for "just a few," but I knew from experience that was dangerous. I had stood the 0400 to 0800 watch and planned to work overtime, since I knew going ashore would tempt me to drink.

The chief mate and I didn't get along, but that day he wanted me to go ashore to mail a $3,000 stock investment for him. He had to stay on board to watch cargo operations. It was 0800 on a sunny Hawaiian morning when the chief mate said, "Darryl, I have a deal for you. I have something really important to mail. If you go ashore and take care of it for me, I'll pay you the overtime anyway."

"I guess I could do that," I agreed.

"I want you to come back at noon. You have to go back to work at four, and I don't want you to come back buzzed. I'm paying you to take care of personal business while I pump the cargo. But I'm not paying you overtime to go drink beer," he lectured.

"Okay, Mate. Don't worry about it. I'm not going to drink beer at 8:00 a.m.," I assured him.

I went to my stateroom to shower and change, thinking the whole time, *Who is this guy to tell me what I can and can't do? I don't have to go to work again until four. He can't tell me to come back at noon. As long as I'm not drinking and I report for duty on time, I'm good to go. Screw him.*

We were discharging the cargo at Barber's Point at the southwest corner of Oahu. The launch boat took people to Honolulu, almost an hour to the east. The only way to get back and forth was the launch boat. I'd have to be careful not to miss it.

As we sped through blue Hawaiian waters en route to beautiful downtown Honolulu, I was still thinking about how the chief mate thought he could tell me what to do. He could give me orders when I was on duty. I respected the chain of command and the need for structure and order. But he couldn't tell me what to do on my time off. He had no right to tell me to come back to the ship at noon. When I wasn't working, I was free to do what I wanted.

Launch boat taking me ashore in Honolulu, Hawaii.

I decided to stay in Honolulu all day and report back for duty at 4:00. As long as I mailed the chief mate's stock options and stayed sober, he couldn't touch me. Then my revengeful, resentful alcoholic thinking kicked into high gear. I figured there would be nothing sweeter than having a few beers at 8:00 a.m. just to rub it in his face. I'd just have a couple, and then I'd have the rest of the day to sober up.

I got off the launch boat at the regular pickup/drop-off point at Aloha Tower, a large clock tower on the end of the pier connected to a shopping mall. At street level, it's the world's nicest parking garage—with a waterfront view.

The launch boat operator instructed the passengers that the normal pickup point had been switched to the other end of the pier because of

Honolulu.

ongoing construction. There had been some confusion between the construction company and the launch boat company, but he assured us it had been straightened out. He also informed us that his office Christmas party was that evening, meaning there would be replacement launch boat captains that night.

It wouldn't affect me, because I was coming back at 4:00. I sauntered ashore and immediately took care of the chief mate's investments. He was paying me four hours overtime, and there was a $3,000 check inside the envelope. I didn't want to lose it.

I walked across the street to a place where they served alcohol in the morning, reveling in the fact that I was disobeying the chief mate's orders. I'd show him. I switched from beer to vodka and orange juice to up the buzz. I'd stop drinking at noon, allowing four hours to straighten up before going back to work.

But I consistently underestimated the enemy—alcohol and alcoholism. I continued to drink, figuring since I was drinking vodka, nobody, including the chief mate, would smell the booze. I'd just buy a toothbrush and mouthwash.

I stumbled around town and stepped into a seedy bar. I wasn't quite done drinking. It was 1:00 p.m.; I'd have one last drink before heading back to catch the launch boat. Before I knew it, my watch said 2:30. I bought a pack of gum and went to Aloha Tower and waited. The launch never showed up.

All I could do was wait another four hours for the next launch. So I did what any serious alcoholic would do: started drinking again. I was in a mess anyway. I wasn't sure if there was any damage control in the world that could bail me out of this disaster.

By 10:00 p.m., I'd been drinking since morning. I hadn't eaten, and I was much drunker than I thought possible. I walked back to Aloha Tower. I had to go to the bathroom, but was too drunk to go anywhere. I stumbled into the parking garage, pulled down my pants and defecated. I'm sure someone paid hundreds of dollars each month for that premium parking space.

I was sober enough to realize I had nothing to wipe myself with. I looked down at my underwear and decided they were my only option. I then deposited the underwear on top of the mess. I vividly remember drunkenly snickering to myself, thinking about the guy who'd pull into the garage in his Mercedes the next day, late for work, and think, *What the heck is that white rag doing in my parking spot?* He'd get out for a closer look, pick up the underwear, and . . .

I was losing my mind, laughing demonically about something that shouldn't be funny, when I should have been back on my 900-foot supertanker tending to my $80,000-a-year job. Instead, I wasn't even worried what would happen to me after I sobered up. I stumbled back to the launch area and sat down, thinking I'd never get back to the ship.

The last launch of the night was supposed to pick up at 11:30 p.m. I had ninety minutes to kill. I sat there, my mind lost in drunken confusion over what had taken place that day. I'd been away from the vessel fourteen hours and missed my watch. I couldn't miss the last launch boat, or surely I'd get fired. The problem was, as drunk as I was, I'd probably get fired if I did make it back. My mind was whirling. And then I passed out.

I woke up just in time to see the launch boat heading out of the harbor and watched as its white lights got smaller and smaller. I found a Harbor Patrol officer and asked where the launch picked up, because it hadn't shown up at Aloha Tower. He explained that because of local construction, it picked up at the other end of the pier. The new spot was in sight of the old one, about a thousand feet away, just far enough to cause a drunken sailor to miss his watch. I later got a statement from the Harbor Patrol confirming that the launch area had been switched, enabling me to spin the story away from my drinking.

I spent the night in a hotel, knowing that no matter what happened when I got back to the ship, it wouldn't be good. I woke up a few times during the night, each time clutching my pillows in fear. I stayed in bed half the next day, too scared to wake up and deal with reality.

That was another big mistake. The captain later told me if I'd been on the first launch at 0730, he might not have fired me. But I decided to sleep off the booze. When I got back to the ship at 1600 in time for my watch, the chief mate was furious. I explained the launch boat confusion, but because the chief mate threatened to inform the company, the captain fired me.

I packed my bags and got off the ship embarrassed, tired, and disgraced. My drinking had finally gotten me fired from a ship. The only silver lining was that I still was not fired from the company. It wasn't long before Maritime Overseas Corporation instructed me to again fly to New York. I was scared out of my mind I'd lose my high-paying job.

At New York headquarters, Captain Ripperger asked me what happened. I defiantly explained the confusion over the launch boat pickup and how the substitute driver had given the wrong instructions. I showed him copies of my requests to the Honolulu Harbor Patrol and the launch boat service asking them to verify the incident.

Ripperger was placed in the unenviable position of having to choose whether or not to fire me with the possibility of facing legal action if I had in fact missed my watch due to circumstances I couldn't control. Of course, there were no blood alcohol tests, because I didn't come back until the next day. He assumed correctly, however, that alcohol had been involved.

"Darryl, I'm going to demote you to third mate," he said sternly.

"I don't think that's fair, Captain. It wasn't my fault the launch boat picked up in the wrong place. I've worked hard for Maritime Overseas Corporation," I defended myself, deliberately skirting any talk of alcohol use.

"Darryl, this is the second time in a year that you've had a major mistake. I suspect alcohol was involved. If it wasn't for the length of your service, I'd fire you outright. You are no longer a second mate."

I knew at that point he expected my resignation.

"Okay, sir."

"I'm also going to penalize you with an extra three months off without work. Maybe that will give you time to think about what happened."

I also knew that at that point he expected me to blow up and quit.

"Okay, sir," I responded. "Is that all?"

"Are you going to accept the assignment as third mate?"

"I'd like a few days to think about it."

I knew he wanted my resignation, but I didn't want to decide until I went home and thought it over—and looked for another job.

"Darryl, if you go back to one of our ships as third mate, you'd better be very careful when you go ashore. There will be zero tolerance for any further mistakes. Are we clear on that?"

"Yes, sir, I hear you loud and clear," I said submissively.

I called Maritime Overseas Corporation and told them I would accept a third mate's position. I could swallow my pride, not drink around the ships, and get promoted again. Still, it was an expensive mistake. I lost three months' pay, and had to sell a piece of land I owned in order to pay my bills. My grand total cost for that one day of drinking was more than $59,000, plus the realization that I probably had no chance of ever sailing as a captain with Maritime Overseas Corporation. Yet I *still* wasn't done with my addictions. I had another fifteen years to go.

I flew home and once again started drinking too much. I spent the summer of 1993 edging back toward being the crazy man I'd been a year earlier, a reckless, angry, out-of-control sailor with an axe to grind with the world.

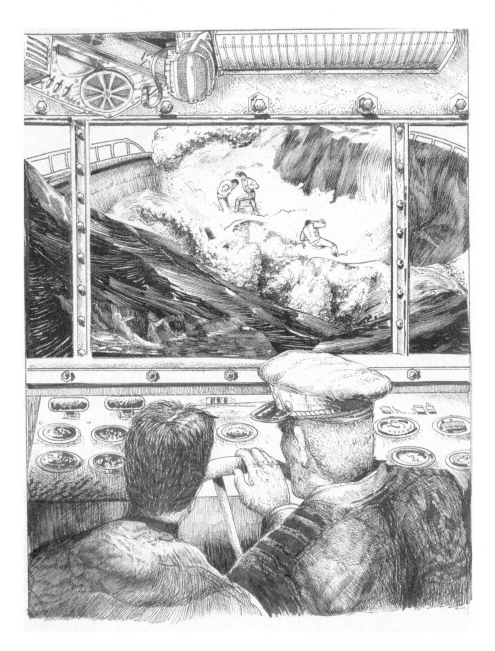

CHAPTER TWENTY-FOUR

ALASKA SNOWSTORMS
AND MONSTER WAVES

Because Maritime Overseas Corporation kept me home an extra three months without pay, I hadn't worked in more than five months. Because I'd been demoted, people who were far behind me on the promotion list moved in front of me. I had sailed as second mate for five years. Going backward was hard on my ego.

Clearly, alcohol was causing me problems with career advancement and finances. But my health was also deteriorating. After years of substance abuse I faced high blood pressure and depression. I was a walking, ticking time bomb. Yet I was a tough old Maine boy, and I wasn't giving up. Maine boys work hard and play hard—unfortunately too hard.

I was again assigned to the Overseas Valdez. After about a week the captain started riding me, but I gave it right back. I was never disrespectful; I just didn't kiss up to him like everyone else. Apparently my attitude surprised him, since I was still vulnerable in my job.

We were on the bridge once when he said in amazement, "I can say one thing about you, Darryl, you're no ass-kisser."

"Captain, I just want to be left alone to do my job to the best of my ability."

He tested me every day, and every day I passed with flying colors. One time there was a hurricane in the Gulf of Mexico, and he asked me which was the navigable semi-circle as opposed to the dangerous semi-circle. I told him we should stay to the northwest of the hurricane. Since that was the correct answer, he walked off.

Two Arctic sailors.

Snowy path on ship in Valdez, Alaska.

Another time we were approaching Tampa, where there are several large course changes, which I executed with the captain standing in the window, observing silently. The transit went perfectly. The captain knew I was good at my job. If I didn't screw up by drinking or losing my temper—and tell him to go fly a kite or something—I'd probably survive.

Piloting the S/T Overseas Valdez, in front of the radars.

I made one error that trip. We were sailing from port with a tugboat tied to the stern. Fifteen minutes after leaving dock, though not yet dismissed by the captain, I left the deck. Since the captain was riding me so hard, I didn't want to talk to him anyway. Normally officers don't leave the deck without talking to each other first—my mistake.

One of the mates came and yelled to me that I forgot the tug. I quickly went to check, but the mate had already let the tug go. The captain upbraided me for that. That's what happens when officers don't have good working relationships, if one of them is walking on eggshells.

In fact, mistakes are more frequent when supervisors are overbearing, something of which I was also guilty.

After the trip the captain gave me a satisfactory deck officer evaluation, indicating that I had an attitude problem but that I was competent and handled my job professionally. I complained to the port captain, who reminded me that the evaluation wasn't negative and that it didn't say I was incompetent.

I got off the Valdez on July 27, 1994, after one of my most difficult trips at sea, only to self-medicate my tired body and mind for three months straight. I was running low on cash and nearly ready to ship out again, when the telephone rang.

The MOC personnel manager said they needed me in Valdez on the Overseas Alaska. One of the third mates had a family emergency. We typically didn't relieve each other in Alaska for two reasons: First, it was more expensive to fly to Alaska than to the West Coast; second, snowstorms through the mountain passes from Anchorage caused many canceled flights. Missing a ship was a worry.

When a sailor gets called and told "I need you on the ship in three hours" or something similar, it's known as a "pier head jump." This time, I pleaded with the personnel manager, "Is there any way I can get the first flight out in the morning? I have lots to do first." The truth was that I needed one more night of drinking before I was ready to go to sea again.

"Okay, but get on the first flight in the morning."

It was time to get a case of beer. I packed my sea bags, drank beer, paid bills, cleaned out my refrigerator, and called the people I cared about, who were amazed I had to fly to Alaska the next day. *Welcome to my life*.

I got about three hours of sleep. I made it from Portland to Seattle with no delays, but things quickly went downhill. Snowstorms were raging in Alaska, and I regretted taking that additional night; I had no time for flight delays or cancellations. If I missed the ship, "the prince of darkness" would surely can me.

I informed the pilot that I was joining a supertanker that would sail without me if he didn't get me to Anchorage on time. He made a valiant effort to shave off some flight time, and we landed in Anchorage ten minutes before my connecting flight. I ran to the gate, but the plane was already taxiing toward the runway.

I was distraught. I could make the seven-hour trek in a rental car, but the area was in the middle of a blinding snowstorm. I visualized sliding off the roads and getting stuck in a frozen wilderness.

I was desperate. I decided to put some heat on Alaska Airlines to send me to Valdez via taxi. I walked up to the ticket counter, still hung over and sweating. If I had traveled the day before like the company wanted, I would have been in a hotel getting a good night's rest. But things were working out just the way they should, given the circumstances I'd created for myself.

After I informed the ticket attendant I had missed my connection, she politely explained airline policy: Put people up in a hotel, give them a meal ticket, and get them on the first flight in the morning. When I insisted more forcefully, she called out her supervisor.

Out walked a drop-dead gorgeous redhead with an attitude to match her looks. I went through my story again, and she repeated the standard company policy.

"Ma'am, that option is unacceptable. I have to join a ship leaving Valdez before sunrise, and I'll get fired if I'm not on board."

She seemed to take pleasure scolding me. "You should have traveled yesterday, sir. This is Alaska, and snowstorms and travel delays should be expected."

"What's the other option, sweetheart?" I asked sarcastically.

"The other option, sir, is to rent a car and drive to Valdez. You could be there in less than seven hours and still make the ship."

"Ma'am, I've been traveling for eighteen hours through three airports, and now you want me to drive through a blinding snowstorm in mountain passes I've never driven through? Why don't you provide me with a taxi? I'll sleep in the back and leave the driving to a professional who's used to slippery roads and knows where he's going."

"Sir, we can't provide that kind of transportation. That would be over $1000 in cab fare."

"I've got an idea, ma'am," I spouted, my voice still full of sarcasm. "You think I'm okay to drive seven hours in a blizzard on dangerous mountain roads because of delays caused by Alaska Airlines. Then for nine hours I'll be piloting a 900-foot supertanker carrying 500,000 barrels of crude oil. If there was a screw up because of my exhaustion, I'd be happy to tell the *Anchorage Daily News* that Alaska Airlines wouldn't provide safe transportation to Valdez. How would that be? You remember the Exxon Valdez, don't you? That little oil spill up here on a ship just like mine."

She looked concerned. "I'll be right back, sir. Let me call my supervisor."

Finally I was getting somewhere. The redhead came back ten minutes later and picked up a microphone.

"The first cab driver who can take someone to Valdez tonight will get two free round trip tickets anywhere Alaska Airlines flies," she announced.

She thanked me for being patient and handed me a flight voucher for the cabbie. I took my luggage outside and jumped in the waiting taxi.

"It's gonna be a bitch of a drive over and back, but my wife will be happy with me when I tell her we're going to Mexico next week," the cabbie said.

I tried to stretch out on the back seat to rest, but sleeping was a pipe dream. The guy drove 90 mph on slippery, bumpy roads, and I was scared he'd spin out and go off the road. After a few hours, I gave up and started a conversation.

"That was quite the oil spill, the Exxon Valdez," I remarked, curious to know what the locals thought.

"Sure the heck was. All the fishermen and locals are pretty upset about it. The good thing is, Exxon stepped up to the plate and helped the fishermen buy new boats and gear."

"People don't realize that Exxon really did step up to the plate," I answered. "If it had happened to a smaller oil company, there might not have been billions to spend on cleanup. A smaller company might have claimed bankruptcy and walked away. Plus, the new boats and gear that replaced ruined vessels meant some people actually ended up with better equipment."

"I saw guys putting in claims if they had any kind of registered boat and fishing equipment, whether or not it was in the water," the cabbie said. "Exxon paid the false claims, even if the guys hadn't fished for years."

"Wow, you don't hear that side of the story," I said, adding, "The captain shouldn't have left the bridge, especially with icebergs around. You start making bad decisions when you're drinking. I've made plenty myself."

"We've all made bad decisions when we were drinking," he agreed. "But when you're navigating massive supertankers, you shouldn't be drinking at all."

I shrugged. "One of my captains likens the Exxon Valdez to a car driving along a southbound two-lane highway, going off the road, over the meridian strip, crossing the two northbound lanes, and then slamming into a big green highway sign. That's how bad they screwed up going around the iceberg. They went left to avoid it and never came back to the right. It's pretty hard to screw up that badly. I've been through there many times, and you have a ten-mile-wide hole to navigate through."

"Well, they're paying through the nose now. It'll cost them a lot of money before it's all done."

We finally reached Valdez. We stopped at the gate, I showed my ID, and the guards looked through my sea bag and briefcase. We drove to the dock, where I tipped the driver and thanked him.

I climbed the gangway and went up to meet the captain, a nice old guy with three decades of seafaring experience. Pilots, mates, and sailors jokingly called him Captain Hollywood because his girlfriend was

Hugh Hefner's secretary. Hefner apparently called him Captain Bob. The captain often shared fascinating stories about visiting the Playboy Mansion, including how he watched movies in its theater. In his office he had pictures of himself with Hugh Hefner, Kimberly Conrad (Hefner's wife), and other celebrities.

One time as we were underway to San Francisco, the captain sent me to meet the pilot boat. The pilot asked, "Isn't this Captain Hollywood's ship?"

"Yes, sir, it is."

"Does he really go to the Playboy Mansion?"

"Yes, he does. He's got all kinds of pictures of Hugh Hefner in his office."

"Wow, I'd love to see those."

"Before we get to the bridge we can pop in his office. Please don't tell the captain. I'm not sure how he'd feel about that."

"Don't worry, I won't say a word."

I showed him the many pictures on the walls and desk in the captain's office. He was fascinated. I finally had to drag him away before the captain realized we were up to something.

On the bridge, the first thing out of the pilot's mouth was: "Hi, Captain. The mate showed me the Playboy Mansion pictures in your office. Very interesting," he laughed.

The captain was a nice guy and didn't seem to mind. I was unhappy with the pilot for breaking his promise, but let it go. I was also interested in the captain's stories. He said some of the girls talked to him about their problems. He consoled and comforted them; he was older, and they probably cherished his wisdom and compassion.

The work tour wore on, and before long winter storms became more common. There were many days when sleep-deprived, grumpy sailors reported for duty. We got into a rough storm one night, and the ship was rolling side to side. The captain slowed the vessel, because 35-foot waves were crashing over the deck.

In big storms there are two scenarios that affect big tankers differently. When leaving Alaska the ship is full of crude oil, and the vessel sinks deep into the water. The distance from waterline to main deck is called the vessel's "freeboard," which is much less when the ship is loaded. A lower freeboard causes the ship to be more stable, but it also means that the deck is much closer to the sea, meaning storms can cause more damage.

When the vessel is empty, or "in ballast," the cargo tanks are partly filled with seawater to ensure the rudder and propeller are submerged enough to be effective. Because we're only half the weight, the freeboard is greater, meaning even big seas don't come on deck, but during a storm the vessel gets tossed about like a cork. The ship is also more affected by wind, since greater freeboard acts like a giant sail.

The night of that ferocious storm, we were loaded and our freeboard was about twenty feet. That meant a 35-foot sea could easily crash over the decks. In rolling seas it could be worse. I turned on the deck lights to make sure the vessel wasn't sustaining damage. Normally we didn't run with deck lights on; they're bright enough to block the view of the horizon and approaching ships. The lights were turned on only in extreme weather, and we used radar to avoid oncoming vessels.

We secured the outside decks for the night, posting signs on every level: "Decks secured, absolutely nobody outside!" These signs ensured that we wouldn't have to worry about a man being washed overboard.

When seas get that high, tens of thousands of dollars of damage can occur. Pipelines can be bent and hydraulic lines can be ripped off the deck, causing hydraulic oil to mix with the sea. I've seen thirty-inch manifold valves bent so badly they were inoperable. I've also seen cracks open inside cargo tanks from the heaving, pounding seas. Extra care has to be used in slowing the ship and changing course to prevent too much water washing over the deck. When that can't be avoided completely, extra eyes are needed on deck to watch for damage.

Winter storm in the Gulf of Alaska.

The wind howled and the ship banged, creaked, and slapped the ocean throughout the night. There were many long, tired faces when the sun finally came up. The captain, chief mate, and I looked the deck over with binoculars for damage. The chief mate spotted something. "I think I see something adrift way up forward by the No. 1 center cargo tank."

"I see it too," the captain said. "Looks like a five-foot section of quarter-inch diamond plating. It could get swept into the pipelines and cause damage. We need to send some men to take care of that, Mate. Take the chief engineer and the boatswain. Call me when you're ready to go outside. Stay away from the sides, secure the plate or put it inside the fo'c'sle, and we'll deal with it later."

The chief mate turned to me. "Radio me if you see any really big waves coming."

"Will do, Mate," I said. "You should wear life jackets. It's pretty bad out there. At least if you go over the side you'll have a chance with a life jacket on."

"We will. I'll call you when we're ready, Captain." The chief mate left the bridge to get the other men.

"Okay, let's see. Let's turn the vessel around, and after that we'll slow down," the captain said. He seemed to be thinking aloud.

"Are you going to swing her around and put the seas on the stern, Captain?" I asked. "I think that's the safest way to go—keeping the seas as far as possible from the men."

"Yes, that what I was thinking. But I think we can go directly into the seas and slow down. Then we won't have to turn around and then back around again after we're finished. If I slow way down, the seas shouldn't come up over the bow." The captain seemed to be asking for confirmation.

"I think that's the wrong move, Captain. I would turn the ship around and put the seas on the stern. It would be a lot safer for the guys."

"Call the engine room and tell them to go dead slow ahead. I'm going to head straight into the seas. They aren't big enough to come all the way over the bow," the captain ordered.

"Okay, Captain," I said, shaking my head. I called the engine room and ordered them dead slow ahead.

The vessel slowed even more. The seas hadn't come over the bow, and he felt he'd made the right decision. But I was an experienced deck officer, and I knew it was the wrong decision. The captain had more than thirty years of experience, and I wasn't going to disobey him. But I would watch carefully.

"Chief Mate, I've slowed the vessel down, and it looks safe on deck. Are you and the other men ready to go?" the captain asked over the radio.

"Yes, sir, Captain. We have life preservers on and radios," the chief mate answered.

The three men opened the starboard main deck watertight door and made their way around the house and to the middle of the ship, following the pipeline forward to the loose diamond plate. Since the captain had changed course and pointed the bow into the seas, there was no problem with seas coming from the sides. The men made it safely forward, but the bow began dipping dangerously, and I was afraid a big wave could crash onto the sailors.

"Captain, the seas are close to coming over the bow. I think we're making a serious mistake here with this course. I recommend they take cover inside the fo'c'sle and we turn the vessel around, then have them go back outside to finish," I said.

"They'll be okay. It will only take a minute to get this done," he insisted.

I watched the seas build. Suddenly a huge wave came toward the ship, and the bow nosedived.

"Here comes a big one, you guys!" I screamed into the radio.

The vessel scooped up the monster wave and threw it onto the men. The chief mate and the boatswain took cover under the overhang of the fo'c'sle deck. It looked like they were standing behind a waterfall. The chief engineer wasn't so fortunate. He hesitated and the giant wave crashed onto him and knocked him off his feet.

"The chief engineer is down, Captain! The wave is swallowing him up!" I yelled.

The captain was stunned. He changed course, but it was too late.

"Here comes another big wave," I screamed into the radio.

Just as the chief engineer got up, the next wave swept him off his feet and carried him fifty feet to the side of the vessel, slamming him into the railing. His face took the brunt of the impact when he hit a vertical stanchion. If it hadn't been for the railing, he would have surely lost his life. I doubt we could have turned around and rescued him. The seas were too big to launch a lifeboat; doing so would have put additional personnel at risk. Once a man goes overboard in those circumstances, the chances of survival are slim. A helicopter rescue would take hours, and we were in the Gulf of Alaska, where hypothermia can kill a man quickly.

"Captain, the chief engineer is almost overboard," I screamed as the captain swung the ship to a safe course. With the seas behind us, the water drained off the deck. The chief engineer ran for his life, holding his bleeding face. Through the binoculars, I could see that he was in shock.

The look of fear mixed with the instinct for survival on his face is an image I will not forget.

"Chief Mate, get off the deck. Come back and attend to the chief engineer. Forget the steel plate. It's too dangerous out there," the captain yelled over the radio.

"Roger that, Captain." The chief mate led the boatswain along the pipelines back into the safety of the house.

The chief engineer had deep lacerations on his face and his front teeth had been shoved backward. We used the satellite phone to call an onshore hospital. The doctors asked us to treat him for shock and warned us not to bend his teeth back to their normal position for fear of blocking his airway. We then transported him to a hospital, and he stayed home many months as his body and psyche healed. We were lucky no one was lost to the sea that day. We also learned an important lesson about seamanship: No man's life is worth trying to minimize damage to a vessel to save money, unless the damage itself is life threatening.

The Gulf of Alaska and the Bering Sea are some of the most ferocious waters on the planet. Men have been lost overboard, never to be found again. That was not the only time I experienced high seas and 80 mph winds, pitching into the air, riding the crest of a wave, then suddenly diving into the trough. People think because a vessel is 900 feet long it will ride over the waves. That's not true. The ocean will toss any size vessel around, depending on its ferocity and direction. The ocean is inherently dangerous, which only added to the stress of a job that included a harsh environment, big and complicated equipment, and many lonely months at sea.

There were no other incidents or drinking issues that trip. We pulled into Tacoma, Washington, on January 28, 1995, the day I was due to get off. I was scheduled to work until 8:00 p.m. as the ship discharged crude oil.

Todd, an old friend who had moved to Seattle from Maine, arrived at 7:00, excited to go out and party. We both loved alcohol, cocaine, and women, making us a dangerous pair.

As he signed the visitor's book, he laughed. "Wow! Look at how big this frigging ship is. It's a trip they let *you* run this thing."

We toured the ship, and I left him in my room with a plate of food and a movie going. I finished standing watch with no problems. As Todd and I sat in my room talking, various crewmembers came by to say goodbye. Before I knew it, I'd been sitting in my work clothes almost two hours after being paid off. Suddenly the chief mate burst into my stateroom.

"Darryl, I need you outside. We have an oil spill to clean up!"

"You're kidding, right?" I said, smiling.

"No, Darryl, I swear to God! We've sprung a leak on a dresser coupling on one of the pipelines. I know you're paid off, but I need you."

My jaw dropped; he was telling the truth. "No problem, Mate. I'll be right out." I turned to Todd. "Sorry about that. It should only take a few hours. I'll be back as soon as possible."

"No problem. Sometimes you gotta do what you gotta do."

Sure enough, a pipeline was leaking. The chief mate had shut down the cargo discharge and called "all hands on deck." We used absorbent pads, kitty litter, shovels, buckets, and trash barrels. We tightened the dresser coupling bolts, and soon the vessel was pumping oil again. When we finished, I walked into my room, and Todd looked up and laughed.

"You got oil all over your face and mouth, man!"

"That'll teach me to sit around and BS with people when I've already been paid off."

I used Gojo, an oil remover, to get the crude oil off my body. I was feeling good about getting off the ship and drinking some beer, when suddenly the ship started shaking.

I stuck my head out of the shower and yelled to Todd, "What the hell was that?"

"I don't know. I thought maybe it was an explosion from the oil spill."

"I don't think so, man. I think that was an earthquake. Let's get out of here before they need me for something else!"

I dressed quickly and grabbed my sea bag. A group of men were on the main deck, talking.

"Was that an earthquake I just felt?" I asked.

One of the sailors laughed. "It sure was, Mate. First the oil spill, then the earthquake. I wonder what's next?"

I stepped onto the gangway, and it immediately dropped five inches and crashed onto the deck. I grabbed the rope handrail and looked back. Nobody had noticed that the earthquake had moved the gangway onto the steel fishplate, a coaming standing five inches above the main deck intended to keep spilled oil out of the water.

"I have to get off this ship!" I yelled.

I learned a lesson that night. Sailors always joked how once you're done with your ninety days, you should get off the ship right away and not look back. Don't answer your cell phone, just run fast and far—before something happens and they ask you to stay.

Todd and I immediately drove to a liquor store. We stayed up all night snorting cocaine and drinking. The next day we planned to watch Super Bowl XXIX, the San Francisco 49ers vs. the San Diego Chargers, at a sports bar. I tried my best to continue partying until the game started. But I was exhausted by my three-month work tour. I had one beer and couldn't do it.

"I have to go outside and sleep in the car, man."

"What!? The game is just starting!" Todd laughed.

I stumbled outside, crawled into the back seat, and passed out. I didn't wake up until Todd banged on the window. The game was over.

I partied a few days with Todd, then flew home to relax on my vacation. Except, I didn't know how to relax. I was either working or drinking, drinking or working.

GLENN CHADBOURNE

CHAPTER TWENTY-FIVE
CHAOS AT HOME

I wrote a letter to Maritime Overseas Corporation asking them to end my penance as third mate. I had stayed out of trouble through two works tours. With support from several captains, I tried to convince the company they'd spent too much money training me to keep me stuck unused at the bottom of the ladder, that my experience was valuable. I asked for another opportunity to prove my worth. And I still hoped to become captain someday.

Through the demotion, I had finally gone beyond one kind of denial; I was no longer oblivious to my drinking problem. For twenty-two years I never honestly looked at my drinking. No matter how striking the evidence of my alcoholism, I didn't see the truth.

Now I had reached the point where I realized I was spinning out of control, but I felt I could still drink if I was vigilant. I swore I wouldn't drink vodka because of the terrible things I did afterward. But there were still many times when I drank beer only—then sought and found cocaine, and spent many days a complete mess.

Somehow I always bounced back. I always got out of trouble at work, legal problems were solved with the best lawyers, and medical problems were fixed by doctors. Continuing to drink was worth all the hassles. I took care of the junk so I could drink the way I wanted to drink.

So there I was in 1995, meaning every word I wrote to the company. I was serious about my career. I'd do anything to get back on track. I was on the Overseas Philadelphia when I received a good recommendation and was promoted to second mate. The captains liked me. I was a competent, hard worker; they just had to keep me reigned in.

I flew home on July 3. Jen and I had broken up some time before, so when one of the captains from Maine invited me to a cottage on Sebago Lake, I brought my new girlfriend. We went out to a bar that night and had fun, though the captain's wife was leery of the whole scene. The captain bought me shot after shot, and before long I went into a black-out. I woke up at the cottage with no memory of how I got there. There was vomit all over the bed. *Man, I messed up again!*

I turned to my girlfriend. "What happened, Susanna?" I wanted to know what I'd done during the blackout. I needed to know how to cover my tracks with the captain.

"You were trashed. I got you in bed, and you threw up during the night. I couldn't wake you up, so I gave up," she said, sounding disgusted.

"I've got to get up and fix this. Maybe I can scrub the bedspread in the lake and hang it on the clothesline before anyone gets up."

I tiptoed through the living room, out the front door, walked into the cold lake, and started cleaning vomit off the bedspread. It wasn't work-ing. The front door of the cottage opened, and the captain's wife came out and sat down in a chair near the fire pit overlooking the lake.

"Good morning, Darryl. What are you up to?" she asked a little sar-castically.

"I guess I had a little problem last night. Sorry about that. I don't even remember it," I said, as if my lack of memory would somehow make my actions acceptable.

The captain walked outside. "What's going on out here? Doing a little laundry, Darryl?"

"It's your fault; you were feeding him shots all night!" his wife scolded.

Susanna came outside. The captain said, "Darryl, you and Susanna take my Audi and go to the Laundromat up the street."

I wrung out the wet bedspread and sheets and put them in a garbage bag. Off to the Laundromat we went.

"Oh, my God, that was embarrassing!" Susanna said.

When we returned, I apologized again and chalked it up to just one in a string of incidents I'd rather forget.

I went back to sea on November 29 to the Overseas Chicago. We loaded 640,000 barrels on the 890-foot long ship and steamed south from Valdez to Hawaii. During that trip we endured the worst storm I ever experienced.

It normally took a week at full steaming to get to Oahu. But this time, the weather maps looked bad. The captain kept trying to get in front of the storm as the weather continued to deteriorate for several days. The storm was bearing down on us. We weren't going to make it.

We battened down the hatches and tied everything down with double ropes. The boatswain took some men to the fo'c'sle, where we kept supplies: neatly stacked and stowed drums of lubricant, boxes of rags, spare parts, motors, tank cleaning gear, lockers full of paint brushes—everything needed to maintain a ship. The men lashed everything down extra securely, especially the dozens of fifty-five-gallon drums full of lubricating oils and degreasers. We were in for a rough ride.

After a full day spent securing the ship, the captain gathered the crew for a safety meeting: "This will be a rough ride for a couple of days. I've slowed to bare steerage way. The steward department should be careful when cooking. Let's not get burned or injured. Be aware that the ship could take a big roll at any time."

The captain's voice was firm and stern. "Tie down everything in the engine room. The decks are secured, the fo'c'sle, and everything throughout the house. The bridge informs me that the seas are now crashing over the ship, so nobody goes outside until further notice. No exceptions. We'll stow food waste in the main deck passageway until the storm is over. Go back to your rooms and secure all loose gear."

In my room, I took everything off my desk and put it in my bureau drawers. I tied down my recliner and desk chair. I took everything in the bathroom, put it in a box, and wedged it behind the recliner. Then I got some sleep. It was the best decision I made at the time; I didn't sleep soundly again for two days.

The storm intensified and the wind howled at near hurricane force. The captain advised the mates to keep the deck lights on at night so we could see any damage. The seas crashed onto the deck, sending seawater and foam through the air. It's fascinating to watch, but dangerous. The ship was almost twenty years old, and it made creaking noises that made even the most hardened sailor cringe.

I was on watch that night as the vessel dove down into the seas and scooped up water like it was shoveling snow. It was nerve-wracking enough that I called the captain several times. We changed course ten degrees to ease the strain. After my watch, I put my mattress on the floor of my cabin so I wouldn't get rolled out of bed. I slept several hours before I woke up again.

I decided to read a Stephen King novel. The howling winds and the slamming seas made me feel like I was on a ghost ship. I was getting a rise out of reading something scary—the storm increased the horror. But I finally got too spooked and put the book away. After that sleep came intermittently. I wouldn't advise anyone wanting a good night's sleep to read Stephen King in 40-foot seas and 60-knot winds.

I was awakened several times by the loud pounding of the seas against the vessel: Bang! Thud! Whack! *Where's my lifejacket and survival suit?* Then I remembered the dream I'd just had: The ship had pulled apart down the middle like a giant zipper. I was jolted into thinking that this storm was dangerous. I got dressed and headed to the bridge.

It wasn't yet time for my watch, but I was concerned. If we were going to sink, I wanted to be the first to know. It was going on two days since we'd last been outside to look around. We'd been boarding heavy seas the entire time, and a ship can only take so much for so long.

I found the captain on the bridge looking out the windows, along with the mate on watch and the helmsman. I walked over to the cof-

Storm in the Gulf of Alaska.

fee pot and filled my cup. I was going on watch in an hour; I might as well stay up.

"Couldn't sleep?" asked the captain.

"That last bump was a bad one. I was concerned, so I got up," I stated honestly.

"It woke me up too. I changed course, so we're riding a little better now," the captain explained. "The storm is right on top of us, but it should move away today. Once the seas subside we'll check for damage." Each winter, it wasn't unusual for several tankers to sustain tens of thousands of dollars in damage.

The weather finally let up; it was safe to walk the decks. The chief mate, the boatswain, and I went up to the bridge.

"I want you three to be the only ones outside," the captain instructed. "Each of you take a UHF radio and stay in contact with me. This should be a quick look around."

We grabbed handheld radios and coats and went to the athwart ship passageway door. Once the captain changed to a safer course, we inspected the thirty- and twenty-four-inch pipelines, valves, and electrical cables. We found some damage, but no major problems. We then inspected the steering gear room to make sure it was dry and walked to the fo'c'sle, an enclosed area beneath the bow the size of a big house supported by a dozen huge steel pillars. Directly above the fo'c'sle on the outside deck sit the anchors, anchor windlass, and mooring line winches. We climbed the 15-foot ladder to the bow to inspect the equipment there.

The chief mate quickly looked around and immediately went back down the ladder and entered the fo'c'sle. I didn't think anything of his quick departure until I heard his radio call.

"On the bridge of the Chicago, Captain, can you hear me?"

"Go ahead, Mate. This is the captain. What did you find?"

"Um, I think you better come up here, Captain. We need to talk."

That was weird. He didn't tell the captain what he wanted to talk about.

The captain radioed for me to come to the bridge. My curiosity was up. The chief mate had obviously found something of concern. I scurried back down the deck and scaled the stairs to the bridge. The captain gave me the con and quickly walked up the deck. He called again, asking me to call the chief engineer and first engineer to the fo'c'sle.

After twenty minutes, I watched the four officers walk down the deck—about the length of three football fields. I could see them talking.

On the bridge again, the captain ordered: "Darryl, the doors are dogged back down tightly. Swing her back on course."

"Roger that, Captain."

I still didn't know what was up. Then the satellite phone on the bridge rang, one of two on board; the second was in the captain's office. When the satellite phone rang, it was usually the home office or some important official call. Standard procedure on the bridge was to let it ring three times and pick it up only if the captain didn't answer. It rang only once.

After an hour the captain called a safety meeting. A third mate relieved me on the bridge, and we mustered in the mess hall.

The captain said, "Gentlemen, we're not in serious danger, but we sustained significant damage in the fo'c'sle. Half a dozen steel pillars that support the bow are bent and cracked. The ship is seaworthy, but needs to be repaired and inspected. We'll pull into Honolulu for a few days for repairs. In the meantime, we have a bad mess up in the fo'c'sle. Over a dozen drums of oil and grease broke free. Chemicals got knocked over, and a lot of supplies got mixed into the mess."

The crew listened in amazement, knowing what was coming next.

"Let's get a good night's sleep tonight and be ready to clean up the mess tomorrow. That'll be all."

The storm pulled away, and all spare hands were called to the bow. There was more damage than anyone had imagined. Gear was mixed in with oil and other lubricants. Many of the large steel pillars supporting the forepeak tank, extending seventy feet down, were bent, cracked, or destroyed. I'd never seen anything like it; neither had anyone else. But this wasn't the only time a ship I was on incurred serious damage from heavy winter seas in the North Pacific and the Gulf of Alaska.

Everyone pitched in to clean up the mess, and no one complained. It took several days, but we got things back in shipshape except for the cracked and bent supports. We steamed on to Honolulu, where repairs were completed. The crew looked on it as good duty, since we could go ashore for dinner, drinks, and to visit the local strip joints.

I finished the tour and went home and hung out with Susanna, who by that time had moved in with me. We were friends and lovers, and on a lot of nights, drinking partners. Things were just okay between us. I was an active alcoholic and drug abuser, and we had our disagreements. Several times, we were involved in drunken fights.

In July of 1996, I wanted to see an ex-girlfriend and convinced Susanna it was all very platonic. The stated purpose was "to catch up, just as friends." I met Kathy at J's Oyster Bar in downtown Portland. We immediately started drinking. Before long we were at my house ripping each other's clothes off. We then got dressed again and continued drinking. I thought Susanna was out of town for the night.

It was late. Kathy didn't want to go out again, but I had the urge to do some cocaine, so I jumped in a cab to score some. That night I snorted lines and drank vodka, a deadly potion that always got me in trouble. Nevertheless, I told myself it would be different this time.

After drinking and snorting cocaine for many hours, I headed home to a situation I never saw coming: two girlfriends in my house at the same time, both drunk. The police report from that night reads:

PORTLAND POLICE DEPARTMENT
INCIDENT REPORT
NARRATIVE

CASE ###########

ON 07-28-96, AT APPROXIMATELY 0332 HRS. I (OFC. DAVID DUMOND) WAS DISPATCHED TO ######### AVE FOR A REPORT OF A DOMESTIC DISTURBANCE. THE COMPLAINANT, SUSANNA NEWMAN[1], REPORTED HER BOYFRIEND, DARRYL HAGAR HAD ASSAULTED HER AND WAS NOW UPSTAIRS WITH A SHOTGUN. NEWMAN WAS CALLING FROM THE BASEMENT WHERE SHE WAS HIDING.

OFFICERS RESPONDING TO THE SCENE TOOK UP A PERIMETER AROUND THE RESIDENCE. WHILE OUTSIDE THE RESIDENCE I COULD HEAR A MALE LATER IDENTIFIED AS

---

[1] The report has been duplicated word for word, but some names have been changed to protect privacy.

HAGAR, IN THE LIVING ROOM YELLING FOR "SUE" TO COME UPSTAIRS AND CALL 911. COMMUNICATING WITH NEWMAN VIA DISPATCH, OFFICERS WERE ABLE TO GET NEWMAN TO EXIT THE RESIDENCE THROUGH THE BACK DOOR. AS SOON AS NEWMAN WAS OUT OF THE RESIDENCE OFFICERS MADE ENTRY INTO THE RESIDENCE AND FOUND HAGAR SITTING IN A CHAIR IN THE LIVING ROOM. HAGAR WAS NOT ARMED AND COOPERATED WITH THE OFFICERS COMMANDS. HAGAR WAS DETAINED IN HANDCUFFS UNTIL OFFICERS COULD LO-CATE AND SECURE THE FIREARM.

WHEN QUESTIONED ABOUT THE FIREARM HAGAR DENIED ANY KNOWLEDGE OF A FIREARM BEING DISPLAYED. HAGAR STATED HE HAD A SHOTGUN BUT HAD NOT SEEN OR TAK-EN IT OUT IN MONTHS. HAGAR STATED HE BELIEVED THE SHOTGUN MIGHT BE IN HIS BEDROOM CLOSET. SERGEANT WENTWORTH CHECKED THE CLOSET AND WAS UNABLE TO FIND THE SHOTGUN. HAGAR STATED IT MAY BE IN THE FRONT CLOSET BUT ONCE AGAIN IT WAS NOT THERE. AS SGT. WENTWORTH SEARCHED FOR THE SHOTGUN I SPOKE WITH HAGAR TO DETERMINE IF A CRIME HAD TAKEN PLACE. OF-FICER STROUT SPOKE WITH MS. NEWMAN.

NEWMAN ADVISED OFFICER STROUT THAT SHE AND HAGAR HAD GOTTEN INTO AN ARGUMENT AFTER HAGAR HAD GONE UPSTAIRS TO THE SPARE BEDROOM WITH HIS EX-GIRL-FRIEND. NEWMAN STATED THAT HAGAR HAD ASSAULTED HER, PUSHING HER, PUNCHING HER IN THE FACE AND CHOK-ING HER. NEWMAN STATED AFTER BEING ASSAULTED SHE GRABBED THE SHOTGUN BUT HAGAR TOOK IT AWAY FROM HER. NEWMAN STATED SHE FLED TO THE BASEMENT AND WAS NOT THREATENED WITH THE SHOTGUN.

HAGAR STATED THAT NEWMAN HAD BEEN JEALOUS BE-CAUSE HE HAD AN EX-GIRLFRIEND OVER. HAGAR STATED HE AND NEWMAN HAD ARGUED BUT AT NO TIME HAD ANY ASSAULT OCCURRED NOR HAD HIS SHOTGUN BEEN USED OR DISPLAYED. HAGAR WAS ARRESTED FOR DOMESTIC VIO-LENCE ASSAULT AND WAS TRANSPORTED TO CUMBERLAND COUNTY JAIL.

NEWMAN ADVISED HAGAR HAD GONE DOWNSTAIRS TO THE FIRST FLOOR WITH THE SHOTGUN AND SHE HAD HEARD A DOOR CLOSE BUT DID NOT KNOW WHERE HE HAD PUT THE GUN. OFFICERS BEGAN A SEARCH OF THE EXTERIOR OF THE RESIDENCE BUT COULD NOT LOCATE THE SHOTGUN. WHILE SEARCHING THE LIVING ROOM WHERE HAGAR HAD BEEN SITTING I FOUND THE SHOTGUN UNDER THE LOVE SEAT. THE SHOTGUN WHICH WAS NOT LOADED WAS CONFISCATED AND TAGGED INTO PROPERTY.

I TOOK A STATEMENT FROM MS. NEWMAN IN WHICH SHE RE-PORTED THAT AT ABOUT 0230 HRS. SHE WENT TO HAGAR'S HOUSE. NEWMAN STATED WHEN SHE ARRIVED HAGAR'S EX-GIRLFRIEND, KATHY REID, AND A MALE NAMED JOE WERE THERE. NEWMAN HAD BEEN OUT LOOKING FOR HAGAR WHO SHE BELIEVED WAS OUT GETTING SOME COCAINE. NEW-MAN STAYED AT THE RESIDENCE AND TALKED WITH KATHY AND JOE WHILE AWAITING HAGAR'S RETURN. AT APPROX. 0300 HRS. HAGAR RETURNED HOME. NEWMAN STATED THAT HAGAR WAS HIGH ON COKE. WHEN ASKED HOW SHE KNEW THIS SHE STATED SHE COULD TELL BY HIS EYES, HIS MAN-NERISMS AND HIS LATE RETURN HOME. NEWMAN STATED SHE HAS SEEN HAGAR THIS WAY WHEN HE HAS BEEN HIGH BEFORE. HAGAR AFTER COMING HOME SPOKE WITH JOE FOR A SHORT TIME AFTER WHICH JOE LEFT. A SHORT TIME

LATER KATHY SAID SHE WAS GOING TO BED AND WENT UPSTAIRS TO THE SPARE BEDROOM. KATHY WAS STAYING WITH HAGAR AT HIS INVITATION. HAGAR AND NEWMAN REMAINED DOWNSTAIRS TALKING.

AFTER TALKING AWHILE NEWMAN AND HAGAR WENT UPSTAIRS AS WELL. NEWMAN THOUGHT THEY WERE GOING TO BED BUT HAGAR WENT TO THE SPARE BEDROOM WHERE KATHY WAS STAYING. HAGAR TURNED TO NEWMAN AND TOLD HER TO LEAVE, THAT HE DID NOT WANT HER THERE. WHEN NEWMAN QUESTIONED HIM HAGAR REINFORCED HIS STATEMENT AGAIN TELLING HER TO GET OUT. NEWMAN HURT AND ANGRY SLAPPED HAGAR ACROSS THE FACE. HAGAR GRABBED NEWMAN BY THE THROAT AND STARTED CHOKING HER AS HE PUSHED HER BACKWARD OUT OF THE ROOM. HAGAR RELEASED NEWMAN AND WENT BACK INTO THE ROOM WITH KATHY CLOSING THE DOOR BEHIND HIM. NEWMAN REMAINED AT THE DOOR TRYING TO PUSH IT OPEN. HAGAR CONTINUED TO PUSH THE DOOR KEEPING IT CLOSED. UNABLE TO GET THE DOOR OPEN NEWMAN STAYED AT THE DOOR YELLING AT HAGAR TO OPEN IT. HAGAR FINALLY OPENED THE DOOR AND NEWMAN WALKED IN. HAGAR GRABBED NEWMAN AND PUSHED HER THE LENGTH OF THE ROOM PINNING HER TO THE CLOSET. HAGAR REPORTEDLY THEN PUNCHED NEWMAN ON THE LEFT CHEEK WITH A CLOSED FIST. WHEN HAGAR RELEASED NEWMAN SHE FLED TO THE FIRST FLOOR.

NEWMAN WENT TO THE FIRST FLOOR WHERE SHE GRABBED HAGAR'S SHOTGUN FROM THE FRONT CLOSET. NEWMAN STARTED BACK UP THE STAIRS BUT WAS STOPPED BY HAGAR WHO WAS COMING DOWN THE STAIRS. HAGAR GRABBED THE GUN AWAY FROM NEWMAN AND TOOK IT

DOWNSTAIRS. NEWMAN WENT TO THE UPSTAIRS BEDROOM WHERE KATHY WAS GETTING DRESSED. KATHY TOLD NEWMAN SHE WAS LEAVING AND THAT THEY NEEDED TO GET THINGS WORKED OUT. KATHY LEFT THE ROOM AND WENT DOWNSTAIRS TO LEAVE. HAGAR ATTEMPTED TO GET KATHY TO STAY BUT WAS UNABLE TO. KATHY LEFT THE RESIDENCE. HAGAR UPSET ABOUT KATHY LEAVING BEGAN YELLING AT NEWMAN. NEWMAN TOLD HAGAR SHE WAS GOING TO CALL THE POLICE AND WENT TO THE LIVINGROOM PHONE TO CALL. HAGAR FOLLOWED NEWMAN AND UNPLUGGED THE PHONE TO KEEP HER FROM CALLING. NEWMAN RAN TO THE UPSTAIRS PHONE BUT HAGAR FOLLOWED AND UNPLUGGED IT AS WELL. NEWMAN FLED TO THE BASEMENT WHERE SHE WAS ABLE TO USE THE BASEMENT PHONE TO CALL POLICE.

IN MY CONVERSATION WITH HAGAR I OBSERVED HE WAS VERY INTOXICATED AND APPEARED TO BE UNDER THE INFLUENCE OF COCAINE. BOTH OF HAGAR'S EYES WERE FULLY CONSTRICTED.

HAGAR AND NEWMAN HAVE A HISTORY OF DOMESTIC INCIDENTS. ON 03-05-96 NEWMAN REPORTED HAGAR HAD ASSAULTED HER. ON 03-07-96 HAGAR WAS SERVED A NOTICE OF TEMPORARY CEASE HARASSMENT. ON 04-29-96 POLICE WERE CALLED TO REMOVE HAGAR FROM NEWMAN'S RESIDENCE AT ######### ST, AND ON 09-25-95 POLICE HAD TO KEEP THE PEACE WHILE NEWMAN RETRIEVED HER KEYS AND PURSE FROM HAGAR'S HOME.

NEWMAN WAS ADVISED OF THE DOMESTIC VIOLENCE LAWS AND HER RIGHTS AND WAS PROVIDED A WRITTEN COPY. A CONDITION OF BAIL WAS SET STIPULATING HAGAR HAVE NO CONTRACT WITH NEWMAN UNTIL RESOLUTION OF THIS

CASE IN CRIMINAL COURT AND HE REFRAIN FROM USING ALCOHOL OR DRUGS.

Portland Police Department   *Ofc. David Dumand #92*

I had an argument with Susanna that night. When she got the unloaded shotgun, I took it away and hid it. When the cops showed up, I was so drunk I couldn't remember where I'd put it. The police seized the gun. I was the only one arrested—for domestic violence.

I'm not making excuses for my behavior; I deserved to be reigned in, and I'm truly embarrassed by the domestic violence. I also realize how lucky I was that I wasn't shot by some police officer passing by as we struggled with the shotgun or later when the police surrounded my house.

The D.A. ultimately said there were no grounds to convict me of domestic violence, since I was the homeowner, I didn't get out the gun, and Susanna wasn't injured. Though I wasn't convicted, the arrest remains on my record.

The police called later and told me I could have the gun back. I told them to keep it. I was drinking too much and doing too many drugs to have a gun around. And because of the cocaine, I was afraid the detective would get to know my face and follow me around.

CHAPTER TWENTY-SIX
SECOND MATE DOWN

I returned to work on October 6, 1996, joining the Overseas Chicago as second mate. No one in the company knew I'd been arrested for domestic violence. The work tour went well. Once again I pledged to turn my life around, keep my nose clean, and get a good job evaluation. I went above and beyond what most guys would do to make up for the pitfalls of being a crazy alcoholic at home and for my mood swings at sea. I was temperamental, always obsessing about how things should be done, and hard to get along with—traits of untreated alcoholism and drug addiction.

I stayed on the ship until December 11 and got off in Hawaii, a great place to end a work tour, since the company paid our transportation home and we could make our own arrangements. I saw it as a free vacation except for the hotel expense. I'd done it before and knew it was both enjoyable and dangerous.

Honolulu is a beautiful city, but like any other it has its rough areas, and I was good at finding them. I was an accident waiting to happen, but somehow was never arrested outside of Maine. My behavior was incredibly disgusting. I'd get off the ship, start drinking, run into some undesirable person, and buy some cocaine. The rest involved prostitution, seedy bars, and even seedier people. I'm lucky to have lived through it all. Nobody from the ship knew about my unsavory behavior. I had to protect my career, and I had my pride, so I hid a lot.

That December, the captain and chief engineer also stayed in Honolulu, the chief engineer just for the night and the captain for four days. I had reservations for a week. They asked me to go out with them, but I wanted to chase women and drink the way I needed to. I said I'd meet them for brunch the next morning.

I hit some strip joints. Honolulu allows the dangerous mix of full nudity and alcohol, not typical in the rest of the country. It was exactly what I was looking for. I drank until 4:00 a.m. then passed out in my hotel. The alcohol hit me hard, because I hadn't had a drink in almost three months.

The phone rang at 10:00 a.m. I was still asleep—and hurting.

"Good morning, Darryl, it's the captain."

"Hey, Cap. How ya doing?" I mumbled weakly.

"You're still in bed. Get up! We're having brunch with the chief engineer at Duke's and then I'm taking him to the airport. We're outside on the patio next to the beach. It's a gorgeous day," the captain said brightly.

"Okay, Captain, I'll see you in an hour."

I felt like throwing up. *Man, why did I agree to meet them? I'm feeling really bad.*

I drank some coffee, showered, and turned on the news. I somehow managed to hold down the coffee, which made me think I'd be all right at breakfast. My colleagues liked me, and I didn't want to change that by embarrassing them. I found them sitting on a deck near the beach drinking Heinekens. Seeing the beer made my stomach churn.

I was turning blue just thinking about drinking, but maybe a little hair of the dog would settle my system. We saluted our safely finished work tour; we had successfully carried three million barrels of crude oil without spilling a drop. I took a big swallow of beer, then another. Suddenly I looked like a blowfish with my mouth full of vomit. The chief engineer started laughing, but the captain was more excitable.

"You better not! You better not! Run over to the railing, Darryl. Quick!" he yelled.

I ran fifteen feet to the railing and threw up on Waikiki Beach. The beer came up first, then the coffee. I turned around and both the captain and chief engineer were laughing, but the rest of the patrons were horrified. I buried the vomit in the sand with my sneaker.

"I'm not feeling well. I should be in bed," I shrugged.

In my mind it was just another story for the ship. I was already legendary as the hardest worker, the hardest partier, the most unpredictable, and for having the craziest things happen to me.

A captain once told me, "The only person I worry about getting pissed off and quitting on the spot is you, Darryl." But a sailor can't just walk off a ship, especially an officer. Regulations require a certain number of licensed officers and certified crewmembers for a ship to sail legally. If an officer quit and held up a vessel, the Coast Guard could revoke his license. It rarely happened.

We drank a few more Heinekens, and the captain left to take the chief engineer to the airport. I hung out with the captain a few more days, eating out, surfing, and snorkeling. We took a jeep to the North Shore to see the Banzai Pipeline, watching the huge breakers and world-class surfing competitions. We drank a few beers, but I watched myself.

In those four days, I never once told the captain how I struggled with alcohol and drugs. I never shared my father's suicide with him—or with hardly anyone else at work. I didn't want to look like I was making excuses, and I certainly didn't need anyone's pity. I kept my home life at home and was careful not to reveal anything that could be used against me later.

After the captain flew home, my hesitation about partying left as if by magic. I drank excessively every day. The night before I left, I packed my gear. I had learned to plan ahead for the aftereffects of drinking. If I drank too much, I'd still be ready to fly—in any condition. I knew myself well enough to prepare for the worst. Most of the time the worst is exactly what happened.

I had time for one more place for my last partying in Honolulu. I looked up at the sign in bright flashing lights: "Miss Saigon Passion," a joint with good-looking Vietnamese girls who did shows totally nude. As I went in, the bouncer stopped me.

He was all business. "Everyone must give a credit card and sign the receipt ahead of time. If you don't use your credit card, we'll rip up the receipt."

"Wait a minute. You want me to sign a blank credit card receipt and trust your nude bar before I even use it?" I asked in disbelief.

"Some people walk out on their bills. Don't worry, it's all on the up and up."

"Whatever," I said drunkenly. Someone swiped my Visa from First National Bank of Damariscotta, Maine. I signed the blank receipt. I hoped nobody I knew would see the receipt with "Miss Saigon Passion" at the top. It was my boyhood town, where rumors spread like wildfire.

I ordered a Budweiser and watched the girls dance. It was a low-end place where the women simulated sex acts, like squatting down on a beer bottle. I shouldn't have been there in the first place, but there I was.

The next thing I knew, I was waking up at my hotel. It was mid-morning; my flight was at noon. I didn't remember how I got back to the hotel. At that time, blackout drinking was a dangerously frequent occurrence, a sign of my worsening alcoholism that I ignored for years.

I rifled through my pockets. No money, not even a dollar. That was always a bad sign. I had my driver's license and my Visa card. *Whew!* Then I found my Visa receipt from Miss Saigon Passion. I had spent $200 drinking, and—*what the hell! No way would I leave a $400 tip at a bar!*

I was very hung over and had a twenty-hour travel day to look forward to. I dreaded both the flight and telling the sex club story to Visa to get the charge removed. But I had to do it; $400 was a lot of money.

I called Visa from the airport and spoke to Shelley, explaining that a nightclub had put a fraudulent charge on my card. Shelley asked the name of the club. Completely embarrassed, I told her.

"One more time, Mr. Hagar. I'm not sure I heard that right."

"Miss Saigon Passion."

The woman giggled hysterically. After everything else, now the Visa lady was laughing at me.

"I don't think it's very funny, Shelley. It's also unprofessional. I made a mistake, got scammed, and you're laughing about it?" I yelled.

"I'm sorry, Mr. Hagar," she said, still giggling. "But you have to admit, it's pretty funny."

"I don't think it's the least bit funny, and I feel like talking to your boss," I yelled again.

"Okay, I'm really sorry. You caught me by surprise. What you have to do is call the bank that issued the Visa card."

"Okay, thanks," I said, completely disgusted, and slammed down the phone.

There was no way I was telling that story to someone who might know me or my family. They'd tell everyone in town, and I'd be a laughingstock. I decided I'd rather eat the $400. *Oh, well. Another lesson learned in the school of hard knocks.* I flew home suffering through yet another hangover.

In April 1997 I was again aboard the Overseas Chicago. We had carried our final load of crude oil to Los Angeles. We were due to clean up the vessel, complete shipyard repairs, and carry out an inspection period. After discharging the oil, we went out to sea and used high temperature/high pressure water to clean the massive oil tanks. We then blew oil vapors out of the tanks with an inert, non-explosive gas. Oxygen blowers displaced the inert gas so we could inspect the tanks.

It's dangerous work. You first climb down a set of slippery ladders. It's dark inside the tanks, and the oily residue is extremely slick. You also have to watch out for the sumps, four-by-six-foot holes aft where the liquid pools for pumping.

A pumpman, third mate, and I went into the tanks carrying buckets of tools to do inspections and tighten nuts and bolts on dresser couplings. There was still a foot of water covering the bottom; I hadn't called the chief mate to have him suck the tank dry.

As we were working, the ship rolled, and a bucket of tools slid away. I reached out to grab it and stepped into the water covering the sump. I fell almost five feet. My hip hit the thick steel side, and pain immediately ran through my body.

"On the bridge! On the deck! We have a man down! We have a man down in the sump, and he's hurt. We need help!" the pumpman cried into his radio.

The third mate ran over to help me out of the hole. I tried to climb out of the sump as the third mate hopped over the pipeline and somehow landed in the sump right next to me.

"We have two men down! I need help right now!" the pumpman yelled into the radio.

The bridge rang a general alarm for all hands on deck to make a rescue.

"Darryl, are you okay?" the pumpman asked.

I was able to pull myself out of the hole. I knew I was seriously hurt, but everything was still attached. "I'm okay. Check on the third mate," I said.

The third mate wasn't injured. "I'm okay. I think we'd better worry about Darryl. I landed in the water. He fell on steel."

My hip was killing me. I needed to get out of the tank fast. The people above wanted to put me in a litter and winch me out.

"Nobody is winching me out of this tank! I'm not gonna be hanging seventy feet in the air relying on a piece of rope. I'll walk out!" I said forcefully into the radio.

I limped over to the ladder and with help managed to climb. At the top, several crewmembers hoisted me out. I looked at my leg; it was starting to swell. I would have a hard time working for awhile.

I hobbled to the ship's hospital. They cleaned me up and reported an emergency via the satellite phone. It was decided we'd see how I responded overnight. The leg was iced and I was given pain medication. My leg seemed okay. The next day I stood bridge watches all day. I hobbled around to look at the radars and take a position and then sat in the captain's chair.

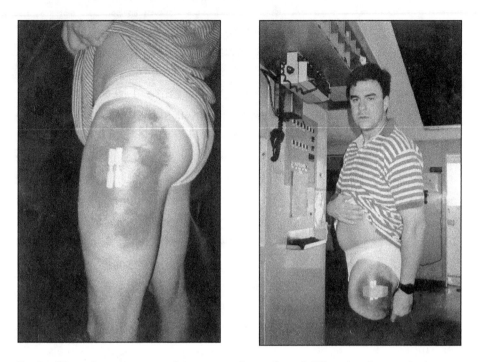

Left: Showing my massive contusion after falling in the tank on ship. Right: On the bridge the day after my fall inside the tank.

The crew continued tank inspections around the clock and to ready the ship for repairs. We would go either to Astoria, Oregon, or Port Angeles, Washington, for repairs and Coast Guard and ABS inspections, so we headed north. We were more than a hundred miles offshore.

The second night my leg changed for the worse. It swelled from my hip past my knee. My hip bone was screaming in pain, and my leg turned strange colors. The chief mate came to check on me.

"How are you feeling? A little better?" the chief mate asked wishfully.

"Actually, Mate, I'm doing a lot worse. I'm worried about infection and losing my leg."

He looked at the injury. "It looks like it's doing okay."

"Are you kidding me? Look at my side. It's screwed up. I'm in a lot of pain. I need to get off this ship before there's permanent damage." I was angry that he had the gall to tell me it looked okay.

He advised me to get some rest. I told him I'd like to talk to the captain. The chief mate was concerned about my well being, but I also sensed he was worried about not having dried out the tanks.

The captain was concerned and used the satellite phone to call the hospital. An hour later he surprised me. "We've decided to get you to a hospital as soon as possible. We're headed for the sea buoy outside the Golden Gate Bridge. A boat will take you ashore to San Francisco."

I told him he'd made the right decision, and he agreed. We would arrive the next morning. Someone would pack my gear and bring me my meals so I could stay off my leg.

"If you need anything, let me know," he said with compassion.

"Thank you, Captain. I'll be able to come back when my leg is better, right?"

He assured me an accident wouldn't affect my standing with the company.

That night my leg was throbbing and screaming in pain. It was twice its normal size. I had to wear coveralls; my leg wouldn't fit inside my pants.

An X-ray revealed signs of infection, but nothing was broken. I had a hip pointer (a bruise to the bone) that I can still find when I press it. I was given an antibiotic, and I flew home to recuperate. I endured the long and painful cross-country flight with the aid of several alcoholic drinks.

My leg and hip eventually healed, and I went back to work. Maritime Overseas was good to me. They paid me for all missed work and took care of all my travel and medical bills. They were always a good company to work for, even if they didn't realize they had an alcoholic mate who needed help.

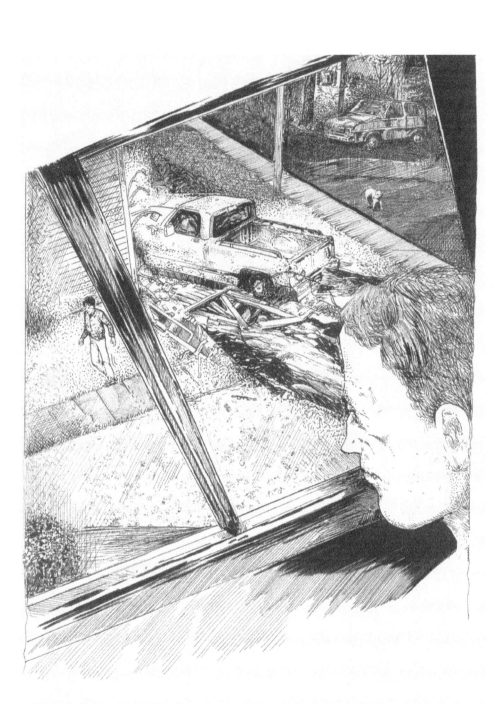

GLENN CHADBOURNE

CHAPTER TWENTY-SEVEN
MY OWN (ALMOST) OIL SPILL

I'd been home for awhile when I realized that two approaching events in my life were on a collision course. I was due to go back to work, and about the same time I'd be observing my thirty-fifth birthday.

I'd have to be careful about how I celebrated so I wouldn't screw up my return to work. Plus I had another worry—I drank more each time a new work tour got closer because of my anxiety about going back to sea. I didn't want to be in jail when I was supposed to be on an airplane flying to a vessel.

I got word that I was to rejoin the Overseas Chicago on April 2, 1998—my thirty-fifth birthday. At first I was disappointed, but I still had a few days before I flew out, so I would celebrate early. I was going to whoop it up; you only turn thirty-five once.

After my second OUI the Coast Guard had given me a warning, and I promised myself I wouldn't drink and drive. For five years I faithfully took cabs. Yet as time passed, I again flirted with drinking and driving. Before long I was doing it regularly. I had set a new clock on the next time bomb, and it was ticking away.

I jumped in my red 360 V-8 Dodge Ram four-by-four with its "Old Salt" vanity plates. My friends joked that I should sell it because all the cops were out to get me for spreading red paint all over Portland. I had drunkenly run into a few things and had been on high speed police chases in my infamous truck.

I drove to a bar on Portland's East Side. I should have taken a cab, since I planned to get drunk celebrating my birthday. But in my alcoholic denial, I told myself I'd catch a cab home. My friend Belvis met me at the bar and bought me a birthday drink. Vodka was my liquor of choice. My best friend, Pusherman, had nicknamed my Absolut and orange juice "high juices," because when I drank them I got very high, very unpredictable, and made very poor decisions. Another buddy, Go-Go, bought me a few more high juices. I was soon feeling no pain. We partied the night away, and before I knew it everyone was going home. I was the last one at the bar.

It was past midnight. I decided I was too drunk to stay, but okay to drive home. I jumped into Old Salt and drove three miles around Back Bay, past the University of Southern Maine, to my neighborhood. I live in a two-story Cape Cod home with a full basement. Because I live by a large college, all the properties are on half-acre lots, and the driveways separate the crowded houses. I turned into my driveway much too fast and—CRASH!

I didn't realize what was happening as my half-ton truck smashed into the side of my own house. I found out later that I caused $1,000 in damage to my truck and $500 to my house.

I looked at my truck for two seconds and decided to deal with it in the morning. I didn't pick up the debris in the driveway; I was too drunk to bend over. I stumbled into the house, turned up some rock music, and drank a 16-ounce Budweiser. I heard pounding at the back door. Barely able to focus, I opened the door, beer in hand, expecting to see a buddy.

Two uniformed Portland police officers stood in the open doorway.

"Are you Darryl Hagar?" one of the officers asked as Led Zeppelin blared loudly in the background.

"Yes, I am. Come on in, and I'll turn down this music."

"Mr. Hagar, is that your red pickup in the driveway?"

"Yes, it's my truck. What about it?" I responded defensively.

"We just received a phone call that you were drunk and you just ran into the side of your house."

"Who said that?" I asked aggressively.

"It doesn't matter. Were you just driving that truck?"

I was drunk, and I did stupid things when I was drunk, but I still knew how to play the game.

"Hell, no! I haven't driven that truck for three days!" I insisted.

"Mr. Hagar, we know you drove drunk and ran into the side of your house." The officer was trying to get me to admit to driving drunk.

I yelled, "I'm telling you, I haven't driven that truck in three days! I want you out of my house right now! I'm calling my fucking lawyer!"

Although the Portland police knew of my crazy drunken behavior because of my arrest for domestic violence in 1996, I hadn't been convicted. They probably hoped I'd crack, thinking this was their chance to finally bust me. But this time there were no eyewitnesses; my neighbor heard but didn't see the crash. I suspect the officers felt the hood of my truck and knew I was lying, but they couldn't prove it, so they left.

As drunk as I was, I clearly remember thinking I was too wild and crazy not to have a lawyer on retainer, and I promised myself I'd call one the next day. But I never did. I locked the doors and turned off the lights and stereo. Then I crashed, hoping the police wouldn't bother me again.

I woke up with my head pounding, trying to remember how I got home. I finally remembered celebrating my birthday on the East Side. Suddenly I recalled talking to the cops, but I couldn't remember why. I looked out the window at my truck. *Oh, my God!*

As I ran to inspect the damage, I began to remember bits and pieces. I had clipped the side of the house, scattering debris all over. The right side of my truck was smashed, the mirror and front light busted out. The oil tank fill pipe had received the most damage. I inspected it and then ran into the basement to make sure there wasn't an oil spill. The tank was intact but had been moved several inches. I went back outside and quickly picked up most of the debris; after all, the cops could come back for a second interrogation. I then called the oil company and anxiously asked the technician to send someone to replace the fill pipe as soon as possible.

"What's the problem with it, Mr. Hagar?"

"You want to know the truth?" I asked with a hint of sarcasm.

"Of course. We need to know what happened in order to fix it correctly."

"I was celebrating my thirty-fifth birthday last night and pulled into my driveway too fast and rubbed the side of my house. I knocked it completely off. That's between me and you, okay?"

"Oh, sheesh. Okay, Mr. Hagar, I'll send a couple of guys right over."

I was hardly able to believe what I'd done. But despite always having to do damage control because of my drinking, I never considered quitting. I never thought to slow down and examine my actions. My family had tried to tell me to slow down or stop. My job had told me to change or face dismissal. Even my drinking buddies worried about how crazy I got when I drank. My denial was unbelievably strong. I really didn't think drinking was the problem.

I blamed my drinking on my dad's death, my career in the Merchant Marine, on going away to sea for months at a time, or on the fact that I was high strung. I drank to manage all that. I didn't know that alcoholism is a disease or that when it progresses into the late stages, it's very difficult to stop.

I was also a typical drunk in that I didn't think. I was lucky I didn't run over someone's kid or hit some vehicle head on. I could have driven into somebody bedroom while they were sleeping. I could have spent years in prison for vehicular manslaughter. I could have killed someone.

The oil company techs arrived. They were amazed at what they saw: a heavily damaged truck, a broken oil system, and a hung over Merchant Marine officer. Within a few hours everything was repaired, replaced, and in good working order. The only thing left was my damaged vehicle. I drove it to an auto body repair shop and said I didn't have insurance; I'd pay cash. My insurance was already crazy high from my two OUIs. I'd eat the accident and use it as a lesson to myself to not drink and drive. If I gave myself an expensive penalty, it just might keep me from getting behind the wheel when I was drinking.

I always quickly fixed my messes and just as quickly went back to the same behavior. What I needed was a twelve-step program to open my eyes to what I really was. I was and am an alcoholic, and I simply cannot take the first drink. When I drink, all bets are off. Nothing is beyond the realm of possibility, including whatever worst case scenario I could think of. And I'm sure that had I not reached bottom, I would still be attending the school of hard knocks.

But in this instance, what lesson had I learned? The cops lacked an eyewitness. The oil company made repairs. The shop fixed my truck like new. I thought I had another good story to tell, and I continued to drink.

What's more, I *never* considered what my poor neighbors had to endure during the worst of my alcoholism. For that I'm deeply apologetic. I asked my neighbor, Hal Cozens, a Jet Blue Airline Pilot, to tell me candidly what it was like to live next to a drug addict and alcoholic for years. I wasn't surprised by his statement, but with typical alcoholic mentality I carried resentment over his remarks for a few days.

Darryl was a neighbor we didn't really know. As a neighborhood, we only knew he was home because of the constant partying at all hours—with no respect for anyone who lived around him.

I lived next door, across the driveway. Many times I was awakened at night because the police had arrived to retrieve cab fare Darryl hadn't paid. Darryl also locked himself out repeatedly. He came home drunk and opened his noisy garage door. Or he'd set an aluminum ladder against his house, jimmy open a second floor window, and squeeze in.

There were carloads of people coming and going and all-night parties on his back deck. I often looked out my bedroom window to see women peeing on my front lawn, people throwing beer bottles in my yard, and rowdiness at all hours, both inside and out. I saw drug paraphernalia on his kitchen countertops, along with lots of tempers flaring, slamming doors, and drunks stumbling in and out of his house.

Although tempted many times, neither I nor my family ever contacted the police. The neighborhood knew when Darryl was home from sea; that's when the parties began and the delivery trucks came. We knew we were in for at least two months of hell. Besides the loud partying, I was aware of the heavy drinking, confirmed the next morning by the noise of Darryl filling trash bags with empty beer cans and liquor bottles.

The neighbors across the street—a married couple, both college professors—expressed a lot of anger about the situation at his house and that they wouldn't continue to tolerate all the late-night partying and hollering.

Darryl's physical appearance changed after he first moved into our neighborhood in 1990. He looked like a train wreck when he was home from sea, putting on a lot of weight and looking rundown. He also became belligerent with anyone who challenged him or suggested he was in the wrong.

My family was negatively affected by Darryl's constant unruly behavior. One day, people from his house cut flowers off my mom's lilac bushes. She was beside herself that people could be so rude. My nephew saw cocaine used in Darryl's kitchen and saw a couple having sex in a pickup truck in Darryl's driveway.

My whole family hated to see Darryl return from sea. We all said, "Oh shit. Three months of hell until he goes back to his ship." The sky would blacken upon his arrival, and the day Darryl left again the sky would clear, the sun would come back out, and life would return to normal until the next round. It was three months of peace and quiet and then three months of pure hell. This went on for fifteen years.

One night in 1998 I was awakened by a loud crash. It was late, more like early morning; I thought there'd been a car accident right in front of my house. I saw nothing in the street, so I looked out a side window, and there was Darryl's truck. I thought, Damn, he hit the house! *He tore off the oil fill pipe and the phone/cable junction box. He got out of his truck, obviously drunk, and stumbled into his house. I couldn't believe it!*

Shortly thereafter the police arrived and woke me up by beating on his door. I figured one of our neighbors across the street had called them. I'm not sure what the police did once they got inside, but I don't remember them arresting him.

I was once again left to shake my head in disbelief! The next day I saw the oil repairman at the house and later the phone repair service. Later Darryl explained to me he did more than $1,000 in damage to his truck that night and hundreds of dollars of damage to his house, driving home drunk once again. It was just another chapter in the soap opera of living next door to Darryl. I kept thinking, What will it be next?

I finally decided it was time to put up a fence to separate Darryl's property from mine. If nothing else, it might force the girls to pee on his side and keep the beer cans and bottles where they'd been consumed. It helped, and I wished I'd done it years earlier. —Captain Hal Cozens, *Jet Blue pilot and neighbor*

I finally grasped how awful a neighbor I'd been, and how I had negatively affected my entire neighborhood with my chaotic, unruly lifestyle. I had no grounds for resentment against anyone who ever had to deal with my drunken behavior. It's truly amazing how blind an alcoholic can be and how easily I justified my actions. But that kind of thinking didn't come to me until long after my thirty-fifth birthday. I had a long way yet to go.

Captain Hal Cozens, Jet Blue Airlines pilot and my neighbor.

GLENN CHADBOURNE

CHAPTER TWENTY-EIGHT
BABY CHANGES

Once again I went back to work with my tail between my legs after weaseling out of yet another potential OUI. I knew I was getting out of hand. On the Overseas Chicago I hoped to dry out and get my act back together.

My friends used to tell me I was lucky; when I was on the ships for three months I didn't drink, allowing my body to rest. By contrast, they drank and drugged twelve months a year. It's possible that the ill effects of alcohol and drug abuse were slowed by going to sea. Just the same, I partied for three months at home, doing damage to my liver, lungs, and brain.

The stress of running 900-foot supertankers took a toll and did its own long-term damage. When I returned to sea, I worked seven days a week, twelve hours a day, eighty-four hours a week, for three months straight, consumed gallons of coffee, and handled stressful events daily.

Picture a bunch of guys working and eating together—and often screaming at each other—for months on end in huge floating steel prisons. The men are isolated from the public. There are no newspapers, no TV, no women, and—after the Exxon Valdez—no booze. The ships quickly turned into pressure cookers, where the goal was to do everything faster and better, with no way for the men to blow off steam other than at each other.

The result for me was high blood pressure, controlled with medication, and a screwed up stomach and throat, resulting in acid reflux disease. Then there was the constant depression that went untreated for years. I'm still not sure which did more damage: the stress of the job for six months or the destructive partying the other six months.

At sea again, I had time to reflect on how badly I'd screwed up. During each vacation my behavior seemed to get worse. I'd been careful for years about not drinking and driving, knowing the Coast Guard wouldn't tolerate a third OUI. Now I was sliding backward, trying to "control" my drinking and driving. It wasn't working. I knew I had to come up with a solution. I considered trying to quit drinking and drugging altogether.

My work tour lasted from April 2 to June 26, 1998. When I went home I decided to see if I could control myself. But after just a few days, I found myself in a bar again, drunk. One night during that summer of 1998 I was in a bar called Raoul's Roadside Attraction, very drunk and feeling amorous. My old girlfriend Jen walked in, wearing tight little shorts and a sexy top, looking pretty hot to me.

It's difficult to estimate the number of times Darryl and I split up since we started dating in 1993. One time Darryl called from sea trying to rekindle our relationship. But I had decided I could no longer continue with this dysfunctional relationship and his constant partying. If Darryl was partying, I wanted to party with him; I wanted to drink more and more as time passed. Drinking got us into a lot of trouble. We fought a lot. That was part of the lifestyle: constant dysfunction. Eventually I became so dependent on him emotionally it was sick. He was all I had, all I wanted, and it wasn't healthy. I was so proud when I was finally strong enough to live my life without being his girlfriend.

In 1998, Darryl had been home a couple of months, and we hadn't spoken. I was doing my own thing; he was doing his. One night in a bar I saw him from across the room, and he smiled. It was the strangest feeling. We had never gone that long without speaking. I missed him.

We went to my apartment that night. Sitting on my couch, he told me he loved me and wanted to be with me. He had just needed time to realize it. We'd been drinking, but these were all the things I wanted him to say! He said them all on his own. Knowing him the way I did, I believed him. I really did.

The next day, Darryl said the same things. He sounded so sincere. He wasn't the kind of man to say "I love you" often; if he talked that way when he was sober, he meant it. When he was sober, I'd never known Darryl to say something because he thought I wanted to hear it. So I really listened. I told him I'd try just once more. It was all I had left.

Within two days he asked me to move in. Two weeks went by, and Darryl said, "I want to give you a baby." For years I'd asked Darryl for a baby. We weren't married, and I wasn't the type to trap him into pregnancy, so I pleaded with him at times. To hear him tell me this of his own will, to hear him tell me that he loved me and only wanted to be with me, was like a dream. He was the only man I had ever loved.

We started trying to get pregnant right away. I was ovulating at the time and took a pregnancy test just two days after trying. It was positive! We were both a bit in shock. Darryl has since told me he was in denial. He wanted me to take another test a couple of days later, which also came back positive. Darryl still wasn't convinced and told me to go to my doctor.

When I came home and told him the test was positive, I think he was more convinced. In denial still? Maybe. We were both somewhat shocked and excited. I mean, a baby? Us? It was all happening so fast.
—Jennifer

That night at Raoul's, it wasn't long before I was hitting on Jen. I made out with her at the bar. Then we went back to her place and made mad, passionate love all night. She asked me if I wanted to have a baby with her, like she'd done in the past, but this time was different. Without saying anything, I actually considered it. Maybe a baby was what I needed to finally stabilize my life. Had the answer been right in front of me all the time?

We had never used birth control, but never had any close calls or worried about getting pregnant. I used the pull-out method, and it worked well in our case. She didn't know it, but suddenly I was seriously thinking about giving her the child that she had begged for over the years. I had never taken her request seriously. My reaction was always, *Yeah, right, who me? A baby? I don't think so.*

But that summer when she asked again, it hit me like a ton of bricks: *I need to be a dad to save my own life.* At the same time I figured my lifestyle was so out of control that the last thing I needed was to get married. A wife gives her husband a hard time when he drinks too much and marriage can often bring as much chaos as it can stability.

So that August I rented an oceanfront room at the Brunswick Hotel in Old Orchard Beach. Jen and I made love all weekend, on the bed, on the bathroom sink, on the balcony outside under the stars, and I didn't pull out once. Of course, being a raging alcoholic and cocaine addict, I didn't give a lot of thought to the responsibilities of being a dad.

Jen soon came to me with news that would change my life forever.

"Darryl, I think I'm pregnant," she said nervously, looking for my reaction.

"Why do you think that, Jen?"

"I just know. I feel different. I'm going to take a pregnancy test. Do you want to go to the drugstore with me to get one?"

I was speechless for a few moments. Though I had thought having a baby would stabilize my life, reality hit me hard.

"Darryl, do you want to come with me or not?" Jen asked.

I finally said, "Okay, let's go to the CVS across the bridge in South Portland."

My head was spinning. *Is this really happening?* At the store, Jen jumped out and said she'd go in the bathroom and take the test. She came out after fifteen minutes and showed me the test strip.

"I'm pregnant, Darryl, look!" she said excitedly.

The strip had a faint red stripe on it.

"It's not red like the directions said. It's supposed to be a solid red stripe. I don't think you're pregnant," I said.

"Darryl, are you kidding me?" Jen yelled. "You said you wanted a baby. We've been having sex and not pulling out. And now I'm pregnant, and you're in denial. For godsakes, Darryl, will you grow up?!"

I asked her to take another pregnancy test a few days later. This time it showed a solid red stripe. I now began to accept that we were going to be parents. I was going to be a daddy.

"See, Darryl? I told you. We're gonna have a baby!"

Jen went to the doctor, who confirmed what we already knew and put her on a nutrition/vitamin plan. She immediately quit smoking and drinking. She had never done drugs, so that wasn't a concern. Soon Jen's belly began to grow. My belly stayed full of booze.

I went back to sea September 24 and stayed on board until two weeks before Christmas, giving me a lot of time to think about having a baby. I was nervous about becoming a father and still in denial about my drug and alcohol issues. Soon I'd become responsible for the life of another human being. But I could barely keep myself alive. How would I be able to raise a child?

Jen had an ultrasound and called while I was in Alaska, excited to tell me that the doctors had seen a penis. We were going to have a boy. I was very pleased. Jen knew I wanted to have a son. What she didn't know was the reason. I knew with my lifestyle I might not be around long; I wanted to leave behind a legacy, a son to carry on my name.

When I arrived home that December I tried to drown myself in alcohol. I was confused about having a child, and my substance abuse increased. I was medicating myself around the clock—and getting drunk more than once a day.

I drank in the morning and kept going until I passed out in the afternoon. Then I woke up and drank half the night away. I'd come home drunk out of my mind and crank up the stereo, blaring Lynyrd Skynyrd, the Allman Brothers, Bad Company, Led Zeppelin, and Eric Clapton. I never once considered Jen's feelings. After being awakened by the music, Jen would come downstairs, and we'd get into a bad argument about how disrespectful I was. She eventually stomped off to bed. I continued to play music.

In denial and drunk again, wearing an Alaskan red fox Arctic hat.

Jen gained forty-five pounds. She and the baby were healthy, but she was uncomfortable and I wasn't supporting her the way I should have been. In truth, I was a mess. I had no soul, no conscience, no spirituality. The devil lived inside me, and he was happy with me. All the crazy things I did when I was drinking and how I treated Jen during the pregnancy are what bring me the most guilt today.

That winter I only stayed home seven weeks. I needed to make extra money since I expected to be home longer when Jen had the baby. I sailed first on the 700-foot gasoline tanker Overseas Vivian and then was sent to the 900-foot crude oil tanker Overseas Boston because of a temporary lack of work, causing me to bump the regular second mate down to third mate. That ship had a reputation for being cliquey; it would likely be a tough trip.

I had seven years more experience than the younger second mate. I told him it was nothing personal and that I remembered helping train him years earlier. He was understanding, but the captain was upset that the company had demoted his permanent second mate for a guy he'd never met. As a result, the captain's spite spilled out at me every day. Once he even yelled at me because he'd lost his pen.

We were in pilotage waters, and I went over to the pilot and said quietly, "Would you get that upset if you lost a pen? Look at the way this captain acts. Another guy with tankeritis. He's half crazy from being on these tankers too long. And everyone pays the price."

The pilot just shook his head. I wasn't the easiest man to get along with either; sometimes I deserved to catch grief, but not for a lost pen. The problem for the captain was that I was a competent mate. I had years of experience and was worth my salt. Plus I learned the vessel as quickly as I could. I went down to the pump room on my own time to study the intricate pipelines and the direction the oil flowed so I'd know what valves to open and close and when.

I stayed on the ship for a month, hoping to do a long work tour. We were still at sea when I got a call on the satellite phone.

"Hi, Darryl, this is Jen."

"What's happening? Is everything okay? Is the baby okay?" I asked, surprised and anxious.

"I'm okay. The baby's okay. But I wasn't feeling good, so I saw the doctor. He put me on bed rest. I need you to come home and help me." She started to cry.

"Okay, Jen, I'll tell the captain. I'm sure the company will find me a relief. I'll let you know what they say. Just take it easy, and I'll be home soon, okay?"

"Okay, Darryl, thank you," she said sincerely.

I talked to the old man. He said he'd call the company right away. After a few minutes he came to my stateroom.

It was the first time the captain had treated me humanely. "Darryl, the company understands. We'll be in Port Angeles in a few days, so don't worry." He said I could call Jen on the satellite phone to let her know when I'd be home.

"Thanks, Captain."

The satellite phone cost $10 a minute, so it wasn't used much. But in emergencies, the company and the captains were understanding. I called Jen and told her to I'd be home soon. Of course, I drank the entire flight. At home I hugged Jen. The doctors had put her on bed rest because she was dilated to four centimeters, and it was still too early for the baby to come.

I tried to be as available as I could for Jen, but alcohol and anxiety about parenthood ruled me. Jen wasn't able to do much, so I helped with meals, laundry, grocery shopping, and housecleaning. At one point she thought she was having the baby. The hospital said it was a false alarm, but the nurses said it would be soon.

Since everything apparently was fine, I decided to go to a sports bar a quarter mile from home to watch the Boston Bruins play the Carolina Hurricanes in the Stanley Cup playoffs. The Bruins hadn't won an NHL championship since Bobby Orr in 1972, and I was excited about their chances. A Bruins fanatic, I wasn't going to miss the game.

I asked Jen, "Is it okay if I go down to Bleachers and watch the hockey game?"

"Yes. Come home after the game, please. I'll call you if I go into labor."

"If you start having contractions, call the bar and ask for the 6'1" guy in a black Boston Bruins jacket."

"Just make sure you come right home after the game," she insisted.

"I will." I kissed her and walked to the bar.

Bleachers was packed with screaming fans. It was a great game, and I was enjoying myself. The game was tied and there were just a few minutes left, when I noticed the bar manager was on the phone. His eyes worriedly scanned the crowd.

Suddenly he shouted, "Is there a Darryl Hagar here?"

I nudged my way through the noisy crowd, and he handed me the phone. It was Jen. *Shit, now what?*

"Darryl, I need you to come home. I think I'm having the baby to-night." She was crying.

"Okay, honey, calm down. Are you having contractions?" I asked, one eye still on the TV screen. The game had just gone into overtime.

"Yes, I'm having contractions. My water hasn't broken, but the contractions are strong."

"How far apart?"

"Three minutes."

"I'm going to watch the rest of the game," I said. "If the contractions get closer or your water breaks, call and I'll run home. Don't worry; I'm close by."

"Okay. Just come home right after the game, please. I love you."

I ordered another 22-ounce Budweiser. The bar manager looked at me in disbelief. I later asked Jen what she said to him. When she told him to look for a tall guy wearing a Bruins jacket, he said there were ten guys like that. She then yelled, "I'm pregnant and having a baby right now!" That's when he yelled my name.

The Bruins scored, and the crowd went crazy. I was jumping up and down high-fiving, while Jen was at home having contractions. Clearly, I was a sick man. My decision-making was so screwed up, I couldn't even stay with the mother of my child as she was about to have my baby. Neither did I care that my son would likely be born while I was intoxicated. Alcoholism had made me an evil man.

I'm ashamed of what happened next. The Bruins won, and I went to my favorite bar for one quick drink at last call. I didn't have a cell phone, and Jen didn't know where I was. She wouldn't be able to contact me if she needed to. I had a tall vodka and orange juice and then headed home. Jen was lying on the couch. She didn't know I'd gone to another bar, and I didn't tell her. I was half drunk when I walked in and asked how she was doing.

"I'm not doing well. I need to go to the hospital!"

"Calm down. I'm here. How far apart are the contractions?"

"About three minutes."

"Let's try to get some rest. You're still not ready, honey. I don't want to drink and drive, and I don't want to be under the influence in the hospital. The nurse said you wouldn't be able to talk if you were having the baby right away. Let's see if you can sleep."

I talked her into going upstairs, but she moaned and tossed and turned and kept bugging me to take her to the hospital. After a few hours, I had sobered up. We drove to Maine Medical Center, but after a few hours the contractions stopped and they sent her home.

The doctors told us that having sex would induce labor, so on May 3 at 9:00 a.m. we made love. Within fifteen minutes, Jen began having contractions. I knew this was it. We got her checked into the hospital. She had two female doctors. One was an intern, the other an experienced baby doctor. Tired of false alarms, I took the experienced doctor aside.

"Jen is as big as a house and a week past her due date. We've already been in twice on false alarms. Why don't we induce labor? It's going to get worse for a vaginal birth if she gets any bigger."

Dr. Jenkins didn't want to commit to inducing labor just yet. So we waited another two hours, which turned into four hours, then six . . .

The night passed, and the sun came up. The contractions stopped. *This is getting crazy. I need a beer.* I again asked the doctors to induce labor, but they still wanted to wait.

Eight hours, ten hours . . .

She'll understand if I call one of my buddies to bring some beer to the hospital parking lot, won't she?

I was an alcoholic starving for a drink. I was cranky, impatient, and certainly not doing Jen any good. I had two options: Try to move things along or go get a drink. Enough was enough. I demanded they induce labor.

Dr. Jenkins said, "Maybe you're right, Darryl. Let me talk to Jen and to a senior doctor, and we'll decide."

They decided on the induction and shot Jen up with medication. She went into labor again and soon got considerably more uncomfortable, though they gave her something for the pain. The baby started to move down slowly.

Twelve hours, fourteen hours, sixteen hours . . .

I was about out of my mind. Obviously I had it easy compared to Jen, who was sweating, shaking, and very emotional. If only I hadn't been a hardcore alcoholic, perhaps I would have been enjoying the madness. My mom had once told me she would like to be a fly on the wall during our son's birth. She was positive I'd pass out. Little did she know it wasn't watching the birth that that was making me woozy; it was the lack of alcohol.

I need a drink like you read about it, and there's no way I can sneak off. Fuck me.

Eighteen hours, twenty hours . . .

Oh, my God, I'm gonna lose it. I was being tortured on what was supposed to be the happiest day of my life. *God give me strength.*

Jen finally started pushing. The nurse and I held her legs. I could finally see the crown of my little son's head.

"Do you have a flashlight so I can see better?" I asked the nurse.

"In the nightstand next to the bed," she said, not at all surprised by the question.

With the flashlight on, I could see a wet little head with lots of hair. My heart raced and the sweat poured down my face. *Oh, my God, this is a trip! Maybe my mother was right, and I'll pass out.*

Twenty-two hours, twenty-four hours, twenty-six hours . . .

Jen pushed for five hours. Still no baby. Dr. Jenkins brought in the senior doctor, and he immediately took control.

"All right, Jen, we're going to have this baby now," he said forcefully. "We're all done fooling around. I want you to roll over on your side and push as hard as you can."

Jen rolled over and pushed for thirty minutes. There were three doctors, three nurses, and several aides in the room, all encouraging Jen on. I knew it was getting close; the doctor was right between Jen's legs.

"Doctor, can I look over your shoulder? I'll stay out of your way, but I don't want to miss anything. I've never been through this before."

"Absolutely, Darryl. You're going to cut the umbilical cord, correct?" he asked.

"That's right."

He turned back to Jen and said, "Push, Jen! Push harder!"

The baby's little head started poking out. When she stopped pushing, the baby's head went back inside, and I let out a big sigh. Then she pushed again, and his head pushed farther out. I held my breath, hoping this was it. Back in his head went again. Sigh! Things went on like that for awhile, and then Jen pushed really hard. The baby's shoulders were stuck. The doctor encouraged her to continue pushing, and out the baby came all at once.

One of the nurses had given me scissors. The doctor held up the baby and the umbilical cord, which had clamps on it two inches apart. I put the scissors on the outside of one of the clamps and the doctor yelled, "No, between the clamps!"

"Okay, sorry!" My hands were shaking a little as I put the scissors between the clamps and cut the cord. The baby was dark and a little blue, and I was worried. There were no sounds from him yet, which made me nervous. A doctor whisked the baby away, placed him on a padded table, and suctioned his mouth and nose. Out came a loud cry, and I let out a deep sigh of relief.

The little guy (actually, *big* guy) weighed 9 pounds, 9 ounces and was 21½ inches long. His collar bone had been broken during birth, and his breathing was rapid and irregular. They assured us his little cone-shaped head would round out to normal. Darryl II had a rough ride coming into the world and was probably glad it was over.

I walked over and said to my newborn son, "Hi, buddy. This is Dad. You did it, man. Are you okay?"

The baby immediately turned his head toward me. I don't know if he could see me or not, but he definitely recognized my raspy, low voice. Maybe it comforted him, but after all the loud parties and music, I feared he was thinking, *There's that crazy voice I've been hearing for the last nine months*. Maybe not, but when I spoke, he turned his head in acknowledgement. It's one of those things you just know deep down. I loved him immediately with all my heart. Alcoholic or not, my love was real and deep.

I touched his hand and let him squeeze my finger. My emotions were getting crazy, and I took a deep breath. I couldn't believe that with the way I'd lived my life, God had given me a normal baby. After all the drugs and alcohol I had put in my body, God had still been good to me. Of course Jen didn't drink or smoke during her pregnancy, and I love her for that. She had done a great job.

The nurse cleaned Darryl up and wrapped him in a blanket. She put a little hat on his coned head and put him in Jen's arms. Jen wept and the three of us embraced: Dad, Mom, and Baby. After about an hour I called my mom, who was very happy to have another grandchild. She promised to visit the next day to welcome her new grandson into the world.

It was after 11:00 p.m., and because of the baby's irregular breathing

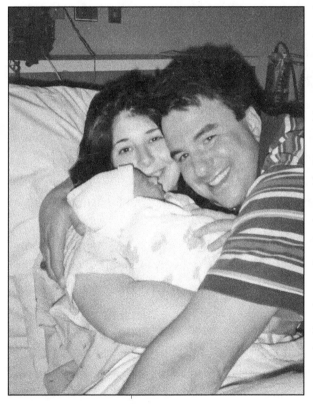

they needed to keep him in an incubator during the night close to the nurses' station so they could monitor him closely. They set up an extra bed for me, and I spent the night in the hospital. We slept intermittently until the nurse brought the baby to us the next morning.

Jen and I took turns holding Darryl II, showering him with love and kisses. Then family started showing up. I was the proudest dad ever.

Our new son.

"Are you okay if I go home now?" I finally asked Jen. "I'm wiped out. I've been here almost forty hours."

"Of course, Darryl," she said. "I'll call you if there are any complications." She reminded me to be back at the hospital early for Darryl's circumcision. "I want you there with him. That's a scary thing for a baby; he needs his parents. And they won't let me go," she insisted firmly.

"I'll be here bright and early," I said, kissing them both. Of course, I didn't go home. I went to a half dozen bars, handing out cigars and partying like a drunken sailor.

The phone rang and rang.

What the hell is that? Am I dreaming? I thought.

"Hello," I said weakly.

"Darryl, are you forgetting something?" yelled Jen's voice. "Get your ass down here! Darryl II is getting circumcised in half an hour!"

My throat and mouth were dry. My head pounded. It was the next morning, and I was at home.

"Okay, Jen, calm down. I'll be right down. Tell Dr. Jenkins to wait for me."

Shit, it never ends, I thought selfishly. There I was, an active alcoholic trying to be a dad.

My head was throbbing. I could feel booze coming out my pores. I smelled and tasted leftover alcohol vapors. I had a question about the circumcision, and I knew in my condition I'd have to be firm to be taken seriously.

I rushed to Maine Medical Center and went to the operating room. Darryl was already there. I wondered if anyone smelled the alcohol fumes following me around. I walked up to Dr. Jenkins, a tall, pretty redhead who could be a little intimidating.

I said, "I have a close friend whose son was circumcised here. There were complications, and he had to come back and have it done a second time. I want to make sure my son only has to go through this once."

"Don't worry, we'll only have to do this once," she assured me.

"I'm just concerned, because he was just born. His penis is so small it would be easy to mess up."

"Darryl, his penis is not small."

Her comment floored me. "Oh, okay," I said, thinking to myself, *That's my boy!* I was almost ready to pat myself on the back.

I put my little finger in Darryl's little hand, and he squeezed it. "Good morning, buddy. This is going to hurt a little, but it'll be over fast. Daddy is right here for you. I'll make sure you're okay."

Dr. Jenkins lifted the circumcision device, which looked like a corkscrew with a thimble on the end. Leave it to my alcoholic mind to think a medical instrument looked like a wine bottle opener. The doctor gave Darryl a shot of pain medication. He cried like anyone who had a needle stuck in his penis. Darryl cried again during the procedure, but after a short time settled down and went to sleep. Jen cried when she saw him. We had a beautiful baby boy. Somehow we both felt that this child's birth had saved our lives.

I continued to believe having a baby would solve all my problems. I now had a son to be responsible for; that should slow down my drinking. I'd finally get sober and start acting like the man I had always wanted to be. That came true eventually, but in the near turn things were about to get worse.

A young nurse taught us how to put on a diaper and asked me to try. I felt she was screening us to see if we could handle our parenting duties. I was working hard to hide my alcoholism and because I was nervous, my hands shook like crazy. The nurse gave me a look of disgust after my first feeble attempt, but eventually I got better. I suspect she smelled alcohol on me.

Darryl was diagnosed with some breathing issues; he later developed asthma for which he needed medication. But after a few days, Jen and I were able to take him home. We had made the spare bedroom into a nursery, nicely decorated with Looney Tunes characters.

Jen was an awesome mother. She breastfed, changed diapers, and sang and rocked the baby to sleep. She was also doing the laundry and helping clean the house. I tried to stay in the present. I changed diapers, got up in the middle of the night in the beginning, helped clean the house, and ran to the supermarket for baby needs.

Despite my good intentions, my drinking problem didn't vanish. Overwhelmed with anxiety about being an alcoholic, drug abuser, Merchant Marine officer, and dad all at the same time, I drank every day. I thought I was ready for parenthood, but it became apparent early on that I wasn't. I maintained for a month and then spun out of control once again. I thank God he was looking over us during those turbulent times.

I was sitting on the couch one evening breastfeeding our one-month-old son. I heard a car pull up to the house. In a second I knew it was Darryl, and I knew what he'd been doing. The details didn't matter; he'd been drinking and that was enough to make me vigilant. It had become second nature to recognize the warning signs.

Instantly I had a knot in my stomach. His disposition was unpredictable; if he was drunk it was best to be on guard. Sometimes he was foolish and senseless, but he was almost always obnoxious and sometimes quite intimidating.

It wasn't uncommon for a lamp or some other object to come flying across the room. There didn't have to be a reason for it, and usually there wasn't even a trigger. It also wasn't unusual to be sitting in total silence and suddenly have a can of beer come soaring at my head. I experienced this behavior many times.

Darryl knocked on the front door and shouted, "Open the door!"

Where's his key? *I wondered. He was probably so drunk he didn't realize he had the key in his pocket.*

"Hang on"! I shouted. I wasn't in any condition to jump up immediately.

But Darryl didn't wait. The next thing I knew there was a loud crash followed by shattered glass all over the living room floor, within feet of our newborn. It happened so fast I don't know if Darryl dove through the window or if he just smashed the glass and opened it. It wasn't a total surprise for something like this to occur, but I wasn't expecting it. Darryl frequently did things without thought for the consequences.

He told me he "blacked out" nearly every time he drank. I never doubted it. Being the adult child of an alcoholic, and realizing that alcoholism is a disease, I'm sure Darryl never would have intentionally put our baby in jeopardy. Not intentionally. But what if he accidentally harmed our child? What if the shattered glass had made contact with our son? We were all quite fortunate that evening. Things could have been much worse. —Jennifer

I was fortunate not to have hurt either my son or Jen. Though I'd scared her, she had nowhere else to go. I apologized and promised the craziness around the baby would stop. I reeled myself in for a month. I stayed at home and prepared myself mentally for my next work tour.

One warm June night when Darryl was about two months old, I took him outside at the full moon. Years before, I had watched the TV series *Roots* starring LeVar Burton. In it the newborn Kunta Kinte is raised to the night sky by his father, who speaks a blessing over him in the middle of an African field. I had a moment of spirituality and wanted God to bless our new baby. I stripped Darryl naked, took him in my hands, held him above my head, and asked the Creator to guide my son throughout his life.

"God, please watch over this little boy. Make him a king among kings. Make him a great man someday. Be with him every day. Please, oh Lord, even as I struggle with my demons, please help him in his life—when I'm not there with him. Amen."

It might seem eccentric or bizarre, but I prayed in all sincerity and with all my heart. I really did love that little boy. If I couldn't take care of him as I should, I prayed the Lord would be there instead.

GLEN
CHADBOURNE

CHAPTER TWENTY-NINE
ALL POINTS BULLETIN

I was due to fly to the S/T Overseas New York on July 4, 1999. The day before, I was packing my sea bags and hanging out with Jen and Darryl, who was one day shy of two months old. It was my first time going to sea since he'd been born.

I drank beer that day to relieve my worry about going away for ninety days. Jen didn't seem to mind as long as I didn't drive, and I had no plans to leave the house. I was trying to be a responsible employee and dad. I needed to stay in control so I could readily assume the con of a 900-foot, 90,000-ton supertanker.

Jen went out with one of her girlfriends, and I was watching Darryl. That was okay with me, since I had things to do. I had finished packing, when the phone rang.

"Hagar, ahhh! Hagar, what are you doing?" my friend Jazz, a 300-pound truck driver, screamed into the phone. He obviously had a buzz on. I could hear other people in the background.

"What's up, brother?" I asked. "Who's there with you?"

"Pusherman and Go-Go. Why don't you come over, man?"

The way I liked to describe Pusherman, Go-Go, Jazz, and me was "out of our freaking minds." We would drink anything, smoke anything, swallow any pill, or snort anything anyone put in front of us. The only thing we didn't do was needles.

"I can't come over, man. I'm flying to the West Coast tomorrow to join a ship."

"We know that, man. We got plenty of beer, and we're cooking lobsters. We want you to come over and say goodbye before you leave."

"I can't, man. I have my son right now."

"Bring your son over," Jazz pleaded convincingly. "We'd love to party with him. We can put him in the shade on the deck."

"I don't know, man. Jen would probably get pissed. I've had a few beers." But the wheels were turning inside my brain. *Hmm. Maybe just a couple of beers and a lobster, and I can say goodbye to my buddies.*

"C'mon, man. You only live a mile away. You can take it easy. We want to see you!" Jazz said sincerely.

"All right, man. If I don't stay too long it'll be all right, and you can see the baby."

I knew I was taking a risk, but my alcoholic mind was weak, and I always chose the wrong thing. This was a typical decision at that time in my life. I thought, *This is a little slippery.* But by that time my entire existence was a slippery slope.

I put the baby seat in my truck, the same one I had run into my house the year before. One of the captains I worked for once joked that the city of Portland wasn't big enough for me. I knew what he was insinuating, and he was exactly right. In truth, there probably wasn't a city on the planet where I would blend in unnoticed.

When I pulled into my friend's driveway, Go-Go yelled, "Hagar!"

I got Darryl out of the truck and put him on the deck in the shade. Pusherman came out and gave me a hug, Jazz high-fived me, and we started to party.

I gave Pusherman his nickname, because all he ever wanted to do was party and score drugs. He always pushed his desires on the rest of us, although we were pretty easy to convince. Pusherman knew all he had to do was put alcohol in me, and I could be talked into anything.

Go-Go got his nickname because he was an energetic, crazy French-American wild man who would do anything at any time. Jazz got his nickname because he was so cool, though he had a serious drinking and drug problem.

Pusherman used to make a bet about who would die first: Would it be Jazz, because he was such a big man and loved his drugs and booze; Go-Go, because he got off on taking dangerous risks; or me from running my mouth off at the wrong guy with a gun? We all lived life dangerously. Ultimately it was Jazz who died early from drinking, drugs, and diabetes. But it could have been any one of us—many times.

My friends checked out my son and made faces at him. Darryl just looked at us, four crazy grown men acting like teenagers in front of a two-month-old baby.

After a few more beers and lobsters, I lost track of time and how many beers I drank. I had only planned to stay half an hour, but I'd gone way past that. I needed to get Darryl home before Jen found out I was out partying with the guys. Just the mention of us together made her nervous. I also knew I should be careful what I did when I had my son.

I buckled Darryl into the truck, realizing I had a pretty good buzz on. I just needed to get home before Jen did, and everything would be fine.

As I pulled onto my street, I saw a police car in front of my house. *Oh, shit. She called the cops.* I immediately had a decision to make: stop or don't stop. I could pull in and try to act sober, hoping they wouldn't arrest me. But I was going to sea the next day. I imagined explaining: "Um, sorry, I can't join the ship today. I'm in jail for endangering a child's welfare." I decided to make a run for it.

The police were inside, so at least I'd have a head start. Jen didn't miss much, so I assumed (correctly) they'd see my big red truck go by. I gunned it, whizzed by my house, ran a stop sign, and took off like a madman. *I'll be lucky to get out of this one. The only chance I have is to outrun the cops and sleep it off somewhere.*

I assumed (correctly) they would put an All Points Bulletin out on me. I looked down at the sleeping baby. I would just concentrate on losing the cops. I took side roads and headed away from the city toward the town of Gray. One of my buddies had a house there where I could hide the truck, sober up, and then call Jen to ask her to call off the wolves.

I drove at crazy rates of speed. Soon I was pulling into my buddy's driveway. I parked Old Salt out back and took the baby inside. Luckily, the house was unlocked. I tucked Darryl in bed upstairs and jumped in the shower to wash away the smell of alcohol. I brushed my teeth a few times and went to lay down with my son.

I didn't think of anything besides getting out of the situation as cleanly as possible. I'm ashamed to admit that I didn't consider Jen's feelings. Nor was Darryl at the top of my list of worries; I'd left so quickly I couldn't even give him a bottle or change his diaper. I was only worried about getting out of the mess I'd created.

I slept for a few hours and woke up feeling more coherent. I decided to call Jen.

"Hi, it's me. What's going on?" I asked innocently.

"Where are you, Darryl? Is the baby all right?"

"Yes. Why wouldn't he be all right? I'm visiting some friends," I lied.

"Where are you, Darryl?" she screamed.

"I'm up in Gray at my friend's house."

"I know where you are," she said, hanging up.

I knew the cops were headed my way. I brushed my teeth again and then woke up the baby. I was sitting in the living room when a Cumberland County sheriff's deputy knocked on the front door.

"Are you Darryl Hagar?" the deputy asked.

"I am. What's the problem, Officer?"

"What are you doing here?"

"I brought my son up to see my friends. Is that a problem?"

"I have to take the baby. His mother is worried about him."

I thought, *I don't think he'll arrest me. He didn't catch me driving drunk. You better be a good actor and make believe you're getting screwed because he's taking your son against your will.*

"You can't take my son. I'm not breaking any laws. I have rights!"

"I have to take him. Put his child seat in the back of the cruiser and buckle him in. He'll be safe. I'll take him back to his mother."

The wheels were still turning in my brain: *If he allows me to buckle my son in, he can't say I was drunk.* My diabolical mind worked quite well when it came to getting out of trouble. I buckled Darryl into the cruiser and stood in front of the deputy.

"I just want to say one thing, Officer, before you take him away," I said sarcastically.

"What's that?"

I smiled. "Take it easy on my son. He's only two months old, and it's his first trip in a police cruiser."

If the officer's eyes could have killed, I would have been dead at that moment. He glared at me, got in his cruiser, and drove off.

I was so caught up in my alcoholism I had no respect for myself, my son, his mother, or even some poor sheriff's deputy just doing his job.

Now what was I going to do? I called the buddy who owned the house and told him the whole story. He told me where there was a fifth of vodka in the cupboard. By the time he and his wife arrived home from work, I could barely talk. I crashed there that night.

The next day I didn't have to be at the airport until afternoon, so four of us took my buddy's boat out on the river. After spending the day drinking, my friends took me home to get my sea bags. Jen wasn't there, and I didn't get to kiss my baby son goodbye.

I shipped out for three months on the S/T Overseas New York, and by the time I got home, Jen had moved out of my house. She had lived there for the first five months of Darryl's life, but told me he wasn't going to live around an alcoholic father. She'd had to endure that crazy lifestyle as a little girl with her alcoholic father. She wanted a better life for her son.

A normal person would have begged Jen to stay. But I was in the full throes of drug addiction and alcoholism. I couldn't take care of myself, let alone a baby. And when I returned home again, the only thing that mattered to me was seeing the bottom of a bottle and a pile of cocaine on a mirror.

CHAPTER THIRTY
KEEPING SECRETS, BARROOM BRAWLS, AND KISS-AND-TELL

Still in denial, I drank heavily during my next vacation. Yet I loved my son very much. I didn't deny that I was a dad; I denied that the life I was living was out of control. The pressure of having responsibility for another life drove me even further over the edge; the complete opposite of what I had intended.

That winter I reached a point where I had no regard for life, people, family, or neighbors. I was going to hell, but I was going down partying hard. Nothing mattered but the next drink and drug. Somehow I managed to get through Christmas with a new baby and stay sober around my family.

Apparently that gave me a green light to rip it up afterward. On December 29, 1999, I went into a bar to enjoy some post-holiday cheer and commenced drinking a ridiculous amount of vodka. I drank through supper, and as the evening wore on I grew louder and more obnoxious. I was self-medicating my anxiety, which ironically was caused by my chaotic life with alcohol.

One of my friends from Maine Maritime Academy, an engineer who also worked on oil tankers, drove his Harley into the parking lot and came inside. He was known as "Sammy the Bull," a man built like a brick house, 220 pounds of rugged muscle. Sammy was a nice guy, and we usually got along well.

I greeted Sammy and said, "Bartender, whatever Sammy wants. I'll have another vodka and orange juice!"

The bartender brought our drinks, and I gave her a $5 tip. I thought I was a big shot, often buying rounds for everyone in the bar and always over-tipping. I was later told that when I got really drunk the bartenders often took advantage. I'd hand over $20 for a couple of drinks and forget about the change.

Sammy and I started out talking about work and where we were sailing next. We liked the money but commiserated about having to leave for months and work like dogs. Then as one drink led to another my temperament changed. My unhappiness floated to the top, especially when I drank vodka, and I often got angry and mean.

I started getting belligerent, and the bouncer, a tough guy who liked to fight, started watching me. He wore spiked rings and had used them. But I also liked to fight when I got that drunk, and I was fearless.

For some reason as the night wore on I felt like calling Sammy names. The evil in me came out when I was drunk. Sammy probably could have killed me in a fight, but in my drunken state I didn't care.

"Hey, Sammy the Mule, want another drink?" I asked sarcastically.

"Darryl, why don't you let me give you a ride home?" Sammy asked, like the good friend he was, knowing it was the vodka talking.

Instead of taking Sammy up on his generous offer, I continued to act like a drunken idiot.

"Sammy the Mule, when you going back to sea again?" I said, smiling drunkenly.

The bouncer edged closer. I noticed he was just a few barstools away.

"Sammy the Mule, you want another drink?"

The bouncer walked over and stood inches from me, salivating for a fight. "Darryl, you've got to go."

"What's your problem? I'm not doing anything."

"C'mon, you gotta go," he said, grabbing my arm. "You're bothering people, and you've had too much to drink."

"Fuck you, man! Don't grab my arm, you asshole!" I yelled.

The bouncer quickly pulled me across the room and out the door. Within seconds we were fist fighting. We went at it for a few minutes, but I was too drunk to fight anyone, let alone a skilled fighter itching to give me his best. He threw me to the asphalt, and I stuck out my right hand. My wrist took the brunt of the fall, and my forehead fell forward and smacked the pavement.

I got up and he threw me to the ground again. I noticed my wrist was badly injured and ran over to my pickup. I barely remember driving off. I was mainly worried about avoiding further bodily injury. I knew I was too drunk to fight, but the thought of being too drunk to drive never crossed my mind. I sped down the road for about a mile, thinking the bouncer would chase me. That was stupid drunken reasoning; he didn't care about me as long as I left.

I suddenly came up to a red light, but it was too late to stop. I blew right threw it, and the blue lights of a police cruiser immediately went on behind me. I knew I'd have a tough time getting out of this one. I haphazardly pulled into a parking lot, and the officers knew I was drunk before they even checked me. The four-page police report from that night is not very flattering.

I stumbled out of the car, trying to stand up straight. Two officers approached, one male, one female. I told them I'd been at a Christmas party and had driven my mother home because she was drunk and I was helping her out. When I read the police report later, I couldn't believe I'd used my mother as an excuse for driving drunk.

The male cop was aggressive, which only fueled my drunken rage. When he made me do the sobriety tests, I called him a "commie." He responded by handcuffing me, pulling the cuffs up, twisting them, pushing me against the police car, and yelling at me.

I'm sure a verbally abusive drunk makes it hard for cops to maintain composure, but beating up the drunk might not be the answer. Alcoholism is cunning, baffling, and powerful, and alcoholics are cunning, resourceful, and sneaky.

At the jail, I became loud and belligerent, so they threw me in the drunk tank, where I banged on the door and ripped off my shirt. Eventually I passed out. In the morning, my eyes opened. I had pants on, but no boots and no shirt. I was in some kind of jail cell. My wrist was swollen and sore. I had a big bump on my forehead. I hopped up, and it all started coming back to me. I remembered the two police officers and my truck.

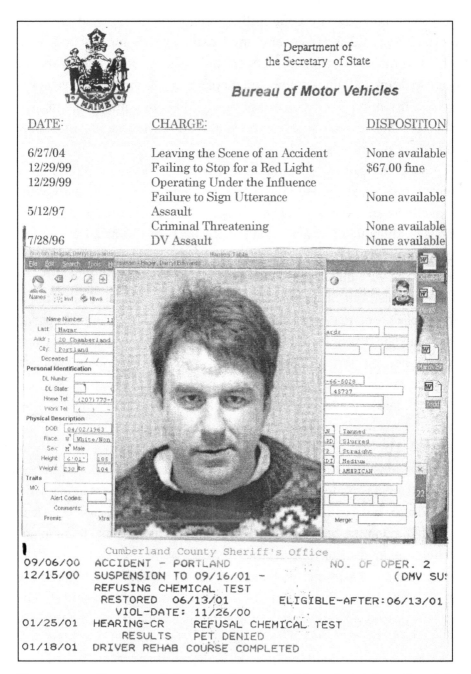

Department of
the Secretary of State

Bureau of Motor Vehicles

DATE:	CHARGE:	DISPOSITION
6/27/04	Leaving the Scene of an Accident	None available
12/29/99	Failing to Stop for a Red Light	$67.00 fine
12/29/99	Operating Under the Influence	
	Failure to Sign Utterance	None available
5/12/97	Assault	
	Criminal Threatening	None available
7/28/96	DV Assault	None available

Cumberland County Sheriff's Office

09/06/00	ACCIDENT — PORTLAND	NO. OF OPER. 2
12/15/00	SUSPENSION TO 09/16/01 –	(DMV SU:
	REFUSING CHEMICAL TEST	
	RESTORED 06/13/01	ELIGIBLE-AFTER:06/13/01
	VIOL-DATE: 11/26/00	
01/25/01	HEARING-CR REFUSAL CHEMICAL TEST	
	RESULTS PET DENIED	
01/18/01	DRIVER REHAB COURSE COMPLETED	

From my police record through the years. Mug shot taken the night of December 29, 1999.

Oh, hell! I'm gonna get my third OUI, and it'll ruin my career. I need a good attorney to get out of this, or the Coast Guard will yank my chief mate's license.

I called a friend to come get me and was given a "no consumption of alcohol" order. I was irritated as the deputies at the front desk returned my possessions. Then they handed me my $600 14-karat gold Maine Maritime Academy class ring. It's big and shiny with a black onyx center and an engraved gold anchor. I wore it everywhere.

At that moment my evil alcoholic twin decided to make an appearance. I said, "You guys know what that is?"

The deputies looked at me.

"That's a Maine Maritime Academy graduation ring."

"Yeah, so what?" one of the deputies snapped, clearly annoyed that I was again being a jerk.

"You know what that ring means?"

They looked at me, knowing something arrogant and unpleasant was coming.

"It means I make more money every year than all three of you put together, but I don't hold that against you."

I was a full blown alcoholic, but I couldn't be convinced of that—not with an OUI, not by a broken wrist, and certainly not by publicly embarrassing myself.

I went home and slept off the effects of the alcohol. When I came to, I tried to figure out how to squirm out of this latest OUI. I decided to see my doctor and tell him I'd been strong-armed by the cops. If I could get him to document the injury and state that the cops did it, I could probably get off. I hadn't taken a breathalyzer, so there was no hard evidence about how drunk I was.

I was afraid I wouldn't be able to sell my police brutality story if I had other injuries. The doctor might figure out I'd been in a barroom brawl or call the police to get their side of the story. To hide the abrasion on my forehead, I wore a baseball cap. As I waited to see a doctor, I pulled my cap down a little farther.

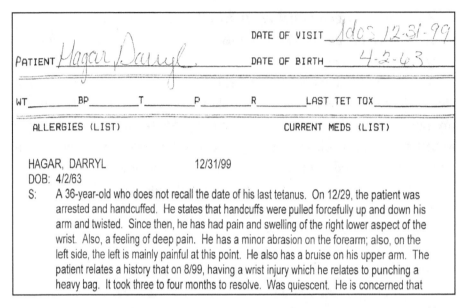

DATE OF VISIT ___Idos 12-31-99___

PATIENT ___Hagar Darryl___   DATE OF BIRTH ___4-2-63___

WT_____ BP_____ T_____ P_____ R_____ LAST TET TOX_____

ALLERGIES (LIST)   CURRENT MEDS (LIST)

HAGAR, DARRYL   12/31/99
DOB: 4/2/63
S: A 36-year-old who does not recall the date of his last tetanus. On 12/29, the patient was
      arrested and handcuffed. He states that handcuffs were pulled forcefully up and down his
      arm and twisted. Since then, he has had pain and swelling of the right lower aspect of the
      wrist. Also, a feeling of deep pain. He has a minor abrasion on the forearm; also, on the
      left side, the left is mainly painful at this point. He also has a bruise on his upper arm. The
      patient relates a history that on 8/99, having a wrist injury which he relates to punching a
      heavy bag. It took three to four months to resolve. Was quiescent. He is concerned that

Doctor's report indicating my broken hand from being handcuffed.

I told the doctor my story, and he ordered X-rays. My wrist was broken. He put on a splint and referred me to a surgeon. But I was more worried about my chief mate's license and my driver's license than about my health. I decided to do another work tour and see the surgeon when I got home. I sucked it up and kept quiet. If the company knew about my injury, there was no way they'd let me work.

Just ten days later I flew to Valdez to join the S/T Overseas New York. I had been drinking excessively in the days leading up to my departure. After fifteen hours of traveling, I arrived in Valdez exhausted, shaky, and hung over. I just wanted to get on board and rest before I went to work. I asked the cab driver if he knew where the Overseas New York was. He wasn't sure, but he thought it was Berth No. 4.

I went through security. At Berth No. 4, I looked up. The ship was almost done discharging dirty ballast water and was in as light a condition as possible before she started loading, meaning I had a steep climb up the gangway with a heavy sea bag and no wrist splint. I bulled my way up, panting at the top like an overheated dog desperately in need of water. I was sweating profusely. I sat down on a mooring bitt and caught my breath.

Then I saw the captain who fired me from the Overseas Juneau—for being drunk and missing a watch in Hawaii—walk toward me. He was now the captain of the Overseas Chicago, a sister ship to the Overseas New York. I wondered, *Did he get transferred?* Sister ships are identical. I wasn't sure what the hell was going on.

He yelled, "Darryl, you're on the wrong ship! The Overseas New York is at Berth No. 5!"

Oh, my God. I'd gotten on the wrong ship! He probably thought I was half in the bag.

"Can you call me a cab?!" I yelled back.

He waved an acknowledgement, then turned around and walked back toward the ship's house. Obviously he didn't want to talk to me. That was all right; I didn't want to talk to him, either. I took a deep breath and threw my sea bag over my shoulder, steamed that I'd have to climb another steep gangway.

I laughed, wondering what my captain would say. I wasn't surprised to discover he already knew of my error. After hearing my explanation, he breathed a sigh of relief; he needed me. After all, he had given me an evaluation saying I was the best second mate in the fleet. I knew the ship inside and out, and Mainers are known for hard work. The captain assumed I wasn't drunk because I got through security, but I'm sure my reputation made him skeptical.

The work tour went well. I called home weekly to see how Darryl was; being away from him made me sad. Though I drank alcoholically around him, it didn't lessen my love for him.

In late April the ship had some problems and needed an overhaul, so the company scheduled repairs at Gray's Harbor, Washington. We got the shipyard workers set up and then sauntered ashore for beers. I partied hard that night, ending up in a bar with a live band and hot local girls. I was people-watching when my eyes met those of a tall, pretty brunette. She was definitely checking me out. I walked over and introduced myself.

"I'm Roxanne," she said. "You're not from around here, are you?"

The Overseas New York was the biggest ship ever to dock at Gray's Harbor, and everyone in the small town had seen it. "I'm from Maine. I'm a ship's officer on that huge ship on the waterfront. What do you do?"

"I manage a local bank. I worked my way up to manager and do pretty well," she said proudly.

"Good for you. If I need a loan, I'll come to you," I joked.

Roxanne and I danced the night away and met for coffee during the day. We went out to dinner one evening. We were both drinking, and I was frisky from being on board almost four months. The evening went well, and I knew Roxanne wanted me, but it was close to midnight, and I didn't think she was up for spending the night with me.

Out of the blue, she smiled slightly and asked, "Do you want to see where I work?"

"Sure," I said gleefully, sure at that point that she was hitting on me.

We drove to the bank, walked through the doors, and quickly embraced in a long, passionate kiss. Soon we were tearing each other's clothes off. I couldn't believe this was happening to me. *There is a God!*

There were clothes trailing from the front door, across the lobby, through the different floors of the bank, up to the bank manager's office. We were both naked as I picked her up and put her on her desk and started making love to her. At one point she was on top of me grinding away while I was lying naked in her office on the carpeted floor. This went on for over an hour before she must have gotten nervous that the police might come.

As we were getting ready to leave, she smiled and asked, "Do you want to watch what we just did?"

I was floored. She was kidding about replaying the tape, but that's when I realized that of course there were cameras inside the bank.

"Will anyone see the tape?" I asked, more worried about her job than about me.

"No. It's a twenty-four-hour tape. It gets recorded over every day. The action will be recorded over tomorrow; don't worry."

I suddenly had a feeling I hadn't been the first to experience Roxanne's brand of late-night fun in the bank.

Of course, I had to brag about it to my captain and shipmates. I hardly ever repeated stories when drinking was involved, but this one was too good. I admit to embellishing. I said we had sex in the safe, giving a new meaning to the term "safe sex." Because the guys had all heard my crazy sea stories from other people, they believed me.

I wasn't one to make up stories. I didn't need to. If anything, I tried to keep my wild episodes quiet for fear the office would find out. There were many true stories that I denied.

I flew home in April of 2000; I had managed not only to protect my broken wrist but to keep the injury top secret. Then I spent time with both my son and the bottle. I'm not sure which was more important to me; at that point, they were running neck-and-neck. One thing is for sure at that point, my addictions owned me.

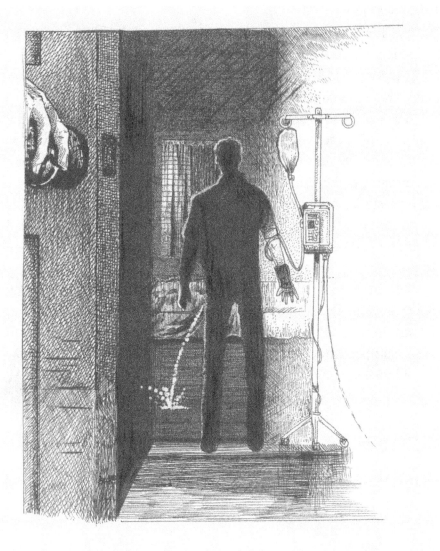

GLENN CHADBOURNE

CHAPTER THIRTY-ONE

BROKEN HAND, BROKEN STOMACH, BROKEN MIND, BROKEN LIFE

I met with my lawyer and gave him the medical report that said I had been arrested and handcuffed by Portland police officers, resulting in my broken wrist. I was manipulating the system to get out of the OUI. I'd do whatever it took to continue in my career—except stop drinking and using.

My lawyer was expensive and very good. He felt I had a good chance of getting out of the OUI. Yet as my DMV hearing crept closer, I still acted irresponsibly. The night before, I stayed up half the night doing cocaine and drinking with friends. I couldn't stop, even for something that important. That night I tossed and turned, worried that I might smell like alcohol in front of the DMV officials.

In the morning, I looked in the mirror. The reflection showed a man with dark circles under his eyes, stubble on his chin, and a pained expression from an aching head. I quickly showered, shaved, and brushed my teeth several times. Since my driver's license had already been revoked due to my earlier OUI and other traffic violations, I took a taxi to the DMV.

I was nervous, but I had cleaned up well enough to disguise having been up to no good the night before. Outside the meeting room, I sat down to wait next to an attractive woman dressed in shorts, blouse, and sandals.

She looked at me inquisitively. I said, "I guess this is where people go to meet with the DMV?"

"Yes, it is," she said politely.

"Are you here for a traffic violation also?"

"Darryl, I'm Jessica Brown, the arresting officer."

I was embarrassed. "Oh, jeez! Sorry about that. It was dark that night. I didn't recognize you in civilian clothes, Officer. I'm sorry about that night; I was having a difficult time."

I was floored that I hadn't recognized her. She obviously remembered me. The partner who had roughed me up wasn't there. I've always suspected he dodged the meeting because of how aggressive he'd been. Or because I had such an outstanding attorney.

I asked, "What's happening now? I hear my lawyer talking. Why aren't we inside?"

"I have no idea. The DMV official and your lawyer are the only ones in there. They told me to wait outside. Darryl, I understand why you have a good lawyer. I know you have an important job and you need to protect your career."

"I have to do what I have to do, Officer. I'm sorry this whole thing happened. But I will try to be more careful in the future." I halfway believed myself.

After a few minutes, my lawyer walked out and whispered in my ear, "We're all set."

"We're all set? What do you mean?"

"Let's talk outside." Outside, he said, "They dropped the OUI charge and charged you with running a red light. Pay the fine, and your license will be restored."

"Wow, you're kidding me! That's it?" I said, amazed.

"That's it. Do you need a ride?"

"I do. If you can drop me off at the restaurant just down the street, I want to get some lunch."

In reality, one very sick alcoholic was planning to have some beer at that restaurant to celebrate the "victory." Now I'm ashamed of so much of that behavior. I thank God I lived through it.

With the OUI hearing out of the way, I went on living my usual lifestyle. But by the spring of 2000, my wrist wasn't healing, and I was worried about being able to go back to sea. Plus, if I needed surgery, then I'd need time to heal. On May 23 I went to see the hand specialist. Dr. Chance confirmed that the wrist was fractured and recommended surgery. He insisted on putting my wrist in a cast, but I stubbornly refused. I was an alcoholic; I knew everything. I didn't want a cast on my hand for people to talk about. I told the doctor I would consider my options and get back to him.

When I finally decided to schedule surgery, I told the company I had fallen in my driveway. The head of labor relations was supportive; I had pulled the wool over the company's eyes yet again.

I arrived at the surgery center on June 7, figuring I could enjoy Maine's summer weather while my wrist healed. The doctor put me under, which I thoroughly enjoyed. The last thing I remember the anesthesiologist saying was, "Just relax, Darryl. Think of lying on a beach with all the bikinis walking by." I went to sleep smiling.

When I awoke my hand was bandaged and felt like it was in a vice. Dr. Chance explained that there were also injured tendons. He had inserted screws, pins, and wires, so I couldn't swivel my wrist, which made me feel claustrophobic. Maybe this would finally teach me to slow down and watch my partying. After all, I'd have to be careful not to use my hand too much or bang it against things. I went home and laid low for a week, my hand finally in a cast.

With broken hand and baby, 2000.

I refilled my Vicodin prescription several times and took the pills twice as fast as instructed. I had never abused prescribed medication before, but liked the buzz I got from mixing Vicodin with alcohol.

At that time, I was watching my son regularly while Jen worked. A buddy, Alan Joiner, was living with me. We had long been partners in crime, many times staying up all night snorting cocaine and drinking heavily. But after I broke my wrist, Alan lectured me from time to time. "You have it all," he said. "And you could lose everything." He reminded me that I had a son, a nice house, a good job, and plenty of women. He feared I had completely lost my mind. I disagreed. I thought things were going okay. I was drinking a lot, but my wrist was healing.

Despite Alan's warnings and my doctor's instructions, I drank like always and used my hand as if it wasn't broken. Then five weeks after the surgery, my wrist started to ache. One night I looked at my hand and was horrified to see a pin had popped out through the skin.

The next morning, I drove to the surgery center. Of course, the doctors had no way of knowing they were dealing with a man with a severe drinking problem. Under a local anesthetic, the pin and devitalized tissue were removed, and the wound was irrigated and bandaged. Afterward, they put me on a powerful intravenous antibiotic. A nurse came to my house, inserted a PICC line on the inside of my elbow, and showed me how to use the IV machine.

Each day for a month, I took a bag of Vancomycin out of the refrigerator and hung it on the IV machine. I had to go through a complicated process of disinfecting the line, bleeding off air bubbles, and hooking it up to my arm. When I pressed the start button, the machine pumped antibiotics into my body for an hour.

The nurse came every week to check on me. It wasn't long before she noticed the beer bottles around the kitchen. She could also smell alcohol on my breath. She was polite but firm when she told me my life was out of control, that I had a son to worry about, and that I should be careful about drinking too much.

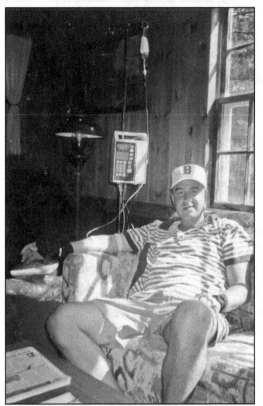

Hooked up to the IV machine.

I told her I was getting a handle on it, but as the weeks passed my drinking got worse. I was often totally drunk when running the IV machine at night. There were several times I could barely remember doing it, and more than once I passed out and woke up with the IV bag completely empty and the machine still running. Alan kept an eye on me as much as he could, but there's only so much a person can get a stubborn alcoholic to do.

Then in early September when the weather was still warm, some friends planned a camping trip to Cow Island, one of several islands in Casco Bay just outside Portland Harbor. On it are two uninhabited Revolutionary War era forts that make a terrific place for camping, swimming, and partying.

I wasn't about to let a broken hand keep me from having fun, so I decided to take an oral antibiotic for the weekend rather than staying home to infuse the IV. Somehow I don't think the doctor would have approved.

We ferried two dozen people to the island, along with fishing gear, Nerf footfalls, and beer. I caught the first boat going over. I was still relatively sober as I set up my tent, drank beer, and prepared to have a fantastic time. By the time everyone arrived, we had created a "city" of more than a dozen tents.

I brought along a big bag of cocaine, and stayed up all night drinking and snorting lines. Consequently, the next morning I was one of first people in the United States to see the sun come up over the Atlantic Ocean. Pusherman, Go-Go, and a few others were also awake. I was still drunk and high when, an hour after sunrise, I decided to jump in the ocean.

I took two cans of beer and walked to the beach down a slippery, sandy hill. The path from the premium camping sites to the beach requires a walk along the steep concrete fort walls. The bad thing about the old forts is the ten-foot drop to the inside. On the way, I jumped up to the two-foot-wide wall to get off the sandy trail and slipped, almost falling into the ten-foot pit. In the process, I hit the cast on my right hand hard against the wall. I pulled myself back up, but because I was drunk I didn't think much about my hand.

I continued, more carefully, to the beach and dove into the cold water. It felt good to sober up a bit and get all the grime off my body. As I sat down to put my sandals back on, I noticed I had broken my cast. I knew I'd have to get it replaced, but I'd worry about that later.

I passed out in my tent and slept eight hours, only to get up and start drinking again. We partied all weekend and really had a great time. I went back to the mainland hung over, with a sore wrist and a wet, broken cast.

Looking back on that period in my life, I'm now convinced that I was bordering on insanity. The drugs and alcohol, being a new dad, and running 900-foot supertankers six months of the year was taking its toll. My roommate, Alan, had a similar perspective about how my life was going at the time.

The weekend at Cow Island was loaded with tons of alcohol and cocaine. Darryl was the first on the island and the last to leave. He was drunk the whole weekend. He went swimming with his cast on and acted like he didn't have a broken wrist with pins and screws holding him to-gether. I came home Sunday morning. Darryl came back Sunday night.

Sunday night we watched the Red Sox game. Darryl's cast was start-ing to come off anyway, so that night we ripped the rest of it off. We could see a lump that was apparently a metal pin. He then hooked himself up to the IV machine with one end connected to the wall socket. Darryl suddenly said he had to take a piss. He got up but could only go as far as the IV cord allowed. He turned away from me, opened his fly, and began to pee on the hardwood floor. He turned to face me, continuing to pee.

I yelled, "What the fuck are you doing?"

Darryl walked back to his chair and sat down. He seemed amazed at the pin popping out of his wrist. He pulled it out, showed it to me, and put it on the table. I got out a mop and cleaned up the mess. Darryl had no reaction whatsoever; to him it was like any other moment in time.

I knew Darryl was on his way out; I was watching him die. We had partied together for years, but something was different. It was like he'd given up on life. I felt so bad about it that I wrote Darryl a three-page letter telling him he was going to kill himself, either from the wrist infec-tion or by driving drunk, probably killing someone else in the process.

I wrote, "You're going to lose your son, your house, and everything else you worked hard to get." Darryl didn't read the letter. He was in total denial. —Alan Joiner, roommate and close friend

I now realize that many people were concerned for my welfare. But nobody could reach me. I didn't think my problem was serious enough to quit drinking and drugging. If you had to live my life, you'd drink and use drugs too.

Dr. Chance was frustrated that I wasn't giving my surgeries a chance to heal and told me, "You'll lose your right hand if you're not careful. These casts have only been lasting a month on you. Usually it's one cast per operation, and you've broken two."

I sheepishly admitted fault and asked how the X-rays looked, con-cerned they'd have to re-do the operation. My fears were well-founded.

Only the right wrist is broken.

Once again the doctors went to work on my hand. After several hours in recovery Dr. Chance came in to see me. He explained that my fall had badly damaged my wrist bones and the infection had eaten away the bones where the screws and pins were attached. He thought the bones should be removed.

"This will cause your hand to fall back just a little to the next set of wrist bones."

"You mean you'll take bones out, throw them in the trash, and one of my arms will be shorter than the other?" I asked anxiously.

I was out of control and didn't even know it.

"Nobody but you will know that your right arm is a little shorter than your left."

We got a second opinion, which confirmed the need to remove the bones, but having surgery meant I'd eventually regain almost all of the original strength and motion in my right hand. I agreed and scheduled the surgery.

Dr. Chance and everyone else at the surgery center always treated me respectfully. Unfortunately I didn't respect my own health. The pronounced four-inch scar on my right wrist, the result of four surgeries, is a constant reminder of just how out of control I was.

I called the new company I was working for, which had recently been created by my employer and two partner corporations. In 1999, Maritime Overseas Corporation, Keystone Shipping Company, and British Petroleum formed Alaska Tanker Company. At the time, MOC split its employees into two groups. MOC operated the smaller product tankers that carried clean oil, such as gasoline, diesel, and aviation fuel. Initially, I was selected to go with that fleet. The other fleet consisted of the much bigger crude oil supertankers to be operated by Alaska Tanker Company.

Since there was still plenty of oil coming out of Alaska, I asked to go with that fleet instead, thinking I'd have more job security. The Exxon Valdez oil spill in 1989, followed by the Oil Pollution Act of 1990, required that single-hulled ships and all ships with double bottoms but not double sides be phased out before 2015. I figured the ships carrying Alaskan crude would be phased out slowly, since most of them had double-hull bottoms. The smaller gasoline tankers were almost all single-hull ships. I thought that fleet would be gone earlier, but the company began building ten double-hull product tankers. The people who worked on them were actually promoted faster.

The personnel manager at Alaska Tanker Company wished me the best with the surgery. Yet the "new and improved" Darryl was showing signs of not being any different at all. Though I had accepted responsibility for being out of control, I continued to hold myself hostage to drugs and alcohol. I was only able to survive that turbulent period in my work life because my medical records and police records were confidential.

Then in addition to my wrist woes, my stomach started to bother me. I went to see a gastroenterologist and was diagnosed with gastroesophageal reflux disease, known as GERD. The acid reflux was constant, and it caused me to cough a lot. It got worse whenever I lay down. The doctor saw acid burns in my throat and referred me to a surgeon.

The doctors went in two different times to look around, discovering that the one-way check valve that connects the throat to the stomach was leaking; I needed stomach surgery. In layman's terms, they'd go in through my navel, wrap my lower esophagus around the top of my stomach, and sew it in place, creating a new and improved valve.

I opted to first have my wrist surgery and then as soon as I had recuperated enough I'd have the stomach surgery. The logic was to let them both heal at once and miss less work. And then I'd clean up my act.

On November 16, I had the infected bones taken out of my wrist, opting for a local anesthetic. The staff worked together efficiently and professionally. I had grown to love these people; they had really tried to help me throughout my ordeal.

I was curious, so I asked politely, "Dr. Chance, can I see inside my wrist before you sew it back up?"

"Sure, Darryl, let me get to a good point in the operation, and I'll let you see."

Several minutes passed, and the nurse pulled back the curtain. I looked down and saw my exposed flesh, tendons, and bones. Suddenly my right index finger started moving in a "come hither" motion. I shook my head in disbelief, and all the doctors and nurses laughed. One of them had a hold of the tendon that controlled my right index finger and was gently tugging on it to make it curl up and down.

"You guys are freaking me out!" I joked. They laughed again. I knew then I wasn't going to lose my hand.

I asked, "Can I keep the bones you took out as a little reminder?"

"We're way ahead of you, Darryl," Dr. Chance said, handing me a small vial with tiny bones inside. "There isn't much left of them," he said pointedly. "Now let's sew you back up."

I scheduled my stomach surgery for December 27. Plainly, my health was deteriorating as a direct result of my addictions, yet I was still in denial. I was already overboard, struggling not to drown in the aftereffects of alcohol and drugs, yet I wasn't even attempting to reach out for a life ring.

GLENN CHADBOURNE

CHAPTER THIRTY-TWO
LICENSE AND REGISTRATION, PLEASE

As far as I was concerned, my life was going in the right direction again. But I underestimated my alcoholism. It owned me. And I had no intentions of fixing *that* problem.

I was still healing from wrist surgery when I went to Damariscotta to visit friends and family. I had already consumed more than ten beers and hadn't eaten any supper when I made the unwise decision to drive Old Salt to Schooner Landing, a bar where a friend was playing with his band, The Boneheads.

At the bar I had a few mixed drinks and a half dozen more beers. I remember several people asking with concern if I was all right. I told them I was fine and kept drinking. At some point I went into a black-out, in which an alcoholic can appear like he's aware of what's going on, when in fact he has absolutely no idea what he's doing and has no memory the next day of what he did.

I don't remember leaving the bar, but I later found out that when I backed up my truck in the parking lot I sideswiped a vehicle so badly that the owner couldn't open either the front or back passenger doors. Someone saw me do it.

Since I only have partial memory of that night, I can only assume that at the time I realized I had hit another car and should leave quickly. Apparently I left the parking lot without anyone in law enforcement knowing I was operating under the influence. I then drove about five miles toward a buddy's cottage in Edgecombe. Suddenly I saw the red flashing lights of a fire truck.

Oh, man! What am I gonna do now? There must be a fire up in the woods.

I saw a fireman holding a stop sign, and the internal debate began.

He's not a cop, so if I don't stop, he can't arrest me. If I stop he'll know I'm really drunk. But if I don't stop, he'll probably call the cops. Maybe I should try to act sober and talk to him. What should I do? Forget it! I'm outta here!

I floored the accelerator and passed the fireman as he waved his arms for me to stop. I saw him talk into his radio and knew I had to quickly get out of Dodge. But when I rounded the corner, I couldn't believe my eyes. There were blue lights, red lights, and yellow lights flashing. Some young guy had rolled his vehicle, and emergency vehicles were everywhere. Of most concern to me was the Lincoln County Sheriff's cruiser blocking my way. I hit the brakes and crept forward slowly, thinking my only chance to get through the situation was to play dumb. If I turned around, I'd be admitting guilt. I stopped ten feet from the cruiser, and an officer walked up to my window.

"What's going on here?" I asked, trying to sound sober.

"Sir, have you been drinking? Let me see your license and registration, please," said the sheriff's deputy.

I can barely remember that night; I was going in and out of a blackout. I know I was belligerent. I was told afterward that when Sergeant Sceviour asked for my driver's license and registration, I shuffled through my glove box and handed him a Visa card. He told me to get out of the truck and arrested me. I was also told later that because I was threatening him and because I had a cast that prevented him from using handcuffs, he called for a cruiser with a caged window to prevent me from striking the officers in the front seat.

I remember thinking drunkenly, *I'm being caged like an animal. Don't they realize I'm a Merchant Marine officer home on leave?*

The police report dated November 26, 2000, states many things I don't remember. Later, it made me sick to read about my behavior that night.

Police report, third OUI:

```
11/26/00                 Spillman Data Syste ɜ, Inc.                      1072
14:53                        Deputy Repoi                    Page:      2


Charge: Criminal OUI  Title 29-A  Section 2411

Arrested : Darryl E. Hagar  DOB 040263     Witness/Fire Police :

            20 Chamberlain Ave.             Richard E Cougle DOB 080831
            Portland, Maine 04101           219 Acedemy Hill Road
                                            Newcastle, Me 563-1178

Vehicle Involved: 1995 Dodge Ram Pickup, Red in Color, Maine
                  Registration OLDSALT

Narrative :

   On Sunday, November 26, 2000, at approximately 0100 hours, I was
investigating a motor vehicle collision on the River Road,in the Town of
Newcastle, involving a vehicle which had rolled over, causing injuries
to the two occupants within the crashed vehicle. As the vehicle was
upside down, partly within the roadway, the River Road was closed as
numerous emergency vehicles were blocking the roadway. As a result, the
Newcastle Fire Chief assigned Fire Police Personnel to moniter and stop
traffic coming in from the east and west sides.

   While investigating the collision, I was advised by Fire Police
Attendant Richard Cougle,via radio, as to the fact a Red Dodge pick up
had failed to yield to his instructions, and was approaching the scene
heading west bound at a high rate of speed. Investigation found Mr.
Cougle had on a reflective vest, had a red wand flashlight, and had a
red rotating light activated on his vehicle on the east end of the scene,
approximately a forth of a mile away. Mr. Cougle also had a portable
stop sign visable advising the subject to stop at his location. Mr
Cougle advised he was concerned as he thought the truck may speed into
the scene causing another collision.

   Upon walking to the east side of the scene on the River Road, I
observed the red truck pulling up to the rear of a fire truck, which was
parked within the west bound travel lane, near my patrol car which had
blue lights activated. I approached the now stopped truck, and noticed
it was bearing Maine registration OLDSALT. I approached the drivers side
door area to the truck and noticed the truck was occupied by a sole
male.

   As I stood near the drivers door,I noticed the male subject was
looking straight ahead, with his eyes partly closed. As the subject did
not react to my pressence, I shined my flash light at him to get his
attention.I instructed him to roll his window down which he did. As he
did, I noticed and could hear the heat to the vehicle was on high, and
could feel the heat coming from within. At this point I began to smell
the strong odor of an intoxicating beverage coming from the vehicle
interior. I noticed a open knocked over bottle of Budweiswer beer on the
passenger seat. As the subject looked at me , he stated in extremely
slurred speech,"whats going on here". I advised him there had been an
accident and asked him if he observed the Fire Police back down the
road. The subject stated,"I saw him,I'm just tring to get down the
```

road".

While speaking with the subject, I noticed he had a cast on his right
wrist area. The subject had extremely blood shot eyes, and was so slurred
in speech, I could barely understand him. At this point I asked him to
step from his truck. As the subject did, I noticed him to stumble and
watched him grab onto the door for balance. As he walked to the front
of the truck, I noticed him to stumble again as he was unsteady on his
feet. I asked the subject for his drivers license and he reached into
his front jeans pocket and pulled out a credit card and handed it to me
I advised him that the card was not his license and he stated, "it must
be in the truck".

With this I asked the subject for his name and he stated, "why, I
have'nt done anything". I asked him if he had been drinking and he
stated, "no". While standing in front of him I could still smell a strong
odor of an intoxicating beverage coming from his facial area. At this
point I asked the subject if he would submit to several field sobriety
tests. The subject stated he would. The tests were observed as stated.

TEST 1) Standing, head back - Subject swayed side to side - subject
                           stepped to the rear to keep balance

TEST 2) ABC,s - Subject stated ABC and stopped. Subject refused to
                continue.

TEST 3) Finger to nose - Not used due to cast on hand

TEST 4) Heal to Toe 9 steps - Subject took 2 steps and stopped

At this point the subject became angry and stated I had no business
making him do the tests. He stated, "your gonna pay big time".

Based on the information supplied by Mr. Cougle, the subjects
condition, and field tests results, I advised the subject he was under
arrest for Criminal OUI. The subject was then identified as Darryl E.
Hagger.

At this point Sgt. Clayton Jordan, who was also on scene, walked over
to assist. As the subject had a cast on, I reached out and touched the
cast to determine in hand restraints were applicable. Upon doing so the
subject yelled out, " you just assaulted me". The subject refused to
follow instructions and was extremely beligerant.

With this Deputy Ronald Rollins arrived on scene and Mr. Hagar was
secured within his patrol unit. Mr. Hagar was transported to the County
Jail via Deputy Rollins.(see attached report)

Sgt Jordan then stood by the subjects vehicle, which I turned off, and
awaited Colby's Towing to arrive in order to remove the vehicle from
the scene for safe keeping.

Upon arriving at the Lincoln County Patrol Division, I was met by
Deputy Rollins who walked Mr. Hagar in from the Detention area. The
subject was seated near the intoxilyzer and asked to submit to a breath
test. The subject stated he was not interested in taking a test

stating,"your gonna pay , your gonna pay". At this point I began to read Mr. Hagar the Implied Consent Form. Mr. Hagar was read each requirement. He verbally stated he understood the first sentence, however stated he did not understand the next three. I read the form again and he laughed at me stating, " I don't understand" At this point I again asked him to submit to a test and he stated,"I'm not taking a test for you", as he again laughed. Mr. Hagar was asked to sign the green refusal form and he again laughed stated,"I am signing nothing, you are gonna get yours".Mr. Hagar who was extremely beligerant was then returned to the Detention area.

Mr. Hagar was then booked into the County Jail and issued a USAC for Criminal OUI. Upon asking him to sign the summons, he flately refused, again stating,"your gonna pay". He then began yelling, "why did you smash my head against the wall, why did you assault me".

Mr. Hagar who refused to cooperate with Correction Deputies was then placed into a holding cell in order to sober up,in order to complete the jail process paperwork.

Court Date: January 17, 2000 at 1030 hours.

Sgt. Dave R. Scviad
Responsible LEO:

Approved by:

Date

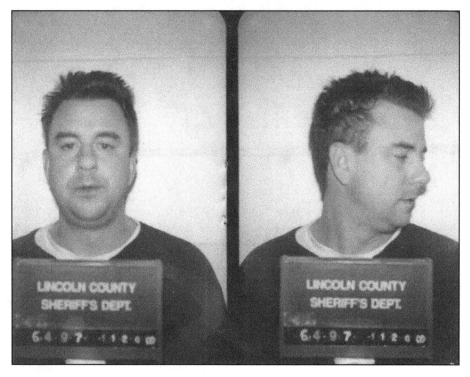

Third OUI, November 26, 2000.

I woke up in the morning to jail cell bars. Once again I would have to get my high powered lawyer to fix things. My friend from Edgecombe posted bail.

"Are you okay, Darryl?" he asked.

"I'm okay, man. I don't really remember what happened."

"Sergeant Sceviour said you were smoked last night. He said you were so drunk you had no idea what you had just done, and you could barely stand up."

"I've got to get a handle on myself. I'm getting way out of control," I said sadly.

I picked up my truck from where it had been towed. The damage to my truck consisted of a black stripe on the left front bumper, but the paint didn't match the white vehicle I had allegedly hit. I suspect that I did in fact hit the white vehicle and that the heat of rubbing the two vehicles together had left the stripe. Or I may have rubbed my truck against the rubber strip on the white vehicle's two doors. I wasn't charged with a hit and run, although it was reported that way in the local newspaper.

This time I was unable to manipulate my way out of the OUI, and state-mandated alcohol counseling was required to have my driver's license restored. But before I could do that, I had to first take care of my medical needs.

Eleven days after my arrest I had my stomach operation. I hoped it would finally solve my constant problem with acid reflux. But if the doctors had been privy to how I really lived, they would have quickly realized that my health problems were directly related to my lifestyle. They would have told me to stop using alcohol and drugs. They might have recommended I find a less stressful job.

But I never let anyone get close enough to know they should recommend those actions. I continued drinking and using, going from one chaotic event to another, dodging bullet after bullet. If I kept on that way, one of those bullets was eventually going to hit me. God only knew if I'd survive when it happened.

The surgeon, Dr. Cobean, proclaimed the procedure a success. When I came to, I looked down. My stomach was bandaged and there was the cast on my right hand. I felt like a robot in a repair shop. A nurse assured me I was would be all right.

"Can I ask you a blunt question?" I asked.

"Of course."

"When can I have sex again?"

"I'd worry about healing before I worried about sex," she said, obviously uncomfortable. She walked off.

I knew it was a sensitive subject, but I really wanted to know. I didn't want to mess up my stitches by having sex too soon. I really didn't think the question was unreasonable.

I was advised to keep to a strict diet of soup, ice cream, and frappes. But like everything else I did in life, I didn't follow directions. I stayed on the liquid diet, mainly beer and soup, for the first week, but then as my stomach healed I started experimenting.

When I ate a bite of steak or bread, I stood up facing the wall and leaned against it with my head buried in the bend of my elbow to allow gravity and my throat muscles to push the food down an inch at a time. As the days went by, force feeding stretched my surgery out sooner than anyone Dr. Cobean had ever operated on.

Like everything else I did in life, I bulled my way through—twenty-seven years of drugs and alcoholism, twenty years of navigating tankers, my father's suicide, no matter what it was. A captain once told me, "You're not a refined, high-tech mate; you're a hard-working, hands-on, bull-your-way-through mate. You always make it happen."

That's why it didn't surprise me that I healed faster from surgery than anyone else. I was used to discomfort and pain. My body had gone through a lot, and a little more abuse wasn't that big a deal. After a month I was eating like I had before surgery. Dr. Cobean was amazed at how quickly I made the transition to eating meat and bread. I laughed to myself, thinking, *Little do you know.*

I wanted my driver's license back, so I told the state-mandated therapist I wasn't drinking and that I wouldn't repeat past mistakes, all the while wearing a cast for an injury caused by excessive drinking. Because I had maintained my job with the same oil company for fifteen years, she believed me and agreed to write a letter to the Coast Guard. I was in survival mode and manipulating the system; that's what alcoholics do. I had to protect my interests in whatever way necessary to keep the status quo.

Gradually, I healed. I was hanging out with my son while Jen worked. I planned my drug and alcohol use for when Darryl wasn't with me. Alcohol was running my schedule.

At the time, I was worried because doctors couldn't figure out why at eighteen months Darryl still wasn't walking. Jen and I practiced with him and he showed progress, but he couldn't quite get the courage to walk on his own.

Wellness Health Associates, Inc.

February 16, 2001

RE: Darryl Hagar
     DOB: 04/02/1963

To Whom it May Concern:

This letter is written in support of Mr. Hagar and to help alleviate any concerns about renewing his United States Coast Guard Merchant Marines Officers License when the time arrives.

Mr. Hagar was required by the State of Maine to complete treatment as a result of receiving an OUI (operating under the influence) on November 26 of 2000. I saw Mr. Hagar for a total of six sessions over a six week period and completed a full history of his alcohol use as part of my assessment. He entered treatment with a positive attitude and exhibited motivation to accept all responsibility for his actions and make sure that this type of negative behavior is not repeated.

Mr. Hagar has worked in the Merchant Marine business, without incident, since his graduation from Maine Maritime Academy in 1985. He has worked his way up in responsibility over the years and does not take his job lightly. He honestly verbalized his dedication to providing the highest quality work he can, and was very upset that he allowed any off duty behavior to have a potential negative impact on his career.

My final diagnosis of Mr. Hagar's relationship with alcohol is problem use, in that, it has caused him a problem in the form of an OUI. I do not feel that Mr. Hagar suffers from alcohol dependency in any stage of the disease. The OUI appears to have been an isolated and unfortunate incident, one that I feel Mr. Hagar has learned a valuable lesson from and one he is assessed as low risk to repeat.

I have, in good conscience, signed the DEEP paperwork that will enable the State of Maine to reinstate his license to drive a motor vehicle. In closing, I would like to state that I understand the scope and magnitude of Mr. Hagar's job responsibilities, and also write this letter of support in good conscience.

Sincerely,

BA, LADC

Darryl's physical therapist thought the signals from his brain were not reaching all the nerves in his legs and feet, and she used techniques I doubted at first but found fascinating. She laid him across big rubber balls and allowed him to climb and roll around on them. She also placed him on his stomach and used a large feather to tickle the back of his legs to stimulate the nerve endings.

While Darryl was in physical therapy for his legs, I was in physical therapy for my wrist. I still had no driver's license, so I jogged two miles to therapy. It was good for my mind and body. At the time I was also going to the gym, further strengthening my body.

One day in March of 2001 when Darryl was twenty-two months old, Jen brought him to where I was rehabbing my hand. We took him to a long hallway with wall-to-wall carpet and Jen held him while I walked ten feet away and kneeled down. I think he knew what was happening, because Jen started him off toward me, and then he began to walk on his own. He teetered and tottered, but made it the whole ten feet, laughing the whole way.

We laughed and cheered as Darryl finally reached that important milestone. It was incredibly cute when Darryl laughed that day; we had been working with him for months, encouraging him, and he was so proud to walk in front of Mom and Dad. Jen and I were ecstatic.

City dock, Valdez, Alaska.

In April 2001, I flew to Port Angeles to join the Prince William Sound, an older 900-foot 125,000-ton crude oil carrier. I had been out of work for almost a year; it was nice to be back on the payroll. Alaska was such a beautiful place to sail into and we always loaded our oil there.

After hauling crude oil up and down the

Valdez, Alaska.

West coast for a few months we discharged 802,000 barrels of crude oil in Long Beach and sailed to Singapore for shipyard inspections and repairs. En route, we would clean the tanks. We Finished discharging 802,000 barrels of crude oil and anchored in the harbor to take on bunkers, stores, food, and tank-cleaning supplies.

Because the vessel was nearly thirty years old, she didn't have a fixed crude oil wash (COW) tank cleaning system. The COW allows high pressured crude oil to be sprayed in the empty cargo tanks, knocking the sludge free. Pumps then suction out the residue. It's one of the ways large crude oil tankers get the sludge out of their oil tanks in preparation for shipyard inspections or repairs. Without a COW system, the alternative was to wash the tanks with high-pressure water. That kind of cleanup is labor intensive. It's a 24/7 job that can take up to two weeks.

The cleanup got off to a bad start and only got worse. One of the able-bodied seamen didn't join the ship as planned, and one of the two pumpmen aboard went drinking in Tijuana and never came back. We were shorthanded from the beginning.

Anchored in Long Beach/Los Angeles Harbor.

Then the captain along with other officials decided to use high-temperature seawater to clean the tanks. The steaming hot water melted the oil off the sides of the tanks, but as it cooled it congealed at the bottom. The crew had to get into the tanks and shovel the muck into buckets, which then had to be winched up and out. The sludge was dumped into 55-gallon drums, sealed, and tied aft to a railing, set for disposal in Singapore.

The crew called it "the cleanup from hell." Day after day we descended 70-foot ladders into dark, oily tanks the size of a seven-story apartment building. It was like descending into the dark belly of a huge beast. Each day we put on white industrial throwaway suits and came back up completely covered in black sludge. The summer temperatures sometimes topped 120 degrees Fahrenheit in the tanks. We shoveled that sticky, oily mess for close to a month.

I worked eight hours every day in my capacity as second mate, navigating the ship. I then worked four hours overtime in the dreaded oil tanks. It was the hardest, most labor intensive thing I've ever done. But the physical labor turned out to be a great way of rehabbing my wrist and getting my body back in shape. As difficult as it was, we got the ship ready for the shipyard without anyone completely losing it. Guys came close to throwing punches, but cooler heads always prevailed.

When we finally entered the Straits of Singapore, my navigation work had been right on schedule to the hour. I was a good navigator. It's rewarding to set courses and take a 125,000-ton supertanker on a multi-thousand-mile journey, arriving exactly where and when planned. Through the use of computers and GPS satellite navigation we could figure our position on the planet within inches and calculate our time of arrival to the minute, three weeks in advance.

Having a good work ethic served me well through the years. The captains I worked under always knew I was on top of things and diligent in my duties. As long as they kept me sober they knew they had no worries, and as long as we were at sea, I was sober. More than one captain jokingly said about me, "Good worker at sea, needs guidance in port."

The night before entering the Straights of Singapore we set a pirate watch and kept our deck lights on at night. We boarded a pilot, who guided us to an anchorage outside the entrance to the Port of Singapore, where dozens of local laborers descended on the vessel to work around the clock for days to finish cleaning the remaining 20 percent of the tanks. We then boarded another pilot who took us to Keppel Shipyard, where the ship would undergo expensive repairs for a month.

After a few days some of us sauntered over to Orchid Towers, where prostitution is rampant. On the bottom floor of a set of tall office buildings are shopping malls, souvenir shops, and restaurants. But the next four floors are full different kinds of bars, and the bars are full of prostitutes. It's known throughout the world as the "Four Floors of Whores," especially to sailors, soldiers, and businessmen.

The four floors each house three to five bars, each with its own personality and regular women from all over the world. There's the Texas Bar and the Manila Bar. Some bars have women of mixed race and nationalities. One floor has a bar with a live band in an auditorium that holds more than a thousand people. I can only imagine the money from sex that place generates.

Prostitution isn't exactly legal in Singapore, but it's not exactly illegal either. The government probably gets its cut, and the girls go through a health screening. Illegal immigrants are not tolerated.

My buddies and I visited Orchid Towers on many nights, and I eventually shacked up with many different women. It wasn't long before I ran out of money, so I had to hit the captain up for a draw. During foreign shipyard periods the men spent a lot of money on drinking and prostitutes, so the captain got more requests for money than usual.

I was standing in a draw line, embarrassed because the captain knew how much each man was spending. I knew he was keeping an eye on me. The port captain was with him, watching the men file through.

Our captain asked, "How much do you need, Second Mate?"

I didn't want to have to keep coming back for money. "I'll take $1,000, please, Cap."

The port captain asked, "What are you guys doing with all your money? Guys were getting big money the other day too."

"I don't know about everyone else, but I'm going to take advantage of the cheap prices here and have a couple of nice suits tailored."

The port captain bought my story, because he didn't work around us every day; I suspect our captain wasn't quite so gullible.

I spent the money in just a few days, drinking and sleeping with exotic ladies of the evening. At the end of the day the lure of beautiful women and cold beer got the best of me and I inevitably headed to Orchid Towers. One night I was out with the guys and drank an incredible amount of vodka and beer. I picked up a beautiful brunette. She talked me into leaving, which turned out for the best. I was already far more drunk than I should have been, and I had to work the next day.

At the hotel, I barely remember paying at the front desk and buying the standard condoms, soap, and towels. We went to our room, got undressed, started kissing—and I passed out.

A few hours passed, and I awoke to the lovely brunette shaking me gently. "Mr. Darryl, I have to go."

The sun was coming up. *Ah, man, I gotta work and I'm wrecked. Oh, well. I'm going home tomorrow.* Unbelievably, the woman hadn't taken my wallet and disappeared after I passed out. Of course, some women from Orchid Towers hope an American sailor will fall in love with them and take them home.

I gave her $100. She left, and I showered and tried to get dressed. I got as far as putting on underwear and had to lie down to prevent myself from vomiting. I waited a few minutes, managed to put on socks, and had to lie down again. It was one of the worst hangovers I'd ever had.

I somehow made it to the ship while it was still early and bulled my way through the day. I put the bridge in order for the new second mate so he wouldn't come in blind and have to figure everything out on his own.

The following day I showed the second mate my plans for navigating the ship back to Alaska. I was finally done. I then went down below, where the captain gave me a work evaluation, which was good, but not perfect. I received excellent marks for navigation skills, managerial skills, knowledge and management of cargo oil systems, and my ability to run the ship smoothly. I rated average on computer technology. That hurt my feelings a bit, but it was true. When I got home I enrolled in several computer classes and came back stronger in that area. I was a drunk, but I was a proud and relentless drunk.

I flew home on July 16, 2001, with connections to Tokyo and Chicago. The trip took twenty-four hours. One of the third mates flew home to New York at the same time, so we drank together for several hours. Our contract called for the officers to be flown business class or better, so we were up front with big, comfortable leather reclining seats and freealcohol. I was always a little uncomfortable about that when the regular crew was in crowded coach seats in the back, but it was what it was.

My son and me at the airport after a long trip at sea, 2002.

At home I was greeted by Jen and Darryl, who was almost two and a half. Jen was always great about picking me up at the airport so I could be welcomed home by my son. Even though we were no longer a couple, we tried our best to get along for Darryl's sake. I owe her my gratitude for that. Going home to a little boy who screamed "Daddy!" and ran into my arms at the airport made for some of the fondest memories of my entire life.

I took Darryl home for some dad-and-son time. The first week home with him was the only time in my life I could relax and be a normal human being. On the one hand, I was a hard-working, foul-mouthed Merchant Marine officer, sailing around the world and acting like a pirate. Then I'd get a brief respite when my heart opened up to a little boy who helped me hang onto my sanity because of my deep love for him. Then in a few short weeks my alcoholism and drug addiction owned me again, and I moved to the dark side until my next voyage. It was a rugged life,

Returning home from sea, 2003: my other savior.

and it hardened my soul. I wasn't sure I'd ever become just a normal man with a loving wife and children and a little peace and serenity.

Then I flew to Philadelphia on August 10 to complete two courses required for my job: Medical Person in Charge and First Aid Responder. On cruise ships with their thousands of passengers, having a doctor on board makes sense. But the ships I navigated had twenty-three-man crews, so the company trained crewmembers for medical emergencies.

The training was informative and rewarding. One day we talked about substance abuse. We were taught "how much is too much" and how to recognize if you have a drinking problem. I even took a twenty-question alcoholism test. If you scored above a nine, you might have a drinking problem. I scored a *twenty-nine*. Even with the evidence right in front of my nose, I didn't think I had a problem serious enough to require professional help.

I drank every night after being in classes all day. Near the end of the week I stayed up way too late and drank way too much. I stumbled back to my hotel and passed out. My alarm rang early. I showered, brushed my teeth, and drank coffee, but I still felt intoxicated. I looked in the mirror at my red, half-open eyes. *I hope today it's something easy. If I'm lucky, just listening to lectures.*

But that day we worked closely with the nurses. The schedule included practicing CPR on a dummy, using the heart defibrillator, inserting an IV needle into an orange, and stitching up a wound on a dead pig.

I did well the whole day until we got to the pig. I made the incision, started sewing, and got confused about how to close the wound. I had to ask for help. I was embarrassed, because all day long people had been telling me I smelled like booze. I decided to be upfront and tell the nurse I'd had a long night, that I hadn't intended to drink so much, but that's what happened.

She ignored my comment and showed me several times how to tie the knots. I got them right after a few tries, but I was still embarrassed. I regretted drinking the night before. Not only was I ruining my health, I was ruining my reputation. Although I cared what people thought, I couldn't control myself.

Of course, that night I went to the bar again for a little hair of the dog.

CHAPTER THIRTY-THREE
ENVIRONMENTAL PROTECTION

One day I was watching my two-year-old son after a night of heavy drinking and drug use. I sobered up enough to fool Jen that I was okay to watch Darryl. But whenever I came down off cocaine, the next day I was always irritable. I called it a "coke over" instead of a hang over. Darryl was cranky that day, and when he wouldn't do what I asked, I shook him a little, and he struck out at me with his little two-year-old hand. In response, I slapped him across the face, and he cried.

What I did is a perfect example of why people abusing alcohol and drugs shouldn't be allowed to watch even their own kids. Drug abusers and drunks have volatile minds and overreact to perfectly normal situations. Drugs and alcohol unsettle the brain. Patience becomes non-existent, creating potentially dangerous and life-threatening situations.

In addition to being volatile, my body and brain were becoming saturated. I liken it to how brine affects a cucumber. You can turn a cucumber into a pickle, but you can't turn a pickle back into a cucumber. Once you're pickled, you're pickled.

The only thing that kept me from becoming permanently pickled was going back to sea. After a few days on ship my mind cleared. At sea my body cleansed itself. After three months of hard labor and using my brain every day, I was back to normal. Those periods of abstinence saved my body and soul.

Once I walked down that gangway, all hell broke loose. A fog settled in my brain for three months of drinking and drug use. That battle raged within me for twenty-seven years. As I grew older my body no longer recovered as it had when I was young. I was thirty pounds heavier, starting to gray, and I needed daily medications for my medical conditions.

I was sinking lower and lower, reaching a point of no return. I blacked out nearly every time I drank. I got up in the morning and drank until I passed out in the afternoon. I'd wake up after dark, not remembering if it was morning or night. When I figured out it was nighttime, I was happy. I could get drunk all over again. Getting drunk twice a day was a progression downward into a very bad place.

For the first time in my life, I worried about people thinking I was a drunk. Whenever someone knocked on my door, I hid my alcohol. I stockpiled cases of beer in the refrigerator and the basement. I worried about running out of alcohol in the middle of the night when the stores were closed, so I kept a case of beer and a bottle of booze tucked away for "emergencies."

If we had a party at my house and the beer ran low, I hid cans in the butter drawer or behind the milk in the refrigerator, in the oven, in the cupboards—wherever I thought my friends wouldn't look. But I had friends just like me, people like Pusherman who also hid beer or tried to find my stash.

I was starting to realize that I drank differently from most people. It intruded on my consciousness that maybe I did have a problem. At the same time, I tried to maintain some sense of sanity around my son. He was the one thing in my life that saved me. I really loved him and tried hard to control my drinking so Jen wouldn't take him from me. She has always been a great mother and naturally was concerned for Darryl's safety. That forced me to tone down the drinking around him.

Yet I never asked God to relieve me of the obsession to drink. Many times I lay awake at 5:00 a.m. suffering through cocaine withdrawals, unable to sleep, thinking I was having a heart attack. I said many prayers asking God to help me, but asking God to keep me alive wasn't the same thing as asking him to help me get clean. At some point all drug addicts promise God that if he'll just help them this one last time, they'll never do it again. They'll change their lives forever. I quickly forgot those promises after the withdrawals and hangovers went away. Then I'd make another promise during the next binge or crisis.

As my addictions progressed, I broke other promises to myself. For years I was disciplined enough to stop using drugs a week before I went back to work, because of drug testing. That resolve began to dwindle.

Stop the madness!

The Coast Guard requires drug testing on all individuals on vessels in the U.S. Merchant Marine. That includes mandatory pre-employment, post-accident, probable cause, and random testing, although random testing seems to unwittingly push addicts to use harder drugs with their quick trip out of the bloodstream instead of the less dangerous marijuana, which sits in the fat cells for weeks.

Addicts typically know how long it takes the body to rid itself of each substance. My drug of choice, cocaine, takes seventy-two hours, meaning that if you know when to quit it won't show up in your urine. Drug users know how to work the system to greatest advantage. I suspect airline pilots, CEOs, doctors, firefighters, police officers, teachers, even judges know how to beat a drug test. I know people who drank liquids designed to mask drug use—I once bought a bottle, but never used it. Sometimes people succeed in manipulating the system, sometimes they don't: The only sure way to pass a drug test is to not do any drugs.

For years I was diligent about not doing cocaine for a week before I went back to sea, leaving myself a four-day buffer. Eventually I justified using right up to the three-day cutoff. When I started smoking crack, I did it the night before I flew to work. Of course, as my addiction progressed, at first I *did* crack cocaine. Then I didn't want to do crack cocaine, but did it anyway. Then I had no choice: I had to do crack cocaine.

After another rough vacation filled with drinking and drugs, I flew to LAX airport on November 3, 2001, to join a ship in Long Beach, California. Until then I'd been doing cocaine every day—snorting it, smoking it, and all the while worrying about drug tests. The insanity of addiction is that you know right and wrong, but you can't make the right decision.

I was experienced enough to know that the Port of Long Beach was a prime opportunity for drug testing. I arrived around noon but stayed at the airport for five hours, just in case. I arrived at the ship after 5:00 p.m. to find out the drug testers had just left. If I had shown up right after I landed, a urinalysis would have indicated cocaine. I had outmaneuvered the system yet again.

During that work tour, we ran up and down the West Coast, loading crude oil in Valdez and discharging near Seattle, San Francisco, and Los Angeles. For the most part, our ships went where British Petroleum owned refineries. When British Petroleum bought ARCO, we included ARCO refineries on our itinerary. The mergers of big oil companies controlled which company's ships hauled crude oil to which refineries.

I had an uneventful trip except for one storm in the Gulf of Alaska. It was very cold and windy, with a lot of sea spray. When we pulled into Valdez in the middle of the night we were in for a big surprise. The entire 900-foot supertanker was covered in three inches of solid ice. The captain called "all hands" to warm up the mooring winches and exercise the frozen valves and equipment.

Having been awakened early, I was grumpy as I walked out onto the frozen supertanker. My frustrations skyrocketed as we tried to use the equipment. Nothing worked. We had to chip ice with hammers and hatchets and pit hot steam on valves and motors to melt the ice. It was a nightmare. I felt like we were at the North Pole or on some reality TV show. We dressed in Arctic gear—snow suits, snow boots, gloves, fur hoods, and face masks covering as much skin as possible. The work wasn't for the physically or mentally weak; this was the Merchant Marine at its toughest.

On that same work tour, I found myself talking to some recovering alcoholics on board. Several men had significant sobriety. Their stories of old drinking and drugging days were exactly like mine. Perhaps I wasn't so special and unique.

For the first time in my life someone offered to help me. A seaman, sober twenty years, offered to take me to a twelve-step meeting when we pulled into Port Angeles. I had never seriously considered the twelve-step program. The only time I'd ever gone to meetings or to see an alcohol counselor was after an OUI conviction, and that was only to get my driver's license back.

Even the ropes are frozen.

Nothing works when it's this cold.

But I took my new friend's advice. As we walked into the meeting hall, I felt like a hundred pair of eyes were on me, though there were really only twenty-five friendly people there. They circled the room and finally got to my buddy, who confidently introduced himself. Then it was my turn. I spoke words I'd never said before: "Hi everyone, my name is Darryl, and I'm an alcoholic." It was a tough decision. As I waited my turn, I had gone back and forth about whether to say those words.

"Hi, Darryl. Welcome!" the people responded in unison.

Wow! That wasn't so bad. The earth didn't shake. Lightning didn't strike. Maybe I am just another drunk who's never admitted a drinking problem. When I finally admitted it aloud, the only one surprised to hear it was me.

That was the only time I ever went to a twelve-step meeting while on board a ship. I wasn't done drinking. I needed to go back home and let the booze prove to me yet again that I was, in fact, an alcoholic.

I flew home on February 24, 2002. I still went on frequent drug and alcohol binges, but I maintained enough not to get arrested or break any bones. In those days, that was a miracle.

We celebrated Darryl's third birthday on May 4. I headed to Port Angeles on May 26 to shuttle oil up and down the coast on the Prince William Sound. One time we stopped in San Francisco, a beautiful city to see from the ocean. We boarded a pilot, who took us under the Golden Gate Bridge, south of Alcatraz, and then due east under the Bay Bridge. We docked at Anchorage No. 9.

Dropping anchor on a supertanker is an event. A weight equivalent to a multi-ton dump truck hangs on the end of a massive chain. When you let off the brake, smoke and sparks fly everywhere. Each time we dropped anchor I had to signal the boatswain to put on the brake at just the right time to ensure the anchor wouldn't pull the chain out of the chain locker—thus losing it to the sea. I did it a hundred times and could relate many tales about dropping anchor in various weather conditions and in different ports around the world.

After we docked, I took the first launch ashore, where I ran into two San Francisco ship's pilots out chasing women and drinking beer. Both had guided the Prince William Sound several times. At first we got a kick out of running into each other. We drank several beers together. But what was supposed to be "just a few" for me turned into double digits. And what started out as fun turned into an experience I didn't remember ending. When I awoke the next morning, I didn't think much about it; I had blacked out many times.

But the next time I ran into the pilots, they were distant. I knew from experience they must have seen the alcoholic Darryl come out that night. Whatever had happened, they clearly didn't want to have anything to do with me. I shrugged it off as just another bad drinking experience. I suspect they felt they had dodged a bullet—word could have reached the Coast Guard, the oil company, or their maritime pilot's association that a mate on a supertanker had gotten drunk with a couple of ship's pilots.

In the summer of 2002, the Prince William Sound pulled into Seattle's Todd Shipyard for several weeks of repairs. It was good duty. We could go ashore at the end of the day for dinner and drinks, plus the Boston Red Sox were in town playing the Mariners at the new Safeco Field. The third engineer, who was from Boston, had scored two tickets.

At Safeco Field we immediately gravitated to the beer garden at center field. It opens right before the game starts, and we were first in line. We grabbed a table overlooking center field with an awesome view and had a great time hollering for Boston along with a few hundred other Red Sox fans.

I went into another blackout that night and woke up on the ship to wet jeans and a wet spot on the floor of my stateroom that smelled of urine. I realized I could no longer control myself when drinking and decided it was time to be more careful. Clearly my drinking was getting worse. I was blacking out more, I couldn't control my bladder, and

Todd Shipyard, Seattle, Washington
(with the Space Needle in view across Puget Sound).

I sometimes woke up covered in vomit. I also constantly thought about alcohol; it had become an obsession.

I knew I'd have to shower, brush my teeth, use mouthwash, and brush my teeth again before I went to work. I also chewed gum because I could still smell the beer. I knew people would be able to smell it on me; I often got comments that I should brush my teeth again.

On August 24, I got off the ship and flew home. Jen had brought Darryl to the airport, and he came running into my arms. Those were the happiest moments of my year. I wished I could make time stand still. People in the airport always smiled as they watched a little boy run into the arms of his returning father. I looked forward to those moments and still cherish the memories. Each time my son welcomed me home, I realized again why my life was important. I had this little guy to set an example for. I was in a battle to survive, to ensure that my son had a father while he was growing up.

I spent time with Darryl while Jen worked, but was having a hard time staying sober. For the most part, I was pretty good when I was with him. I partied when Darryl was with Jen, and I didn't when he was with me.

A night I'll remember forever occurred a few weeks later. I had Darryl for the day while Jen worked at her nursing job. That day I hooked up with my buddy Bulldog, who told me he had some good cocaine. I bought a gram. I was tempted to do a few lines, but decided to wait until the next day when Darryl wasn't with me.

Darryl and I had dinner and played and read together. After I put him to bed, I drank a few beers. At that point I really wanted to do some cocaine. I knew Jen might call and check in on Darryl, so I did just a few lines so she wouldn't detect anything.

After drinking a few more beers and doing a few more lines, I got the brilliant idea to call Jen before she called me. That way I wouldn't be too screwed up when she talked to me. The problem with that grand plan was that I my body was so saturated, using even a little affected me noticeably. When I called, it took Jen about ten seconds to figure out what I was doing.

"Hi, Jen. I'm just checking in," I said nervously.

"What's going on? Is Darryl in bed?" She was surprised to hear from me. Usually she was the one calling.

"He's in bed. We had a good supper. I read to him and tucked him in."

Her voice rose. "What's the matter with you? You sound weird. Are you doing cocaine?"

"Of course not. I'm just watching the Red Sox," I said defensively.

"Are your friends over there doing cocaine while my son is upstairs sleeping?" she yelled.

"Nobody's here, and I'm not doing any drugs."

"You're lying! I know when you're doing drugs! I can hear it in your voice. I'm coming over to pick up Darryl, you asshole!"

She showed up ten minutes later, screaming and yelling. I deserved it, and the guilt set in. She stomped upstairs and scooped Darryl out of bed, still asleep in his pajamas.

"I should call the cops on you! You're not seeing him until you quit drinking and drugging!" she yelled, slamming the door.

I started thinking I was going to lose my son. It was the first time anything in my life had prompted me to think about changing—but could I do it? I was weak, and I was in love. I was in love with my son, but I was also in love with drugs, alcohol, and the wild life.

My addictions were so entrenched that I knew I'd have my hands full trying to quit. My body had gone from being able to do three grams of cocaine followed by drinking, with nobody knowing I was doing drugs, to not being able to do a couple of lines without peering out the window to see if the cops or the DEA were after me. My friend Go-Go often joked: "The definition of paranoid is when you pull up behind a police cruiser and you think he's following you." I was already there.

Jen remained upset with me. My actions had negatively affected her work schedule. I was paying child support, but she still needed to work, and she couldn't trust me to watch Darryl anymore. She thought Darryl was better off in daycare than with a daddy consumed by alcoholism and drug addiction. In order to see him again I had to swear on a Bible I would never do drugs around him again. I kept that vow. I still did plenty of drugs, but not while I had Darryl. I knew Jen was serious about keeping him from me. Darryl was the last thread of sanity I had going, so I cleaned up just enough to keep him in my life.

I went back to sea and worked through the holidays. I sailed through the winter before getting off the vessel to attend an Alaska Tanker Company leadership safety conference for a week in March of 2003. The conferences made me nervous, because they served free alcohol every night starting at 5:00 p.m. They also served free wine during after-dinner presentations about the new $200 million 900-foot double-hulled supertankers they were building.

Among the ships' officers there was debate about whether the company served free alcohol to loosen up the officers so they'd tell the higher-ups how they really felt about company operations. My take was that the company understood the pressures of going to sea, so they allowed us to let our hair down at conferences. Due to the Exxon Valdez, that kind of "relaxation" was restricted on the ships. The conferences gave officers a chance to socialize without fear of reprisal. Of course, they knew there were guys like me who drank too much, but they certainly didn't recognize us as alcoholics.

The CEO of Alaska Tanker Company, Anil Mathur, was at the conference, as well as the COO, the office management team, captains I had sailed under through the years, chief engineers, other company officers, and Bob Malone, BP's American regional manager. When Congress called the oil companies to testify on Capitol Hill, Bob Malone represented British Petroleum. Half of the captains, engineers, and mates were still at sea running the ships; they would attend a second conference later that year. A skeleton crew ran the company's home office in Beaverton, Oregon.

One night, a gentleman gave a presentation and then invited audience questions. After having a bottle of red wine and several beers, I felt the need to speak up. I said into a microphone: "What's the plan with the passage plans?"

The presenter looked at me and paused, confused by the question. Deck officers in the audience explained that the passage plans were navigation waypoints and details of passages and track lines where our ships ran. Since the ships were new, I knew the computers were new, too. My drunken logic told me that meant the computers were empty, thus no passage plans. It made perfect sense to this drunk, but everyone looked at me like I had two heads.

He finally answered, "The captains of the new ships will decide what to load onto the new navigation systems. I assume they'll copy the information in the current ships' computers and download them into the new computers."

Several guys in the audience laughed and shook their heads, knowing I was half drunk. I skated by without a reprimand.

After another night at the free bar, I woke up to a wet bed. I didn't have time to strip the sheets and hoped the maid would think I spilled water. I showered and went to the scheduled meetings. I returned to my room later that morning, thinking about drinking a beer to take the edge off, but I decided having beer breath might get me in serious trouble, so I opted for water. On the way I ran into the maid.

"Hi, sir. Is everything okay? Is the room all right?" she asked.

"Yes, everything is fine. I'm sorry the room was such a mess this morning. I spilled some water in the bed," I said, embarrassed.

"I know, sir. I saw it and cleaned it up. Do not worry. Everything is fine." She smiled and walked away.

The conference ended. I went home and spent a few weeks with Darryl before going out and getting drunk with my friend Jazz. That night for the first time I used OxyContin, a pain-reliever similar to morphine. When I woke up I was hung over and having chest pains. I seriously considered calling 911 to report a drug overdose. OxyContin obviously hadn't agreed with me. I'm lucky I didn't die that night.

After several days I still wasn't feeling well, so I called my doctor about the pain in my chest. Against my will, she called an ambulance. I freaked out, thinking they might give me a drug test I would probably fail. I heard sirens and went outside to meet the ambulance. Two EMTs took my vital signs and transported me to Maine Medical Center. I hadn't had a heart attack, but was told I had an irregular heart rhythm. I later took a stress test and passed with flying colors.

For my next work tour in April 2003, I learned that for the first time in my twenty-year career I'd be sailing as backup to the regular chief mate. He would be in charge of a tank cleanup, and I'd be in charge on deck when he was sleeping. We discharged our remaining oil in Long Beach, and set sail for Singapore.

We put in long, hard hours, but it was rewarding to finally sail on my chief mate's license, to be trusted with the daunting task of cleaning a 900-foot supertanker. Alcohol had destroyed the self-confidence necessary for advancing my career, and my crazy lifestyle had hurt my dream of becoming captain. I was comfortable as one of the company's best second mates, but I had always felt apprehensive about the greater responsibility of being full-time chief mate. I couldn't share these fears with anyone.

Of course, during that work tour I still had the security of having the regular chief mate to call if there were problems. I sailed as backup chief mate for two weeks. When the bulk of the cleanup was over, the captain asked me to move back to second mate.

We pumped the tank-washing residue into slop tanks and planned a stop in Manila for shore disposal. Until the late 1980s, oily slops were legally pumped directly into the ocean, but the laws had changed. There weren't many facilities that could handle the hazardous waste, and disposal was expensive. The decision to deviate to the Philippines made my job more difficult as ship's navigator. The captain had me pull every applicable chart, bring them up to date, lay out the new courses, choose new waypoints, and enter the information into the navigation computers.

I was relieved by the third mate at 0800 on the morning we approached the Philippines. It was foggy and the ship and small-vessel traffic was incredibly heavy. I asked the captain if he wanted me to stay on the bridge as an extra set of eyes. He thanked me for offering, but told me to go rest; the chief mate would need me later when they were pumping the oily slops ashore.

We boarded a pilot and anchored in Manila Bay. I slept a short time and went back on duty as we cleared customs and immigration. After many hours of negotiations and planning between the captain and a ship's agent, an oil barge pulled alongside, mooring lines were passed between the vessels, and the oily slops were discharged through a six-inch hose.

Arrangements were made for another barge to come out the following day to finish the disposal. The next day, we waited. The captain finally called the agent to ask why the barge hadn't arrived. The agent assured him it would come the next day.

The oil barge again failed to show up. We sat at anchor wasting time and losing $50,000 a day in extra expenses. The captain was frustrated and angry. From my point of view, being there a few more days meant an opportunity to visit Manila, known for its beautiful women and flourishing sex trade. The lure of beer and exotic women was strong. It took all my inner strength to resist temptation, but I made the right decision for once and stayed on board.

The agent finally found a company to haul the oil away, but he wouldn't disclose where they would dispose of the oily slops. He told the captain not to worry about it, but the captain yelled at him. The captain knew the oily slops would go straight into the ocean as soon as the barge was out of sight of our vessel.

The captain threatened to pick up anchor and do the disposal in Singapore. It would be more expensive, but was the right thing to do. The agent said we couldn't leave the Philippines before being released from customs and immigration. The captain threatened to heave anchor for Singapore, released or not. The agent came out early the next morning with the paperwork.

The captain's actions made me proud to work for him. Alaska Tanker Company and British Petroleum have zero tolerance for oil pollution, and the captain had followed their environmental protection guidelines, no matter what.

I was on the bridge the entire transit out of Manila. The captain was one of the company's most competent seafarers, and we worked together like a well-oiled machine. He made course changes as needed to avoid traffic. I told him if we were in the center of the channel and indicated how close we would come to passing vessels as we made adjustments.

We remained right on target. The captain and I handled every ship, boat, and vessel smoothly and calmly, one at a time, always dealing with the closest first.

After we hit the open ocean, the captain surprised me by coming up to me, beaming. "Darryl, you did a very nice job this morning. We make a great navigation team. That was intense traffic. We handled it like we were out on a Sunday sail."

I was surprised because he was always happy with my work and always thanked me. I supposed that after going through the environmental corruption nightmare at Manila and leaving at the busiest time of the morning, he was greatly relieved. I thanked him genuinely, and he instructed me to set safe track lines to Singapore.

"Aye, aye, Cap," I said, smiling. It was nice to get a pat on the back once in awhile.

GLENN CHADBOURNE

CHAPTER THIRTY-FOUR
SARS, SEX, AND SINGAPORE

When Alaska Tanker Company had decided to take the thirty-year-old Prince William Sound to Sembawang Shipyard in Singapore for an $11 million overhaul, many in the crew had been concerned about SARS (Severe Acute Respiratory Syndrome).

Before the vessel left the United States, the ship's officers met with company officials to voice our concerns about traveling to Asia, where SARS was epidemic. The company assured us the Singaporean government was closely monitoring outbreaks throughout the region and that we'd be safe. I felt uneasy since I was responsible for my son, but the company seemed to be on top of it.

After responsibly discharging the first portion of the tank-washing slops in Manila, we steamed at full speed and several days later entered the Singapore Straits, where a pilot maneuvered the vessel to an anchorage. A few hours later a neat-looking 200-foot coastal tanker pulled alongside to discharge the remaining oily slops. What a difference it made, being in a modern country.

We had a few days to go ashore in the evenings, and as soon as we got to the ferry terminal we passed through a government health check station. Everyone infected with SARS ran a fever. If your temperature was normal, they allowed you to pass.

I spent that first night in Singapore drinking with some of the crew. It was like a scene from an old movie with sailors toasting each other and singing. After several hours, we stumbled back to the dock and caught an open-air launch. One of the guys had a fantastic voice and started singing. We each cracked a beer and sang together on the way back to the ship. It's a memory I'll always cherish.

I went ashore often, each night sleeping with a woman I picked up at Orchid Towers. I now realize that the strong lure the prostitutes had on me was the beginnings of sex addiction. It was easy to "buy" any gorgeous woman I wanted. The pull got stronger with each passing day.

After several days a pilot guided us to Sembawang Shipyard. The Prince William Sound would be shifted into drydock where repairs and inspections would be completed. Then the Prince William Sound would be shifted from drydock to a regular dock and sit in Singapore until the company found work for her. There was too much tonnage, i.e., too many ships and not enough oil demand. From time to time vessels were taken out of service.

Dry-docked supertanker, Singapore.

It was June, and I would fly home in a few days. I was tired from the shipyard preparation and vessel cleanup. But I had one last evening off and several hundred dollars in my pocket, so I went to Orchid Towers. I chose a sexy brunette with a knockout body who seemed like a nice girl.

**The S/T Prince William Sound in
dry dock, Singapore.**

I drank heavily. The brunette dragged me out on the dance floor, and I thought I was the disco king. I was loud and foolish, just one of many men acting that way, but probably the drunkest person in the bar.

We went to a hotel, and I continued to imbibe. The next thing I knew, I was face down on the bed passed out. I tried to come out of it, but was only semi-conscious. My eyes were open, but my body wasn't responding. I tried to get up and fell back down.

I saw the brunette take all the money out of my wallet. I tried to tell her to stop, but I couldn't speak clearly. I reached out and mumbled something. She looked at me, money in hand, and ran. "You snooze, you lose" was just a phrase I'd heard my whole shipping career without ever thinking about what it really meant. When I woke up later to see my empty wallet on the floor, I understood. I ran outside. Two men were sitting nearby, and when they saw me they laughed. I had to assume they knew what had happened with the prostitute.

The woman had seemed innocent enough that not trusting her hadn't crossed my mind. Of course, she was nowhere to be found. I went back to the room and passed out again. I got up in the morning dry-mouthed with a pounding headache and sick stomach.

I thought, *I didn't sleep with her. At least I don't have to worry about disease.* That's how I thought throughout my drinking career: *At least I didn't get arrested with drugs . . . At least I didn't get an OUI . . . At least I didn't run over someone's kid.* Being rolled by a prostitute was just another event I ignored in my denial.

I took my bruised ego back to the ship and had to retrieve money out of my stateroom to pay the cabbie. I told no one that I'd been ripped off by a lady of the evening. I still had my pride. I flew home the following day.

I made it out of Singapore without SARS, HIV, or an STD. Aware of my developing sex addiction, I saw being disease-free as a major accomplishment. Yet the lure of cheap sex with gorgeous foreign women gave me nightmares. I worried one day my luck would run out. Perhaps God in his infinite mercy was looking out for me, no matter how unworthy my behavior. Perhaps he had greater plans for me. If I had gotten what I deserved, I would have contracted every STD known to man. I slept with too many prostitutes and bar women to keep track.

I spent June and July with my son, not knowing where or when I'd return to work. The Prince William Sound was still laid up in Singapore, and I no longer had a home vessel. That worried me. I had bills, mortgages, and a child. I also had a drug and alcohol habit that needed funding. I called Alaska Tanker Company to see where they would put me after my summer vacation, knowing I had to take whatever they offered.

The personnel manager at Beaverton headquarters said it looked like they wanted me to fly to Singapore to join the Kenai as it underwent repairs for a month.

My first thought was: *Oh, my God! A month of drinking and prostitutes might be the death of me! Should I turn down the job?* Singapore is a beautiful, clean city with thousands of pretty women from all over the world. Sailors *requested* duty at Sembawang Shipyard. Why would anyone want to turn down what amounted to perfect duty? But I was afraid of what I might do to myself. I was concerned I'd catch HIV some night in a drunken stupor. Yet if I told my personnel manager about my fears, the company would force me into rehab or—worse—fire me.

I knew I wouldn't turn the company down. I'd just have to try not to drink and chase prostitutes. Deep down I knew that wasn't probable, so I hoped I'd use condoms. But I hardly ever practiced safe sex. I hoped God would continue to put his umbrella of protection over me. I prayed often, asking God to be with me and guide me, despite my crazy, alcohol-riddled life.

I chose not say anything and had nightmares for more than a week. I dreamed I contracted HIV and was dying. I dreamed I told the company I couldn't go because I was an alcoholic and didn't trust myself in a worldly city like Singapore. I had dreams of getting drunk, getting into fights with the locals, and being tossed in a foreign jail. I dreaded going to sleep.

More than once, as I waited for my work tour to start, I considered calling Alaska Tanker Company and asking for other duty. But I knew that would raise red flags, so despite my doubts, I flew to Singapore on August 30, 2003, in preparation for breaking out the S/T Kenai in October. I got drunk two different times on the twenty-hour flight, but no matter—the airline liked high-paying business class passengers.

I had never laid eyes on the captain of the Kenai. That was good. I had a rugged reputation around the fleet, and just maybe he wouldn't know of me. I intended to work hard to impress him.

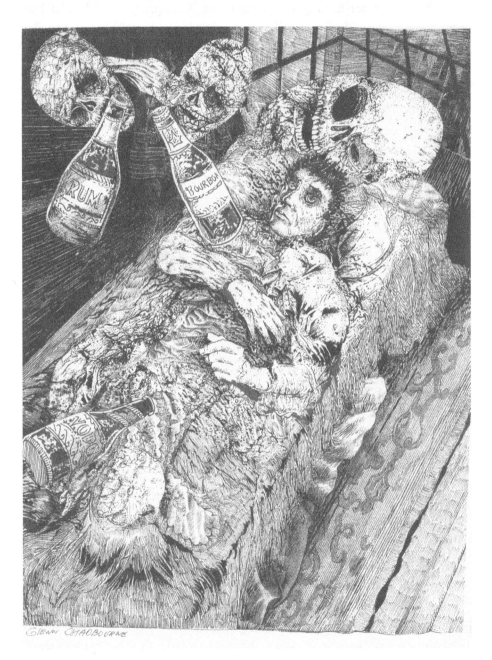

Nightmares of drinking and using drugs.

But as I walked up the steep gangway I was exhausted from traveling and still feeling the effects of partying for three months. I was sweating profusely in the tropical climate and my bags felt like they were full of lead weights. I walked into the captain's office so out of breath I couldn't introduce myself. I walked back out the door and got a drink from the scuttlebutt. As I walked back in, the old sea captain looked at me inquisitively. I apologized, and we introduced ourselves.

He explained that the ship wouldn't be moving for weeks, so there would be no sobriety checks at the gangway. He didn't care if the men went out and enjoyed themselves as long they made it back by the end of the night and got up for work the next day. The captain had no idea the potential his new second mate had for causing pandemonium, and he had just given me a green light. I was scared of what lay ahead.

Nevertheless, I settled in and did a good job. I updated the navigation charts and publications and the ship's safety and life-saving equipment. Always a team player, I got permission to go to my permanent

On the stern, S/T Kenai, Sembawang Shipyard, Singapore.

ship, the laid up Prince William Sound, to share the navigation plans I had prepared for the Kenai.

The first assistant engineer on the Kenai, a friend, went with me to the Prince William Sound. I looked around the bridge and deck and he walked through the engine room. I left the navigation paperwork in a folder in the captain's desk. I also removed more than a hundred charts that would be outdated by the time the vessel was broken out of layup. I ordered new charts flown in so she would be fully prepared to follow the Kenai back to the United States.

One of the higher-ups in the office criticized me for not focusing solely on the Kenai. But all the calculations were exactly the same; I could solve two problems at once for the second mates of each vessel. I was concerned with all of our ships, especially my permanent one, and I took care of her like a baby.

I did it because of my dedication to Alaska Tanker Company and to the captains I worked for, and because of the pride I had in my job.

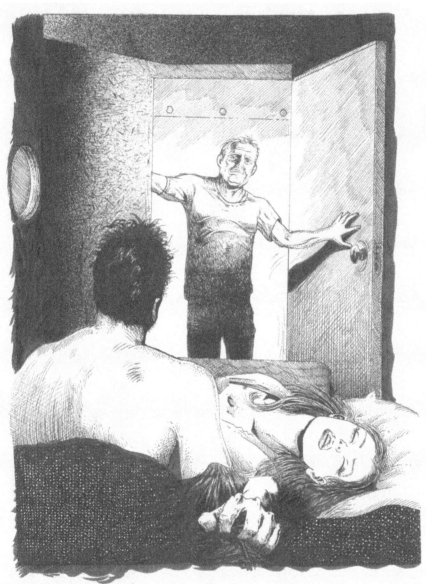

GLENN CHADBOURNE

CHAPTER THIRTY-FIVE
FINDING TRUE-LOVE IN ORCHID TOWERS

For the first seventeen days on the Kenai I continued to work hard. I managed to keep my nose clean. For seventeen days, I managed not to mess up. We were continuing to make repairs and the ship was now in drydock.

Many nights I went to Orchid Towers to drink and find prostitutes. Several times a week I took out hundreds in cash from an ATM. I spent the night at a hotel then got up around 0430, so I could get ready to work at 0600.

After my eighteenth day on the Kenai, I taxied into town. It had been a long day at work, and I was thirsty. I also felt a magnetic pull between me and the exotic prostitutes that was eerily similar to the pull of drugs and alcohol. Once I experienced a little, I wanted more and more.

We were not out to sea, and every day I spent a good deal of my time on dry land, but I was being pulled further and further adrift into a current of my own uncontrolled addictions. It's a twenty-minute drive from Sembawang into town, and not once anytime I took that ride did I ever think of my four-year-old son at home or that what I was doing might be wrong.

That night I got some cash and headed to my favorite disco in Orchid Towers where live bands often played the classic rock I liked so much. Walking into the bar was like window shopping. I strode by groups of women, pausing to see which flavor I wanted to taste that night. The women were also checking out the men. I was still young and easy on the eyes, and women wanted me to pick them. Sometimes this caused a little competition. It was fun watching them flaunt their stuff, trying to get me to come over.

The S/T Kenai in dry dock, Singapore.

It didn't take long before I found her, an exotic Thai woman I'll call True-Love. Perfect body, beautiful skin, beautiful white smile that invited me to take her home and do things to her I can't write about. I walked up to her. She smiled and wrapped both arms around me as if we were reuniting after years apart.

I took her to a table and ordered drinks. After having a few, we went out on the dance floor and were rubbing up against each other. She tried to get me to leave with her. I wanted her, but I teased her, telling her I wasn't ready. We continued drinking. I put her in my lap and put my hands all over her body.

We were rubbing our bodies against each other more than just sug-gestively, when the police charged in. They rounded up all the girls, including True-Love. The girls with legal paperwork were allowed to stay; the rest went to jail. It was quite a show. I was surprised when things picked up right where they left off.

My Thai hottie and I started thinking about getting a hotel for the night; a clean, private room in Singapore can be had for about $50.

That's exactly what we should have done. But, I was having too much fun, and I soon became very drunk.

I went into a blackout. I don't remember leaving Orchid Towers, but I do remember pulling up to the gates at Sembawang. I told True-Love I was the captain of the big American ship—did she want to go make love on my ship? She was thrilled to be with such an important man.

The guard at the front gate asked, "Can I help you?"

"We're going to the American ship—the Kenai."

The guard looked at me. Obviously I was American. He looked at my date. Obviously she wasn't and was scantily clad to boot. Black fishnet stockings, pretty dress, high heels, the works. Terrorism was a concern, especially around Americans.

"What is your position on the Kenai, sir?"

Sometimes even my friends couldn't figure out how drunk I actually was, so I'm not surprised that I was able to fool an unsuspecting security guard. Evidently I was quite convincing when I said, "I'm the captain. Now let us through, please. We're tired and need to get some rest."

He waved us through. I paid the driver, and for the rest of my days I'll never forget what happened next.

First, we had to get up the ladder in the dry dock. Then we had to walk up the ship's gangway, where True-Love's spiked heels kept poking through the spaces. We were both drunk and laughing and having a good old time. Not once that night did I stop to think what the real captain would say if he found out. I was a troubled alcoholic. I'd had seventeen days of controlled chaos, and on day eighteen in paradise, I had a meltdown.

We sneaked in through a side door and made it to my stateroom without anyone noticing. But I had forgotten that all the bathrooms on my deck had been treated with a special epoxy resin paint. All but one were unusable for a few days, and my Thai princess had to pee. I walked her down to the spare stateroom with the working bathroom. While I waited for her, I decided to lie down and rest my eyes for a minute. That was the last thing I remember until the next morning.

I had passed out in the wrong room. In the morning, the captain headed for the one useable bathroom on deck. There, instead of what was supposed to be an empty bed, he discovered two sleeping figures. "Passed out" would be the correct terminology. The captain quickly realized someone had a woman on board, which was utterly off limits. When he told me sailors could go ashore freely as long as they made it up the gangway at night, he hadn't meant a man could bring a lady of the evening as a guest.

The next thing I remember was the third mate bursting into the room: "You guys gotta wake up! The captain is really pissed off. You've got to get her off the ship quick before he loses it!"

I looked down by the edge of the bed and saw a pair of work boots. The only problem was they weren't mine, and that confused me. I looked around and saw my Thai hottie, who was trying to figure out what was going on. I jumped out of bed and started getting her dressed in her fishnet stockings and mini-skirt. I knew I was in big trouble this time.

The Thai girl started crying, knowing now that I wasn't the captain and she wasn't supposed to be there. I gave her some money, threw on a boiler suit, and hurried her out through the side door. As we reached the gangway, I heard applause, laughter, whistles, and yells. I looked back over my shoulder, where three men were leaning against the ship's railing.

The first assistant engineer and the company safety awareness man, both my friends, were laughing, taunting me, and in general adding to my stress. The third man was a Singaporean shipyard foreman who got a front row seat to the antics of another "ugly American." He also appeared to be enjoying himself.

Every day afterward, the safety man laughed at me about the incident, although initially he was serious when he asked, "What if she'd had a bomb, Darryl?"

I looked at him, shaking my head. "When's the last time you heard of a whore having a bomb?"

I finally got True-Love down to the dry dock and down the ladder. I kissed her goodbye, and she walked off looking frightened. She had a half-mile walk to the front gate, and there were thousands of Singaporean shipyard workers pouring in for the morning shift. I was so caught up in my alcoholism that I never considered the young woman's feelings or safety.

Later, I was told that a security guard saw her and put her inside one of the security shacks until the shift change ended. He was worried that one of the thousands of men riding bicycles would get run over by one of the thousands of men driving trucks if someone gawked at a scantily clad lady of the evening.

The captain must have decided to let me sober up for a few hours, because he waited until lunchtime before calling for me. I would rate that walk up to see him as one of the scariest of my life.

He immediately gave me the evil eye. "Darryl, what were you thinking? I feel like I've been violated! I'm not sure what action I'm going to take. What do you have to say for yourself?"

The captain was the nicest guy in the world, and I had just betrayed his trust. I felt about two inches tall.

"Captain, in all my years of shipping, I've never pulled a stunt like this. I don't remember coming back to the ship. I never would have done that sober." The truth was that I'd been in trouble years earlier for telling the pumpman I'd break him in half. But this captain didn't know that.

"Go to your room and think about what you've done. I'll let you know later if I'm going to fire you."

"Captain, I'm very sorry. I promise it won't happen again. Please give me another chance. I'll work my ass off and stay out of town. I promise," I pleaded.

For four days the captain made me squirm, holding the proverbial ax above my neck. I wrote him a letter begging not to be fired for my idiotic behavior. I stayed on board after work, knowing he was keeping track to see if I was truly remorseful. I promised to ask for alcohol treatment from our Employee Assistance Program when I got off the ship.

After four days, the captain told me I wouldn't be fired. He signed my letter, acknowledging its contents. The chief mate also signed it as a witness. The captain knew a man of my experience had to have done a lot of good work in order to remain in a highly competitive industry for sixteen years.

To: Captain ███████ S.S Kenai   09/21/2003
From: Darryl E. Hagar 2nd Mate

Dear Sir:

This letter concerns the events of 9/17/03 in which I brought a female guest onto the vessel knowingly breaking the rules. I have the deepest regrets over my lack of maturity and judgement shown over that mistaken decision. I know I have embarrassed not only myself but have violated you sir, as Master of this vessel. Having said that I can only promise you that no further incidents will occur due to my actions and furthermore I will not leave the vessel without your prior knowledge and permission.

I take this matter seriously. Along with my family I consider my job as one of the most important things in my life and my actions have put both of these things at risk. As previously stated, I take this job seriously and if anybody was to review my work file and history, they would see an overwhelmingly majority of excellent evaluations from numerous Captains in our fleet. I will continue to give it my all each and every day and past mistakes will not be repeated.

In closing I would like to finish my full work tour on the Kenai and when I go home on vacation, I intend on speaking to ATC'S Employee Assistance Program personnel to make sure past mistakes aren't repeated. I feel I still have a lot to give to help ATC continue to be a Premium tanker company.

Respectfully,

Darryl E. Hagar
Darryl E. Hagar

Recieved 0824 - 09/21/03 Sembawang, Singapore

master

WITNESSED BY: ███████ c/m

Letter of apology to the captain, Sembawang Shipyard, Singapore.

The captain tortured me for weeks afterward. I couldn't go ashore unless he or the chief mate escorted me, and that was only to pick up toiletries or get a haircut. A few weeks later, the captain flew home, and I went ashore and drank again. The new captain was never told what happened. The True-Love incident eventually became "shipyard lore" that my buddies and I laughed about.

The shipyard period wrapped. It was time for Coast Guard annual inspections, which included lifeboat and fire drills. We had to lower both lifeboats with men inside to show we could abandon ship if necessary. I handled one boat and the chief mate handled the other. It went well, but there was always the fear that the lifeboat wouldn't operate correctly or that someone would make a mistake in front of the Coast Guard.

Next we "fought" a mock fire in the ship's galley to prove our competency to the Coast Guard. We mustered at emergency stations. I was a squad leader in charge of a firefighting team. We suited up in full gear, each donned a self-contained breathing apparatus, and carried fire extinguishers, axes, and flashlights. The captain was on the bridge simulating a command center. High pressure water was pumped throughout the ship and fire hoses were scattered throughout the vessel. The third mate brought a second squad, and at the chief mate's direction, we entered the galley and "put out" the simulated fire. We carried out these drills once a week throughout the year, whether we were at sea or in port.

We passed inspections, the ship was deemed "manned and seaworthy," and we left for the United States. We slow steamed to conserve fuel, and arrived in Alaska on October 26. We then took 800,000 barrels of Alaskan North Slope crude oil to British Petroleum's Cherry Point refinery in Washington State.

I got off the ship and flew home to my son. I had promised the captain on the Kenai that I would get help, but I went back on my word. I wasn't ready to stop drinking. To this day I regret letting the captain down. At the time, I justified remaining quiet because no one at company headquarters knew of the True-Love incident. And the old sea captain had retired. My actions would never affect his career.

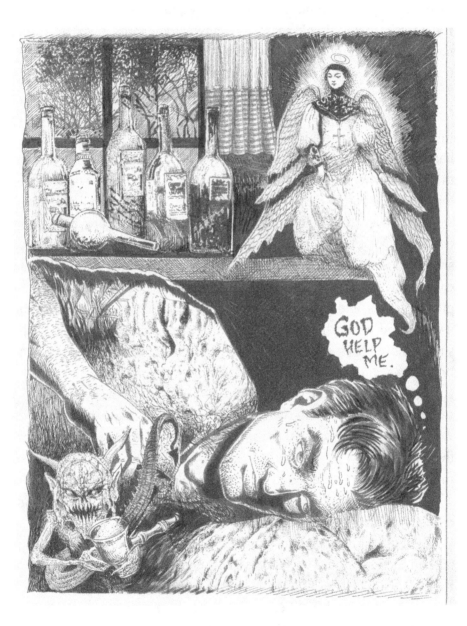

CHAPTER THIRTY-SIX
A SENSE OF IMPENDING DOOM

At home again, I walked right back into my drunken life. I went out one night and was drinking with some guy in a bar. He seemed down and out. I felt sorry for him, so I told him he could crash at my house. We drank all night, and the guy passed out on my couch. I went upstairs for a two-hour "nap." I woke up at 8:00 a.m. and started drinking again. The guy woke up and joined me.

At one point I asked politely, "What do you plan on doing today? Where are you going to go?"

"I was planning on drinking with you today right here," said the stranger I'd met the night before in a bar.

I walked into the kitchen. He followed me, still talking about how he'd like to stay at my house.

"Listen, man," I said forcefully. "I don't mind hanging out with you. But I don't want a roommate. I bought you beer last night. You crashed here, no problem. But you have to figure out what you're doing with your life. Where you're going to live. But you can't stay here. I have a son who lives with me sometimes, and we live alone."

"I don't have anywhere to go, and I'm staying here. I'm not going anywhere. Especially since we have all these beers." He said it as if I would take it lying down.

My hackles rose immediately. I yelled, "I was gonna let you crash here another night, but I decided you're leaving right now!"

"I'm not going anywhere!" he yelled back.

"You know what I'll do to your fucking head?!" I screamed.

I turned around, intending to punch out the glass in my kitchen window. My fist slammed into the wood windowsill.

"Get out of my house, or you're gonna be dead!" I yelled.

By the time I turned around, he had already run to the refrigerator and grabbed a half-full thirty-pack of Budweiser. He ran out the back door and down the street carrying the beer. I never saw him again.

My hand ballooned to where I couldn't make a fist. I put some ice on it and passed out. I woke up several hours later with my hand screaming in pain. I took a pain reliever and kept it iced. The swelling went down the next day, but the hand was still very sore. After icing it another day it felt and looked better, but I had a feeling it might be broken.

I decided to ask my doctor for X-rays in case I needed a cast. I would need time for the hand to heal correctly before returning to work. I'd need to get the cast off so the company wouldn't find out about the injury. I found out my hand didn't require a cast, but it was fractured and would take six to eight weeks to mend.

I tried to be careful with my hand through December and January, allowing it to get stronger. I needed strength in both hands to turn valves on the decks and in the pump room. I hid the injury from my family, just like I hid the truth from the company I worked for. Just like I hid from my doctors how much I drank and the fact that I did illegal drugs. I covered up mistakes, spun stories in my favor, or denied my blunders altogether. I was an old pro at damage control.

I continued to struggle with alcohol, but I promised myself I wouldn't drink on duty. I wouldn't go ashore and have "just a couple." I'd follow a self-imposed restriction not to leave the vessel unless absolutely necessary. I'd be ever vigilant. It amazes me now that I didn't ask myself if I was an alcoholic. It shows just how cunning, baffling, and powerful the disease is.

It's like having a good angel on one shoulder and a bad little devil on the other. The good voice in my head kept saying: *You need to change your life. You've had too many problems with drinking. Stop before it's too late. One of these days you'll make a fatal error.*

The little devil was more assertive and convincing: *Darryl, you're not that bad. You can still drink and be careful. You've been through a lot. You deserve to have a few drinks to unwind. You work hard and have a lot of responsibility. Enjoy yourself. If you screw up, you can wriggle out of it. You always do.* But an alcoholic who listens to the devil in the bottle always loses.

More and more I felt close to the end of something. Would I finally crash and burn? Would I make a mistake fatal to myself or someone else? Perhaps I'd end up in prison for the rest of my life. Would I finally break down and admit that I was out of control? I was thinking about alcohol and drugs 24/7 and moving into a more dangerous place. I started asking God for help. *Save me, oh Lord, before it's too late.*

My hand healed, and I was given orders to fly to Singapore to join the Prince William Sound. British Petroleum and Alaska Tanker Company had found work for her—great news for those permanent to the ship.

I arrived halfway around the world tired and haggard. At Sembawang Shipyard, I threw my sea bag on my shoulder and climbed the gangway. I walked aft to the house, climbed the stairs, set down my sea bag outside the captain's office, knocked, and entered.

The captain and I exchanged greetings and he asked about my vacation and my son.

"I saw that you were on the Kenai and that you left navigation plans in my desk. I'm glad you were still thinking about this ship. Thank you," he said sincerely. Then his expression became stern. "I also heard through the grapevine that you had a little incident on that ship. What happened there?"

"Do you mean the prostitute, Captain?" I asked sheepishly.

He was polite but firm. "Yes, I mean the prostitute, Darryl. I'll tell you up front; if you bring a prostitute on board or have any drinking issues while I'm on board, you *will* be fired. Is that clear to you?"

The captain knew I did good work and that I took my job seriously. By warning me he had heard what happened on the Kenai, he ensured I wouldn't repeat it on the Prince William Sound.

"Captain, I swear that was a mistake that will not be repeated. I don't know what I was thinking, but you won't get anything but hard work from me."

"Okay, Darryl, as long as we're clear on that."

"Aye, aye, Captain."

For the most part I behaved myself during that shipyard period in Singapore. I dabbled with the ladies some, but I was very careful not to bring any back to the ship. I took them to hotels. I controlled my drinking so I wouldn't miss work or smell like booze. I was being watched, and I was vigilant.

Me under the supertanker.

The shipyard work was complete, and we sailed the Prince William Sound back to the United States. I came to be known as "The Singapore Connection," because I had made five trips to Singapore and had the most experience navigating the huge supertankers back and forth from the States.

Yet my life continued to spiral out of control. One time after I flew to a vessel, I noticed my leg and hip were hurting. I had been very drunk the last few days of my three-month vacation, and I didn't remember falling. The day I returned to work I was fine; the injury didn't worsen for a day, and at first I didn't recognize how badly I was hurt. There was no significant bruising; the damage was internal. But after I had traveled around the world, my leg started killing me.

Lucky for me we had a young captain filling in who didn't know my reputation. I was able to hide my limp the first day, but after a terrible night of uncomfortable sleep with a swollen leg, I could hardly walk. There was no way to hide it anymore. I knew my leg wasn't broken, so I just limped around the ship. People asked me about it. The chief mate and the captain talked to me about the injury, and the captain asked several times if I wanted see a doctor. I insisted I was fine.

I told everyone I'd been raking loam and had fallen on the corner of my backyard deck. The captain grudgingly did not insist I get medical attention. Although the leg got worse, I still didn't report it; I knew it had been caused by my drinking, and I didn't want to answer a doctor's questions.

To complicate the situation, a British Petroleum vetter was on board to inspect our operation. He was there to make one trip with us at sea to watch us work, go through our paperwork and drills, and write a report about the vessel and our competence in running it. I knew he would come up and inspect my charts, waypoints, and voyage plans. I wasn't worried about my work; it was topnotch as always. I was worried about limping in front of him. The man had been a sea captain. He knew what sailors do when they aren't on board.

We set sail. When the vetter inspected the bridge, though embarrassed, I gave him the explanation I'd given everyone else. He observed the ship and crew and seemed pleased with our operation. I thought I was in the clear; as far as I knew, no one had said anything negative about the gimpy second mate.

On the third day of the vetter's tour, I went to the officers' mess and found him there. We were alone. He was at the captain's table, and I sat in my usual spot at the junior officer's table.

"Hi, Captain, how are you today?" I asked politely.

"Hello, Second Mate. I'm fine, thank you."

"How's the vetting going?"

"Going well. Just about finished."

"Have you found anything disturbing about the ship?" As soon as the question was out, I knew it was a mistake.

"Just the second mate," he replied bluntly.

"You know what, Captain? I've got almost twenty years' sea time with this same outfit. I figure I must be doing something right," I said angrily.

"I know you are, Second Mate, but you asked the question."

That was the last I heard about it. Apparently I hadn't disturbed him enough to write it up in his report. He disembarked at the next port, and I never saw the man again, but it wouldn't surprise me if he remembered the conversation. He couldn't assume in his report that my hurt leg was caused by drinking, but I'm quite sure he assumed it personally.

After that, I became keenly aware that I would soon have to do something about my drug and alcohol problem. The sense that the end was approaching grew even stronger. Either I would die in my addictions, or I would throw myself a life ring and go to rehab.

GLENN CHADBOURNE

CHAPTER THIRTY-SEVEN
I AM KING

At home, I again began to get drunk more than once a day. I drank coffee in the morning and by 10:00 a.m. I had switched to beer. By 2:00 p.m. I was drinking vodka in some bar I could never remember leaving. I would wake up on my couch and try to figure out if it was morning or night. When I figured out it was nighttime, I'd go to the Old Port and get drunk again.

It didn't take much to get drunk the second time, and sometimes bartenders wouldn't serve me. But there are many bars in Portland; it isn't hard to find someone to pour a drunk a drink. After passing out again, I'd wake up trying to figure out what had happened and what day it was. The man takes the drink—then the drink takes the man.

One day after getting drunk twice, I woke up a foot from my bed, fully clothed. I couldn't remember how I got there. I picked myself up off the floor, muttering, "Man, Darryl, how bad is your drinking getting? You only had one more foot to make it a cushy bed, and you passed out crawling."

I was entering uncharted waters. Here I was passing out more than once a day, when I had to go back to work within a week. I was not ready for a 900-foot supertanker.

Despite these realizations, I called my friend Go-Go.

"Hey, Darryl, what's up? When you going back?"

"Not for another week, and I'm thinking about one last blowout. Can you get in touch with Bulldog and see if he can set us up? I'm buying."

Bulldog was a mutual friend who could score some blow. To us, Bulldog was just another really good friend and a good person. But like the rest of us, he had a drinking and drug problem. A rugged six-foot, 230-pound guy, he could knock the crap out of anybody in Portland. Many had tried to best him; none had won. Bulldog had served more than five years in federal prison for cocaine possession.

Bulldog once told me a story about a guy who owed him money for cocaine. After trying to get his money to no avail, Bulldog took the guy and duct-taped him to a tree. He poured gasoline on the guy and asked again if he was going to pay. Bulldog then lit matches next to the gasoline-covered druggie, who was crying like a baby. The guy paid him.

That night, Go-Go, Bulldog, and I met at a bar. We partied together for an hour until we got an overwhelming urge for cocaine. In the bathroom, we laid out lines on the back of the toilet. When one guy came out of the stall the next went in. We then decided the lines weren't cutting it.

"Let's head over to my house and smoke some of this stuff," I said.

"Now you're talking my language," said Bulldog.

It was a rainy, windy night, perfect for smoking crack. Nobody would bother us, and we could do whatever we wanted. At my house, the crack operation started. We each grabbed a beer and went to work. The first thing I always did was pull down the shades. We didn't want the neighbors watching and calling the cops. Then we got the necessary supplies together.

"Let me find a 16-ounce soda bottle and some tin foil to make the crack pipe," I said.

"I'll light the cigarettes to make some ash for the pipe," said Go-Go.

"I'll get a spoon and a lighter. Where's the baking soda, Darryl? I need a glass of water too," Bulldog added.

Within minutes we had all taken the first hit of crack, which was really the only "good" one. It was all downhill after that. We tried to get the same high we got from that first hit, but it took more and more crack to get back to that point. But once we started doing cocaine, we didn't stop until either the cocaine or the money ran out.

We had bought a quarter ounce with the idea that we could sell some and therefore party for free. That was always the intent, but it never worked out that way. That night, we stayed up for hours smoking. Then we got paranoid. All three of us thought we heard someone coming in.

"What was that?" I glanced up from the crack pipe after taking a big hit.

Bulldog immediately went into a karate stance. If somebody was coming through the door, he'd take them out in a blink. Go-Go peered through the blinds, and I got up and opened the door.

"It's just the storm blowing the tree branches!" I said. "We've got to chill out before one of us has a heart attack!"

I felt relieved and foolish. We laughed, but every time the wind blew, we looked toward the window. We knew we wouldn't be able to sleep that night. By that point in my life I was used to the routine: Try to slow down on the cocaine, drink more beer, and, if I needed it, there was always the Nyquil.

"You guys, it's 4:30. I'm going to bed. You're welcome to spend the night," I said.

"We're calling a cab, Darryl," Go-Go said. "We'll get out of your hair."

I went upstairs and tried to sleep. I tossed and turned for awhile and decided to go downstairs and grab a few beers. I walked down the dark steps, not wanting to turn the lights on in case any of my neighbors were up early. In my crazy, paranoid head I figured they would know I'd been up all night drinking and drugging. I went to the fridge and grabbed two beers. *What the hell.* I turned around and grabbed two more, just in case. I didn't want to walk downstairs again.

I tiptoed back upstairs as if someone would hear me if I made too much noise in my empty house. I then decided to drink some Nyquil before going back to bed. It was typical behavior when I did too much coke and couldn't sleep: Drink lots of beer quickly and follow that with Nyquil. Then drink more beer and, if necessary, more Nyquil. Usually there were about three bathroom breaks between all that madness. Invariably I passed out.

In those days, I always kept at least two bottles of Nyquil in the house to use as a sedative after all-night cocaine binges. If I drank enough, it would knock me out. I eventually got to the point where I couldn't smell Nyquil without wanting to throw up. It was one of the darkest times in my life. Partying meant beer, vodka, cocaine, marijuana, and Nyquil, in that order.

I had a weird premonition that I was building toward something bad. Would it be a nervous breakdown or dying from a heart attack, leaving my son fatherless? Would I drunkenly run over someone's kid and spend the rest of my life in jail? Something bad was going to happen; I could feel it in my bones.

I had two days left of vacation, and I spent them drinking away my dope sickness and my hangover. I got dressed and showered both days, but that was about all I could do. I was either sleeping or drinking.

The night before I was due to leave, Jen brought Darryl over to spend the night. She had agreed to drive me to the airport in the morning. Because I wasn't home, she put Darryl to bed. When it got late and I still wasn't home, she climbed into bed with him.

I arrived home very late and stumbled upstairs where Jen and Darryl were sleeping.

"Hey, I'm home. Wake up," I slurred.

Jen said, "Darryl, you're going to wake the baby. Quiet down."

"Don't tell me to quiet down in my own house! What are you doing here anyway?" I had forgotten she was giving me a ride to the airport.

"Darryl, you're a mess. You have to fly early in the morning. Go sleep in the other room and sober up. I'll wake you up in a few hours."

"No, I'm sleeping with my son on my last night. Why don't you sleep in the other room?" I said belligerently, hauling her out of bed. She put up a struggle. Darryl woke up and started crying.

"Leave her alone! What are you doing to Mommy?! Get out of here, Daddy!" Darryl screamed.

Jen scooped up Darryl and left the house. I didn't see him again for three months.

Alone and very drunk, I went downstairs and opened a beer. *Fuck them. Fuck them all*, I thought drunkenly. I put on some music and sat in my chair, trying to decide whether I could handle getting packed and traveling across the country half drunk. *I can do it. I can do anything. I'm a king among kings in my world. I'll go back out to sea and work like a madman.*

I drunkenly went back upstairs. I packed the dirty underwear lying on the bedroom floor, the dirty clothing I had worn to bars in the last week, and the clothes I had been wearing while smoking crack with friends. I was too drunk to do laundry. I laughed to myself. *I guess the TSA will have to go through my dirty underwear this time.* I had no respect for anyone or anything, especially not for myself.

I drank until the sun came up, listening to music and napping in my chair. For reasons I still don't understand, I found a black marker and a yellow legal pad. I wrote three words in big bold letters and taped the paper above the fireplace.

I called a cab and grabbed my sea bag. I went to turn off the living room light and looked at the sign I had left for "whomever" to see in my absence. I laughed. It was perfect. I ruled the world. It didn't matter if I was drunk on booze, high on cocaine, committing domestic violence, or navigating 900-foot supertankers. I thought that I ruled. Laughing, I read the sign one last time:

> # I
> # AM
> # KING

What a way to spend my last week on dry land: drug-saturated and paranoid. I had a five-year-old boy who loved me, yet I had spent my time smoking crack with the boys. It seemed I had a death wish. The guilt from that is still with me today, and I hope I never forget what I did. If I can always remember how bad it was, I might just stay clean.

I was meeting the Prince William Sound later that day at the BP refinery at Cherry Point, Washington. Because I had napped on and off for a few hours, I figured I could get through airport security. I hoped to drop off my luggage with TSA and walk off before they could associate the drunken sailor with the luggage laden with dirty underwear. I wanted to at least have a fighting chance of getting through the gates and meeting my ship. Missing it was something I couldn't afford to do.

I came up with a brilliant idea. Instead of showing security my driver's license, which had a star stamped through it to designate my OUI, I'd show them my Merchant Mariners Document, a plastic, official-looking photo ID card. Issued by the U.S. Coast Guard, it listed my Merchant Marine credentials. I figured it would probably get me a little leeway with the Transportation Security Administration.

As I got to the front of the security line, I was stopped.

"Male pat down," the TSA official yelled out. "Sir, step over here."

I kept my mouth shut. I wouldn't have a chance if warranted any extra attention.

"ID and boarding pass, sir." The TSA official looked me over.

I handed him my MMD, which he looked at carefully.

"Sir, we need to go through your carry-on luggage. Take your belt and shoes off, please."

I followed his directions without uttering a peep. I needed to get to my ship; work was the only thing keeping me from spinning totally out of control.

"I'm going back to a ship for three months," I finally said meekly.

"Yes, I saw that from your ID. Did you have a late night last night?" he asked.

"A little bit. I've been nervous about going back out and leaving my family," I said, hoping he'd cut me some slack.

He went through my bag, then took a wand and went over me with it. Then he went through my bag again. He looked at me. He was an older man who obviously felt sorry for me.

"Sir, go to your gate. Try to get some sleep on your plane and take it easy today."

"Yes, sir, I will. I'll sleep the whole way." I let out a big sigh of relief. "Thanks again."

It had worked, although I had pushed the envelope yet again. I boarded the plane and was out like a light as soon as I sat down. I woke up as the plane touched down in Chicago. The shakes had started. *Oh, no.* Detox had set in. I was sweating the booze and drugs out of my body, trembling, and suddenly nauseated. I felt like an eighty-year-old drunk. It was not going to be a pleasant day.

I ran into the nearest men's room and puked my brains out. My hair and shirt were soaked with sweat. I was in no shape to go back to work. I had to think: *Let me call and see where the vessel is. Maybe it got into a storm on its way south from Alaska.*

I dialed the shipping agent's number and got an answering machine with the ship's schedule and ETAs. The ship was not delayed, but was shifting to a dock at the U.S. Oil refinery in Tacoma for a partial discharge. It would stay there overnight and then shift to Port Angeles.

I could catch the ship outbound at Port Angeles. That meant I had a day and night to lie in a hotel. By that time I'd be ready to go back to work. I figured God was once again watching over me. Though the captain would worry about where his new second mate was, I thought I could pull it off. I would lie. Tell the captain I missed a flight. They wouldn't want me in my current condition anyway. I breathed easier. Now I could detox in peace.

I boarded the flight to Seattle, still sweating and shaking. In Seattle I felt just as bad as I had five hours earlier in Chicago. I caught a cab for a $200 ride from Sea-Tac to Port Angeles. The captain wouldn't like the transportation reimbursement, but I reasoned I was actually doing the company a favor.

In Port Angeles, I asked the cabbie to stop at a convenience store, where I picked up a six-pack to celebrate not having to go straight to the ship. My hands were shaking again; I needed a beer to settle me down.

In my hotel room, I cracked a beer. I took one swig, ran into the bathroom, and vomited violently into the toilet. I tried another drink and ran back into the bathroom. This time I only had the dry heaves. I was experiencing alcohol poisoning.

Eventually I was able to get two of the beers down. I felt a little better, but I didn't want to drink anymore. I was getting to the point of quitting drinking altogether. I had already said that to myself many times, hung over. But this time seemed different. This time I was worried I was going to die. I had cheated death many times, but until now quitting had never been a serious option.

The next day I called the shipping agency to find that the ship was sitting at anchor in Port Angeles loading bunkers and stores. The stores would take all day to load.

I looked at the four beers left in the six-pack and left them behind. Something was different this time; I never left beer unconsumed. I was suddenly aware that I was sick, and I knew I had to get help soon. But first I had to face the captain, and that put my nerves on edge.

I took a launch boat out to the supertanker at anchor. As usual, I got half-hearted hellos from the regular crewmembers. I was a tough boss and a hardcore worker with a no-nonsense attitude; sailors always regretted the day I came back on board.

The crew had no idea of the double life I lived. Many moons before, an old seaman had told me: "Mate, you never tell anyone about your life at home. That's your personal life, and what happens at home should stay at home. If you don't, it will come back and bite you every time. You tell one guy something that happened to you, especially if it was bad, and everyone in the crew will know about it. And it will be used against you when they need it."

I stuck to that rule. Imagine if the captain, the officers, or the crew knew about my escapades involving drugs, alcohol, prostitutes, guns, police arrests, and all-night cocaine binges. Nope. I shared it with no one, no matter how close they were to me. They knew enough already from the things that happened on the ships. Let them assume the rest. I certainly wasn't going to feed the rumor mill.

I knocked on the captain's door.

"Hi, Captain. Darryl Hagar reporting for duty, sir."

"Nice to see you again. Our paths haven't crossed in many years."

"Sorry I'm so late. It was a weekend and I couldn't let you know I was joining at anchor. I missed a flight and figured it was better to rest and catch the ship outbound," I lied to my old friend. As always, I thought: *I have to do what I have to do.*

"I figured as much. I was afraid you might be in some bar in Tacoma."

"Nope. I'm going to make a major decision in my life very soon, but I'm not ready to talk about it."

"I'm here if you want to talk about anything. That's what they pay me for. Nothing is off limits."

I went to my stateroom to unpack, wondering how much work gear I had forgotten. As I looked for some work clothes, I realized how irresponsible I had been. I would be on board up three months. There were many items I needed as we traveled to the Arctic north. I had forgotten a winter jacket, long john bottoms, boot socks, shampoo, and dental floss. I had also failed to bring music CDs, which I'd sorely miss.

Then, as I pulled out the last of my gear, I realized how low I had sunk. I had forgotten my Bible. *I guess I don't even need God anymore.* For twenty years I had always brought along my childhood Bible, a modern-language version called *The Way*. There was a special section in the front with words of comfort for anyone going through hardship that I referred to often. I always had that Bible by my side, both on the ships and at home. I had been so drunk I had forgotten the one thing most important for my inner strength. I was getting a very strong message: My priorities were all messed up. I had progressed into such a drunk that I couldn't remember what was most important to me.

God finally had my attention. Maybe it was time to look at my life. I reflected on the way I was living. Maybe it was time to stop the madness. I was reaching a point of no return. I stood at a crossroads. I could either change my life and save it or progress even further into alcohol and drugs and perhaps never recover. The clock was ticking. I needed to think.

I was in my twenty-sixth year of drunken, drug-addicted madness, and it was catching up to me faster every year. I was barely keeping my head above water. I didn't know it then, but my notorious career of ships and booze was coming to an end. I would one day thank God that both were out of my life.

GLENN CHADBOURNE

CHAPTER THIRTY-EIGHT
YOU HAVE TO SURRENDER TO WIN

I was impressed by the Prince William Sound, my home away from home for the next three months. Built in the mid-seventies, it was the world's first double-hulled oil tanker. By contrast, the Exxon Valdez was single-hulled; after the infamous oil spill in March 1989, all oil tankers in the United States were required to have double hulls by 2015, making the Prince William Sound a gem of a ship well ahead of its time.

It was November 30, 2004. I was still tired and not feeling well after my last cocaine and alcohol binge. I went to relieve the second mate, who didn't care what shape I was in. When you're due to get off after a three-month work tour, any warm body will do.

We took a relief tour of the vessel, then headed up to the bridge and went over all the equipment, charts, and passage plans. It amazed even me that I could be a drunk and drug addict one week and in charge of a 900-foot supertanker the next. I went to work as if nothing unusual had happened in the last few days, but was reminded of my drunken irresponsibility every time I had to don the old, battered winter jacket that belonged to the ship.

Again I thought seriously about quitting drinking. I reflected on how bad I was getting during my time off. The pain now outweighed the pleasure. I wasn't having fun with drugs and alcohol anymore; they were having fun with me. I decided when I went home again I'd attend twelve-step meetings. Maybe with help I could control my drinking so I wouldn't have to give it up completely. I resolved to try to change my life. I knew it wouldn't be easy. I would ask God to help me. I had been drinking and drugging for twenty-seven years, but I would try.

A windy day at sea.

On the ship, I felt safe. I couldn't get drunk, I couldn't score drugs, and I didn't want to. I was at "sea-hab" again. It also felt good to be making money again. I'd earn $13,000 dollars a month on this voyage, and I needed it. I literally went through money like a drunken sailor. It cost a lot of money to be a drunk and a junkie.

We loaded crude oil in Valdez and discharged at refineries in Washington State, San Francisco, Los Angeles/Long Beach, and Hawaii. We supplied our customers with crude oil they had purchased from British Petroleum or supplied BP itself. I played an important role in carrying the oil safely, and it was a satisfying job. Despite a serious drinking and drug problem off the ship, I did fantastic work on board. I might have a flotilla of personal demons chasing me, but I felt I could work them out with my own relentless effort.

Still, each time I went back to sea it was with untreated addictions and a chaotic mind and personality. On the ships, I worked night and day to make up for my shortfalls, primarily my dysfunctional personality.

Through the bridge windows, Valdez, Alaska.

I worked extra hard to please the captain and the company. I was successful. I did excellent work and gained twenty years' valuable experience. In turn, I taught many younger officers how to run a super-tanker safely. We had many challenging and dangerous situations on these ships, including horrific winter storms to navigate through, and an experienced sailor worth his salt was invaluable.

They had to put up with my rough-around-the-edges demeanor, but that's how I operated. I was certainly unique; I was both the hardest working guy on board and an untreated alcoholic and drug addict. I lived a double life.

I completed my work tour and flew home on February 9, 2005. I decided I would try to quit drinking after I blew off some steam for a week or two, so I had a few beers on the plane. I still thought of the time when I first got off the ship as my "decompression time." Of course, the irony of it wasn't lost to me: Over and over again I went quickly from being able to walk a straight line on a ship, even as it was tossed around in rough weather, to having wobbly legs onshore due to a belly full of beer.

Heavy seas on board the S/T Prince William Sound.

What had kept me going the past few years was seeing my son and the sheer joy of his unconditional love. When Jen picked me up at the airport, Darryl always waited for me to come through security, yelled "Daddy!" and ran into my arms.

It was one of the few things that could still touch my heart. But Jen couldn't forget me pulling her out of bed like a drunken madman three months before. She wanted nothing to do with me. That was the price I paid for what I'd done. My favorite part of going to sea—coming home to the people I loved—was denied me, and I deserved it. This time there was no joyous little boy there to greet me, nobody to give me a ride home. I gathered my bags and jumped in a cab. My mind quickly started working. Should I get some beer, or should I see my son? Beer or son. Son or beer.

"Pull over at the next convenience store, will ya? I gotta get some beer," I said loudly.

But my guilty conscious was eating me alive. Something told me this twelve-pack wouldn't be an enjoyable one. But I was past the point of no return. Drinking was no longer fun; it had become necessary.

I paid the cabbie and looked at my dark, empty house. This was no way to come home after three months at sea. I had been alone on the ship; now I was alone at home. What a life. Why had I chosen to have a son? So I wouldn't be alone and to gain some stability in my life. He was five years old, and my life hadn't changed a bit.

I unlocked the door and walked inside my cold, dark house. I flicked on a light in the kitchen and opened a beer. I took a long pull on a bottle of Budweiser and thought, *This isn't so bad after all*. I walked through the hallway and into the living room.

In the dark, I looked around the large room with its oak hardwood floors, large-screen TV, and beautiful brick fireplace. I turned on the light, and my heart skipped a beat. I couldn't believe my eyes. I would end up in the insane asylum for sure. I walked over to the fireplace and looked at the sign I had drunkenly taped above the fireplace mantel three months before:

I
AM
KING

I stood frozen, my mind racing. Was I that out of touch with reality? Was I turning into a total mental case? An alcohol-crazed lunatic? I tore down the sign, crumpled it up, and tossed it into the fireplace. I started a fire to destroy the evidence. I felt sick to my stomach, and yet here I was drinking again the first chance I got. God save my soul; I couldn't save myself.

I drank every one of those twelve beers. I justified my drinking and drugging based on the stress of going to sea. While there was some truth to the idea, it wasn't a free pass to go overboard. I wasn't allowed to drink and drive, ravage, plunder, and pillage just because I had the stress of working for Big Oil.

I woke up the next day feeling guilty. I had told myself that this vacation would be different, and I had every intention of trying to change. I was free from my floating prison and ready to try something new. I knew where there was a twelve-step meeting nearby and decided to give it a shot.

The meeting was inspiring. I heard many eerily familiar stories about drinking patterns, drug use, loneliness, chaos, dysfunctional families, and despair. I was certain I was in the right place, and I sensed a spiritual awakening in my mind. Maybe I could pull this off. Maybe I could actually fight this thing. Have half a chance of getting and staying sober. The meeting wrapped, and somehow I was tempted to head to the beer store. One minute I felt I could change and the next I felt "not yet."

I went home and drank all night. I was due to see Darryl the next day, so I made sure to tell Jen I had gone to my first twelve-step meeting in more than a decade, the first I'd ever gone to of my own free will. As I sat there drinking for the second night in a row, I wondered how I had gotten in so deep. I'd been such a good kid, a great athlete, and a good student in high school. Where had I gone wrong? Yet here I was, choosing alcohol and drugs over my son for a second day.

The next morning, I brushed my teeth aggressively to hide the booze smell, gargled with mouthwash, and brushed my teeth again.

When Jen and Darryl arrived, he yelled, "Daddy!" and ran up to me.

"I missed you, and I love you, bud," I said, scooping him up and hugging him tight.

He had forgotten all about what happened the last time I'd seen him, but Jen had not. She told me I would have to stop drinking or lose my son. She really meant it this time. I decided I would try my best to quit.

As I spent time with Darryl that summer, I tried unsuccessfully not to drink around him. At first I went to twelve-step meetings on the days he wasn't with me. I drank only when alone. But as the summer progressed, I found myself drinking every day. Eventually I was drinking in the mornings, whether I had Darryl or not. Once in awhile Jen stopped over unannounced. I hid my beer behind my chair and quickly chewed some gum. It got to the point where I was hiding alcohol in my own house and peering out the windows to see if anyone was watching me.

I was losing my mind, and I knew it—but I couldn't stop drinking.

Too sick to drive to the store a half mile away, I often called my friend Matt early in the morning to ask him to bring me some beer. My hands would be trembling. I needed my "medication" to make it stop. I kept getting worse and I kept trying twelve-step meetings. They would work for a little while, but I hadn't suffered quite enough yet to quit.

One day I was on a mission to catch a buzz, so I grabbed some beer. Before long I was drunk and tracking down my old running mates. We scored some cocaine and headed over to our favorite crack house in Portland, owned by a guy we called Zookeeper. Soon we were hitting the crack pipe.

Zookeeper's house sat directly on the street, and I worried about the cops storming in. As we continued to get high that night we got paranoid, so we moved to the dark, damp basement, where there were a few chairs, a couch, and a coffee table set up solely for the purpose of smoking crack.

I noticed Pusherman was hitting the pipe pretty hard and said, "Take it easy, man. You just did a big hit, and you're trying for another one."

"I didn't get that one," he insisted.

"Okay, but I think you got the first one," Zookeeper said.

Pusherman did another hit and suddenly turned gray. He looked confused.

"You okay, Pusherman?" I asked, concerned about my buddy.

He didn't say anything, but finally started breathing again.

"You okay, man?" I got up and shook him a little.

"I'm okay," he said. "I thought I was having a heart attack for a minute there."

"Sheesh, you're scaring me, man!" I paused. "Give me that crack pipe. My turn."

We took turn after turn with our sick game. The adage "one is too many and a thousand ain't enough" was still true.

Go-Go was getting paranoid down in that crack den. He looked around, listening for noises that weren't there. He did a huge hit and looked at me.

"Darryl, if you had a heart attack and died, would you have a problem with us dragging your body outside somewhere?" he asked sincerely.

"You're freaking me out, Go-Go. Stop talking like that!" I yelled.

"I'm serious, Darryl. You never know. If anyone died, we'd have to get rid of the body so the house wouldn't get busted. Otherwise all of us would be in deep shit. You'd be dead anyway. What do you care?"

"You're serious."

"Yeah. I've already asked everyone else."

I finally said, "I don't care. Drag me outside and leave me by the road so at least they'll find me. But enough of that talk. Leave me alone and hand me that pipe."

I couldn't believe he had said that. But when I thought about it later, I realized in the logic of crackheads and junkies, it's not an unreasonable thing to ask your party partners. Nobody wanted to call the cops and tell them somebody had overdosed at his pad. Nobody wanted to call 911 while everyone was high on crack and have the ambulance and cops show up.

Later, a friend from Boston told me that if somebody overdosed wherever he and his friends were using, they would throw the person out of the apartment window, no matter how many stories up they were. Sometimes the person was dead, sometimes still alive. He told me about the Orchid "shooting gallery" on Dudley Street in Boston. He sometimes saw guys get tossed out of apartment windows in the Columbia Point housing project. It was eerily similar to what Go-Go had suggested. All of it was sick, sick, sick.

I walked home, went to bed, and tossed and turned all night. When I got up to use the bathroom, I didn't turn on any lights, afraid the neighbors knew what I was up to.

Cocaine abuse leads to paranoia. It also causes terrific let downs that turn into suicidal thoughts, which I had quite often when I was abusing every night. I'm also amazed that I don't have any drug convictions. Those aspects of partying were scary, but I was an addict so I put up with them. That an intelligent person could do the things I did shows how powerful and evil drug addiction and alcoholism really are.

I asked God to help me get through the night without having a heart attack. It was my typical junkie promise to God. If he helped me through the night, I'd clean up my act. The promise lasted until the next time I used. I repeated that prayer many, many times.

I'm so grateful that we have a forgiving God who accepts us despite our shortcomings. While I was still using, even then I knew God was listening and that someday I'd make it up to him. Somehow I was sure of it. I often recalled the vision I had years before: If I survived my crazy addictive lifestyle and lived to talk about it, I would share my story with the hope of helping people—so help me, God.

I survived the night and continued on with my reckless behavior.

I was still off the ship when the time came to attend a required Alaska Tanker Company safety conference. I had attended in 2003 and 2004 and hated them. I was uncomfortable knowing former captains and co-workers would be there; they knew about my crazy partying ways. Some resented my ability to survive in the highly competitive and conservative oil business. I was one of few in the industry who said what I thought and did what I said. Consequently, I had a big target on my back.

Plus, there was all that free booze. Imagine a large group of drunken sailors talking too much, telling sea stories, and arguing company politics. It was like having a company Christmas party five nights in a row. I usually put on a good performance all five nights, arguing with engineers, embarrassing my shipmates, and ordering drink after drink.

At the 2003 conference, I tried to sleep with some of the female office personnel. In 2004, I did. In 2003, I was told to slow down on the drinking. In 2004, the hotel maid was the only one who knew I wet the bed. In 2003, I hid my alcoholism from our CEO, who was and is a great man. In 2004, I drunkenly told him, "Sir, you remind me of Gandhi. Of course, you're the only Indian I know." He didn't know me well enough to realize how bad an alcoholic I was. Yet the excellent work evaluations I received lessened the impact of my negative behavior.

Understandably, I was apprehensive about attending the 2005 conference. I knew that under the influence I was capable of doing or saying anything to anyone. I was worried about my job, worried about my lack of self control, worried even more about my health. I couldn't slow down the drinking and using, and I didn't think I could stop. But I was too tough not to attend the conference, so I got ready to go.

I stayed up half the night drinking, trying to calm my nerves so that the next day I'd appear normal to my co-workers and management. That's good alcoholic thinking: *Drink more so you won't shake and nobody will realize you're a drunk*. I passed out that night. I got up early on May 9, 2005, and hurried to gather my things. I flew to Chicago, where I would catch a connection to Portland, Oregon. After that I'd take a shuttle to Washington State.

I was a little nervous on the flight, so I had a few beers to calm down. It was 9:00 a.m., but I was an adult. I could have a beer if I wanted to. I drank three beers between Maine and Chicago, putting me right back in the condition I'd been in the night before.

In Chicago I found an airport bar where an older Asian man was serving drinks. I decided to ramp it up a bit.

"Bartender, I'll have a vodka and OJ. In fact, make that a double." That would hit the spot. I started feeling much better. Maybe the conference would work out better than anticipated.

"Coming right up, sir. What kind of vodka?"

"Absolut. Only the best, man," I said, laughing.

"There you go. Where are you headed?"

"I'm attending a company conference in Washington State tomorrow."

It was lunchtime and I hadn't eaten all day. I had two more drinks and thought about how much I had begun to dislike my job. I traveled all the time, I had to make believe I liked all the Big Oil people, I was stressed under corporate pressure, and I had turned into a drunk at home. What a life.

I was getting pretty buzzed, and my flight was coming up, so I said drunkenly, "I'll have a beer this time."

"You sure? I want them to let you on the plane," the bartender said, sounding genuinely concerned.

"I'll be okay. I'll sleep on board."

I finished my beer and said goodbye. I bought some gum to mask the smell of alcohol and made it onto the plane. I intended to take a nap and sober up, until a work mate I hadn't seen in awhile came walking down the aisle.

"Hey, Dave, how's it going, man?" I said excitedly, sticking out my hand.

"Darryl Hagar—how are you? Anyone sitting next to you?"

We sat next to each other, and like a good drunk I talked my buddy into drinking with me. Before long the flight attendant cut us off. I was a mess again.

"Dave, I'm thinking about not going to the conference," I confessed. I was suddenly tired of stressing over working for the oil company, and I was sick of my drunken life. After twenty years, I was ready to quit my job.

"What are you talking about, Darryl?" he said, not believing me.

"I'm seriously thinking about quitting. I can't take it anymore, man."

"C'mon man, you're just drunk. You'll feel better in the morning. When we land, we'll grab our luggage and take the shuttle up to Washington. You can check in and hit the rack. You'll be fine in the morning."

What had started out as fun turned into my buddy not being able to listen to what I was saying. The plane landed, and we headed toward the shuttle van, where we were joined by another ship's officer from Alaska Tanker Company.

"I'm serious, man. I think I'm done," I told my friend with conviction. I was physically exhausted. Spiritually bankrupt. Emotionally a mess. Mentally broken. I knew I wasn't proceeding on to the conference.

"I'm going to check into the airport Marriott," I said, on the verge of tears. "I'll decide tomorrow if I'll show up."

"It's only five days," the other officer said. "Then you can fly home and quit if you feel like it. At least you'll get five days' pay."

I just couldn't do it. All I could think about was drinking some more and quitting my job. "Nope. You guys go ahead. I'm checking into the hotel." I shook their hands and walked off with my luggage.

I had hit a brick wall. I had just hit bottom without realizing it was coming.

I checked into the hotel, drank a beer from the mini bar, and contemplated my life. What was I doing? If I didn't show up tomorrow and the company found out I was dodging the conference, I'd be fired. I finished my beer and walked to a liquor store to buy more. I filled the sink in my room with beer and ice, and decided to save it for later. I wanted to drown my sorrows at the hotel bar.

It wasn't two hours before I had offended everyone in the hotel bar and was shut off. They told me to leave, and I stumbled back up to my room, where I had twenty-four cold beers waiting for me. I drank the night away, knowing I would have to make a decision the next day.

My options were to quit the company or ask for help. Tell them thanks but no thanks or finally fight the demons that had been chasing me for twenty-seven years. Maybe I could get my drinking under control if I didn't have the stress of running ships all over the world.

I drank another half dozen beers and passed out half-dressed.

I woke up and tried to figure out where I was. I then remembered I had to make a decision in the next few hours. Quit my job or go into alcohol and drug rehabilitation. I wasn't thrilled with either choice. I crawled back under the covers. Either decision was scary, so I put it off for a few more hours.

I dozed, moving in and out of consciousness, worrying about what to do. I knew the best thing for me was to get help and save my job. It's not really what I wanted, but it was clearly the safer choice. If I quit, I could continue drinking and drugging, but I would end up having to sell my house and spend my retirement savings. And I'd probably die young.

Then I did what any good alcoholic does when he's worried, nervous, and has to make a decision. I opened a Budweiser and drank the whole can. I ran into the bathroom and threw up. I was shaking, trembling, sweating, and the only cure was the hair of the dog. I splashed some water on my face, threw on a bathrobe, and opened another beer. I finished the beer, opened another, and finished it as quickly as I could.

The beer calmed me down and gave me enough courage to call my employer.

"Good morning, Alaska Tanker Company," a woman answered politely.

"This is Darryl Hagar. I'm a second mate with the company. I was hoping to talk to the head of human relations, Art Balfe."

"He's at the ATC Leadership Conference in Washington State. Just about everyone from the office is there. Can I help you?"

"It's kind of embarrassing. I need some help with alcoholism. I've developed a bad drinking problem."

"I'll ask Art Balfe to call you."

Relieved, I hung up and drank another beer while I waited. I couldn't believe I had finally surrendered. After twenty-seven years of drinking and drug use, I was going to my first rehab. I felt an enormous sense of relief, as if a 10,000-pound elephant had finally been lifted off my back.

The phone rang a few minutes later. I took a deep breath.

"Hi, Darryl. Art Balfe. I hear you're having some personal problems."

"Thanks for calling, Art. My drinking has progressed pretty badly, and I can't take it anymore. I'm tired of living this way. I hurt all over: my head, my heart, even my hair."

"I'm proud of you for being man enough to ask for help. We'll do everything we can to make you well."

"I should be at the conference right now, but the pressure kind of took me over. I can't go see anyone there," I said emphatically.

"You don't have to go to the conference. Don't worry about anything but getting help." He asked me if I wanted to get help in Portland, Oregon, or if I wanted to go back to Portland, Maine. I wanted to go home, and he offered to book a flight that day.

"I can't fly today, Art."

"Why not?" He sounded surprised.

"I'm half drunk right now. I had to have some beers this morning to get the courage to call you."

He told me he would arrange a flight the next morning. "Will you be okay today by yourself?" he asked sincerely.

"I'm okay. I feel better now that I've finally made the decision to get help. I should have done it years ago."

I woke up on May 11, 2005, as the sun was rising. After a few seconds I remembered I had called the company and was flying home. I went into the bathroom and looked in the mirror. My hair stuck out in all directions. My throat was dry, and my stomach was churning. My hands were shaking. I ran to the toilet and threw up violently. I sat down and started having diarrhea. I threw up again between my legs.

I got into the shower with my head pounding. I knew I would have a hard time traveling. I tried to wash away the stench of alcohol and vomit, but after I toweled off I realized the smell was coming out of my pores. My body was trying to cleanse itself. I was shaking and sweating. I had the d.t.'s. I'm sure my blood pressure was sky high, and I was white as a ghost. I felt like I was going to die. But I had felt that way many times before, so I sucked it up and got dressed. I called the front desk and made arrangements for a shuttle to the airport. I took my bags downstairs. The shuttle driver was an older man.

"How are you, sir? Going to the airport?" he asked.

"I am. When are we leaving?"

"In about five minutes. Have a seat right up front if you want."

"I'm not feeling so good. I think I'll get some fresh air and jump in when you're ready."

"You don't look too good. Are you okay?" he asked, genuinely concerned.

"I just made a monumental decision about quitting drinking and going into a rehabilitation center. I'm stressed out and hung over," I admitted.

"Oh, my God, I hope you'll be okay. I think you're doing the right thing." He hurried to the front desk to see if there were any more passengers. Apparently he thought it was best to get me on my way quickly, because he came right back out and said he was ready. We were leaving early.

"Let's go. No one else for this trip."

They want to get me off their property before I have a heart attack or die on them. He seemed nervous as he drove me to the airport, but also genuinely worried about me.

I was still sweating and shaking and got more than one second look, but was able to get through security and onto the plane. I discovered I had the center seat between two large men.

"Excuse me. I'm in the middle seat."

The gentleman next to the aisle stood up. I took the center seat and said hello to the man seated by the window, who politely asked how I was.

"To be honest, not very good at all. It's a long story." The three of us engaged in some small talk, and I could tell they were trying to figure out what was going on. I was shaking, sweating, sighing a lot, and obviously emotionally distraught.

"Are you going to be okay?" one of them asked.

"Listen, guys, I'm going through a life event that I'd rather not talk about. I'm not very good company. I'm going to shut my eyes. I'll be fine, but you'll have to cut me some slack."

"Sure, no problem," they both said.

It was an uncomfortable flight. My seatmates were uneasy, and all I could do was pretend to sleep. I wish I could have heard what they told their wives when they got home. I'm sure they figured out a few things. I smelled like booze and had full-blown d.t.'s.

We managed to get to Chicago without incident. I hurried off the plane and straight to an airport bar. I would not go through another flight shaking in front of strangers.

When I walked in, the bartender looked at me and laughed. It was the man who had served me before catching my connecting flight to Oregon. I didn't recognize him.

"Did you make it through the other day?" he asked.

"What do you mean?"

"You were so drunk the other day I didn't think they would let you on the plane," he said, laughing again.

"Sorry about that. I forgot about you until now. Give me a tall 20-ounce beer."

He brought me a beer, still curious about what had happened. I realized I must have put on quite a show.

"I made it through. I know I was drinking too much. I'm headed back home now." I paid for my beer, trying to steady my hand—to no avail.

The smile on his face disappeared. "I couldn't believe how drunk you were. You had no idea what you were doing." The old man knew I was medicating myself and walked away to give me some privacy.

I raised the beer to my lips and took a huge drink, hardly able to keep the beer from spilling. The memory of that moment will stay for me as long as I live. I finished that beer and ordered another. As it turns out, one day at a time, God willing, that second beer I drank on May 11, 2005, at Chicago O'Hare Airport was the last beer I would ever drink.

I was all done.

GLENN CHADBOURNE

CHAPTER THIRTY-NINE
DETOX AND REHAB

At the age of forty-two, I finished what I now believe was the last beer of my life. I thanked the bartender and went to find my departure gate. I again started to sweat and shake. I found a bathroom, knelt down in a toilet stall, and threw up.

I washed my face with cold water and looked in the mirror. The reflection wasn't pretty: I was white as a ghost with sunken eyes, sweaty hair and face, and a broken spirit. I stuck my entire head under a running faucet, toweled off the best a person can in an airport bathroom, and went back to the gate to wait.

I sat there shaking like a leaf, thinking about how I had reached this point in my life. I wondered where my life was headed. Could I get myself together and raise my little boy, or would I succumb to alcoholism and drug addiction? I would give it my best shot. A tremendous burden had been lifted just by admitting I had a problem. Now it was up to me to change. I'd have to ask God to help me every day; Lord knew I needed as much help as I could get.

It was embarrassing boarding the plane with my hands shaking. I sat down and quickly fell asleep. Once we landed in Portland, I was severely tempted to go straight outside and hail a cab. I needed to be home in my own bed more than I needed my gear. But I toughed it out and waited until my bags arrived on the luggage belt.

In the driveway at home I looked through my briefcase for my house keys. They were nowhere to be found. I walked around back and tried all the doors and windows. I couldn't believe it. I had finally made it home, I was hung over as a bastard, and now I couldn't get in my house. I went through my luggage; still no keys.

I got a ladder out of the garage and leaned it against the house. I couldn't believe I had to do this. God must be teaching me a lesson; he didn't want me to get off too easy. I pried open a window and slid into the house. I grabbed my luggage out front and went back upstairs to shower.

It hurt to wash the slime off my body. It hurt to brush my teeth. It hurt to move. I was an utter mess. I toweled off and collapsed on my bed. My dreams that night were wild and vivid and included being drunk on ship and passing out on watch. In one dream I tried to wake up, but I just couldn't. The ship was going to crash; the oil was going to spill! *Wake up, Darryl, you're drunk again!*

After a restlessness night, I opened my eyes and lay there thinking. *I'm at a crossroads. My time is now. Here's my chance to regain control and finally move forward.*

My company had told me to call a medical facility that would process my paperwork. I was nervous as I dialed the number, but relieved I was finally getting help.

A young woman named Lisa answered the phone, and I explained my situation. As I gave her the information she requested, I tried to remain patient. I wanted to tell her to get me the fuck to a facility already; the shakes were coming back. I either needed a drink or to get some help.

"Can we move this along? I'm not feeling well." I said.

"We have to go through this for me to help you," Lisa said evenly. "I'm going to ask you now about your drug and alcohol use. Please answer truthfully and be as thorough as you can."

"I'll do my best," I said impatiently.

"How long have you been drinking alcohol?"

"Ummm," I counted it up in my head. "Twenty-seven years."

"How long do you think you have had a problem with drinking?"

"Since day one. I passed out in my own vomit the first time I drank."

"Have you ever tried to stop drinking before? Tried to drink only beer or just on the weekends?"

"Yes to all the above. I've been arrested ten times. I've had numerous surgeries for problems caused by alcohol. I've been in trouble at work and at home for drunkenness and drug abuse."

"What kind of drugs were you using?"

"Everything but heroin. I have a pretty serious problem with cocaine. I've been a drug user my whole adult life. Cocaine, LSD, mushrooms, marijuana, speed, crystal meth, pills, hashish, OxyContin, downers, uppers, and everything in between. Everything but needles."

"What is your biggest problem?"

"I think if I quit drinking, the rest will go away. When I start drinking, I start making bad choices. I've never done hard drugs without drinking first."

"Darryl, you do know you'll be given drug and alcohol tests, and if you test positive you'll be dismissed from your job."

"Yes. I have no plans to drink or use drugs."

Lisa made arrangements for six visits to a drug and alcohol counselor. After that we would decide what other help I needed.

I got on my knees and asked God to help me. I knew I was in the struggle of my life. I knew I couldn't do it alone. I knew God was with me. But I could do this if I worked at it hard enough. I wanted this. I needed this.

After six visits with a therapist we decided I needed to go through rehab. I went to Mercy Recovery Center and filled out forms and answered more questions about my drug and alcohol use. They told me I was a candidate for their Intensive Outpatient Program and that I could begin as soon as my insurance gave the green light.

I was told to go home and they would call me. I decided to attend twelve-step meetings in the meantime. I looked in the yellow pages and called a hotline number. A young man answered and told me to come to the office; he would give me all the information I would ever need to find twelve-step meetings. In addition to the meeting lists, he gave me some words of advice and comfort. That man eventually became my second sponsor.

I eagerly jumped in my car. I took a deep breath, said a quick prayer, and walked into the meeting. I felt like every eye was on me, but later learned that wasn't the case. Everyone at twelve-step meetings has his own issues to deal with. Meetings are part of a fellowship where everybody accepts and supports one another.

I found a chair against the wall. I was out of my element, so I decided to sit back, watch, and listen. At the front of the room sat a huge, bearded, tattooed, pony-tailed biker. He rapped a gavel on a desk.

"Hi, everyone. I'm Larry, and I'm an alcoholic," he said confidently.

"Hi, Larry," everyone said simultaneously.

Larry shared his story of drugs, alcohol, women, fights, arrests, and health problems. Here was a guy completely different from me in looks and speech, but our stories were very much alike. Perhaps I wasn't unique. Perhaps I wasn't alone. Maybe I wasn't the only one this crazy.

Larry told the horror story of his past and then talked about how beautiful it was to surrender and attain a year of sobriety. His family was happy he was still alive, and he was able to enjoy his children with a clear mind. He thanked God he'd made it. He got choked up, and the next thing I knew, the big Harley Davidson biker was weeping in front of fifty people.

Man, if this guy can get sober and find peace, so can I. If he's willing to humble himself talking about his feelings in front of a bunch of people, maybe there's hope for me. I immediately connected with everything he said. I felt the same regrets and, somehow, the same sense of hope. The idea resonated that we can't change yesterday, but we can live today and thrive tomorrow. I would ask God to help me do this.

I went home and spent the afternoon and evening with my son, who had turned six a week earlier.

I sat down with him and said, "Darryl, Dad has decided to change his life. It will be hard for me to quit drinking beer, but I'll try. I'm going to a hospital every day, and they're going to help me."

"Okay, Dad. Why are you going to a hospital?"

"Because Dad can't stop drinking. I need the doctors and nurses to help me. They'll teach me how to live every day without drinking and how to be happy with my life, and with you, without drinking beer. I hope you'll help me too, Bud. I love you more than anything in the world." I gave him a kiss.

"I will, Dad. And Mom will help you too."

"I'll make a deal with you. If you stop sucking your thumb, I'll stop drinking beer. We'll quit together. Do you think we can do it?"

"I think so, Dad. I'll try."

We went through the day, and I could tell Darryl wanted to suck his thumb. I could see the wheels turning in his little head. He was trying to resist the comfort of that little thumb. I was very proud of him; he didn't put it in his mouth all day. Later that night I read to him, tucked him in, and he said his prayers. I went up to his room a few hours later, and his thumb had made its way back into its usual nighttime position. I reached over and gently tugged it out of his mouth.

We repeated that scenario a few times, but never while he was awake. He knew that quitting drinking was a decision important to both our lives. He knew the connection between quitting the thumb-sucking and quitting drinking would help his dad. He stayed true to his word. He never sucked his thumb again; from that day, I didn't pick up alcohol.

I continued to go to meetings every day; some days I attended two. I was having terrible cravings for alcohol, and the only thing that quieted my mind and put me at ease was to get around other people who were struggling. It helped to hear how they stayed sober. I was told to "keep coming back," get lots of phone numbers, get a sponsor, and work the twelve steps.

A few weeks passed, and I still hadn't been accepted for rehab. Though Mercy Hospital's assessment was that I needed the program, my insurance company wasn't sure that I was a candidate, since they'd already paid for six therapy visits.

I got on the phone with Alaska Tanker Company and was told the group plan was not set up for expensive rehab. I couldn't believe that I had finally surrendered, finally admitted to myself and the world that I needed help, and the oil company had no program available. It was an absurdity that a company partially owned by British Petroleum, one of the world's oil majors, couldn't flex their group policy to allow one of their officers to get well.

This was post Exxon Valdez. The captain of that ship had a drinking past eerily similar to mine, with multiple drunk-driving events. Even after that, apparently the industry had not yet learned its lesson. If a sailor came forward on his own accord and asked for help, I thought the oil companies should be eager to assist him.

I spoke with Mrs. Smith, the intake coordinator at Mercy Recovery Center. She set up a conference call with Alaska Tanker Company and the insurance company. I was ready to let them have it.

Mrs. Smith explained the situation. "Darryl is a long-term employee of the company. He came forward on his own, asking for help."

"Ummm, we're trying to work this out," said the official from Alaska Tanker Company.

The insurance rep was not any more helpful. "The group rate does not cover long-term rehab. I'm sorry, Mr. Hagar, but that is the situation."

"You're telling me that you can't figure out how to make an adjustment for two weeks of rehabilitation? You're telling me Alaska Tanker Company can't afford $5,000 for one of its key personnel? I'm coming forward asking for help," I said.

"It's sad that you gentlemen can't figure this out for a man definitely in need," Mrs. Smith scolded.

By that time I was angry enough to challenge them. "I can give you another option: I can go back out and drink and break my hand four more times like I did in 2000, and you can spend another $75,000 fixing my injuries. And then I'll just go back to sea and navigate your 900-foot supertankers and try not to drink. How's that?"

I had done what I felt needed to be done. I had strong-armed them in as public a way as I could manage. I knew I'd crossed a line with the oil company; there was an unspoken agreement that nobody challenged them and survived. But my sobriety and my sanity took priority over any job.

"Darryl, I'm sure we can work something out. I'll call you at home," the ATC official said.

I received a call later that day. I would be going to Mercy's two-week outpatient program, four-and-a-half hours Monday through Friday and six hours on Saturday with my family.

The following Monday I drove to the recovery center and signed in. I went to a room where ten other alcoholics and drug addicts sat in a circle. A small blonde, Nancy Adair, was running the group. Nancy was one of several licensed alcohol and drug counselors who worked with us to help us understand the illness. I credit her with saving my life.

Nancy was assigned five of the clients, and I thank God I was one of them. She taught me that I could live a clean and sober life and do it happy, content, and free. When I walked into the room that first day, I could feel Nancy's eyes on me. Not only did she take in my outward appearance, but I had the sense that she was also trying to figure out what was going on inside my head. It was almost as if she was talking to me telepathically, asking me "What's wrong?" and "How can I help you?"

I wasn't the least bit intimidated or embarrassed. I wanted her to figure me out. I wanted someone to take a close look at me and tell me why I was so far overboard. I welcomed all advice, education, suggestions, and information. I asked questions that would help lead her to the answers to why I was so insanely addicted. I was finally ready to help myself. I was ready to open up my heart and soul to Nancy and the other counselors and doctors. I was ready to look inside and fix what was broken.

What I learned was that nothing was broken; I had an illness, a disease called alcoholism and addiction. I had a mental obsession and a physical allergy to drugs and alcohol that was there when I was young and will be there when I'm old. I came to understand that alcoholism/addiction is a chronic disease that is genetic and biological. It's passed on through families—and that means the alcoholic/addict is not a bad person. It means the alcoholic/addict is a sick person. It means the alcoholic/addict has to understand that he can't use drugs or drink safely. It means the alcoholic/addict will have the problem for the rest of his life.

I'm not making any excuses for my past. I knowingly raised the bottle to my lips. I knowingly put a rolled up dollar bill in my nostril and snorted lines of cocaine. I knowingly took painkillers, mushrooms, LSD, and smoked pot until I couldn't see straight. I'm not a dumb person, but I did a lot of dumb things, and I blame no one but myself. I don't blame my friends who urged me to party with them. I don't blame the stress of running ships with a bunch of hardened men or being away from my friends and family for months at a time. I don't make excuses that I didn't realize I was an addict or an alcoholic.

I *was* in denial for years. I sincerely believed I could handle my lifestyle, even with my frequent screw ups. I still had a good job. I didn't do bad things like throw rocks at old ladies or break into people's houses. I was only hurting myself. It was my way of medicating myself, my way of making it through all life's issues.

In rehab I realized that once I admitted I was powerless over drugs and alcohol, I finally had a chance to get the disease under control. I can't change that I'm an alcoholic/addict. The disease is cunning, baffling, and powerful. It cannot ever be totally removed, but it can be managed with continual recovery work.

With each passing day in the program, the feeling grew that my life was being resurrected. On the first Saturday, I selected a friend from the twelve-step program to join me. I wasn't ready for my family to come, and I felt comfortable with someone who had gone through all this before. He was understanding and supportive and willing to go through five hours of education and group therapy with me.

My favorite day was when we were asked to write a letter saying goodbye to our "drug of choice." I had two: alcohol and cocaine. Some drug addicts are not alcoholics, but for me alcohol was the gateway that led me to consume everything else. What I mainly used when I was drunk was cocaine. In the letter I knew I would write about alcohol, but I also needed to say good riddance to cocaine. Alcohol had taken my mind and my money, but cocaine had taken my soul. I loved every one of the fifteen minutes it took to write that letter.

> 30 min/8
> I'm sitting at my
> desk in the big chair
> & have brought in 2 of my
> employees for dismissal
> instead of n.
>
> Write a letter saying GOOD
> BYE to your drug of choice.
>
> Alcohol
>
> Good Bye Old Friends
>
> Dear Anheiser + Smirnoff, Bud beer vokka (and your evil cousin Cocaine)
>
> I am putting you both on notice that you both will not be brought back. 7 weeks ago I decided to put you on a leave of absense because of your conning intentions of ruining my life. You have been very successful in your endeavor and I have given you the benefit of the doubt because of the good times we've had together.
>
> As I grow and become to realize your poisons and intentions, I am effectively + Immediately Firing you. Hopefully you will not try to Fandangle your way back into my life. You have managed to take 20 years from me and I'm tired of living this way.
>
> By the way, your Cousin Cocaine said he'd pick you up when you leave, Tell him he's Fired to, and that I'm tired of him Fucking with my life too.
>
> Pick up your belongings + your last check as you leave. Darryl

Goodbye letter to drugs and alcohol.

On the second Saturday I asked my sister to accompany me. It was an emotional day. Karen Ann talked about how year after year she had watched me destroy myself. Her children had been deprived of a responsible uncle, unable to be involved in their lives. I was uncomfortable hearing about my disease from my sister's perspective, but it was an important step in my recovery. I loved my sister for her honesty and her ability to forgive the past. She was proud that I had finally asked for help; in fact, my entire family was supportive of my newfound sobriety

As the program ended, Nancy Adair went above and beyond in making up a five-page treatment plan for me that included going to daily twelve-step meetings, finding a sponsor, and group therapy. I also planned to see a therapist, Phil del Vecchio, who turned out to be not only an important part of my recovery, but a great friend. I was ready to move on from rehab to the outside world.

Attending Mercy Hospital Recover Center had been one of the best decisions of my life. I believe God steered me there to prepare me for a future that would include speaking about the insidious disease of drug addiction and alcoholism—and about how even a man overboard can change.

GLENN CHADBOURNE

CHAPTER FORTY

GOD HELP THE MAN IN THE MIRROR

Not long after my journey of recovery began, I was flipping through channels on TV and came across a preacher from Texas named Joel Osteen. What he said made me sit up and take notice. His message was if you ask God for forgiveness and try your best, he will change you and reward you with an abundant life. If you believe you're an overcomer in Christ, then you'll act like an overcomer and *become* an overcomer. He talked about committing whatever you do to the Lord—and then your plans will succeed.

When I heard Joel's broadcast that night, I had reached the point when I wanted more than just to navigate supertankers around the world. I had a very good retirement setup, a nice home and car, money in the bank, and a beautiful son. It was a very good life, but it wasn't enough. I was also looking for fulfillment, forgiveness, inspiration—maybe even greatness.

I needed more than financial success; I needed to feel I was making a difference in other people's lives. Joel had said, "The best way to solve your problem is to get your mind off what's wrong in your life and help somebody else." I realized the same principle can be found in the twelve steps.

I had already made my money; it was time to sow some seeds elsewhere. I came to believe that devoting the rest of my life to God, to my sobriety, to my family, and to helping others recover from drug and alcohol addictions was the best way I could serve God. I also decided the only way I could stay clean was to hit my recovery just as relentlessly as I had once hit the partying. Going to more than a hundred twelve-step meetings in the first three months of sobriety saved my life. The fellowship kept me strong when I was scared, gave me answers when I was confused, and provided support when I felt alone.

The program also increased my faith in a power greater than myself. I had always believed in God, but I had strayed so far from my faith that only daily meetings and the reinforcement of watching Pastor Joel could bring me back. Going to church once a week wasn't enough for this alcoholic. The twelve-step program brought spirituality back into my sick head.

I also began meeting with my therapist. Phil helped me understand that what I'd been through with my dad had contributed to my addictions. I suspect Phil had never had a client quite like me; we both knew we had our hands full.

Alaska Tanker Company supported me fully and wanted me back at work when I was ready. I'd go back when I felt strong enough. Attaining and keeping sobriety was paramount. I was nothing without it, and I wasn't about to let anything or anyone threaten it.

I met my first sponsor, who had been sober ten years. I could tell immediately that he had a close connection with a higher power. We worked together on the twelve steps, and I started keeping a journal. Every day I wrote—about how alcohol and drugs placed my life and the lives of others in jeopardy and about how I had lost all self-respect.

My sponsor taught me how to forgive myself and helped me realize that I was powerless over drugs and alcohol. He showed me that I had to look back at my past before I could talk about the future. It suddenly was clear that if I refrained from using, I'd be clear-minded enough to deal with the life issues I'd never worked on. Drugs and alcohol had enabled me to forget about reality and mask pent up feelings. Those emotions now streamed out of me.

I worked tirelessly and I felt better every day, except for one thing: Not only was I still craving drugs and alcohol, I was obsessing about them. Every beer commercial, every convenience store I drove by, every restaurant I walked into—there was alcohol all around me. I'd watch a baseball game and see a Budweiser sign in left field. I'd be walking on a sidewalk and see an empty twelve-pack stuffed in a trash can. I had dreams about using cocaine or going to the liquor store for a half-gallon of vodka and a case of beer. Now that I wasn't drinking, alcohol was in my head every second of every minute of every hour of every day.

It was driving me insane. A twelve-step meeting, talking to my sponsor, and therapy slowed down the thoughts for a few hours, but then they came rushing back.

One day in the midst of my obsessions, I went into my downstairs bathroom and looked in the mirror. I said aloud, "Dude, you're fucking nuts!"

I had lived in the same house for fifteen years and had looked in that mirror many times after being up all night doing cocaine. Not once under the influence had I ever told myself I was nuts. What was happening to me? I had given up all the bad stuff, so why was I feeling this way?

Scared and confused, I prayed, "God, you have to relieve me of the cravings and the obsession with drugs and alcohol. I'm asking you, dear Lord, to take them from me. I know there'll still be plenty of problems if you do, but I promise I'll deal with all that junk. Just quiet my head and let me be at peace."

I went directly to a meeting. Once again I felt refreshed. I went home and slept comfortably. The next day I met with my therapist in the morning and my sponsor in the evening. They both told me to stay the course; things would get better.

I picked up my son, and we spent the night and the following day together. It was such a joy to reassure him that Dad would always be there for him and have confidence that I could follow through on my promise. Jen picked him up, and I attended a twelve-step meeting that night. I slept peacefully without nightmares. In the morning, I went outside to enjoy my coffee. I thought about the day ahead. I'd write in my journal and hit a meeting later that night. That's when I realized what had happened.

Since I had stood at the mirror and prayed three days before, I'd had no cravings and I had not obsessed about drugs and alcohol. I had just experienced a miracle! People might say I was losing it, that I was bending the truth, or that I had suddenly become some kind of religious fanatic. None of that was true. I had just sincerely asked God to relieve me of my burden, and he had answered my prayer. It wasn't on par with parting the Red Sea, but I had experienced my own little miracle, and for that I will forever be grateful.

After that I occasionally had dreams about drinking or doing cocaine. I sometimes still thought romantically about alcohol when I saw someone having a glass of wine with a lover in a movie. Those thoughts will always be there, but they're intermittent and fleeting. From that day forward, I no longer obsessed about or craved alcohol every second of the day. I know in my heart that God listened to me and helped me. He loves us all and is always waiting for us to ask him in.

I shared that story many times at meetings. The more people I talked to, the more I realized my little miracle was not unique. Many others had been relieved of their cravings and obsessions after asking God for help.

During that first year of recovery, I had a checkup and told my doctor about my past. I wanted to be tested for STDs and HIV. Dr. Merrill was supportive, and all the tests came back negative. Despite my risky behavior, I had been spared. I let out a big sigh of relief. At my most undeserving, God had been merciful. Perhaps he had bigger plans for my life.

I began to think I could handle going back to sea. It had been five months since I'd asked for help. I felt good and believed going back to work would further my stability in recovery. Alaska Tanker Company was pleased with my progress. I called the captain with whom I'd be sailing to ease his fears. I now had my feet on solid ground and would do a good job for him and the company.

I flew to Port Angeles, Washington, on October 15, 2005, to join the Prince William Sound. Weeks went by, and work went well. I got along with the crew and worked well with the chief mate. I even gave a talk about rehab and quitting alcohol to the deck gang. I had come full circle

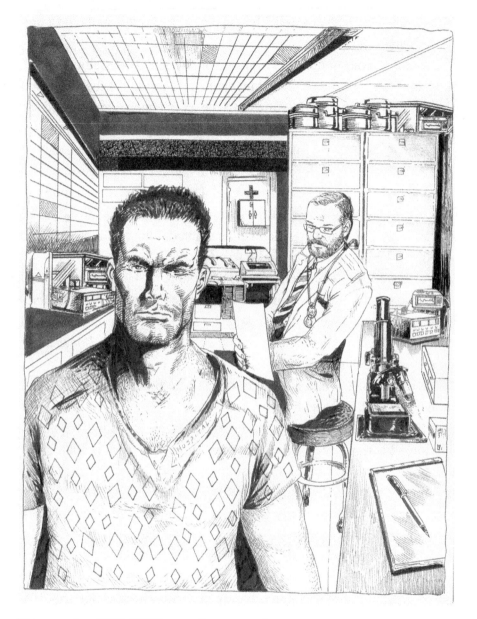

Requesting STD/HIV tests from my doctor.

in all ways but one. I still wasn't interested in becoming chief mate. I had enough on my plate just maintaining my sobriety. But the captain wanted more. He had expressed his displeasure about it in the past and was showing it again.

One day I was standing in front of one of the radars along with a pilot from Puget Sound. The captain came over to look at the radar, and instead of saying "excuse me" he gave me a hip check that knocked me away. He'd done the same thing once before, and I suddenly realized that his hate for me was real. The first time hadn't been an accident. Was I that bad a guy? I'd always been a handful and for that I was sorry. But I'd made major changes to my behavior. The company was supportive; wouldn't the captain forgive me? The captain "owned" the ship while he was running it; he could do whatever he wanted. I kept both incidents to myself, but I felt intimidated and uneasy.

We docked, and a new chief mate came aboard. He asked me about what I'd gone through and what I did to stay sober. I got out a twelve-step book while we were on the bridge, and he looked at it. He thought what I was doing was good but seemed skeptical about the book. I told him about the shoving incident.

He looked at me and said, "Darryl, you're bigger than him. Deck him next time he shoves you."

I was surprised. I didn't think he expected me to actually punch a superior officer, but then again, anything could happen on board. The climate on the ships was like something I'd once heard from a former classmate: "Ships are basically stable, but it takes a lot of unstable men to run them." The ships really did make men a little nuts, and the men who chose to sail on them were not average. A person had to already be a bit off-kilter to want to sail for weeks away from land and society.

A few days later I was on the bridge and had the con as another sailor steered the ship. The chief mate came up to look out over the deck. We were standing together having a cup of coffee, and I remarked, "I'm really tired today."

"Did you get your rest last night?" The chief mate was always concerned that he had a rested crew.

"That's the strange thing. I got seven hours of sleep before we loaded the ship. I should be feeling great."

"I tell you what, Darryl. Why don't you take a mental health day? Don't work overtime. Go down to your room, get out your twelve-step books, hum and meditate, and flog your main member," he said half-seriously.

I couldn't believe what I'd just heard. First the captain shoved me twice, and now the chief mate was making fun of my sobriety. He had always treated me respectfully, so I blew it off as a joke and didn't reply.

But a week later when we again were on the bridge together, he smiled and repeated his bad joke word for word. That time I blew up and yelled at him. He left the bridge muttering about losing his job. I was deeply hurt; the man had always been my friend. I suspected he and the captain were trying to drive me off the ship. The only two people on board who could ruin my career seemed to be trying to get me to over-react. I thought about quitting on the spot; it wasn't worth the added stress, and my sobriety was being put at risk.

I toughed it out a few more weeks. When the captain was due to get off the ship, he gave me a less-than-satisfactory evaluation; perhaps he thought he could finish me off. Afterward he knew I was angry and seemed to realize I wasn't going to take the harassment lying down. I got the feeling he knew he was in trouble.

I stayed on board, stewing on it for weeks. Then one day I typed an e-mail to headquarters from a satellite communications terminal on the bridge. After five minutes I heard the satellite phone ring. Within sixty seconds, the captain was on the bridge telling me to go to his office and take a call. Two Alaska Tanker Company officials were on the sat-phone, and I explained my beef. The company again treated me fairly.

I finished that work tour on December 27, 2005, and never set foot on another supertanker. Twenty years was enough. The ships had taken my mind and my health. I had taken a step forward, but had been pushed two steps back. I would have to work hard to get back where I'd been in recovery. Now I'd see what I was made of.

At home I joined Amistad, a Catholic Charities mental health recovery group. It was a godsend. The program helped me understand that through all the years of going to sea, working long hours, cursing like a pirate, partying like a fool, and living in chaos, I had never looked at other people's feelings or thought about how good I had it.

The group leaders were in recovery either for substance abuse or mental health issues; they were wonderful people helping the less fortunate. At the first meeting we each explained why we were there and what we hoped to gain. Several people were bipolar or struggling with depression, some had slight mental retardation, and others had issues with substance abuse or overeating.

One of the men was gay; he had been molested as a child. I had always been homophobic, and to my great surprise we became close. He was just a guy trying to recover from the evil someone had done to him. He didn't push himself on me, and I learned acceptance. He had to have known how I'd been before, but I was changing into a man who appreciated that everyone struggles and that we all had to live together.

I attended three twelve-week group therapy sessions, each time meeting new people and gaining more understanding of the kinds of issues people struggled with. I felt God was growing me up and allowing me to help other people. At the same time, I continued working the steps with my sponsor and writing in my journal. I no longer had a problem admitting I was an alcoholic. I had asked God to restore me to sanity and I was willing to turn my life over to him. I was finally ready to do his will and not my own.

I soon discovered that my old lifestyle had really taken a toll. I took a second HIV test, which came back negative, but not long afterward I was told I was "pre-diabetic," probably due to all the years of drinking, drugging, and not taking care of myself. I had broken a lot of bones and killed a lot of brain cells. I was taking medication for diabetes, high blood pressure, depression, and stomach problems.

I began to exercise more, eat and sleep right, and meditate. My health was being restored. At the same time, my sober relationship with my son took off. I coached him in Little League baseball and Portland Recreation basketball. Working with all the little guys was good for my soul. Those activities were as important as therapy—they let me back into the human race and proved that I had human feelings and that I was a good person.

Then I took on the incredibly difficult task of working the fourth and fifth steps with my sponsor. The fourth step is taking a moral inventory, and the fifth is sharing it with God and another human being. I spent weeks writing down all the sex behaviors, arrests, screw ups at work, problems with family and friends, errors in judgment, and bad decisions I had made in my using days. It was a long list. On it there were three things I decided I wouldn't share with my sponsor; I would take them with me to the grave.

But when it came time, I told him everything. For two hours, all the things I regretted from my past came gushing out. It was embarrassing and uncomfortable. It was also very freeing. I felt as if the ball and chain of my past had been cut away, and I had been given a new lease on life.

It was a new beginning.

CHAPTER FORTY-ONE
GOING BACK TO CUMBERLAND COUNTY JAIL

When I arrived at Cumberland County Jail in June 2006, feelings of shame overwhelmed me. I hadn't been sure how to get there. Every other time, I had arrived too drunk to remember going through the entrance. I didn't remember being fingerprinted, processed, or locked up. I do remember being inside jail cells. And I remember how rude, unruly, belligerent, and downright mean I was to the deputies.

I sat in my car, thinking of how much of an animal I'd been. How could a boy from a decent middle-class family—a high school scholar, top athlete, and Merchant Marine officer—become the man I'd become? But alcoholism doesn't discriminate. Drug abuse can take anybody prisoner. Tears came to my eyes. *I only have one life to live, and I've wasted half of it. I'd better move forward.*

I was at the jail, now with more than a year of sobriety under my belt, to learn how to bring twelve-step meetings to the inmates. Located in the heart of Portland, the facility is the largest in the state, employing a direct supervision pod design with a capacity of 560 inmates.

I walked to the entrance, and several deputies outside stopped their conversation. As they looked me over, I wondered, *Do they recognize me? Do they remember the last time I was here? Or the time before? Or the time before that?*

No one said anything, and I walked inside. I passed through a metal detector and was taken to a big classroom. The deputy running the training was strict and professional. While she was talking, I noticed that some of the younger folks were joking and fooling around, distracting the rest of us. I thought, *My days of not taking life seriously are over!*

We took a tour of the facility, and the deputies were happy to show us everything. I was amazed at their professionalism and sincerity. These were the same people I had called "communist pigs." My standard line had been, "You're pretty tough after you have me handcuffed."

The feelings of embarrassment and shame returned. It's amazing how a person's mind gets twisted by drugs and alcohol. All my adult partying life I had no use for cops. Now my eyes were being opened. These were polite, caring people with families, who daily had to deal with out-of-control people like I had been. In the old days I treated them with zero respect. I suddenly understood that law enforcement professionals have a very necessary and important job to do. The longer I was there, the more my respect for them grew.

When we finished the tour I was fully trained and ready to come back and talk with the inmates. I left that day on a pink cloud, thanking God for the opportunity to give something back. I was finally becoming the man I had never had the courage to be.

In July I went back to Cumberland to conduct my first twelve-step meeting. I was paired with another alcoholic and assigned to Pod C1. My partner mentioned that he always felt pre-event jitters and asked if I was nervous. I wasn't. Not at all.

As we proceeded through the jail, we had to stop every twenty feet to pass through another security door. Once inside, we saw thirty-five men spread out around the pod. All activity ceased, and all eyes were suddenly on us. For a few seconds I was unnerved. So much for my nerves of steel. A deputy announced a twelve-step meeting and took us to a room with a steel table and eight chairs. Six men joined us.

My partner and I began the meeting by telling the inmates about the things we had done under the influence and the problems we had caused our families. We had seven OUI convictions between us and had gotten out of eight more, totaling fifteen incidents of drunk driving, not including the dozens of times we didn't get stopped. We shared more of our stories, and each inmate then talked about his life and his plans upon release. By getting down into the trenches with these guys, by talking and listening to them, I felt we could have an impact on their lives.

As I said goodbye to the men, I looked each of them in the eyes. The desperation I had seen when we had entered the room an hour before had changed to hope. The married men who had shared seemed especially sincere. If we could help just those two men, we would actually make a difference in the lives of ten people. If their lives changed, so would the lives of their wives and children.

As we left the jail, I once again was riding my pink cloud. God was alive and well inside me. I no longer needed the momentary high of doing a fat line of cocaine. I was high from helping others, and it was okay to be intoxicated by that. I was finally making a positive difference in other people's lives.

What I realized then was that whether or not I felt up to leading a meeting at the jail, I needed to go. Being of service helped me stay sober. I saw where I could end up if I ever let the insanity of drinking and drugs creep back into my life. It worked as my very own cautionary tale.

I went back in August, wearing a tie-dye T-shirt in an attempt to fit in with the inmates. I wanted the men to know they weren't the only rebels in the world, that you don't have to break the law to be cool.

After I signed in, I saw a friend and asked, "What's the deal with the pod I'm going into tonight? Nobody else wanted it."

"That's the pod with the child molesters, narcs, rats, and junkies."

I was taken aback, but didn't refuse the assignment. If that was the place I was supposed to conduct a twelve-step meeting, so be it. I asked God to give me the inspiration and wisdom to offer hope to these men regardless of what they had done. At first no one showed up. Then one inmate came in and said others would follow. He was a normal-looking guy. He told me he had a nine-year-old daughter and that he had grown up in an affluent family with two alcoholic parents.

Addicted to crystal meth, the man had been caught setting up a meth lab. His alcoholic parents didn't understand. They thought he was weak, that he should just grow up and stop doing drugs. But addiction comes from chemical imbalances in the brain; the only way to correct addiction is through proper treatment.

Three more guys came in. One was a heroin junkie, two were cocaine abusers. I didn't ask why they were in prison. It was none of my business. I was there to advise and guide them and show them that there's hope.

I talked about my long-term cocaine abuse and hardcore alcoholism and how I had eventually received "the power of desperation" from God. Until I reached bottom, until I was desperate enough to totally surrender, I kept using. The shakes stopped, the vomiting and sweats subsided, but the cravings came back. I had to be desperate enough to ask for help. I had to be willing to do *anything* to stay sober. When I wasn't willing, I fell right back into the vicious cycle of addiction.

The men listened, nodding their heads. I hoped that I was making a difference. They then complained to me about the lack of treatment in the correctional centers. All four men expressed a desire for more treatment, but none was available. The heroin junkie said, "I have a plan when I get out. I just won't let my heroin use get out of control like last time." I wondered who would want him living next door while he was "controlling" his heroin habit.

A week later, I went back to Cumberland. Going into Pod C3 I felt comfortable, but then an inmate started making fun of me in front of the other prisoners. As other inmates joined in and laughed at me, I felt rage quickly rise up. I had to stop myself from saying, *What the fuck are you guys laughing at? I'm in here to help, you assholes.* But I quickly quashed that thought. A deputy announced the meeting, and pointed me to the classroom.

I expected the usual one to six inmates. First there were four. Then seven. Then ten. Then twelve, and finally fifteen men. The men started out quiet and apprehensive, but as I spoke I could see them physically loosen up. They pulled their chairs closer and listened attentively. The men raised their hands, asked questions, and talked about their problems. They asked what I'd do in their shoes and about rehab centers and halfway houses on the outside.

The message I took from the meeting was that the men needed to be guided, befriended, and closely followed up on. I realized I should treat them as peers and show them that I thought they could change. Inmates came up after the meeting to shake my hand and tell me their stories. They were looking for advice and were highly concerned about what they should do when they were released.

I knew that the message had been received. It made me feel good. It made me want to continue on a path that included helping others—and therefore myself—maintain sobriety. Whenever I go into jails and prisons, I always come out grateful. I always see and hear things that make me realize why I got sober in the first place.

I went back to Cumberland again on Labor Day. As I signed into C3 Pod, an old buddy immediately ran up and gave me a bear hug. I realized then that God had a plan for that evening. It was Bulldog, my old-time cocaine connection. He was known as one of the baddest guys in Portland; to me, he was the nicest guy in the world. He just couldn't get off the coke. We had spent many nights smoking crack, snorting big fat lines of cocaine, chasing women, smoking weed, and getting plastered on booze. He was a big dude with a bald head and a heart of gold, until you crossed him.

About ten inmates came in, and I ran the meeting like I always did. When I finished speaking, Bulldog told his story, about how messed up his life was. I smiled to myself, because I could tell he was getting to the point of desperation, just as I had. After the meeting, Bulldog told me he was sick of abusing alcohol and drugs and that more than anything he wanted to change. My personal cocaine dealer was scared, lonely, and needed help.

When Bulldog had been in jail a few months earlier, I had called his dad to ask how long his jail term was. Bulldog never knew I had called, because his father wasn't speaking to him. When I mentioned it, Bulldog was surprised that I cared enough to talk to his family. He hugged me, all bad-assed, bald-headed 220 pounds of solid steel muscle, and asked if I'd be his sponsor when he got out. I told him I would if he was serious about recovery.

I left, amazed at what had taken place.

A few days went by, and the phone rang. It was Bulldog. His dad had bailed him out, and he said he was still serious about getting clean. I was skeptical, but invited him to my house the next day. We could talk and then go to a twelve-step meeting. He showed up at my front door right on time.

As his sponsor, I promised him some tough love and explained that what I asked for might negatively affect our friendship. Bulldog had been in jail dozens of times, had been stabbed, had sold and consumed large amounts of cocaine; he didn't need to be pampered. If he was ready, he would do anything to stay clean and sober. I set the rules and said, "If you fail, I'm not sponsoring you, plain and simple."

Bulldog agreed to follow the program I outlined. I explained that if he put half the effort into sobriety that he had once put into getting and using drugs, he had a decent shot, one day at a time, of turning his life around.

We headed to a noon men's meeting that attracts professionals—businessmen on their lunch breaks. Bulldog would see that anybody can be drawn into the dark hole of drug abuse and alcoholism. There's a public misconception that alcoholics are homeless, hungry, broke, and dirty. My friend was about to see that people from all walks of life are represented at twelve-step meetings.

I introduced Bulldog to the people I knew. I asked one of the old-timers, "Who's chairing the meeting?" He said, "You are, if you'd like to." I agreed and thought about what I could say to help my friend.

As I started the meeting, I looked around and saw many familiar faces. I talked about how suddenly the small things in life had become important and beautiful. How I had stored my son's first lost tooth in a bag where I could look at it and appreciate him as a sober dad. How when I was writing out my fourth step he said, "What are you doing, Daddy, writing about drinking beer? Can I draw a picture of when you rolled

Mimi's car the night you were drunk?" How I would keep that picture forever as a powerful tool to help me remember why I was sober.

Bulldog was shifting in his seat when I mentioned him and told the men that he needed phone numbers. I then opened the meeting for discussion. An old friend talked about how beautiful my son was and how far I'd come as a man. He assured Bulldog that they'd be there for him. He also pointed out how important it is to do the work to get sobriety.

I had tested that theory in my own life. A couple of years before, I told everybody I was quitting drugs and alcohol. I gave away all my alcohol, swore off drugs, and told my mother I'd seen the light. A few days later I relapsed. I learned an important lesson: Actions speak louder than words. I no longer brag about my sobriety. I live my life one day at a time, knowing I'm only an arms length away from taking a drink.

I was excited when Bulldog raised his hand. He was sweating and shaking, and I thought he might break down and cry. He said he'd been to meetings before, but had never had the courage to speak. But he knew if he didn't get involved, he'd slip back into using, and he didn't want that. Then he talked about how a few days before one of his best cocaine buyers walked through the door at the county jail to conduct a twelve-step meeting. A light had gone on; he suddenly knew that now was the time.

As offers of support were expressed, this big, bald-headed ex-con shook uncontrollably. Bulldog had just done the most important things a struggling addict can do: Humble himself, admit he couldn't do it alone, and ask for help. I was proud of him.

After the meeting, I told Bulldog that I had once asked a surgeon what she thought about the twelve-step program. She said, "Darryl, if we in the medical field could take a twelve-step program, make it into a pill and bottle it up, we would have done exactly that many years ago." I take my "medicine" willingly and gladly each and every day.

Bulldog told me that many of the men had raved about how far I had come, saying he should stay close to me.

"I'm just another bozo on the bus trying to stay sober," I said. "If I'm successful so far, it's because I'm relentless in recovery. Every day

I get out of bed, get on my knees, and say a prayer asking God to keep me away from taking a drink and using drugs. I actively participate in my recovery by going to meetings and talking with my sponsor. I read about my disease and write about my shortfalls. At the end of the day, I get back on my knees and thank God for keeping me sober another day."

Bulldog and I continued to get together every day as sponsor and sponsee. He talked about having dreams about doing cocaine and drinking and how in them he was upset that he'd failed again. I had experienced the same dreams. Each time I woke up and thought, *Thank God I still have my sobriety*. The dreams were further apart the longer I stayed sober. I assured Bulldog the same thing would happen to him if he stayed clean.

Sponsoring Bulldog after he was released from jail.

The next time we got together, we talked about how often Bulldog had put himself in danger. We both knew a man who was in jail for murder after a night of drinking. The man had said he shot the guy by mistake and then shot him again to put him out of his misery. Then he took the body and buried it in a shallow grave. Both of us had done cocaine with the guy, and I knew he was a wacko. He had been in my house more than once.

Bulldog talked about a time when he and that man had been doing cocaine and the guy had whipped out a pistol. He wanted to know, "What would you do if I asked you for all your drugs?" Bulldog replied, "I'd probably give them to you and come find you later."

Bulldog's story brought me back to how lucky we were. Either Bulldog or I could have been the one in that grave. Looking back on that kind of dangerous behavior showed us just how powerless over drugs and alcohol we were, and just how unmanageable our lives had become.

I could see Bulldog changing before my eyes. Here was one of the baddest dudes in Portland regaining his self respect and learning to enjoy life without mind-altering substances. I felt like an older brother watching a sibling grow up.

At another meeting, several more men offered Bulldog their support. Some told him he could call anytime; it didn't matter what time of day. After the meeting, I could tell Bulldog was on an emotional high. He spoke freely about how good he felt and how he was getting the message. We were the last people to leave that night, because he wanted to talk to everyone.

In the car on the way home, Bulldog said, "These meetings are like getting a fix."

I knew exactly what he was talking about. The fellowship of sobriety was producing a high just like the drugs had done.

I thought, *Here's the guy who once called me a junkie right out of the blue. Now he's talking about getting his fix at a twelve-step meeting.* We were coming full circle, just like God had planned.

CHAPTER FORTY-TWO
ROLLING WITH THE STONES

The chance came along to take Bulldog to see one of my favorite bands, the Rolling Stones. I had first been to a Stones concert in 2002 during the last few years of my addiction insanity. The opportunity to go occurred at a friend's apartment in a three-story building we called the "White House" because of all the cocaine consumed there.

I always joked with my buddies Go-Go, Pusherman, and Bulldog that when you knocked on that door to visit, you never knew when you'd leave. Many times I went there just to say hello and didn't leave for a day or two. Before I knocked, I always paused. *Do you really want to walk through this door?*

Even when I knew I was scheduled to have my son, when I had things to do and places to go, I would still walk through that door, and all my plans would change. I would call Jen and make different arrangements for Darryl; I'd cancel all my appointments and head to the bank to get a wad of hundreds so I could do cocaine all night with a bunch of yahoos. The lure of cocaine was stronger even than the love I had for my own child. The loving father and the coke fiend within me battled from the day my son was born until to the day I surrendered on May 11, 2005.

I was at the "White House" in 2002 with Pusherman when Gary, one of Pusherman's friends, came by to buy a bag of weed.

At one point Gary asked, "Do you guys know anybody who wants to go to the Stones?"

"How much, when, and where, man?" I asked.

"In a couple weeks in the Patriots' new stadium, $175."

"That's a brand new stadium!" It would be the first concert held at Gillette Stadium, the new home of the New England Patriots just outside Boston.

I called him the next day and said I was in. I was pumped. I would finally get to see the Rolling Stones. Gary didn't drink, so I thought it wouldn't be a big drinking event like past concerts, meaning I'd actually get to remember the show.

On the day of the concert, I had a few hours to kill, so I started priming the pump. Gary was late. When he finally arrived I quickly downed my fourth beer, ran to the bathroom, and loaded my cooler into his car. The two-hour ride to Foxborough was a little shaky. We hardly knew each other. He was a pothead; I was a drunk; we were in different places.

"Do you mind if I drink on the way down?"

"Just keep the beers down so I don't get stopped by the cops."

We made small talk, I swigged beers, and he lit up a joint. I passed on that; I wanted to remember the show. If I drank beer and smoked grass, I might go into "the zone," which is what I called my blackouts. I finished half the beer in just over an hour. Traffic started getting heavier. Ninety minutes into the trip, I was pretty buzzed. I was grooving, but then soon became uncomfortable.

"Hey, Gary, can you pull over somewhere so I can take a leak?"

"Let's get a little farther down, and I'll find a place to pull over."

I kept drinking, making my need for a bathroom even worse. I repeated my request.

"Let me find a place."

"Okay. Sooner rather than later, please."

I started getting agitated. I wasn't asking him for much, but because we were running late, he didn't want to stop.

"Gary, I really gotta piss, man. C'mon, pull it over at the next exit."

Traffic was getting heavier as we moved into the flow of concert-goers. I opened another beer.

"Why did you open that next beer? That's going to make it worse."

"I don't know. But I'm gonna piss in your car in a minute, man."

"All right, all right! You fucking drinkers are a pain in the ass."

He was an ex-drinker, and I thought they were the ones who were a pain in the backside. *Everybody gets loaded before a good concert, especially the Rolling Stones*, I thought.

He pulled over, and it took me a good three minutes to empty my bladder. I got back in the car and swilled a couple more beers. My bladder was soon full again, but he had given me such a hateful look that I held it until we got to the stadium.

By the time we arrived, I had finished the twelve-pack for a total of sixteen cans in four hours. Inside the stadium, I bought two more beers. We found our seats, and I stared in amazement. Sitting next to us were five attractive young women from Northeastern University. The one sitting next to me was gorgeous. I remember thinking later how pretty and sweet that young lady was and how sloshed I was—it was another opportunity lost. There she was, the woman of my dreams, and I was drunk out of my mind.

When the Rolling Stones came out playing "Start Me Up," the girls, Gary, and I danced in the aisles and on our seats. Gary lit up a joint and passed it to me. I was drunk enough by that time that I smoked some. I offered it to the girl next to me, and she waved it off.

Gary kept smoking pot, and it wasn't long before the Northeastern girls grew weary of us. They said they were going down front to get closer, but more than likely they wanted to distance themselves from us.

The Stones played about five songs before I went into "the zone." The last thing I remember is a guy in front of us leaving to get a beer. I was too trashed to go myself, so I asked him how much he would sell it for.

He said, "Ten bucks."

I said, "Sold."

He said, "Go get your own beer, man. You're pathetic."

He was right. I had paid $175 to see the Rolling Stones, and I hardly remember a thing. I knew I had a serious problem. Like the Bob Dylan songs says, I was "knockin' on heaven's door." But I didn't care.

I had experienced the Rolling Stones at their best during their 2002 Forty Licks retrospective tour, and I could barely recall it. I've heard that in an alcohol-induced blackout your brain "erases" the memory, and it can never be recalled. I can't say how many times I asked friends, "What happened? What did I do? What did I say? I'm really sorry."

I didn't attend another major concert until 2006, when life gave me a second chance to experience the Rolling Stones during their A Bigger Bang tour. I was hesitant to invite Bulldog, because he only had two weeks of sobriety. When a person first gets sober, there are a lot of confused emotions, memories . . . and temptations. At sixteen months clean, I knew I'd be fine; but I was worried about him.

He jumped up when I asked and said, "Of course I want to see the Stones!"

He had made it two weeks without a drink or drug, so I got the tickets. On September 19 Bulldog slept on my couch so we could get an early start.

As Bulldog's sponsor, I had advised him to attend ninety twelve-step meetings in the first ninety days of sobriety, and he had agreed. He had been to a meeting every day for two weeks and was doing great. To keep that commitment, we'd have to go to a 7:30 a.m. meeting before our drive to Boston. To me, it was quite remarkable. Not only was I going to a big rock concert sober, but I'd be attending a twelve-step meeting beforehand! That's what's called acting responsibly, enjoying life as a sober human being, and finally growing up at the ripe young age of forty-three.

It felt good walking into the meeting that morning. When it was my turn to speak, I shared about the concert.

"I've never been to a rock concert sober. I feel like we're breaking new ground," I said.

People laughed and told us to enjoy the show. I planned to do just that.

On the way, I told Bulldog I wanted to find a park so I could take a nap while the day was still sunny and warm. I lay down, and Bulldog took off.

When I woke up, he still hadn't returned, so I found a park bench and began to reflect on my life. How had it gotten so out of hand? How had I managed to stay alive and somewhat sane? Was it possible for me to be sitting in a park ready to see a Stones concert, sober as a judge? Yes, it was possible.

As I waited for another hour, I began to worry about where Bulldog was. Could he falter and walk into a bar or run into someone on the street selling cocaine? I was like an old mother hen worrying about her chicks. But then suddenly there he was.

"What are you smiling about, man?" I asked.

"I'm just happy to be here."

"What have you been doing? I had all these crazy thoughts that you might have walked into a bar or something."

"Actually, I did walk into a bar . . . to use the bathroom. Then I bought a notebook and pens. I've been writing for over an hour."

"Way to go, Bulldog! I'm proud of you, man."

We drove to Foxborough and hit heavy concert traffic. As we got closer, we saw concert-goers in store parking lots playing Rolling Stones music and cooking barbecue. The booze was flowing as everyone got juiced in preparation to hear the world's greatest rock and roll band. I felt very good being sober. I was turning another page in my recovery.

Bulldog's eyes grew wider as we walked into the 70,000-seat Gillette Stadium. It was about four years old at the time, and he'd never been there. Alcohol was served at every turn, but we stopped only to buy a few T-shirts.

Our seats were twenty-three rows from the stage. Mick Jagger would be so close he could hear us if we yelled at him. The stadium began to fill with an interesting collection of people. Most were in their thirties, forties, and fifties. There were a few in their sixties and even some in their seventies. We saw people dressed in sixties garb: leather vests with bare chests, flower-girl outfits, and tie-dye T-shirts. We also saw business suits and ties—the whole gamut.

They all had one thing in common: They wanted to see the Stones. Some of the people reminded me of myself at the 2002 concert. I had recently been in their shoes and was glad that my shoes had changed. I knew from experience that there was no way that some of those people would remember the concert. They were staggering drunk before the Stones even hit the stage.

That day I learned that you don't have to be sloshed to have a good time. In fact, I remember everything that happened at the 2006 concert, and I'll cherish the sober memories for the rest of my life.

The Rolling Stones took the stage and played "Midnight Rambler," "Monkey Man," "Brown Sugar," "Jumpin' Jack Flash," and "Satisfaction." The crowd was loud and appreciative. After an hour of solid playing and singing, Mick went backstage to change. Keith Richards walked up to the microphone with a sly grin and said, "Hi, Boston. How are ya? I'm good. It's been quite a year." He laughed wildly. "It's nice to see you, literally." He laughed again. He was referring to his accident several months earlier when he fell out of a coconut tree in the Bahamas. He had swelling and water on the brain and had to have surgery, but he looked no worse for the wear.

It was a highlight of the concert for me. I had always adored Keith Richards; I had lived a similar lifestyle. I thought it was awesome to see him joking, laughing at himself, and continuing to play an amazing lead guitar. He has a real zest for life and will always be one of my heroes. Mick came back out and started singing and running all over the stage. His voice was still tremendous and he was as good as always, as were Ron Woods and Charlie Watts.

Bulldog and I had a great time people watching. Two guys in their fifties about three rows down kept swilling down beer and going back for more. Every time they left their seats, they had difficulty finding them again. Each time, I laughed and pointed the way, and each time they laughed right back and stumbled down the stairs.

A woman nearby started bumping and grinding with her boyfriend. After awhile, she went to get some beer. As she put her foot and half her body over the row of seats in front of her, she fell face first into the aisle below. She bounced up quickly, embarrassed. She probably sported a raspberry the next day . . . and wondered how it happened.

Bulldog and I couldn't help laughing. For me, it was like going back in time to other concerts and seeing what I must have looked like to the people around me.

Two guys from Maine were smoking joints right next to us. I took a couple of extra deep breaths. It's a testament to the insidiousness of addiction and how diligent I have to be in my recovery that it smelled so good to me. At the same time, I was a worried about the smoke wafting over to Bulldog. I told the weed smokers not to hand it to us. They got a few looks from some older people, but I wasn't surprised. I chalked it up to typical rock concert behavior.

The whole night was incredible. The Stones played for more than two hours and came back three times for encores. I came away from the concert with this thought: *My God, Darryl Hagar watching the Rolling Stones—seventeen months sober. Thank you, God. I really think I'll make it, one day at a time!*

Not long after that Bulldog didn't get in contact with me for several days. We had made an agreement to stay in touch, and when he didn't call, of course I expected the worst. I even called his dad to check on him. Eventually, the telephone rang.

It was Bulldog. "Hi, Darryl. I've got some bad news. I had a slip."

"Are you okay, man?"

"I'm okay, but I had a few beers, and I've got to pick up some gear."

"Don't drive, Bulldog. You'll just make things worse if you get popped by the cops. I'll come get you."

"No, that's okay, I won't drive for awhile. Can I come over tomorrow and talk?"

"Of course, man. I'm worried about you."

A swarm of emotions flew through me. Had I been too hard on Bulldog? I had asked him to read recovery books, write for fifteen minutes every day, pray, and attend a meeting every day for ninety days. Would he start chasing cocaine and drinking around the clock again?

But Bulldog had made good progress so far. He had a brain full of good recovery work. I hoped that education would bring him back into the program. I asked God to watch over Bulldog while he was trying to decide which way was better, using or not using.

Addicts are an arm's length away from a drink and drugs. That's why recovery has to be the primary focus. The job goes on hold, the family takes care of themselves, not even children should take away the focus on recovery. What kind of parent is an alcoholic? To be a good parent, people must be clean and sober. Their children will benefit later.

I realized I had to let Bulldog make his own decisions, but I could be there to pick him back up when he fell. I got down on my knees. *God, I know that until each one of us is ready, we won't stop. Bulldog spent more than five years in federal prison and went back out drinking and drugging. Obviously he's still not ready. God, help my friend before it's too late.*

A few days later we met at my house.

"Bulldog, when you say you had a slip, I assume that means both cocaine and drinking."

"Well, yeah. I assume everybody who knows me knows they go together."

"I assumed you would say, 'I might as well do some coke too,'" I said.

"That's the way I looked at it. I thought, 'What's the difference?'"

"I think we should try ninety meetings in ninety days. Pray and keep it simple. Write down your meetings for both your father and me to check, and we'll worry about working the steps later."

I hoped that accountability would give Bulldog motivation to get to a meeting every day. He did go to meetings, but he wasn't as connected with me as before. He was struggling with whether he wanted to give up the drugs and alcohol for good.

It's a tough decision that I also struggled with more than once. But I knew if I kept going the same way, I'd end up dead, in jail, or in a mental institution. The choice became very plain: *Sober up or lose everything.*

I tried to influence Bulldog to make the same decision, but everybody has to find his own way. Nobody can make anyone else get clean and sober. It has to come from the heart. Alcoholism took me close to the edge, dangled me around, and threatened to drop me; it was the power of desperation that saved my life. My hope was that Bulldog would get to that same place.

Before Bulldog's slip, we had made plans to see Gregg Allman of the Allman Brothers Band at Merrill Auditorium in Portland's City Hall. Bulldog said he still wanted to go, because he already had tickets. We could enjoy one of rock's legendary hell-raisers and at the same time reinforce our sobriety.

When I picked up Bulldog and asked him how he was doing, he said, "I'm doing well. I've been going to a meeting every day since my slip."

When Bulldog kept blowing his nose, I asked him if he was sticking to that story. He said his allergies were kicking up and that he had a cold. But my nose had been runny for ten years when I was doing cocaine. As my addiction progressed, whenever I snorted cocaine, my left nostril, the one I always used, would be runny nonstop for a week. My mother, who suspected my drug use, often asked, "Are your allergies acting up again? Do you have *another* cold?"

We arrived at the beautifully renovated Merrill Auditorium, which seats 1,900 people and boasts world-class acoustics. We were thirty feet from the stage, and I was pumped to see one of my old heroes. When Gregg Allman took the stage, the audience erupted. He thanked the crowd and said, "Sounds like we got a good bunch. It's gonna be a good show."

Bulldog and me at a Gregg Allman concert.

As he played and sang, "Whipping Post," I looked at one of my all-time idols and suddenly had the old-time cravings. I was surprised.

I hadn't foreseen those feelings returning to me at seventeen months sober, and it was scary to know I still had that inside of me. My disease was calling me to come back and play, but I fought it off. Gregg Allman had partied hard in his day. My feelings of wanting to go back were probably rooted in that knowledge.

Allman sat down behind the keyboards and said, "Thank you. It's nice to be in Portland, Oregon." He immediately paused and said, "I mean Portland, Maine. There's the first mistake of the evening."

The crowd laughed, and he started to play in what turned out to be an amazing concert.

I was surprised to learn something new that night: I'll always have to fight the battle with alcoholism and cocaine addiction. I have it inside me, and I can never let my guard down. I have to remain vigilant and aware of my disease so I won't relapse. I must always remember that some people in relapse never make it back again. I'm now aware of how strong my disease is, how much it wants me back in the old club.

Gregg Allman continued to play Allman Brothers tunes and some of his own. He and the band sounded awesome. Bulldog and I just sat and enjoyed—both of us smiling, laughing, and relishing a rock legend.

About halfway through the show Allman said, "How you all doing?"

The crowd cheered, then quieted down.

"The night is young, no worries," Allman said.

"So are you, Gregg!" a fan yelled.

"That's debatable," Allman said, laughing along with the crowd.

He then played my favorite song of all time: "I'm No Angel." It's a song of rebellion and partying that quickly brought me back to the many nights when I told bartenders, friends, or Jen, "You know, I'm no angel!" Their response: "Tell me something I don't know!"

As Allman sang that song, tears of joy welled up, and I felt overwhelming gratitude. I had gone through twenty years of living as The Man Overboard, and yet somehow I survived. Here I was sitting next to

Bulldog, a dear friend who was also struggling mightily with addictions. Yet I was sober—I had changed my life before it was too late.

Toward the end of my using career, I worried almost daily that I'd take my drinking and drugging too far, that I would end my life or die tragically in some nightmarish scenario. At the end of my cocaine-using days, I often had suicidal thoughts. Each time I detoxed, I'd get up every five minutes to wipe off my sweating face. I'd lay back down, only to endure my racing, cocaine-induced thoughts and emotions.

I closed my eyes, pointed my face upward, and thanked God for still being alive, for being able to enjoy a rock concert in sobriety, and for giving me the courage to tell my story and help others. *Thank you, God. I'm actually going to make it. I think you're going to show me how to make a huge impact in this world. Thank you, God. I love you!* It was a spiritual awakening that was one of the most powerful moments of my recovery.

I wondered if the people next to me were watching me have this moment. It's easy to let yourself become distracted, but that moment between God, Gregg Allman, and me was completely in sync, and nothing could disturb it. Nothing and no one could stop this enlightenment. I said a prayer for my friend Jazz and my MMA and high school classmates who hadn't been as fortunate. Lives had been shortened by drug addiction and alcoholism. But at that moment I had a direct channel to God. Others in the program had told me there would be moments of spiritual awakening; I now understood what they meant.

After the concert, I worried when several days went by without hearing from Bulldog, but before long he stopped by. I was with my sponsor, and Bulldog saw that I was working my program.

After Bulldog left, my sponsor advised me to pray for him, and explained that what Bulldog had learned in thirty days of meetings would make it hard to drink and use with a clear conscience. They say a belly full of beer (or a nose full of cocaine) and a brain full of the twelve steps don't mix. I've heard people describe how as they sat at a bar in relapse, all they could think of was how they were screwing up their lives.

Sadly, some people who relapse never get a second chance; they don't survive. Alcohol and drug addiction picks up where it left off; the disease is in another room doing pushups while you're working your program. The disease doesn't go back to day one, it picks up worse than before.

Bulldog is a quality person with a great work ethic. If he stayed clean and became a drug and alcohol counselor, what a powerful example he could be! I resolved to pray for him every day.

CHAPTER FORTY-THREE
ALL THESE DEFECTS OF CHARACTER

When I first started going to meetings, I knew zero about the twelve steps. I used to read them and think, *What the hell is all this mumbo jumbo?* But after a few months of sobriety, I started to understand their purpose. They were designed to get people to take a deep look at their lives and show them how to live without using alcohol as a life ring. I realized in order to stay sober, I had to change my thought processes, my way of living, and my perspective. I had to trust a program that has worked for millions and the people who went through it before me.

After eighteen months of sobriety, I was fearful about the approaching work I would have to do in Steps Six through Nine, which are about identifying character defects, asking God to remove them, and making amends to all the people I had harmed while drinking.

One meeting I attend, an all men's step meeting, helped me greatly. There, I shared how the thought of making amends to my family didn't bother me; it was the amends I should make to my coworkers. Should I apologize to the captain who despised me so much that he shoved me twice while standing watch on the bridge? Had I driven him to the brink? Was it really *my* fault?

And then there was the chief mate who made fun of my sobriety by saying, "Why don't you take a mental health day, go to your room, get out your twelve-step books, hum and meditate, and flog the main member?"

The roomful of men erupted in laughter. I explained that I had let the comment slide, but the following week when he repeated his inappropriate remark, I had blown up at him.

I asked the men, who had finally stopped laughing, "Am I supposed to make amends? Did I drive them so far over the edge that *I* need to apologize to *them*?"

Several men nodded their heads. I knew deep down they were right. I had caused more harm to my coworkers from my alcohol-poisoned tongue than anything they had ever done to me. But how could I ever find the courage and humility to take the blame for my role? When the time came, I talked to my sponsor, prayed for guidance and strength, and made the hard decisions needed to clean my side of the street.

One of my most besetting defects of character is anger. When I was still drinking and using, I was an angry man, in part because I kept my problems close to the vest. Plus, alcohol and drugs alter the circuitry of the brain. It's my theory that the section of my brain that controls anger and patience became impaired, manifesting in abrupt bouts of magnified anger. Irritation turns quickly to all-out anger. Anger rapidly turns into rage. I'm not sure how or if it can ever be repaired, except by the grace of God.

Alcoholics are emotional, short-fused people. And alcohol didn't mask that I was pissed off at the world. I stored up anger, and when provoked I came unglued. It's unhealthy behavior that I continually ask God to help me overcome.

One time on one of the ships I was particularly irritable and discontent and was flying off the handle left and right. A friend asked me to slow down and relax. He said, "I know what kind of problem you have. It's the same one I've got."

He was a recovering alcoholic who hadn't had a drink for years. He was happy, friendly, and fun to be around because he worked the steps and had learned how to live life. He had a solid program to follow that served him well. I heard his message loud and clear: Not only is it about quitting drugs and alcohol, it's about taking a good look at yourself. What underlying issues were so powerful that I covered them up with alcohol, drugs, and sex for so many years? What he said reminded me of the old saying: "I have found the enemy, and he is me." How true it was.

There have been many instances when the nastiness of my anger has surfaced, even in sobriety. Sadly, it's easiest to take anger out on those closest to me, and I'm a pro at it.

Early in sobriety, I signed up for anger management classes. I attended for a few weeks before I got irritated about how the class was run. I wrote out some suggestions about how to improve the class and sat down with the instructor to talk about them. What started out as an adult conversation between two men ended up being an example of anger *mis*management. I was angry with my anger management instructor and told him where he could stick his class. Later, I ran into the instructor and apologized.

Another example occurred when I took my mom and seven-year-old son to Maine's largest fair in Fryeburg. I told myself I would have no anger incidents while Mom was visiting; she didn't deserve it.

We walked around and had a great time. Everything was beautiful. All my wonderful childhood memories came flooding back. It was like going back to a time when I was young, innocent, and not an asshole.

We went through the funhouse, then on a ride where my mom and Darryl spun around in a bear cage, and finally on one where Darryl drifted around a water canal in a boat.

As we left the boat ride, Mom said, "Oh, shoot! I left my shoulder bag somewhere."

"You serious? What was in it?"

"My medication, cigarettes, clothes."

"Let's go back to the water ride and check," I said.

It wasn't there.

"Mom, let's check over by the funhouse."

We looked all around and found nothing.

My irritation quickly surfaced, and I couldn't help myself. I said, "Can't you hang on to your things?"

"Darryl, I'm getting old. You know I forget things."

"Jesus, Mom! It's like I'm taking care of two kids!"

"Boy, Darryl, you know how to spoil a good time, don't you?"

I was ashamed and embarrassed. When the rage comes out, I feel like such an ass afterward.

We decided to check the fair's security office. Sure enough, somebody had turned in Mom's bag. That made my mother happy, probably more because it got me off her back than anything else.

We drove home and had a nice dinner together—without an apology from me.

A good son would have apologized that day, but I'm pathetic at times. I didn't make amends until the following day over the telephone. In doing so I was practicing the tenth step, which is about continuing to take inventory and when wrong, promptly admitting it.

Incidents like that illustrate that I must continue to ask God to help me be a compassionate and loving man. I've walked a long way into the forest the last twenty-odd years, and I can't expect to find my way out only by quitting drugs and alcohol. I must keep walking persistently and relentlessly in the right direction. Eventually I'll find my way out of the black forest I chose to walk into so many years ago.

The day after the incident at the fair, I sat down with my new sponsor and told him about it. I explained that I didn't know where the rage comes from. I also talked to my first sponsor. He told me that I had to learn to control my temper and not to let insignificant things bother me.

My first sponsor will be forever in my heart because he led me through the most difficult time of my recovery. He took a man full of fear, anger, and confusion and convinced me that there was a better way to live. He helped bring God back into my life. I told this man many times that I loved him; that in itself was a miracle. But after fourteen months, I lost one of the main staples of my sobriety when he moved to Massachusetts.

So I explained to my new sponsor how I'd be sailing through the day beautifully and something would trigger the rage. I was like a stick of dynamite—light the fuse and run, because once it's lit, there's no snuffing it out. It amazed me as much as it did the people receiving the brunt of it. My sponsor told me to ask God for clarity about why I get so angry, what steps to take to control it, and for awareness when anger is surfacing before it actually explodes. I needed to figure out what lights the fuse.

A few days later a recurring problem arose. My neighbor's 120-pound rottweiler woke me at 6:30 a.m. The dog's owner and I had talked about the problem. His response had been, "You should have been awake by now anyway"—the wrong thing to say to a recovering alcoholic and drug addict.

I called Portland Animal Control and started off by politely explaining the situation.

"Has this been reported before, sir?"

"Yes, and I'm sick and fucking tired of it. You warned him before, and he continues to care more about his dog than his neighbors."

"Sir, please don't swear and threaten. It's early here too."

"I'm sorry, but I've been patient with this guy. I've been sober for sixteen months, and he's upsetting my serenity."

"Sir, the animal control officer will be in shortly, and I'll have her call you."

"Thank you. Sorry about the swearing, Officer."

My behavior that morning showed progress. In the past I would have banged on the old man's door and shouted at him or behaved in some other irresponsible manner. This time I was calling the proper authorities and letting them handle it.

I've learned that as long as I don't get my own way, I have a decent chance to stay sober. I also had to learn that I'll never be perfect. The only thing I can do perfectly is admit that I'm powerless over alcohol.

My goal is to be less imperfect, less intolerant, less impatient, less irritable, less demanding, less angry, less demeaning, less rude, less hurtful, less judgmental, less lustful, less self-pitying, less ego-driven. However, I'll always be human and I'll always have faults and make mistakes. My plan is to minimize the bad and maximize the good. I'll do my best to love my fellow man, to live and let live, and to ask God for strength, guidance, and wisdom every day.

GLENN CHADBOURNE

CHAPTER FORTY-FOUR

REVISITING THE PAST

I received an invitation to my twenty-fifth high school reunion. Now that I was sober, it would be great to see my former classmates. When other reunions had come up, I'd always been drinking and doing tons of cocaine, which made me hesitant to see the people I grew up with. In high school, I didn't drink openly. I had partied with my closest friends, but of 120 kids in my class that was fewer than a dozen.

I mentioned the reunion to my sister, Karen Ann, who had been sober eleven years.

"How do you feel you'll handle that?" she asked.

"Drinking won't be a problem. I'm more worried about how I've changed physically."

In high school I was 5'10", 160 pounds. I had since morphed to 6'1", 225 pounds. I'd gone from a clean-nosed kid barely shaving, an excellent athlete, student, and citizen, to an unruly, loud, drunken sailor traveling the world, chasing women, and doing drugs. I was working on getting back in shape, but I was self-conscious about my size.

It was a beautiful, sunny summer day in Round Pond on Muscongus Bay with ocean views and smells and seagulls flying noisily around the moored lobster boats. When I arrived at the Anchor Inn, people were drinking and socializing as if it had been only yesterday since they'd seen one another. I made the rounds, shaking hands and giving out hugs, spending the time before dinner getting caught up. Several people didn't recognize me. I recognized most people immediately. It was like finding long lost friends I'd never forgotten. The experience was good for my soul.

The drinks were flowing, and I was glad to see that most of my classmates could enjoy themselves without going overboard. If I'd still been drinking, I would have gotten louder and crazier, until I wanted some cocaine. I would have been lucky to enjoy the magnificent dinner served that night after leaving to find "the man" and making frequent trips to my vehicle to "get right." I don't miss those days, although in some ways I'll always be envious of non-alcoholics, who can drink responsibly without taking it to the next level, like I always did.

I shared portions of my story with some close friends. I was hesitant, but I wanted to know how they'd react, how they felt about what I'm doing, and if they'd still respect me. Some of my old drinking buddies thought my story was funny, but they all supported me in the fullest.

At dinner I was at a table of ten. Sitting near me were Marcy, Sarah, and Kathy, close friends from high school. I wanted to find out something from these women. I was a single man, still wanting to find the right woman, get married, and possibly have more children. Was that possible with my track record? What woman would be interested in a man so reckless that when his son was about to be born he was watching the Stanley Cup playoffs in a sports bar? What woman would want to associate with a drunken sailor who used drugs his entire adult life? What about the prostitutes? The car wrecks, the OUIs, the reputation? How could anybody ever love me and forgive my past? Who would put up with me?

I asked Sarah how I'd ever meet my soul mate. She was a sweetheart. "Of course you will, Darryl. You'll be able to close this chapter in your life and then move on. Things will work out."

Marcy was listening and reassured me that Ms. Right would come along when she was supposed to. Kathy gave me a big hug and we spent some time catching up. She was astonished by some of my story. I asked her what she thought of me now. She said her opinion hadn't changed.

"Just be true to yourself," she said.

After dinner, we continued to socialize. When I said my goodbyes, I knew I had introduced my high school classmates to the new Darryl Hagar. All my fears were put to rest.

Then, in August I started looking for answers to questions that had haunted me for years. Twenty-three years after my father shot himself, I was finally ready to exorcise the demons that had flourished inside my alcoholic body. Not dealing with my father's suicide had let some forms of insanity take hold in my mind. I had dreams about my dad over the years. The good dreams were happy. But I couldn't make the nightmares stop.

In 1983, when my dad killed himself, nobody recognized that family counseling was warranted. Thinking a funeral would end the grief was shortsighted. The result for me, and ultimately for everyone whose lives I touched, was the havoc I created by becoming a man overboard. Dealing with the trauma when it occurred might have prevented a lot of ugliness that followed.

It took rehab, weekly recovery groups, professional psychotherapy, daily twelve-step meetings, working with a sponsor, and—most importantly—returning to faith in God to effect a permanent turnaround in my life. For years I suppressed my feelings and built a fortress around me that I wouldn't let anyone tear down. But, finally, the walls were crumbling.

It was time to talk to my family about Dad's death. I wanted to know why. How could a man be hurting so badly that he didn't want to be around for his wife and five children? Why wouldn't he want to see me graduate? Did he understand the wreckage he would cause? I wanted to know the specifics: Did he shoot himself in the head? Why hadn't doctors recognized his mental state?

I had tortured myself with these questions for years, though I had never spoken with my family about our mutual tragedy. I was finally ready to learn the details and explore why my father had taken his life. My mind needed relief from the trauma that had been inflicted upon it.

I went to Damariscotta and spoke with my mom, who had been extremely happy when I went into rehab. She understood that getting answers was part of my recovery.

I started by asking, "Why would Dad shoot himself, Mom? Why was he so down?"

"Your father had back surgery at the veterans hospital," she began. "He was a proud man and wasn't recovering as fast as he wanted, and I was working two jobs. Your father felt belittled, embarrassed, and ashamed, since he'd always been the breadwinner. The bills piled up, and I couldn't pay them all on time. He couldn't take it. It was an embarrassment having people call and find out our phone had been disconnected."

"Didn't anybody realize how bad off he was mentally?"

"Your father showed signs of being depressed and desperate, but in those days nobody took antidepressants or had therapy. People toughed it out. He was able to change the oil in the vehicles, mow the lawn . . . so I didn't realize how bad off he was. He wouldn't open up to the doctor. The doctor said, 'There's no sense in him coming back, because he won't talk to me.'"

"Did they tell Dad how long it would take before he could work again?"

"The doctors thought it would take a full year. But they held that information from him because of his fragile mental health. Then as the months passed and he still couldn't work, he became increasingly more fragile."

The anger arose. I was confounded that the doctors would withhold information so vital to a patient's mental health. My father had deserved to know the truth. Knowing why he wasn't healing quicker would have taken off some of the pressure. They should have been straight up with him and let him weigh his options. And counseling and family assistance would have helped him make it through his year of recuperation.

I next spoke with my brother Mark. It was the first time we had discussed our father's death since the day it happened. He had also been supportive of my going through rehab.

I asked, "Did you have any idea Dad was considering suicide?"

"Dad was acting strangely a few weeks before. Mom, Mom's brother, and I went down to the fish stream to talk to him. He defended not telling anyone where he was, but I suspect he wasn't doing too well."

"Did he ever say he was thinking about committing suicide?"

"No, but two days before he shot himself he told me that I was to help Mom with her finances if anything ever happened to him. I didn't know he was contemplating suicide, but afterward I realized that was the reason he said it. He said, 'Your mother has a hard time budgeting her money, so please help her keep things straight.'"

Just before the suicide, another well-respected local man had taken his own life. The incident had shaken the whole community. Mark had asked Dad, "How could such a well-respected and admired man kill himself?" Dad had given Mark a strange look.

"I can still see Dad looking into my eyes, even today, twenty-three years later," Mark said.

I felt sorry for my brother. I felt sorry for my mother. I felt sorry for my two other brothers. I felt sorry for my little sister, who was only eleven at the time and grew up without a father. I felt sorry for myself. The whole situation made me angry.

Mark felt guilty for not recognizing that Dad was planning his own death. Dad had gotten his paperwork in order. He knew the mortgage insurance would pay off the house. He also had life insurance, but it wasn't payable because of the suicide.

Mark told me Dad had been really addicted to cigarettes, but often had to make a decision: orange juice for the children or cigarettes for him? Of course he picked the orange juice. The pressures of being out of work and having no workers' compensation had helped drive him to the brink.

My father would never see my beautiful little boy, and my son would never see his grandfather's loving face. They would have loved each other so much. He didn't see me graduate as an officer in the Merchant Marine, wearing my dress white uniform and high pressure cap, standing on stage with an admiral and an ex-governor. Instead, I succumbed to drug and alcohol addiction, self-medicating my feelings about an event I could never have imagined in my worst nightmares.

Suicide rates are higher in families where one has already occurred, making family therapy essential. I've come close to proving that true, having thought about suicide many times. But having seen the aftermath, I would never do it. People who commit suicide don't realize the mental wounds they leave behind.

"Did he know what he was doing?" I continued.

"Dad knew he was going to kill himself. He went into Karen Ann's bedroom while she was sleeping and gave her a kiss goodbye. She skipped school that day and was pretending to be asleep, because supposedly she wasn't feeling well. Later we discovered that he had left behind a cigarette standing up in the ashtray. It had barely been smoked. It's like he left it suddenly—left immediately after making up his mind.

"Later, Karen Ann said, 'If only I had rolled over.' We all have our individual 'what ifs,' don't we? What if I had realized the depth of his pain and had talked to him? What if we had recognized the coming crisis? What if the doctors had actually done their job and recognized his mental instability?"

I asked how and where he did it.

"He used the 20-gauge shotgun. He drove the truck up to Upper Cross Road in Nobleboro, got out of the truck, and shot himself."

"I'm sorry to ask you this, Mark, but I've wondered for years: Did he shoot himself in the side of the head—the temple?"

"No. He put the shotgun barrel in his mouth and pulled the trigger, blowing off the back of his head."

"Why do you think he got out of the truck?"

"Because he knew we would use it for transportation, for helping the family."

"Did he leave a suicide note?"

"Our brother Randy still has it."

"Okay, I'll ask him to send me a copy. I want to see it," I said to my oldest brother.

"How did the authorities find out?"

"The man who lived at the end of the dirt road heard a gunshot and called the sheriff's department."

I asked about identifying the body.

"Mom and I went to the funeral home. His body was in a hearse. The sheriff said, 'Mark, you don't want to look.' He was mostly covered up, but I looked and walked away. I recognized his body and saw his shoes, and that was enough."

I wanted to know what happened to the truck.

"We sold it, because the family needed the money, and then later on I bought it back, but it wasn't running at that point."

That truck is still on a hill in the woods on my brother's property. Many months before, I had gone through that truck, trying to answer some of these questions myself. At the time I didn't understand why the truck wasn't bloodstained. It's not that I wanted to see something gory; I just wanted my questions answered.

I finally had some of the answers I needed. My mind had been put to rest. I hoped my nightmares would also rest—for good.

Later that year, Darryl and I spent Thanksgiving night at my mother's house. The next day I decided to visit the church where I attended Sunday school in the sixties and seventies.

Damariscotta Baptist Church had been an important part of my youth. Several weeks before, I had made a donation to help finance the rebuilding of the steeple of this historic landmark. I had also written a letter to the editor of *The Lincoln County News* urging other people to donate.

As a boy, I had run all over the old, historic church. I wanted to go back to remember and reflect. Over the years I had revisited the church many times in my dreams, reliving different events and ages in my early religious experience. I needed to go back to a time when I was young, innocent, and pure. Now that I was sober it would be healing to remember the solid foundation I'd been given as a boy.

Having religion early in my life got me through hard times when I had no one to turn to but the Lord. I turned out to be a drunk, but religion helped me never become a thief. I wasn't a criminal. I wasn't a rapist. I was a person dealing with addiction. In order to overcome those problems I went back to my source of strength, hope, and wisdom: Jesus Christ.

Darryl had also just started attending Sunday school; I was excited and relieved that Jen had taken the initiative to take him to church.

On the way, I explained to Darryl about why the church was important to me: "It's where I went to Sunday school when I was seven, just like you."

"Really? Did Mimi take you?"

"She got me up early every Sunday. She was a Sunday school teacher and she also sang in the choir. We went to church after Sunday school. Mimi would sing from way up high in the church, all dressed in a red robe."

"Wow. Can we walk around and see everything?"

"Of course, bud. I want to remember when I was a little boy like you."

Inside the church, we walked into the library. We found a fun book about Jesus and sat on a church pew together. As Darryl was reading to me about Jesus, I thought how truly beautiful a moment this was. Here I was in my childhood church reading a book about Jesus with my son after being in recovery for eighteen months. Tears welled up in my eyes, and I wiped them away.

With Darryl still reading, I closed my eyes and prayed, *God, please forgive my past mistakes. Thank you for this beautiful moment and this beautiful child. Show me how I can best serve you and what my mission should be from this day forward. Make it clear how I can do thy will and help other people struggling with drugs and alcohol.*

We finished reading. As we walked through the church, memories flooded back in droves, not one of them negative. The church had been an important part of my life. I owed it and the community a big debt, and I vowed to do my best to show my gratitude.

Darryl had fun exploring the gigantic building. Upstairs, he went into the Sunday school rooms and looked at the books and artwork, comparing it to his own Sunday school class.

I took him into the sanctuary, which prompted more memories. We were up high, overlooking rows of church pews. I remembered the big pipe organ that had been played so beautifully. I remembered being in the children's choir, wearing a red robe, holding a book of hymns, and singing to hundreds of people. These were powerful memories. As we left, I was keenly aware that I was participating in my own healing and was glad I had come.

A few weeks later I received a letter from a church official thanking me for the donation and the letter to the editor. Who knows, maybe there's still hope for me. I had spent years of wasted time. It was time to redirect my energy to helping others and doing God's will—with the same kind of intensity.

A little while later, my brother Randy sent our father's suicide note in the mail. Reading it for the first time had a profound effect on me. I stared at my dad's penmanship. I hadn't forgotten his writing style, and there it was, twenty-three years later, just as I remembered it.

Dear family

please forgive me.

I love you very much

Dad

The note that broke my heart.

I think about how my dad must have felt writing that note. About how much pain he must have been in. I miss him dearly and have strong, unpredictable emotions whenever I re-read the suicide note. My dreams of him are both full of joy as a child and horror as an adult. Yet I know in my heart that I will see him again in heaven, because he was a good man and a good father.

GWENN CHADBOURNE

CHAPTER FORTY-FIVE
A LIGHT UNTO MY PATH

I had followed Pastor Joel Osteen on TV during my entire time in recovery. He had been instrumental in my ability to keep sober and reconnect with God. Darryl and I headed to Boston to hear him preach at the TD Banknorth Garden, where the Celtics play.

The stadium houses a museum of sports memorabilia. It was amazing taking my son to see the historic sporting achievements of Boston teams and noteworthy individuals. The four sections include keepsakes from the Red Sox, the Celtics, the Bruins, and the Patriots, showcasing uniforms and pictures of present and future Hall of Famers.

I loved it all! Here I was, enjoying life without drugs and alcohol, appreciating all that life had to offer. I had loved sports my whole life. Now that I was sober, I had finally slowed down enough to enjoy the things around me. Every other time I'd come to Boston I had been so intoxicated I couldn't remember much of anything.

I had "seen" the Eagles, the Rolling Stones, and AC/DC, and didn't remember the concerts. In hindsight, it seems my primary purpose was not to hear music but to get as stoned as possible. One time I told a ship's pilot I'd just seen the Rolling Stones. He laughed and said, "We should give you a drug test." How true that statement was.

Walking around quietly appreciating what the arena had to offer was a brand new experience. When we were done, Darryl and I made our way to our seats. When Joel Osteen took the stage, fifteen thousand people stood and cheered.

I had brought my childhood Bible, which I'd been reading and writing in for thirty years. Inside were examples of my penmanship at ten years old—it was very dear to me. I had brought that Bible on every ship I'd ever been on, except for the tour just before I got sober. When I had forgotten my Bible that one irresponsible time, it had been like a message from God: I had put him in the backseat of my life. While everyone cheered for Pastor Joel, I raised my Bible in the air and said a prayer, asking God to bless it and to give me strength and guidance whenever I read it.

Pastor Joel preached about not being fearful of going after your dreams. He said God wants us to make the world a better place, to move forward, and climb higher. For weeks beforehand, I had prayed I'd hear the message I needed to hear. I was struggling about telling my story publicly, worried about the ugliness I'd be sharing with the world.

That night I received inspiration and courage to carry on with my plan to inspire lost men and help them turn their lives around. My mission is clear, and I continue to ask God to stay close and to not let me wander from the path he has set before me.

Not long after, I received a request to volunteer at two Joel Osteen services in Tampa. Could this turn into a chance to tell Pastor Joel how important he'd been in my recovery? I made arrangements to go. If nothing else, it would be a time to get closer to God. I also hoped to find some answers about where I'd been and where my life was headed. I was excited about the possibilities.

In Tampa, I checked into my hotel with a feeling something special was about to happen. The next morning at the Forum, I spoke to an administrator in Pastor Joel's church. He promised to deliver my writing samples through the correct channels with the hope they would be read by Pastor Joel himself. I then spent the day stacking books and videos, folding T-shirts, and moving equipment into position. It was an amazing feeling being with hundreds of volunteers working together happily in the spirit of serving God.

We worked until the venue was ready for the evening service. Then I took a walk and reflected on my crazy life. I thought of my father. He had once taken a trip to Florida to do the same kind of soul-searching. My thoughts must have echoed his: *Where have I gone wrong? What should I do now? Why am I here? What is the purpose of my life?*

Though I had drifted away from God, I now felt he was the answer to my problems. I could lay my burdens on him and ask him for guidance. I would live my life from this day forward as a new man. I wouldn't succumb to the mental illness that had consumed my father. Instead, I would overcome my personal demons by serving God and helping others.

Pastor Joel's message that night was about how he had taken over his dad's ministry because that's what the Lord wanted him to do. Yet he wouldn't rest on his laurels. He would work to make Lakewood Church bigger and better than it had ever been before.

Would I follow Joel's example? I could choose to quietly fade into the twilight, getting by comfortably even if I never worked again. Yet I had no doubt that my life's trials and tribulations could be object lessons, especially for those struggling with alcoholism and drug addiction. I would have to ask God for courage, strength, and wisdom in sowing seeds that could help others. Would I do it? I would.

Pastor Joel also said that God takes our tragedies and turns them into success stories. Wasn't that exactly what I was doing? Taking my darkest hours and asking God to help me turn them into my brightest moments? I wanted to lead by example and help others shine their brightest too.

Joel really hit home when he said if we have faith, God will open the right doors, that much of life is spent waiting for great things to happen, that while we're waiting we must prepare and be patient. That message fell on me like a ton of rocks. I was still waiting for the right woman to come along, someone to push me to aim higher and not settle for mediocrity.

The service was awesome, but I still hadn't met Pastor Joel. I mentioned my desire to a fellow volunteer. He told me Pastor Joel was doing a book signing the next day, so I made plans to go. When I got to the store the following day, there were hundreds of people lined up, with more people arriving every minute. While I was waiting in line, I couldn't help hearing a conversation in front of me.

"I wish I had tickets for tonight's meeting. They're out," said a lady named Polly.

"Why don't you ask God to help you?" a female minister suggested.

I had been given tickets for volunteering, and since I was an usher, I wouldn't need them.

"Excuse me, ma'am. I'm Darryl. I have two extra tickets, and I'd love to give them to you."

"See? God already heard us talking!" the female minister said.

Polly thanked me, and several of us continued to chat as we waited.

When Joel Osteen walked in, he signaled to his people that he would be just a minute. He shook hands with every person in line and said "God bless you" to each of them.

Later, when it was my turn to get my books signed, I approached Pastor Joel and stuck out my hand. "It's such a pleasure to meet you, sir. My name is Darryl."

"Nice to meet you," he said, shaking my hand.

"I'm an alcoholic in recovery for nineteen months, and you've been an important part of it. I've watched you on TV, and you've inspired me. Now I'm helping others struggling with addictions. I speak at jails, prisons, and colleges."

I handed him the letter I had written and my book excerpts.

"I'm writing a book about my life, and I've included you in parts of it. I prayed that you would read these excerpts. I'm trying to write a godly book that will help others, and I hope that you'll read and bless my book."

"I will," Pastor Joel said sincerely.

I was ecstatic. My trip to Florida had given me the opportunity to meet one of the people most important to my recovery. Up to that point Pastor Joel had helped me from afar, but now he had helped me face to face—more than he would ever know.

Pastor Joel Osteen signing a book for me, Tampa, Florida, 2006.

I arrived at the venue at 3:30 p.m. and was assigned to the very top section of seats, which gave me a bird's-eye view of the main floor. I was happy to be a part of Pastor Joel's growing ministry. The ushers would collect money that his church would spend wisely in helping the less fortunate. Osteen's ministry helps thousands of people every week distributing food and other supplies to the poor. For the Indonesian tsunami and hurricanes Katrina and Rita, his ministry provided relief in the form of 3.2 million pounds of food, clothing, and other supplies.

Later, I went downstairs and sat next to Polly and her husband. Polly gave me a big hug.

"Darryl, there you are! I was hoping I'd get to thank you again!"

She introduced me to her husband, explaining that he was in the military.

"God bless you and everybody in the military, sir," I said.

Joel's message was just as powerful as it had been the night before. At the end, I stood and joined in as Joel asked people pray. He asked those standing to pray aloud: "Lord Jesus, I repent of my sins. I ask you to come into my heart. Wash me with your blood. I make you my Lord and Savior. You are now more than my God, you are my Heavenly Father, and I will serve you all the days of my life. Jesus is my Lord. Amen."

I looked to my right and saw tears streaming down Polly's face. It was beautiful to be a part of that special moment.

My journey was complete. The trip to Florida had encouraged me to gather my strength and to go wherever life takes me in helping others to overcome alcoholism and drug addiction.

I believe God has a plan for me, and that's why I'm still on Planet Earth. In 1985, after hearing a man share during a state-mandated drunk-driving prevention program, I'd had an epiphany. My life would go in one of two directions: I'd die tragically, overdosing on drugs and alcohol, or I'd survive to share my experiences with the world.

God still has work for me. After visiting Tampa, I was baptized in the Sheepscot River near my hometown as a representation of God's forgiveness of my past mistakes. I continue to ask God to be with me always, because I know I can't do it alone. My faith had become more important to me than it had been for twenty-five years.

Being baptized in the Sheepscot River, 2006.

GLENN CHADBOURNE

CHAPTER FORTY-SIX
OUT OF THE MOUTHS OF BABES

My son continues to play a major role in my ongoing recovery by giving my life greater purpose. Darryl has been the one constant in my sobriety, because no matter what, he deserves a sober dad. My father's suicide taught me how vital good parenting is and how I need to be there for my son. When I'm around Darryl, I understand just how pure life can be and how easily I could have missed the opportunity to watch him grow up. Being around for him has been worth every second.

When Jen and I decided to have a child, I hoped being a father would save my life. Before then, we were both out of control. In motherhood, Jen immediately became more responsible. My problems were more deeply rooted, and my toxic body and mind required more years of desperate living before I finally surrendered.

One time I was at a twelve-step meeting where a man with twenty-five years of sobriety talked about how in the first thousand days, a person is still a newcomer. It takes about that long for a person's mind and body to fully comprehend sobriety, and it's normal for newcomers to be full of mixed up emotions. At eighteen months sober, I sometimes felt like a brand new baby and at others like a wily veteran.

It took me six years of being a drunken daddy and eighteen months as a sober one to realize that children are truly our most precious gifts from God. My son and I spend enormous amounts of time together. While I'm with him, I sometimes see myself as a loving, beautiful man; at other times, I'm a chaotic madman with a messed-up brain. The big difference is that I now recognize my shortcomings. I'm learning to be the man and father God wants me to be.

One day it was my turn to take Darryl to see his asthma doctor. I picked him up at school with his usual snack of cookies and juice.

"Hi, Daddy, what are you doing?" he asked.

"I'm here to take you to the doctor, remember?"

"What are they gonna do?"

"You're worrying about taking a shot, aren't you? It's just a check-up. They'll check your breathing. No shots, bud."

"Okay, Daddy."

We arrived a few minutes early, so we sat in the car while I helped him with his math homework. It was a beautiful October day, unseasonably warm with the leaves bursting with color. I was with my seven-year-old son being a responsible, sober dad. Life was good. I thanked God I had made it that far.

Inside, the office was packed with kids. A nurse called us into an examination room. The doctor came in and asked a few questions about Darryl's breathing and medication and listened to his lungs. I noticed a sign that said something about "flu shots," and suddenly realized why the place was so busy.

Before I could ask about it, the doctor said, "His lungs sound good. We'll test his breathing. Also, I'd like him to take a flu shot while he's here."

Darryl heard the word "shot" and looked me squarely in the eyes.

"You said I wasn't taking a shot today, Daddy!" The tears started to come.

"I know, honey. Daddy didn't know they were giving flu shots today. You need one because of your asthma."

He put his arms around me and cried. I was deeply touched; somebody in this world needed me to protect him, to tell him it was going to be all right. Somehow, he knew I would. I almost cried with him. It was another moment when I realized God was showing me something important.

"It'll be okay, buddy. They give smaller shots these days. You'll hardly feel it."

That was the best white lie I could come up with on the spot. The nurse reassured Darryl that they had a new device that presses the skin right before the shot to dull the nerves. Sure enough, he did fine. It was the first shot since his birth that I was enough in touch with my feelings to understand that this little boy needed me and trusted me with his well-being. I wouldn't let him down. But I still had more to learn.

A few weeks later, I asked Darryl if he wanted to help me put up a new toilet paper holder. He liked home projects; Bob the Builder was a favorite cartoon character. We gathered the necessary tools, and I explained about the need to do things safely.

"Shouldn't we be wearing our glasses?"

"You're right! Go grab some for both of us."

I laughed to myself. I had been trained on supertankers for twenty years to wear safety glasses, and here my kid was reminding me not to use a drill before donning some.

"This is the drill, and these are the drill bits," I explained after we put on the glasses. "First we pick a size a little smaller than the screws, so when we drill the hole the screw will be tight."

"Okay, Daddy. How about that one?"

"That one looks a little big. Let's try this one." I showed him how to tighten the bit with a drill chuck and how to reverse the drill.

"That's the righty tighty, lefty loosey rule. Right, Daddy?"

"That's exactly right. Good job, bud."

I drilled the holes and mounted the first bracket. I eyeballed the second bracket as Darryl watched.

"Aren't you gonna use the measuring tape?" he asked.

"No, I think that's good enough."

After the second bracket was mounted, Darryl watched as I tried to fit a toilet paper roll into the two brackets. It wasn't wide enough.

Oh, the words you hear come out of a babe's mouth. I knew they were coming, but didn't expect him to be so eloquent: "I told you, Daddy, to measure it. Sometimes grownups don't listen to kids. Kids have brains too, and sometimes they're right!"

I laughed. I couldn't believe my attempt to eyeball the distance had been so far off or that my son was reminding me about safety and advising me to use a tape measure. Our time together had proved more fruitful than I had imagined. I looked lovingly at my son. He was a godsend. *God, I promise to do my very best each and every day. Thank you, God. Thank you, Jesus.*

That year Halloween was another day when watching a child's excitement was a beautiful thing. Jen brought Darryl over after school, and we hung out and did homework. Darryl cut out eyes and used a marker to make a mouth on an old white sheet. Jen helped him get into his ghost costume. He popped out with a loud "Boo!" Jen and I laughed.

Darryl and Jen had candy duty. Darryl's friends came by, and he handed them one piece each. After they left, I laughed and asked him why he didn't just give them a handful; we had plenty. I wasn't sure if he was showing his friends who had control of the candy situation or if he had ideas about eating all the leftovers.

We had fun looking at costumes, talking to parents, and remembering when we were kids. Before Darryl left with Jen to trick-or-treat, I gave his costume a tug and kissed him goodbye through the eyehole. I told him I loved him, he said he loved me too, and off he went.

Just a few short years before, I had spent Halloween a bit differently. I was drinking Budweiser, dressed in a T-shirt that said "Yankees Suck." Darryl and Jen came by. When the doorbell rang I suddenly realized I might be dressed inappropriately. The beer in my hand might not be the best example for greeting the neighborhood trick-or-treaters. I quickly turned my shirt inside out, hid the beer, and pretended not to be under the influence. How things have changed. *Thank you, God. Thank you, Jesus.*

Of course, I'm still a work in progress. One time I raised my voice to Darryl after he didn't respond to my call to come to dinner. He wasn't doing anything wrong, besides being allowed by his parents to watch too much TV. I threatened to take his TV away if didn't pay attention to Mom and Dad. He started to cry.

I lost my temper because I'm ill, which means I have to work that much harder to remain even-tempered. Just as a person healing from a catastrophic injury might have to relearn how to walk, I'm relearning how to live life.

After raising my voice and making him cry, I went and held my little boy. I explained that some TV is okay, but too much of anything is bad.

"Sometimes you get focused on TV and nothing else," I said. "And that's not good for your little brain."

Hardcore alcoholics—whether they're under the influence or sporting a hangover, especially a cocaine hangover—use TV to keep their kids out of the way and to remove the nuisance. Now that I'm sober, I don't use TV as a babysitter. Instead, I'm more aware how parents can both positively and negatively affect a child's development. I'm also aware that I'm fighting my demons not only for myself, but also for my son and family.

At dinner, I told Darryl I was sorry. "Daddy is still trying to get well from drinking beer. You need to listen to Mommy and me, but no matter what, we'll always love you." I promised to do my best not to raise my voice and instead talk about what upset me.

Darryl said he understood and acted as though nothing unusual had happened. After dinner, I asked him to get out his Cub Scout Wolf Handbook. He had a lot to do to earn his Bobcat badge. I had done it as a boy, but didn't remember the details.

We lay down on the couch and practiced the Cub Scout promise. He had already practiced it with Jen. After a little more studying, he pledged: "I, Darryl Hagar the Second, promise to do my best, to do my duty to God and my country, to help other people, and to obey the law of the pack."

I was full of emotion. Was this doing him more good—or me?

I was learning what I had missed in Darryl's early years: how to participate in my son's life. Although I believe I was born with a propensity for addiction, I had been a willing participant. It was only when the pain outweighed the pleasure that I considered getting help. Booze and drugs had ruled my decision-making. My disease had told me that without continual excitement and chaos I'd be bored. I'm thankful that God stepped in and gave me an opportunity to slow down and be there for my son. Since getting sober, I've taken him to Boston Red Sox and Harlem Globetrotter games and on camping trips with the Cub Scouts, among other things.

Sober dad and son at a Red Sox game at Fenway Park, sometime in the fall, 2005.

One night while I was attending a Bob Dylan concert, Darryl left an "important" message on my answering machine about losing a tooth. I was already on cloud nine from seeing an American legend in concert, and my son's message just confirmed to me what I already knew: I never want to go back to my old way of living.

I started coaching Darryl's sports teams, taking him to Sunday school, and watching him grow up and flourish. Darryl's teacher, Andrea

Romer, was selected as one of five finalists for "State of Maine Teacher of the Year." She is a fantastic educator, and we were lucky to have her. Mrs. Romer chose Darryl II as the "Good Citizen" of his second grade class that trimester and told Jennifer and me how important it was for children to have involved, loving parents. I was again being rewarded for being present as a dad, and I dug it. His mom had always been there, and now Darryl had what every child deserves: *two* sober and loving parents.

Darryl II receiving the Good Citizenship Award at Riverton School, Portland, Maine.

Not long afterward, Darryl and I were headed to bed one night. He asked if we could practice blowing bubbles with chewing gum, having tried many times without success. After a few minutes, he magically started to blow his first bubbles. His missing tooth must have played a role. He laughed hysterically after blowing each bubble. It was a treasure watching his pure delight in that small accomplishment. *God, how can such a simple thing bring a dad such joy?*

GLENN CHADBOURNE

CHAPTER FORTY-SEVEN
ON THAT PINK CLOUD AGAIN

My psychotherapist, Phil del Vecchio, asked me to give a presentation at Southern Maine Community College, where he teaches a class on substance abuse. Some of the students were in twelve-step programs. Most were planning to enter the fields of drug and alcohol counseling or social service. As I spoke about my former life of drug and alcohol abuse, the students wrote in their notebooks. I felt good to be sharing with them.

I then invited questions and answers. A young woman asked, "Do you think alcoholism and drug addiction are hereditary?"

"I believe I was born an alcoholic but that it didn't manifest until later and that there are different levels of alcoholism and drug abuse; the more you ingest, the worse you become. There are alcoholics and addicts who have a genetic predisposition to addiction. The genes aren't triggered until they start using. That's why a non-alcoholic can get drunk and not turn into an alcoholic."

A man asked, "Do you think you can make positive things happen out of the horrific things you've told us about yourself?"

"Of course, man. That's why I'm talking to you right now. I hope to pass on the knowledge about just how dangerous drugs and alcohol are and how important it is that people like you get an education and help people struggling with addiction. I'm making my case that people can recover no matter how serious the problem. I'm a living example."

Another woman asked "Do you think if someone doesn't drink he'll still have problems with other drugs?"

"In my case, when I stopped drinking, my drug problems went away. Under the influence of alcohol, I craved other drugs. But not everyone is the same. There are plenty of addicts who aren't alcoholics and vice versa."

Speaking to a college substance abuse class, Southern Maine Community College.

A young woman asked, "Do you think your son will be an alcoholic?"

"Both his mother's family and mine have significant histories of alcoholism, so the cards might be stacked against him. But some children of alcoholics don't become alcoholics. I hope and pray for the best, but it's in God's hands."

Another woman asked, "Do you think your son will learn from your experiences?"

"I worry he'll say, 'Why are you bugging me not to do what you did?' He does remember me being drunk and mean to his mom. He's also old enough to realize the changes I've made by not drinking and how hard I'm working at recovery. I hope he'll learn from my example. I'll continue to explain how dangerous drugs and alcohol are, but eventually he'll have to make his own decisions."

Another young woman asked, "How long were you in rehab?"

"Three weeks in an intensive outpatient program. They wanted me to stay longer. I'm grateful for what Alaska Tanker Company provided, but naturally I was disappointed when they wouldn't cover more time. Does anybody here think the oil companies might be able to afford to keep the navigational officers of their 900-foot supertankers sober?"

The class laughed, and I offered to take one last question.

Phil said, "You know I'm a believer in God, but what about people who are agnostic? Is there something in the twelve steps for them?"

"A person's high power doesn't have to be God; it can be that yellow shirt that man over there is wearing. If that yellow shirt is his higher power, maybe he'll wear that yellow shirt every day!" I joked. "For some, a higher power may be nature, a maharishi, or a belief in the power of goodness. My higher power is God. I believe he's looking down and smiling right now as I'm talking about helping people recover from addiction."

After class, two of the students approached me for advice. One of them asked if I could talk to her son's father, who had sixteen OUIs and was in Knox County Jail. I gave her my phone number. Another student said he was in my twelve-step program. We worked out that we'd been to at least one meeting together. We exchanged phone numbers and agreed to meet later. At that point I needed to go pick up my son. I had to decide whether I should drive my car to his school or float over on the pink cloud I was sitting on.

Later, I got a call from a friend who asked me to help run a meeting for the inmates at Maine Correctional Center in Windham. How things had changed. Instead of being arrested and drunk in jail on a Friday night, I'd be running a twelve-step meeting, sober as a judge.

Maine Correctional Center is a well run, well respected facility housing approximately 650 inmates who are offered intensive therapy and drug and alcohol counseling and who are taught job skills to help them meld back into society.

I had been in the center twice, the first time to speak to the inmates when I was newly sober. Several inmates came up afterward to thank the speakers. That first time ended in one of my first rides on the proverbial "pink cloud," a phrase from twelve-step literature referring to being high on sobriety. It can't and doesn't last, but it sure feels great while you're there.

The second time, I attended five hours of training, learning about the huge challenges we were up against. The program director explained how they had a difficult time staying ahead of new designer drugs so powerfully addictive that rehab and counseling couldn't keep up.

I headed back to Windham in February 2007. I drove down the long country road toward the prison. As I approached, the brightly lit fortifications loomed on the horizon like a small city on a hill, its many buildings surrounded by fences, barbed wire, and razor wire. It was eerily beautiful, with hundreds of brilliant floodlights casting shadows over the surrounding snow-covered fields.

I reflected on the opportunities I had spoiled in my life. I could have been a supertanker captain. I could have fallen in love and had a big family. I wouldn't have soiled the family name, appearing notoriously in newspapers and in government databases for habitual offenders. It's not a life I would ever encourage my son to live. But I would somehow make up for all my mistakes with the help of God's unmerited favor.

I suddenly found myself becoming emotional. Even through the years of addiction I knew that if I was ever strong enough to survive, I'd go on and do my best to help people. I was channeling the energy of all those wasted years into doing what God wanted me to do.

As I got out of my car and walked toward the front gate, I felt eyes on me. I looked up; two guards were watching from a tower. As I was buzzed in, I took a couple of deep breaths. Going into prison still felt surreal, and I asked God to give me strength.

I walked into the hallway, and there was my friend Zoo.

"Hey Zoo, how's my favorite alcoholic?" I joked.

I have the utmost respect for Zoo. He battled alcohol and drugs for many years and was arrested many times. Yet he's one of the most gentle, intelligent, and artistic men I've ever met. His abstracts in wild, bright colors are scattered around the city of Portland, several prominently displayed at natural foods stores. He attends hundreds of twelve-step meetings every year and volunteers at many correctional facilities.

We passed through several barred steel doors, walked down stairs, and through hallways until we found the right room. Two inmates wearing dungarees were making coffee. They welcomed us warmly.

I said, "This room is wild! Look how the inmates have painted all kinds of recovery phrases on the walls: the twelve steps, words of encouragement . . ."

Looking at the murals and recovery sayings gave me hope. It was obvious that people here were working at bettering themselves. Soon, fifty inmates filed into the room. Everyone introduced themselves, and Zoo shared his story.

He had started using as a kid, even before becoming a teenager, which led to trouble at home, at school, and with the law. He did time in different jails and prisons, but went right back to using when he got out. He impressed on the inmates how much his life had changed after getting clean, how he was now a successful businessman, and how happy and content he was. He explained that he had stayed sober for twenty years because of his involvement in the twelve-step program.

I could tell the inmates believed him and loved his story. When it was my turn to share, the inmates looked at me curiously, probably wondering what this clean cut guy would say. Could this guy relate to how hard their lives had been? What did he know? But I did know, and I began to share my wild stories of drug addiction and alcoholism, followed by the more hope-filled stories of recovery. I remarked how amazing it was that the deputies now called me "sir" when I came to conduct twelve-step meetings—the same deputies I had drunkenly called vile names when I got arrested.

As the meeting ended, I was inspired. All fifty inmates came rushing up to thank us. Smiling and laughing, they stayed to talk and ask questions. They wanted what we had. I could see that desire in each man's eyes as I shook each hand.

As Zoo and I walked out of the prison, I was once again riding a pink cloud. I knew God had been looking down and smiling as fifty-two men with drinking and drug problems talked about how we could overcome our addictions.

CHAPTER FORTY-EIGHT
A FRIEND IN NEED

I went to my regular Thursday night twelve-step meeting. It felt good see friends in the program. I looked around the room and joked, "Is there a meeting here tonight?"

"Who are you?" said a guy who always kids around with me. "Oh, it's Darryl. Nice of you to make it."

I was in my seat less than three minutes when my friend Paul walked up. "I need to take a guy with alcohol poisoning to the ER. Will you give me a hand?"

I grabbed my coat and out the door we went. Paul was a mentor with a story similar to mine. He often talked about his struggle with inexplicable anger and how he used to drink and take out his wrath out on the people around him.

"It's Joe," Paul explained. "He used to come to meetings. He called my house and told my wife he's dying. She thought I should take him to the hospital."

Something in Paul's voice made me think he was not exactly enthusiastic about helping Joe.

"It's just that I've been through this with this guy five or six times, and I'm getting sick of it. He was sober, then drunk, then sober—off and on for years. This time he got my wife involved. He told her he had two seizures today and that he thought he was dying. But I've heard it all before. He's the worst case I've ever seen."

"Maybe it's his time to get sober, man. You never know how God works. Maybe he's desperate enough this time."

"I don't know, man. This guy has an unbelievable tolerance. One time his blood alcohol content was over point four, and he was still walking."

As we drove to Joe's apartment I thought, *Wow, I'm helping some-body who's in the same kind of shape I was in two years ago. Maybe God is showing me something right now.*

Paul knocked. The door wasn't locked; inside, the apartment was pitch black. I could hear somebody stirring and moaning. We found Joe lying on a couch in the next room.

"Paul, I'm really sick, man. I had a couple of seizures and bit my tongue. That's what this blood is on my shirt," Joe said, slurring his words.

"We're here to take you to the hospital. Do you remember Darryl from the meetings?"

"Yeah, I do."

"We're here to help you, brother," I said, trying to be encouraging.

"Thanks, man. I'm sick, really sick. I can't stop." Joe started to cry.

Paul asked, "Do you have a bag packed? We should go."

"Yeah, I got a bag right here. But I need a drink before we go."

"No," Paul insisted. "Let's get you checked into the hospital before it gets any later."

Joe stumbled off toward his bedroom. He was laughing now. "What, do you think I'm stupid? You think I'm going to detox without another drink?" Joe kept talking. One second he was cursing, the next laughing, the next crying, at all times slurring his words.

So this is how this works, I thought.

I said, "Let him have his drink, and then we'll haul him out of here. At least he won't have a seizure on the way to the hospital. We'll never shut him up if we don't let him."

Joe took a couple of swigs of vodka, and we managed to get him into the car. On the way to the hospital, we tried to talk some sense into him.

"Joe, you're killing yourself, man," I said. "Paul tells me you have two boys at home. You'll lose them if you don't get yourself together."

"I know, man. I can't get a handle on it. Every day it's the same madness."

Paul said, "Listen, Joe. You have to tell the doctors the truth this time. No lying, no bullshitting. Have you been doing heroin?"

Joe was looking through his pockets.

"Have you been doing drugs today, Joe?" I asked.

"No. Nothing but drinking."

"Cocaine?"

"No"

"Pills?"

"No"

"OxyContin?"

"No"

"Weed?"

"No. Nothing but beer and vodka," Joe insisted.

"Then what are you looking for in your pockets?" I asked.

"I did heroin three weeks ago. Eighty milligram oxies a couple of weeks ago. Making sure they don't find anything I missed."

Paul rolled his eyes.

"You have to tell them the truth or they can't help you," Paul said.

"I'll tell them the truth this time. I'm sick, and I'm all done this time. I mean it."

At Maine Medical Center I walked Joe to the Emergency Room. He lit a cigarette and sucked in the smoke as if it were the last pleasurable thing he'd ever do. As we waited for the doctor, Joe alternated between laughing, crying, being loud, and acting drunk. People stared, but for once I wasn't embarrassed. I had always been the obnoxious drunk with something to be embarrassed about later. This time I felt there was no reason for people not to see and hear how terrible alcoholism is.

Joe's name was called, and Paul and I helped him to the nurse's station, where he explained tearfully, "I have severe alcohol poisoning. I'm really sick."

"He's been doing heroin and OxyContin recently, although supposedly not today," I told the nurse, afraid Joe wouldn't admit everything. I wanted to make sure he got the help he so desperately needed.

Joe repeated to the nurse what he had told us. She found him a bed, and we said our goodbyes.

Paul walked away. I said, "I want to talk to him for a second."

I gave Joe my phone number. "Call me when you can and tell me how you're doing. I want to help if I can. I care about you, man."

"Thanks, Darryl. I'll call when I get straightened out."

I shook his hand. "Paul said your boys are nine and seven. I heard they're great kids. If you can't get it together for yourself, do it for them, man. It's time to step up to the plate. Those boys need a clean and sober dad. I'll pray for you, brother. And I'll help you when you get out."

I walked out of the hospital knowing we'd done a good thing, but it was unsettling not knowing what would happen to Joe. The hospital would straighten him out and then he'd go into detox. After that, only God knew.

Paul was waiting in his SUV. As I jumped in, he said, "He's the worst case I've seen in fifteen years. We just might lose this one."

"I understand your frustration. But a lot of people relapse over and over, and then one day they wake up and quit. Maybe this is the time. We have to support him."

"I've been there every time he asked. It's just hard when you see a guy who's smart, educated, had a good job, had a wife and kids, his own properties, and he threw them all out the window. He was sober for years, and now he's worse than ever."

"I'll follow up with him," I offered. "I've only done this once. Maybe I can get through to him somehow."

A few days went by without a phone call from Joe. I knew the hospital couldn't release the detox location because of privacy laws, so I went to his apartment. Knock, knock, knock. I could hear someone moving around. A dog started barking.

Someone walked by the door. I yelled, "I'm looking for Joe! I checked him into Maine Medical Center the other night!"

The door opened a crack, and an eyeball peered out. His girlfriend opened the door. Sweat was pouring down her face. She was shaking, her nose was running, and she kept sniffing. I immediately thought: *She's high on cocaine.*

"Sorry about that," she said, letting me in. "I was worried it was Joe's friends from the shelter wanting to come up here and party."

"Is Joe in detox?" I asked. "I'm worried about him."

"Yeah. They have visiting hours and a daily public twelve-step meeting if you want to see him." She was still sniffling. Her hands shook and her voice trembled.

I'm in the middle of Addiction Central. Having lived the lifestyle for twenty-seven years, I knew the drill.

"I'm almost two years sober from alcohol and drugs. I used to go to twelve-step meetings with Joe," I said, trying to gain her confidence.

"I'm in drug recovery myself."

Apparently she thought I'd believe that. *Recovery means no longer using. But one soul at a time.*

"If you talk to Joe, tell him to look for me at the meeting. Is there anything I could bring him?"

"He could use some cigarettes."

As I left, I thought, *Here are two addicts living together. Makes it even harder to stay sober. I hope she does recover. But at the same time I hope she moves out of Joe's apartment. That would be best for both of them.*

The only kind of support a man gets from and gives to an addict girlfriend, frankly, is someone to sleep with, someone to yell at, and someone to get another bottle from the liquor store. It was obvious that Joe and his girlfriend were parasites feeding off each other.

The next day I went to the meeting at the detox center. The very last person to come into the room was Joe. I went over to him.

"Do you remember Paul and me taking you to the hospital the other night?"

"Oh, yeah. But that's about all I remember. I'm not feeling too good. It's getting a little better each day, though."

I handed him a pack of cigarettes. I wanted him to know that I cared and that I knew what he was going through.

The meeting started. There was a palpable feeling of hope in the room, a feeling of togetherness, and a spirituality that comes with people praying to a higher power asking for forgiveness, guidance, and strength. I believed I was supposed to be there that day for Joe. During the meeting I asked God to give me words that would have an impact on him. After the meeting we shook hands.

"I'm glad you're here, man," I said with sincerity. "Call me, and I'll go to some meetings with you."

"Hey, man, thanks for everything."

"You have to get it together," I said. "Paul is afraid you're going to die, man. If you can't do it for yourself, do it for your boys. I know you love them. Being threatened with not being able to be near my son is the only thing that brought me back to reality. You can do it. I did."

"Thanks for the other night and for the smokes. I'll try my best."

I wasn't sure if he meant it or not. I was afraid he was using detox to straighten out just enough to make the seizures stop and get some food in his belly before going back out to do it all over again. I asked friends to pray that Joe would get sober before two young boys lost their daddy forever. I was saddened by his situation; he was very close to being gone. I left the meeting that night intent on doing whatever I could to help.

Joe stayed sober for a year, fighting his alcoholism and addictions by going to twelve-step meetings. Then one day when my mom had been taken to Maine Medical Center for some heart issues, I rushed in to see her, and there was Joe in the ER—slumped in a wheelchair, obviously drunk—checking into the hospital for alcohol poisoning.

Alcoholism and addictions are cunning, baffling, and powerful. The disease lay dormant inside Joe, waiting for an opening, a moment of weakness. For this reason, I continually pray for Joe and for everyone struggling with alcoholism or drug addiction.

The disease is waiting to take me too. I must remain vigilant, ready to fight for my very existence. I must always keep in mind that if I go back to drinking I'll never see my son graduate from high school, I'll never grow to be an old man, and I won't finish living the one life God gave me.

MARINE SAFETY OFFICE.

UNITED STATES COAST GUARD 1790

GLENN CHADBOURNE

CHAPTER FORTY-NINE
GRATITUDE, FULL SPEED AHEAD

With all sincerity, I thank God for helping me achieve and maintain sobriety from drugs and alcohol. Today, my life is so much more rewarding than when I was in the midst of addictive behavior.

In that spirit, I knew it was time to come clean with the Coast Guard. Every five years Merchant Marine officers must have their U.S. Coast Guard licenses reviewed and renewed. I went through the process several times and each time was taken in back to "discuss" my OUIs. Each time I assured Coast Guard officials that I was "on top of it" and didn't have a problem.

During the most recent process, I wanted to tell the Coast Guard of my past drug use and alcoholism, and to accept whatever decision they might make about whether I was competent to sail on my chief mate's license. I sent them letters, one from my therapist, Phil del Vecchio, and one from me.

I drove to Boston after completing a physical and getting all my records together. Whatever might happen, I was at peace, even if the Coast Guard took away my seafaring license.

For the first time, I had to go through a security checkpoint at the USCG building. The events of September 11, 2001, had changed everything.

As I handed in my paperwork to the woman in uniform behind the counter, I lowered my voice: "I went through drug and alcohol rehab since the last time I was here five years ago. That paperwork plus a letter from my therapist is also in the package."

"The commander will review it, and we'll call you back up."

To:	The United States Coast Guard	3/5/07
From:	Darryl E. Hagar	

Subject: Renewal of Chief Mate Unlimited License

Subject: Driving Record, Attending Drug and Alcohol Rehabilitation 6/22/05

To Whom It May Concern:

I have three Operating Under the Influence while operating a motor vehicle. The first was in 1985, all state programs completed with license restored. The second OUI was on 8/28/89. I refused a breath test and was convicted and again completed all state programs and license was restored.

The last OUI was 12/15/2000, and I again refused a breath test and was convicted. I again completed all state programs and therapy. As you can see, there was a large gap where I had no issues.

In May of 2005, I reported to my company, Alaska Tanker Co., that I felt I was developing a drinking and drug problem and I requested the help of their Employee Assistance Program. They warmly steered me through that and supported me fully. I had 20 years with the prior company, Maritime Overseas Corp., and Alaska Tanker Co. with excellent evaluations, no oil spills, and good sober work. Also included in this paperwork is a recommendation from Art Balfe, Human Resource Manager of Alaska Tanker Co. Mr. Balfe was the person that helped me enter rehabilitation and saw me change and change my life around. He certainly would not write a letter for me if he had doubts about my sincerity and desires to remain sober.

On my vacations, I felt I was getting out of hand and voluntarily came forward. I decided to take a severance with that company as I wanted to change everything in my life. It's almost been two years since any drug or alcohol usage. I was in denial for many years and that is the reason I always denied having a problem with drugs or alcohol. I have attended over 300 twelve-step meetings in the past two years, I run a twelve-step meeting at the Cumberland County Jail on Monday nights in Portland, Maine, and also have given talks on sobriety in prisons, three colleges, and schools. I am never planning on drinking or using drugs for the rest of my life and practice that one day at a time. I have a sponsor, a therapist, and my family is very involved in my sobriety.

Please accept my sincere apologies for past behavior and accept that I have learned from my past and intend to be a good example for others that go to sea.

Enclosed with my license application is a letter confirming all of this with my therapist of two years, Phil Del Vecchio. Also included is my clinical record when I attended Mercy Hospital alcohol and drug rehabilitation. I can assure you, my sobriety is real and sustainable.

Sincerely,

Darryl E. Hagar

After getting photographed and fingerprinted, I fidgeted in my seat, wondering if I would have to explain myself yet again. It was some time before my name was called.

"Okay, Mr. Hagar, you're all set," the woman told me.

I was confused. "Do I get my new license?"

"We don't do that anymore. If approved, your new license will arrive in the mail in less than a month. Congratulations on your sobriety!"

I left the station amazed at being congratulated by the Coast Guard rep. For the first time in my seafaring career, I'd been completely honest with them. It felt good, and I knew that God had been guiding me.

About a month later I was surprised and pleased to receive my United States Coast Guard Chief Mate's, Unlimited Tonnage, Any Oceans License. I could be the first officer on any vessel anywhere in the world, regardless of size, type, or location. I was elated and relieved. Life was good.

Not long afterward, my son turned eight. How beautiful it was to have him come into my bedroom, lie down next to me, and rub his face against mine.

"Hi, Daddy. It's my birthday," he whispered quietly.

I was awake, but made believe I was still sleeping to see what he'd do. He continued to rub his face against mine and put his arm around my shoulders.

"Daddy, are you awake?" he said quietly.

He was patient. He kept crawling on top of me and moving from one side to the other. I turned over, keeping my eyes closed, pretending I was waking up a little. He rubbed the side of my face with his face again, and I opened my eyes. He was smiling from ear to ear.

God was blessing me at that moment, and I don't take times like that lightly. How could I have missed out on the first five years of his life? I was always present and we had our share of beautiful moments, but this was so much more. It was life changing. I thank God every day for what he has blessed me with.

"Hi, bud. What's going on? Why are you awake so early? Is something special happening today?" I teased.

"It's my birthday! Don't you remember?" he asked, smiling.

He knew I was playing with him. I started wrestling with him and singing "Happy Birthday." He giggled hysterically. We then got on our knees, put our elbows against the bed, and said our prayers.

"I go first; I go first!" said Darryl, as he does every day. "God, thank you for this day. Help people have food and water and clothes. Help people that are sick, people who don't have a home, and our soldiers in the war. Amen."

It was my turn. "God, please keep me from a drink and a drug today. Thank you for this special little boy in my life, and thank you for being with us all the time. Help me help others. Give me your Holy Spirit so I won't be hurtful to others, so I'll be loving to all, and so I'll do your will. Amen"

We went downstairs and had a nice pancake breakfast.

"Do you want to open a few small presents and then after school we'll open the rest?"

"Yesss!" he shouted.

His mother and I had bought him a beautiful new bike, some cool superhero Legos, some pajamas, and other clothes. He opened some small gifts—the little Spiderman characters he loves. He's such a special kid. He could care less if a gift is a $5 dollar boxed toy or a $100 bicycle. He is growing into a little man, and I hope and believe he'll be special and successful.

I thought back to that moon-filled night, when as an infant I had raised him high in the air in the palms of my hands asking, "God, bless this young man and make him a king someday." Years ago, I had watched Alex Haley's *Roots* with my dad. Life had come full circle with my own son. Even then I knew God listens to us. Amazingly, he even listens when we're drunk, high on drugs, in jail or prison, starving, or freezing in the cold. He listens to us all.

If you have faith, God will answer your prayers. He answers my prayers daily. If there's hope for a man overboard like me, there's hope for anybody. I found faith in the twelve-step program.

At 3:00, I gathered Darryl's gifts, picked him up from school, and took him to Jen's, where his new bike was waiting. She brought out a birthday cake with number "8" candles in the middle and eight lit candles around the outside. As we sang "Happy Birthday," I knew deep down that we were doing a good job of raising Darryl. Perhaps he *would* be a king someday. In my mind, he had already achieved that. We then played together and talked about each new toy and how we would spend our summer together playing with them.

Before I left, I gave a Darryl a big birthday hug and kiss. I would see him the next day as the assistant coach of his Little League team, the "Rangers." Coaching was an opportunity to give back to my community and to work on newfound character traits: patience, love, and understanding, which will always be tested at sporting events.

That night I had a date in Lewiston, about forty miles from Portland. We had a nice meal at an Italian restaurant. Her ex-husband was an alcoholic and heroin junkie living in another state. He had been an absentee dad throughout his children's lives and paid zero child support. It's a tragedy how widespread the problem is. So many children are caught in the overspray of self-indulgent addiction. Kids are raised by parents under the influence, neglected, and abused. Many grow up never knowing their deadbeat dads or junkie moms; others live in chaotic households where both parents are using, trying to imitate a normal, healthy life, and not succeeding.

We finished our date and said our goodbyes. The Red Sox were playing, and I decided to step on it on the highway so I could watch the late innings. As I drove, I was daydreaming about helping alcoholics and addicts and pressed on the accelerator more than I intended. I suddenly saw blue lights flashing behind me. I looked down, and the speedometer had pushed past eighty. *Oh, man, I'm busted*, I thought. I pulled over, and a State Police trooper pulled up behind me. I thought back to all the other times I'd been stopped.

I rolled down the window and said, "Hi, Officer," without much emotion.

"License and registration. And your insurance card, please."

I searched through the compartment between the front seats of my Chevy Blazer and found my tattered plastic license with its OUI star. I handed him my registration and insurance card, all current and up to date.

"Is there an emergency for you to be going so fast?" he asked. "I had you going over eighty."

"No, sir. I was just thinking about life since I've been sober two years. My mind just drifted off. I usually pay attention. To be honest, I didn't see you when I went by."

"That means I'm doing my job well if you didn't see me. But we don't want you daydreaming and speeding on the highway."

"I understand," I said.

As the trooper walked back to run my driver's license, I wasn't the least bit nervous. I wasn't intoxicated, and I really had just spaced out for a few minutes. If he wrote me a ticket, I'd accept my lumps. What a difference two years of sobriety and working the twelve steps had made.

The trooper came back and said, "Obviously, you're not out speeding up and down the highway all the time. I look at a man's record, and he's had nine fairly serious violations in his past and now he's been out of trouble for five years. That tells me he's doing something different."

"I *have* been doing something different," I said. I told him how I now spoke to large groups at colleges and jails. "I appeal to the inmates as a parent who struggled with substance abuse and explain how I'm a much better dad now that I'm clean and sober."

"That's good. Inmates are searching for answers, and they need to hear from guys like you."

"I tell them how much better life is now. It's like I'm bursting at the seams with the joy of it all. Recovery is beautiful."

"I'll give you a written warning this time. I can see you've turned your life around. I hope you make a difference. People need to hear from people like you."

"Hey, Officer, I have a strange request."

"What can I do for you?"

"How do I contact the chief of the Maine State Police? I read that Chief Fleming supports advocacy in substance abuse issues."

He said Chief Fleming was an average, ordinary guy and that I should call headquarters in Augusta for an appointment. I thanked him, and he walked away with a smile. Once again, I realized that police officers aren't all on some kind of witch hunt. Sure, there are undesirables in every group. But I was once the undesirable. It was people like me who deserved to be messed with; at least, I used to be.

Now I was experiencing the fruits of sobriety. I was respected in the community, by my family, and now even by law enforcement. I was grateful. It felt good to be turning my life around and to be doing God's work. I was no longer a man overboard. I had my feet firmly back on deck.

CHAPTER FIFTY
THERE ARE NO COINCIDENCES

To celebrate my second anniversary of being sober, I was asked to dinner by a dear friend, Sonya, a savvy businesswoman and marketing guru. I felt blessed to know her; she had helped me make important business decisions—without charging her usual consulting fee. We decided on a late dinner at Falmouth Sea Grill just north of Portland. We wanted to wait until the crowd thinned out.

When we arrived, I was surprised to see the downstairs section still full of several large parties. The hostess escorted us upstairs to a quiet corner table overlooking the Atlantic Ocean. It was dark, but I could sense the sea right next to us, just where I was most comfortable.

Our waitress asked if we wanted a before-dinner drink. I looked at Sonya and winked then told the waitress we were all set. Sonya isn't much of a drinker, and I'd had enough alcohol in my lifetime for a thousand people.

"I can't believe I've been sober two years. What a ride it's been," I said.

"You're doing well, Darryl. Keep it up." Sonya's words encouraged me. Then she leaned over and whispered, "Do you see who's seated next to us? That's Olympia Snowe and her husband, John McKernan."

Was it just coincidence we were seated next to a U.S. Senator and her husband, the former governor of Maine? Or another sign that God was giving me another opportunity to get my voice heard and my story told?

"I'm going to talk to them when they finish their dinner," I said decidedly.

"No, you're not Darryl! They're out with another couple. Don't you go disturbing their dinner." Sonya smiled, knowing I'd speak to them regardless.

I smiled. "I promise I'll wait until they're done with dinner. They're just people, and they could be helpful. We're here at the same restaurant at the same time for a reason. God is one step in front of us."

Sonya and I whispered about how funny it was that we had decided to come to that particular restaurant and how we'd arrived later than normal. But everything happens in life for a reason. I told Sonya how much joy it gave me, after struggling through a self-induced hell for twenty-seven years, to be put in these kinds of situations.

When the esteemed party next to us was finishing dessert and ordering coffee, I took a deep breath and approached the table.

"Senator Snowe, Mr. McKernan, I'm Darryl Hagar. I've been a big fan of yours for a long time."

"Thank you. How are you?" the senator responded graciously.

I shook hands with the four people at the table and introduced Sonya.

"I'm a lifelong supporter of yours, Senator. There's a reason I came over to speak to you. Today I'm celebrating two years of sobriety from severe alcoholism and drug abuse. I'm a Maine Maritime Academy graduate and sailed 900-foot supertankers around the world. I want to tell people about the battle I waged against alcohol and drugs and about how I was finally able to get ahold of myself and straighten out. It's been a long, tough road."

I could tell I had their attention and that they were relating to me. I told them how I speak in jails and prisons and to large groups, and that I envisioned speaking at military bases, schools, churches, detox and recovery centers—anyplace where people want to hear about recovery.

"That's quite a story. What made you finally quit?" asked Senator Snowe.

"I was spent—physically, mentally, emotionally, and spiritually. I was sick and tired of being sick and tired. I asked God to help me, and I called my employer to ask for help."

"Good for you, and I wish you all the luck, Darryl," Senator Snowe said genuinely. "We need people who have experienced substance abuse problems to help people who are still suffering. Congratulations on your two years of sobriety."

"I navigated huge supertankers like the Exxon Valdez for over twenty years, dealing with these issues. It's a tough and demanding lifestyle."

"I'm sure it is. We certainly don't need any more disasters like the Exxon Valdez," said Senator Snowe.

"It's not that people are drinking while they're working. When we come home after three months at sea with three months to decompress and a full bank account, it's easy to spin out of control. I want to speak to the midshipmen at Maine Maritime Academy about the dangers of drinking and drugs. It's a story they need to hear before they start this very unique lifestyle."

"Good for you, Darryl. Keep up the good work," the senator replied.

"I'd also like to contact the new State Police chief, Patrick Fleming. I have three OUI convictions, and I got out of several more. I'd like to talk to him about an anti-drunk-driving campaign."

Governor McKernan spoke up. "I know Patrick. He used to work for me. You tell him I told you to call him. He's a good man; he'll listen to your ideas."

"I'll leave you alone now, but I just couldn't pass up the opportunity to speak with you both. I believe God allowed me to live through the chaos of addiction for a reason."

"You have our full support in your endeavors," the senator said. "It's an important and worthy cause. It was a pleasure meeting you both. God bless you, and take care."

"Thank you. It was my pleasure meeting you all."

As Sonya and I left the restaurant I was once again floating on a pink cloud.

"I'll call Chief Fleming tomorrow," I said enthusiastically.

"Go for it, Darryl. You're full of surprises; that's why you're fun to be around."

My life was changing again. Opportunities were happening on a daily basis. I wondered, *Is this all happening for a reason? Has God already written the script for my life?* Each day I looked forward to what God had in store. No longer did I get up wondering what kind of chaos I would cause. I now wondered who God would put in my path on this new journey of recovery.

I said a quick prayer asking God to give me the right words to say to Colonel Fleming. After several attempts over several days, I finally spoke to him by phone.

"Why don't you tell me what's on your mind, sir?" the colonel asked.

I went over my background and aspirations as I had done with the senator, and he said, "That's quite a story, Mr. Hagar. How do you think I can help you?"

I took a deep breath. "I'd like to sit down with you someday and see what we can come up with to help government, law enforcement, and recovery centers work together instead of against each other. I'd like to get all the parties to talk about treatment as opposed to 'just' jail. Most inmates want more treatment. Meanwhile, they sit in their jail cells, do their time, and when they get back on the streets they commit the same crimes to feed their addictions. State and county governments should offer drug and alcohol rehab, and inmates should be encouraged to participate. If they don't get treatment they won't get well, and they'll reoffend."

"When you think the time is right, I'd be happy to talk about this subject in detail. Call my office and set up an appointment, and we'll see what we can do," the colonel said.

Whew, what a trip! I hope he takes me seriously—because he is definitely going to hear from me again.

Just a short time before I would never have had the courage to talk to a senator or a prominent law enforcement official. Just two years earlier, any encounter I might have had with the colonel would have meant he was running my record and about to throw me in jail.

Later, I sent Senator Snowe a letter confirming the ideas I had expressed to her in person. The senator replied with a letter that made me proud to have her representing me in Washington. I knew then that she cared about all citizens, even alcoholics and drug addicts, and that she understood my mission to help others.

With U.S. Senator Susan Collins.

With U.S. Senator Olympia Snowe.

I also decided to travel to Washington, DC, to meet with both senators from Maine. I first met with Senator Susan Collins and her staff. I related my story and talked about the substance abuse problems in our state, especially the severe problem with opiate addiction. Senator Collins' eyes shone with tears when I shared about my own struggles, and I was deeply touched. She said she would help in my endeavors to help others.

I then met with Senator Snowe. After a few minutes of listening to my ideas, she warmly told me to keep up the fight, that I was doing a great job, and that she would help me in any way she could.

I left Washington feeling that perhaps this small town kid from Maine could make a contribution—and redeem my experiences as an alcoholic and drug addict.

GLENN CHADBOURNE

CHAPTER FIFTY-ONE
ONCE AN ADDICT, ALWAYS AN ADDICT

As time has passed in my sobriety, I have sometimes questioned whether I can once again drink or do drugs safely. The thought has come to me: *Maybe with everything I learned and the tools I've received from the twelve-step program, I can drink differently now. If I'm just aware of how crazy I can get, I can surely remain in control.*

I have also thought, *If I can just control my drinking, I won't go out looking for cocaine. It's been two years since I last drank or used—maybe I'm different.*

But I can't listen to the lies my mind tells me. I must always remember where I've come from, how hideous my disease was, and how it's just laying there dormant, waiting to take advantage of a weak moment. It's waiting for me to believe I can have "just one."

Yet my mind continues to whisper lies to me: *Maybe it'll be different this time.* Wrong!

Deep down, I know better. The temptations are there, but I know where giving in would lead. The first few times, I might actually get away with it. But it wouldn't be long before I'd drink a little more. Then I'd flirt with the idea of scoring just a little coke or smoking a little weed. Before long I'd get drunk and show up on the doorstep of some crack dealer. I'd end up sleeping with some troubled woman with major drug and mental problems that I didn't know about, much less cared about. I'd end up losing my child, and I'd regress back into all the trouble I've worked so hard to overcome.

I won't do it.

All I have to do to stay real is to listen to people's stories at twelve-step meetings. One man had twenty years of sobriety; he was a staple in the recovery community who helped many people through the years. He slowed down on the number of meetings he attended. He stopped calling people in recovery. He could deal with his daily problems by himself. He didn't need a sponsor to tell him what to do. He stopped helping newcomers.

He eventually decided, *Maybe I can drink again.* I later saw this man in a detox center looking like some scared runaway. His face was sunken, his confidence shattered. His experiment with "controlled" drinking turned into two months of round-the-clock drinking and drug use.

At a meeting, his voice cracked and he fought back tears as he shared how he had gotten cocky in his recovery and had let other things in his life take priority. He began drinking to see if he could control it. Within a week he couldn't work, had no place to live, and had lost his family. He stayed in a cheap motel and drank and drugged for seven weeks until he checked himself into detox.

He told us how embarrassing it was to come back as a newcomer. Yet I'm positive his story helped every single person in that room. He was no dummy; he had just forgotten: "Once an addict, always an addict."

I often recalled his message, especially whenever I thought, *I wonder if I can control my drinking? Am I still an alcoholic, or have I changed?*

The answer became quite clear to me on August 16, 2007. As I showered I noticed a small lump on my behind. I forgot all about it until the next day, when I realized it had become inflamed and that the inflammation had spread. When I finally decided to go to the emergency room, it had become extremely uncomfortable to sit, and I realized I'd waited too long. Darryl was with me, so I brought him along. I explained my embarrassing symptoms to the triage nurse.

It's amazing how easily and quickly the old addict-Darryl took over.

"I'm hoping the doctor can give me something for the pain. I'm in a lot of discomfort," I whined to the nurse.

I hoped the doctor would give me something strong. Why not take advantage of my unfortunate medical situation? The wheels continued to turn in my alcoholic mind. If I could convince a doctor to give me a bottle full of painkillers, I could once again catch a buzz—legally. Was this normal thinking? Do normal people look forward to taking strong pain medication just so they can be under the influence?

"Once an addict, always an addict." My addict gene had just re-awakened and was frothing at the mouth. As long as I had a medical problem, I could justify that not only did I need painkillers, I deserved them. It didn't matter that I was an addict in recovery, did it?

In the exam room, I was given a johnny and told to undress. Darryl giggled.

"You have to take your clothes off, and the doctor will see you naked," he said, laughing.

"Darryl, doctors and nurses are used to seeing people's bodies," I said, laughing too. "That's how they can look at what's wrong with you and help you get better, silly."

I lay down on my stomach, looking forward to two things as Darryl played with his toys. One, I wanted to know what the hell was wrong with me. Two, I wanted narcotic-strength painkillers so I could get a buzz started. I had no desire to look for drugs on the street, but I had no reservations whatsoever about taking prescription drugs.

The doctor walked in, and I introduced Darryl. "My son is my side-kick for the summer and goes everywhere I go. He's a great kid."

As the doctor examined me, I said, "This whole thing is throwing me a curve ball. I can't write. I can't sleep. And I'm getting up in the middle of the night to soak in the tub. You gotta give me something, Doc, so I can stand the pain and get some sleep. It's driving me crazy!"

The doctor thought I had a staph infection. He explained that even people living healthy lifestyles get them and that he would prescribe an antibiotic.

I asked yet again, "Are you going to give me something strong for the pain so I can get some sleep until the antibiotic kicks in?"

"Yes, but I want you to be very careful, especially since you're in recovery. They're very strong."

"I wouldn't do anything that would threaten my recovery. It means the world to me," I said truthfully.

I didn't think a prescription painkiller would cause me to fall off the wagon. I didn't care that it would cause me to be under the influence and might threaten my sobriety. I needed it. So much the better that I could catch a buzz.

The dosage for the painkillers was one to two tablets every four to six hours. Taken at maximum strength, there were enough pills to last sixty hours. Anyone taking oxycodone at that strength is either in tremendous, unrelenting pain or is an addict. I was both.

As soon as the pharmacist handed me the drugs, I turned around, opened the bottle, and took two. I drove home, grooving on my newfound buzz. Two pills were supposed to last four hours. I waited an hour and took two more. I had the same old feeling I got from drinking fifteen beers, smoking a joint, or doing cocaine. I was back to my old self— never being high or drunk enough. If I felt this good with four pills in me, I'd feel even better with six.

Darryl went upstairs to play. I put on Stevie Ray Vaughn and jammed to the rockin' blues. I was right back to my old behavior: "Once an addict, always an addict."

The oxycodone lasted just forty-eight hours. After the two days, I was very surprised that I felt hung over. Yet I was thinking of getting more. I was sure I could easily renew the prescription, though the infection was responding well to antibiotics. Should I call the doctor and tell him the drugs were making me constipated and that I needed something else? My addict mind was trying to take back control despite all the recovery work I had done in the last two years. Was I weak enough to give it all away?

Absolutely not. Instead, I learned a valuable lesson on the long, hard road of recovery: Legal or illegal, a drug is a drug is a drug. Booze, pills, cocaine, oxycodone—it's all the same. Addicts must be aware at all times what they're putting in their bodies. Prescribed or not, any drug can lead to abuse. The best advice for anyone prone to addictive behavior is: Be very careful about what you take, how much, for how long, and why.

I now know sobriety is the only way I can thrive. I came close to making a terrible mistake with prescription medication. My old feelings of wanting to be under the influence, of wanting to block life out, came flooding back. I want no part of it. It's a recipe for failure. The old demons haven't vanished; they've just been brought under control, and they'll take me to my death if I let them. But I don't plan to give them a chance to ever rule my life again.

I have to *always* remember that it's not the tenth drink that gets me in trouble. It's not the tenth line of cocaine or the tenth crack hit that keeps me up all night. It's not the tenth painkiller that causes me to want more. It's the first drink, the first line of cocaine, the first crack hit, the first painkiller. If I don't do the first one, I don't have to worry about the tenth one that will always get me in trouble.

I told my archenemy, alcohol, to take a hike. I kicked his evil cousin, cocaine, to the curb. Everything else that alters my mind has to go too. It's all an escape from reality. It's all a way to run away from life. All mind-altering substances are the same and will lead me down the wrong path. A drug is a drug is a drug. "Once an addict, always an addict."

MERCY RECOVERY I.D. BADGE

Security clearance

The Man
Overboard:

CHAPTER FIFTY-TWO

FREELY YE HAVE RECEIVED, FREELY GIVE

After thirty months of sobriety, I was looking for something to further inspire my recovery. After considerable thought and prayer, the answer came to me: Mercy Recovery Center, where I had gotten sober.

I had already gone to Maine Maritime Academy, wanting to educate the student midshipmen about the pitfalls of going to sea, making huge amounts of money, and partying too hard when they returned from a voyage. But academy officials were standoffish. Like an alcoholic in denial, they didn't want to be associated with drug and alcohol use. Apparently the less said the better. The institution was willing to help people who asked, but being proactive might attract the press. It was better to ignore the alcoholic graduate—maybe he'd go away. Never mind that the disease of alcoholism is rampant in the Merchant Marine.

I also had already gone back to the jails. I had talked with the sheriff of Lincoln County and had a long conversation with the chief of the Maine State Police about working on alcohol and drug education and rehabilitation issues. I had made amends to a deputy I had threatened and demeaned one drunken night, and he told me he was proud of me. That was a profoundly moving thing to hear.

Now it was time to return to Mercy Recovery Center. I'd been in the clients' shoes a short time before and could relate to them. I hoped to be an inspiration, as others had inspired me. I was preparing for a new leg of my journey—helping people fresh off the street.

It was October 2007 when I drove to Mercy Recovery Center. Going back turned out to be a cleansing experience. Inside, I introduced myself to the other volunteers and said, "I'm here because this place saved my life."

Hospital staff explained that the detox section housed the clients in deepest crisis. They reminded us they were in varying stages of withdrawal. They also talked about Maine's extensive problem with opiate addiction, number one in the country in the percentage of opiate addicts compared to state population. These were drugs I had flirted with: Oxy-Contin, oxycodone, and Vicodin, although I never tried heroin.

We were advised to be empathetic, to let the patients talk about their lives and fears. It's true: There's a balance between listening, answering questions, and sharing your story, yet all are essential to promoting long-lasting rehabilitation.

The next time I was due to go to Mercy, I woke up thinking how lucky I was to have a son who loved me even though I was a drunk and cocaine addict the first six years of his life. I even enjoy getting him ready for school. The simple things in life are beautiful to a person in recovery. Because we've seen the worst of life, we appreciate any part of life lived in sobriety. I was grateful just being able to get out of bed without having to throw up. I was happy I no longer woke up on my bedroom floor, unable to make it to bed the night before—and not remembering any of it.

I spent the rest of the day writing, sitting by the ocean with my laptop; it felt good breathing the fresh Atlantic air. Being near the sea made me reflect on my life . . . something I never did while drinking.

I looked at two big tankers in port and wondered if I knew anyone piloting ships that day. Two former captains were pilots in Portland as well as MMA classmates. I thought about how different I was from them. I'd been just as successful going to sea, but I ended up in rehab. I could have been a pilot if I had applied myself. The only thing I couldn't change was being born an alcoholic.

Later that day at Mercy, Dr. Publicker, a personable man with more than thirty years of experience in recovery medicine, talked to the volunteers about addiction as a genetically linked disease. He also explained that volunteers play a major role in helping clients get clean. It would be much more difficult to help people without the aid of those who had once been in their shoes. We had a huge opportunity to change lives.

As I waited to speak with clients for the first time, I reminisced about my time in Mercy's rehab, when I'd been scared, anxious, and confused. I knew the clients I would talk to that day were in the same place.

A manager led me to a room, where I introduced myself and looked around at four clients. I could see the desperation and hurt in their eyes, and wished that I could help them. I started by talking about my past and finished by saying, "If a drunk and drug addict like me can turn it around, so can you. You have to want it, and you're worth it. God will help you if you ask. He helped me."

I could see hope in their eyes as they listened intently. I asked them to tell me what they were going through.

Anne was an addict facing four years in prison for selling crack. "My life is a mess, and I'm really scared," she said.

Ben was an alcoholic, who said, "I can't seem to stop. Drinking is all I think about doing lately."

A man in his early twenties said, "I'm Jeff, and I'm an opiate addict. My parents made me go to rehab twice, but I went right back to using. This time I wanted it for myself. I feel like I might actually change this time."

"That's huge, man," I said. "When we do it of our own free will, real change can and will happen. You're on your way, man. I'm proud of you, Jeff."

I felt like the kid was my younger brother—and I had just met him twenty minutes before. If it was powerful having an addict and alcoholic encourage them, it was even more powerful for me. I could feel God's presence working in that room.

The last young guy, Pete, an opiate addict, was slumped in his chair, baseball cap pulled down so he could barely see. I asked him how he was.

"I'm okay. I'm here. I'm just doing the time. They told me to come here," he said grudgingly.

From his response, I wasn't convinced Pete was ready to stop. He obviously hadn't been beaten up enough by his addictions to totally surrender, and that was both a shame and very dangerous.

For the most part the clients seemed encouraged that someone as wild and crazy as me had gotten my addictions under control. I wasn't a parent telling them to stop; I wasn't a therapist teaching them how to stop; I was just another alcoholic/junkie supporting them and their feelings.

I felt stronger for coming to Mercy Recovery Center and giving back. In my car afterward, I prayed, "God, help them. Three want to change, and the other one needs you even more. Help them find peace and sobriety. Amen."

Volunteering at Mercy Hospital Recovery Center, detox.

The next time I drove to Mercy, several volunteers went to the detox meeting room where three people waited, all in pajamas. The first was weeping and having a hard time just living life. Seeing her like that was sad and made me realize there are people with no drug problems, just hardcore alcoholism, which is just as devastating to them and their families.

The second was a heroin addict, cocaine abuser, and vodka drinker. He'd been dealing drugs when a bunch of desperate junkies who wanted what he had and didn't want to pay for it put a dent in his forehead. He seemed dazed. I wasn't sure if this one would live to old age; he was what they call "rode hard and put away wet."

The third was an older man in late-stage alcoholism. He was losing his hair, pale, and had a big red nose and sunken eyes.

One volunteer shared that he used a cane because he almost died in a car accident. Disabled and barely able to walk, he had started drinking and drugging again. He sometimes fell down and couldn't get up, yet was willing to rely on someone eventually finding him. It was powerful seeing a person have the courage to limp into a detox center and share his story.

A new volunteer, Bill, shared that he'd been through twenty-five detox and rehab centers and had lived at dozens of sober houses and halfway houses before he was finally able to put fourteen months of sobriety together. He was living at the Salvation Army in Portland. He had been an alcoholic, heroin addict, crackhead, and pill-head. He got choked up when he talked about what he'd put his family through.

Hearing these men speak reinforced how I wasn't alone in my crazy, destructive, addictive behavior. That day I kept my story brief, because we had so many who needed to share; I was there to listen and learn how I could help.

The next time I went to Mercy, I first picked up Bill, who answered my greeting with: "Life is good. I'm getting a new apartment. My job and girlfriend are cool. I'm sober and clean."

"Let's go help some sick people then," I said.

Inside Mercy, Bill said he wanted to pray in the chapel. I thought that was pretty cool. Here's a guy who had been in rehab twenty-five times, and he was really trying to help himself. I went on to the meeting room, where I was surprised to see an old friend.

"Darryl! Oh, my God! I forgot you had gotten sober. Are you running the meeting today?" Jane asked.

"I am. I was hoping to see you in a place like this someday. Don't worry. It's all good, and it'll get a whole lot better."

It's always amazing seeing someone I used to use with. At first they're uncomfortable, but when they realize I'm non-judgmental and supportive, they quickly warm up and become receptive. Anyone who knew me when I was actively using and then sees me sober realizes that *anyone* with enough conviction and perseverance can get well.

Before long, the rest of the clients filed in. Crack and opiate addiction and hardcore alcoholism were represented. But I could see the worried looks turn to hope as Bill and I shared. The clients even laughed at some of the things we had done in our insane drunk-a-logs.

One of the men was a commercial fisherman, and we bonded right away. He wanted to get sober, but everyone on the waterfront drank and drugged. I told him to lose all the party guys; it was important to attend meetings and find new, likeminded friends. People sometimes think twelve-step groups are some cult that brainwashes nerds. That's totally false. All types go to twelve-step meetings, and plenty of them are cool people.

My friend Jane shared about how her drinking had progressed to keeping a bottle of vodka in her purse or vehicle. It was when someone beat her up that she finally surrendered. She was in a safe place, and I was hopeful she would listen to the therapists and doctors.

By the time the meeting ended, we had given them our message and prayed for them. The rest was up to them.

I encourage anyone in recovery to go to jails, prisons, schools, and recovery centers. Service is one of the most effective ways not only to help others but to keep yourself clean and sober. As for me, I won't ever stop talking to people struggling with addiction—I need them as much as they need me.

GLENN CHADBOURNE

CHAPTER FIFTY-THREE
I THINK I'LL MAKE IT,
ONE DAY AT A TIME

I woke up on May 12, 2008, and looked over at my sleeping nine-year-old boy, whom I'd tucked into my bed the night before. It was three years to the day since I'd gotten sober. I was so proud of my son and so thankful to God that he had given me this gift. My love for Darryl had spurred me on to sobriety. Three years later, he was one of the main reasons I was able to stay clean and dry.

I lay there remembering how wild and crazy I had been the first five years of his life. God had to have been with me, because I shouldn't be alive. I had flirted with death many times. And yet here I was, looking at my beautiful little boy, three years sober.

I don't deserve to be alive. I don't deserve the love my son shows me every day. I don't deserve the love of my family and friends. I don't deserve the economic security and home that I enjoy. I don't deserve my relatively good health after all the things I put my body through.

My son stirred. He opened his little eyes and smiled.

"Hi, Dad," he said lovingly.

"Hi, buddy. Do you know what today is?"

"Today is Monday, and I have to eat breakfast and go to school."

"Yes, it's Monday, but today is our special day, man. It's May 12. Three years ago today I stopped drinking, and you stopped sucking your thumb. We made it three years. How to go, my son!" I said joyfully.

I dropped Darryl off at school, went back to the place where I had first started going to twelve-step meetings, and signed up to chair that day's meeting. I sat in front. One by one, people came in that I had met early in sobriety. It was like a homecoming, and I felt blessed.

I started the meeting and shared my story. I talked about progressively getting better in sobriety, how my head was calming down and my anger, impatience, anxiety, and lack of serenity were receding day by day. My life wasn't perfect. I had gone through some tough months and learned some hard lessons. Though I stayed clean, my old self had sometimes reared its ugly head.

I explained that the biggest mistake in my third year of sobriety was not laziness or lack of participation. Just the opposite. I had gotten so busy trying to save the world that my own recovery sometimes took a back seat. That's dangerous and unwise; I can't help anyone if I'm not healthy myself. After six months of too much volunteerism it was time to make some adjustments. I had decided to stick with what helped me most.

I opened up the meeting for sharing. One by one, my old friends spoke about how they'd seen me grow in three years, how proud they were of me and of my mission to share my story of recovery with the world.

My friend Paulie talked about being homeless, staying at my house, sharing meals together, and how I used to give him rides. He also shared how I'd put him to work when he was out of cash. He said he liked being around "the A-Team." I was tickled that he thought so highly of me. I had come to love Paulie, a great guy recovering from a serious heroin problem.

The time came to hand out chips to mark time in sobriety. Chips are powerful tool, a mark of a person's perseverance and persistence, used to motivate people in their ongoing sobriety.

Alan, a man I'd met early in sobriety who had helped me along the way with invaluable advice, stood up and said, "It's my pleasure to give Darryl this three-year medallion to mark his hard work and effort. I see Darryl all over the city at different twelve-step meetings, at Mercy Hospital volunteering every week, and I've seen him grow as a person and a friend. Congratulations, Darryl. Keep going!" He shook my hand, handed me the medallion, and gave me a bear hug.

The shiny new medallion with its Roman numeral III went into my pocket. I had plans for it. As the meeting wrapped, I felt good. I'd wait a couple of weeks and celebrate one more time. In the meantime, I talked to Jen and Darryl about joining me as I celebrated three years of sobriety at my home group meeting.

Darryl couldn't yet understand how important it had been to me that we had quit something together. Nor would he be able to realize, until he got older, how he had saved my life. How much it meant to me that he could have a sober dad to grow up with instead of a drunken crazed madman for a father.

I sat Darryl down and asked, "Will you come with me next week when I get my three-year chip for quitting drinking? I want you to be there."

"Okay, Dad. I'll go."

"Do you remember when I gave you your one-year chip for not sucking your thumb, and I received a one year medallion for not drinking?"

"It was a yellow chip."

"I'd like to give you a metal chip with a three on it to show you made it three years without sucking your thumb. I'm going to get a chip for not drinking, and I want to give you one to show how proud I am of you. Would that be okay?"

"Umm, okay."

"Will you come up front, or do you want me to walk to where you're sitting?"

"You come to me," he said quickly. Then he asked, "Dad, what about my two-year chip? You never gave me one of those."

I laughed. "I think you were with Mom at Sunday school that time."

I talked to Jen and asked her to attend this special meeting. She was surprised and excited to go. She knew I was serious about my recovery and how much our son meant to me. She was a wonderful mother, and she had been supportive of my recovery. We loved each other as friends and proud parents and were always able to work out our differences for Darryl's sake.

When the time came, Jen and Darryl rode with me. I'd been asked to chair the meeting and was a little nervous. There were more than a hundred people there, and I'd be sharing some personal and intimate experiences. But I was ready. I made room for Darryl and Jen in front, took my seat, and banged the gavel.

"Good morning, everyone. I'm Darryl, and I'm an alcoholic."

I looked out and saw my little boy and his mom watching. I knew Darryl was as nervous as I was, but I knew he'd be all right. He was brave, and he loved his dad.

I took a deep breath and sighed. "I'm a little nervous, but that's okay. It's good for me to get out of my comfort zone. That's when we grow the most. I want to talk about my experience, strength, and hope today.

"My drinking was like most alcoholics, although I always took it to extremes. My drinking would turn into hours of drunkenness. Then days of drunkenness. Then months of drunkenness, until I went back out on ship and sobered up. My alcoholism progressed, and I became more reckless, more unstable, and less healthy. I was turning into a madman."

Then I told the audience how I had tried to drink away the aftermath of my father's suicide. Instead of getting professional therapy, instead of asking God to help me, I turned to the bottle. How my life had spun out of control and stayed out of control for twenty-two years. How I hadn't been able to talk to anyone about my father's suicide for twenty-three years, but after eighteen months in a twelve-step program, I finally was able to talk to my mom and oldest brother. How I planned to talk to the rest of my siblings, hoping it would help us all.

I then talked about Jen and deciding to have a son in 1998, thinking after he was born we would have the answer to life, that we'd have a purpose. How it worked perfectly for Jen, and how it hadn't worked for me. I did not magically get sober because I suddenly had a child.

I shared how I struggled with drugs and alcohol the first five years of my son's life and how Jen finally insisted that I'd lose him if I kept drinking. How I asked God to help me, because I didn't want to lose the most precious thing in my life, my son, the one person who loved me no matter what. I spoke from my heart, which is something I never imagined doing in front of a hundred people.

"I want to tell my son congratulations for not sucking his thumb for three years," I said. "He quit on the day I quit drinking. We made an agreement, and both of us have made it so far, one day at a time."

I looked directly at Darryl, who was sitting quietly, listening and watching. "Darryl, you saved my life. I'll always be here for you. Dad is going to try his best to never drink again and to be the best dad I can be. I love you, buddy, and I want to give you this three-year medallion for helping me stay sober."

The crowd applauded as I walked over to my son and got down on my knees. His mom was weeping. I looked Darryl squarely in the eyes and said, "Thank you, buddy. I love you." He leaned forward, and I kissed him on the lips.

I just might be able to pull this off. I might be able to help others get sober too. God is with me and he knows how badly I want that. He knows I don't want to go back. I fight this battle every day, the battle of addiction. It wants me back, but I'm resisting with all my power and all my prayers.

I continue to work on my recovery by going to twelve-step meetings, working the steps, and making amends for my past behavior to family and friends. Every day I pray on my knees at the foot of my bed: "God, please keep me away from a drink and a drug today. Help me continue to grow as a person, and help me help other alcoholics and addicts find you and recover from this insane disease."

I just might make it. I might grow old enough to see my son graduate from high school. Graduate from college. Meet a woman and get married. I just might get to meet my grandchildren, something my dad never got to do. I'll see them grow up and love their dad, my son.

Darryl II's Cub Scout trip on the Mayflower at Plymouth Rock.

Not long ago, I received an invitation to go to Dallas to tell my story to a convention of four hundred sober people. I had talked to meetings of more than a hundred people, but never that big a crowd or in such a large venue. I was nervous, but excited at the opportunity. I flew to Texas thinking about how I could offer a message of hope and recovery. There would be many people with decades of sobriety as well as people with just one day. I prayed God would give me the right words.

I arrived on Thursday and I would not speak until Sunday, giving me three days to meet people and get a feel for how to best serve the attendees. The other three keynote speakers were older, with twenty to thirty years of sobriety. I had three years—I was definitely the rookie. But I knew I was there for a reason.

I was given a nametag with a red ribbon with the word "Speaker" on it in big gold letters. As I placed it around my neck, I was amazed at the opportunity I'd been given. Just a few short years before, I'd been a drunken mess, fighting in bars, mending from broken bones, and hiring high-priced lawyers to get me out of yet another alcohol-induced fiasco.

Back in 2000 I had urinated on my living room floor in a drunken stupor. Now I was preparing to speak to a room full people about how I finally tamed the beast within. I was calm and focused as I waited for Sunday to arrive.

On Sunday morning, I kneeled at the foot of my hotel bed and prayed for a long time. I thanked God for saving my life and allowing me the opportunity to tell my story. I asked for guidance, courage, and wisdom. I knew God would be with me.

I put on a suit and tie. I looked sharp and felt strong. I followed my host up front and onto the stage, where I was introduced. I told the crowd my name and told them about my journey as a drunken sailor. The crowd laughed at my silly drunk stories, and there were tears when I talked about my inability to get a hold on myself for twenty-seven years.

They were brethren; they understood my disease and appreciated my forthrightness. When I finished speaking, people got on their feet and applauded. A line formed, and people came through to give me a handshake, a hug, a thank you, and words of encouragement. It was a fantastic experience I won't soon forget.

God had reached down inside my soul and planted the seeds of something new. He had given me a second chance at life. I knew that chance came from something far greater than me. That Texas crowd knew what I meant when I said I had reached the point of no return and had to make a decision about living or dying. I had to make recovery priority one in order to be a good dad, a good son, a good brother, and a good person. If I worked a good program, if I kept God close, and if I lived life one day at a time, I could and would remain clean and sober.

My ship had navigated the stormy seas of addiction and alcoholism and had come close to sinking. It had boarded heavy seas and been through a few hurricanes. Although it had been badly damaged, it had made it ashore where it was firmly docked. Repairs were underway. My family and friends had stuck with me through it all. I had a little boy who still loved his daddy and accepted me for being me. I was going to be all right. I was going to persevere.

I was going to make it, *one day at a time*.

EPILOGUE

My memoir was finally written, but it had taken a toll on me both physically and emotionally. People had told me it would be therapeutic, that writing my story would give me a chance to finally purge the past from my body and soul. Instead, I was emotionally worn down to the point of exhaustion by reliving my former life, which had been a living hell. I spent many sleepless nights tossing and turning or consumed by dreams so horrific I wished I hadn't fallen asleep.

A lot of my anxieties had to do with how the public would perceive my past. Would they vilify me? Ask for my head on a platter? Would I shame my family and son with my stories of insanity and addiction? I worried that my alma mater and the oil companies would be angry and ashamed, or that they would take legal action against me. I worried that the public would think I was after my fifteen minutes of fame and a quick fortune, which wasn't true.

Every day for two years, as I wrote I asked God for courage, wisdom, and strength. I also asked God to help me keep my focus on the people who still struggle with alcoholism and addiction. Not to let visions of fame and money take over and distract from the main purpose of this book: to help others see that there is a better way to live, that like me, no matter how low they have sunk, they can still recover.

Ultimately, I decided to push forward with what I believed to be right and let God take care of the rest. I sincerely believed that my story could change and save lives, so I pressed through all the doubts and anxieties. I was ready to send the manuscript to the publishers, but I was still struggling with the "what ifs"—when the phone rang.

An unfamiliar voice that sounded far away called me by name and said, "I'm an oil company executive, a port captain on the West Coast, and I heard about your book and website from someone on board one of our vessels."

Portland Headlight, 2008.

I immediately feared I was in some kind of trouble, and my heart started racing.

"How can I help you, sir?"

"I just wanted to tell you, Darryl, how proud I am of you and how courageous I think you are for writing a book like this, telling your story to the world. I think it has the potential to help many people on ships around the country and even around the entire world."

I was floored. In the twelve-step recovery world, we call these moments "spiritual awakenings."

"I'm so happy to hear that! I've had a lot of tough moments writing about some difficult memories."

"Do you know what I think will probably happen with your book? I think guys will buy it and put it in the bottom of their sea bags right next to their dirty magazines. They'll read it while they're at sea and think about their own lives and behavior. I believe your book will save lives and prevent many accidents and oil pollution incidents. I really do!"

"If that's true, it would make this whole experience worthwhile. That's exactly what I pray for!"

"Darryl, you may not hear much from sailors at first, because they keep these kinds of things quiet, but it wouldn't surprise me if guys call you five or ten years in the future and tell you how your book changed their lives. I want you to know there are people in the industry who support you and applaud your courage and transparency. It's time for someone to write a book like this. I'll be waiting for its release."

I decided to send the book to press. I know there may be rough waters ahead. I realize this might be a controversial book with some hard truth. I am comforted by the fact that God will be watching. I know he is there, **Always**.

GLOSSARY

Able-Bodied Seaman—Unlicensed sailor who steers the vessel and is part of the deck gang working for the boatswain.

Afterhouse—House aft that holds personnel and the galley, with the engine room and pump room deep below.

Anchor Windlass—Machinery on the bow that can heave in the ship's anchors.

Athwartship Passageway—Transverse or crossways passageway on a ship.

Ballast—Seawater loaded into an empty vessel to sink the rudder and propeller and to stabilize the ship with weight.

Bare Steerage Way—Lowest speed at which a ship can still be steered.

Boatswain, Bosun—Highest ranking crewmember in the unlicensed deck department in charge of the sailors. Answers to the chief mate.

Boiler Suit—Coveralls that completely cover the body for safety reasons, i.e., hot liquids, chemicals, etc.

Bollards—A thick post on a ship or wharf used for securing ropes and hawsers.

Boom—Ship's crane.

Bowditch—*American Practical Navigator*, i.e., the nautical "Bible."

Bridge—Navigational center and ship's headquarters.

Bunker Fuel, Bunkers—Heavy fuel burned in the ship's boilers to propel steam ships.

Captain—Ship's master; officer in charge of a vessel.

Chief Cook—Crewmember in charge of cooking lunch and dinner.

Chief Engineer—Officer in charge of the engine department.

Chief Mate—Officer in charge of the cargo and the deck.

Chief Steward—Head of the steward department. In charge of the chief cook and messmen, orders food, cooks breakfast, and is the ship's baker.

Coaming—A raised rim or border around an opening, as in a ship's deck, designed to keep out water.

Con, the—To have the navigational direction of a ship.

Deck Cadet—Cadet training to be a licensed deck officer.

Engine Cadet—Cadet training to be a licensed engineering officer.

First Engineer—Officer in charge of the engine room.

Fo'c'sle, Forecastle—Most forward enclosed area of a ship used for storage of equipment, lubricants, paints, etc.

Freeboard—Distance from the waterline to the main deck.

Galley—The ship's kitchen and eating quarters.

Hawser—A cable or rope used in mooring or towing a ship.

Merchant Marine—The nation's fleet of civilian merchant vessels engaged in commerce and the crewmembers of those vessels.

Merchant Mariner—A person who works professionally on civilian merchant ships.

Messman—Lower ranking member of the steward department who cleans the officers' rooms and galley, and serves meals.

Midship House—The house located in the middle of older tankers containing the bridge and deck officers' living quarters.

Midshipman—Cadet in training to become a ship's officer.

Mooring Bitt—Iron, steel, or wooden posts on a ship's deck around which ropes or cables are wound and held fast.

Mooring Line Winches—Equipment, run on steam or electric power, used to tighten mooring lines.

Officer on Watch—Officer in charge of the vessel during the current watch.

Pilot—Local expert who assists the captain in navigating a vessel in and out of port.

Pilotage Waters—Waters close to shore where an expert pilot comes aboard a ship to guide the vessel.

Port—When facing the bow, the left side of a ship.

Pumpman—Crewmember in charge of running and maintaining cargo oil pumps.

Scuttlebutt—Drinking fountain. Slang: ship's gossip.

Seaman—A crewmember on a sea vessel.

Second Engineer—A licensed engineering officer, mid-rank, in charge of a ship's boilers.

Second Mate—A licensed navigational officer, mid-rank, acts as ship's navigator.

Shipyard—Industrial site with a dry dock where vessels are raised out of the water for repairs and inspections.

Slop Chest—Ship's store where toiletries, cigarettes, soda, candy—and before 1989, booze—can be purchased.

Starboard—When facing the bow, the right side of a ship.

Third Engineer—Licensed engineering officer, lowest ranking officer.

Third Mate—Licensed navigational officer, lowest ranking officer.

TransAlaskan Pipeline—Pipeline carrying oil from Northern Alaska's Prudhoe Bay nine hundred miles to the southern oil loading port of Valdez, Alaska.

Vacation—In the Merchant Marine, refers to the time a seaman is not employed on a vessel.

Valdez, Alaska—Home of the American supertankers.

Vessel Traffic Service—U.S. Coast Guard traffic controllers in charge of controlling shipping traffic in the nation's ports.

ABBREVIATIONS

AB—*Able-Bodied Seaman*
ABS—*American Bureau of Shipping*
ANSCO- *Alaskan North Slope Crude Oil*
ATC—*Alaska Tanker Company*
BAC—*Blood Alcohol Content*
BP—*British Petroleum*
CPA—*Closest Point of Approach*
DUI—*Driving Under the Influence*
DWI—*Driving While Intoxicated*
GPS—*Global Positioning System*
MOC—*Maritime Overseas Corporation*
MMA—*Marine Maritime Academy*
MSC—*Military Sealift Command*
M/V—*Motor Vessel*
O/S—*Overseas*
OSG—*Overseas Shipholding Group*
OUI—*Operating Under the Influence*
PWS—*Prince William Sound*
SARS—*Severe Acute Respiratory Syndrome*
SPM—*Single Port Mooring*
SS—*Steam Ship*
S/T—*Steam Turbine*
T/V—*Training Vessel*
USCG—*United States Coast Guard*
USS—*United States Ship (military)*
USNS—*United States Naval Ship*
VTS—*Vessel Traffic Service*

ABOUT THE AUTHOR

Darryl Hagar grew up in mid-coast Maine with his mother, father, sister, and three brothers. After four years of rigorous training and education, he graduated from Maine Maritime Academy, earning a bachelor of nautical science degree. He holds a United States Coast Guard Chief Mate's License, Unlimited Tonnage, Any Oceans.

As a ship's officer, Darryl sailed for big oil corporations for twenty years, carrying millions upon millions of barrels of petroleum around the world. He was an active alcoholic and drug addict through it all. He got sober in 2005 and left the industry shortly afterward. He currently resides in Portland, Maine, and is the single father of a young son.

Darryl discusses the dangers of drug and alcohol abuse and shares about what he does to stay clean and sober at high schools, colleges, in jails, prisons, and detox and recovery centers, and to other large groups around the country. He plans to eventually speak to U.S. military personnel across the United States.

Darryl Hagar is a shining example of how people with severe alcoholism and drug addiction can overcome their personal demons and ultimately live happy, fulfilling lives.

SPECIAL ACKNOWLEDGEMENTS

GLENN CHADBOURNE's artwork has appeared in more than forty books as well as numerous magazines and comics. His trademark pen-and-ink illustrations have accompanied the works of many of the world's top-selling authors, among them Stephen King. His artwork has been featured in the international bestseller, *The Colorado Kid*, as well as two volumes of King's short story collection, *The Secretary of Dreams*. Chadbourne's work has appeared in the major motion picture *The Mist*, and he has twice won the Maine Press Association first place award for best editorial cartoon. He lives in mid-coast Maine with his wife, Sheila, and their pug, Rocket.

"I couldn't have asked for a better artist to help me draw my life's story. Glenn was always friendly, on time with his drawings, and is very good at drawing anything one could imagine. His prices are more than reasonable, and I highly recommend him to others needing artwork." —Darryl Hagar

Glenn Chadbourne can be reached at *www.cemetarydance.com*.

DEBORAH JACKSON has more than ten years of professional experience ghostwriting and editing a wide variety of material, including fiction and non-fiction books, textbooks, and websites. She also has extensive academic editing experience (dissertations, master's theses, grad papers, academic journal articles).

Her clients have said: "What a terrific job of editing! I'm impressed with you getting inside my mind to make sense out of obscure passages. You did a great job understanding what I intended to say and finding ways for me to say it with economy and vigor." —Dr. John Gay, former missionary to Africa, Cambridge, MA.

"I have sent Deborah diverse projects that demand detailed editing, often within hours. She always predicts my needs and meets them, sometimes even before I know them." —Gabriel Buelna, Ph.D., MSW, Instructor, Chicana/o Studies Department, California State University, Northridge.

"Deborah worked tirelessly and thoroughly editing *The Man Overboard* for me. She was diligent, relentless, and very affordable. I consider Deborah a godsend both to me and my memoir, and I highly recommend her to other authors. She is brilliant, honest, persistent, and easy to work with. Her writing intuition and instincts are superb." —Darryl Hagar

Ms. Jackson resides in Los Angeles and can be contacted through her website at *www.accentonwords.net*.